This School Called Planet Earth

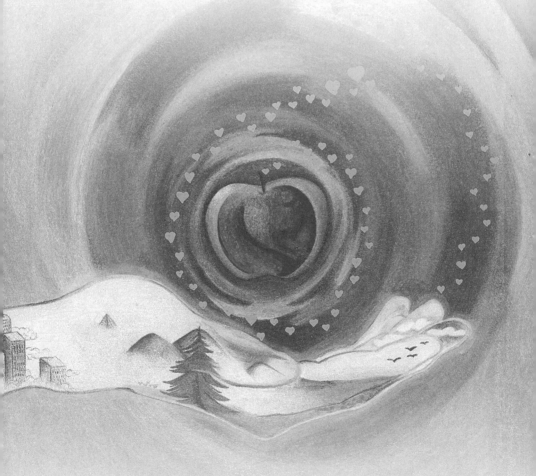

Dr. James Martin Peebles as channeled by Trance Medium

Summer Bacon

This School Called Planet Earth

Dr. James Martin Peebles as channeled by Trance Medium

Summer Bacon

Light Technology Publishing

Cover art by:
Emily Haas

ISBN 1-891824-54-6

Published by:

800-450-0985
www.lighttechnology.com

Printed by:

PO Box 3540
Flagstaff, AZ 86003

Dedication

This book is dedicated to my two beautiful daughters, Emily Lisa Haas and Bobbi Leigh Hillman, with my deepest love. I could not have made it without your love and encouragement.

Special Acknowledgments

To my parents, Ron and Lisa Bacon, for the encouragement to never stop growing. To my brother, Britt Bacon, for teaching me to never give up, and reminding me to laugh. To Bev Scott, for your deep love, devoted friendship, and transcription of this book. To Gordy and Karen Brown, for the great food, great wine, amazing friendship and undying faith in me. To Tom Dongo, for your friendship and for introducing me to Melody. To Mary Cornell, for your courage and inner strength. To Karl Mullings, for your incredible love, friendship and devotion, and for never giving up on me.

Speak thy thought if thou believ'st it;
Let it jostle whom it may;
E'en though the unwise scorn it,
Or the obstinate gainsay;
Every seed that grows tomorrow
Lies beneath a clod today.

If our sires (the noble hearted
Pioneers of things to come),
Had like some been weak and timid,
Traitors to themselves, and dumb,
Where would be our present knowledge?
Where the hoped Millennium?

—*James Martin Peebles, MD, MA, FAS, PhD*

From the preface of *Spirit Mates: Their Origin and Destiny* by J. M. Peebles, entered according to an act of Congress in the year 1909, by J.M. Peebles.

Contents

The Three Principles and Trance Channeling

G od bless you! Dr. Peebles here! It is a joy and a blessing when man and spirit join together in search of the greater truths and awarenesses. My dear friends, as you strive to understand your right to receive and to give abundance in this, your chosen lifetime, we would like to offer you the following principles to be used as tools in tandem:

● Number one, have loving allowance for all things to be in their own time and place, starting with yourself.

● Number two, increase communication with all of life, and with respect.

● Number three, take self-responsibility for your life as a creative adventure, for through your choices and perceptions, you do indeed create your reality.

My dear friends, you have come to the school called planet Earth to discover and dissolve the illusions of separation within self and between life. Certainly it is your labor of love to diminish these very same illusions, wherein you will discover that never in your eternal soul have you been the victim but always the creator.

Trance Channeling Is at the Center of Every Religion

Trance channeling is a total marriage between Eastern and Western religion. Even the process of channeling comes from trance, and trance is a large part of Eastern culture. In various forms, whether it be through chanting, healing work or manifestation of physicality from one place to the next (known as translating from spirit into human form—back and forth you go, taking your body with you), all kinds of Eastern mysticism is involved in the trance process. It was part of my studies when I walked the Earth as Dr. Peebles, in the country of China, for example. There were tremendous trance mediumships occurring there, although it would not have been called this.

This is anything but New Age; this is very old age. Trance is at the crux of every religion, even within Christian culture. Think of communication with angels, with the heavens—it is part of the way in which the Bible was written and part of the way in which the Lord Jesus Christ communicated with the many rather than the few, with the masses. Not only did He minister to human beings in the physical body, but at the very same time, He was found within the heads, if you will, clairaudially speaking to the masses upon the planet Earth. That is how He touched so very many lives—as a result of trance.

So trance in and of itself runs through the core of the existence of humanity. Even within Western culture, trance has been extraordinarily important. When you think about it, it is a part of what chains you to your cars, to your televisions. It is the crux of all entertainment upon the Earth. When you are watching a football game or what have you, you go into a state of trance—that's why it feels so good. That is why trance is eternally fascinating. That is why the masses are beginning to become very much attracted to trance—especially to Summer, in the way she is presenting it to the world as a very normal-appearing individual who does something that is very extraordinary. In fact, it's no more extraordinary than any single, solitary person for whom she channels. That is part of the teaching here: to understand that trance is about the contemplation of God. Prayer is trance.

So it is the perfect marriage of all Western and Eastern traditions; really, trance is at the core of human existence. And trance is absolutely what is occurring for unborn children. What do you think they are doing in the womb there? It is a part of sleep. Reaching out and touching the world is why you are here.

— Dr. James Martin Peebles

My Life on Earth

Dr. James Martin Peebles through Summer Bacon
II June 2005

Dr. Peebles died in 1922 at the age of ninety-nine. He was a writer, a natur-opath, a medical doctor, a spiritualist minister and a mystic. He traveled the world over five times and healed, counseled and ministered to the masses. Dr. Peebles became enlightened during his transition (death) and was then counseled by his guides to continue his work with planet Earth through trance mediums worldwide.

During his remarkable life on Earth, Dr. Peebles performed surgeries during the Civil War era and rode on a mule through gold country in Northern California, where he ministered to gold miners. Dr. Peebles was also fascinated by medi-umship and researched both the psychological and mystical mechanics of the process. He authored several books, one entitled Seers of the Ages. In a short pamphlet entitled "The General Principles and Standard Teachings of Spiritualism" and published by Peebles Publishing Company with no date of pub-lication, Dr. Peebles referred to Jesus Christ as "the great medium." He goes on to say that "our inspired and regal-souled mediums today are mediators, mediating between the world's visible and invisible."

Dr. Peebles is now the wise, witty and compassionate spokesperson for a band of angels. Through trance medium Summer Bacon, this master wordsmith and doctor of hearts has guided thousands of people in profound physical and emo-tional healings. He offers very practical and specific guidance about everything from daily-life issues to universal truths. His kindness and down-to-earth sensi-bility make him a tangible and accessible spirit guide and have endeared him to people from all walks of life.

When I was asked to prepare a biography about Dr. Peebles' life for this book, I was uncertain of how to proceed. The remarkable thing about Dr. Peebles is that he did, once upon a time, inhabit the human form. He has an ability to under-stand our lives in a very sensitive, practical and down-to-earth way. He knows our pain because he has lived on the Earth. He's extraordinarily sensitive and *compassionate. He addresses each us as if we are the most precious of God's gifts upon the Earth, and you can feel Dr. Peebles's sincerity.*

Although there are existing biographies about Dr. Peebles's life on Earth, I know very little about him, as I choose not to read books about him or about metaphysics in order to keep myself as clear a channel as I can possibly be. I do know that Dr. Peebles was a writer, a mystic, a naturopath and a medical doctor. He was a Unitarian minister and a spiritualist. He performed surgeries on victims of the Civil War.

As Bev Scott (my personal assistant) and I discussed how to proceed with presenting the biographical background on Dr. Peebles's life, Bev had a sudden revelation. "Why not ask Dr. Peebles to tell us about his life?" It was pure brilliance! What could be better than getting the scoop straight from the horse's mouth? On June 11, 2005, I taught a seven-hour workshop in Sedona, Arizona, called "The Power of Surrender." I knew I would be channeling Dr. Peebles during the final hour, and I decided to do something I had never done before. I made a special request of Dr. Peebles and publicly announced my desire:

"I have asked Dr. Peebles if he would be willing to talk to you today about his life on Earth. I don't know if he will do it, since I know he doesn't like to focus on his past life existence. But I am hoping he will help me out with biographical information for the book This School Called Planet Earth," *I said. True to form, Dr. Peebles did honor my request, but not without using it as an opportunity to educate and guide us into greater love. Here is the transcript in its entirety.*

We understand that our little channel has a special request here for Dr. James Martin Peebles. Well, all right then. We love you so very much that I am certainly willing to come forth and share about my life of discovery—discovery, my dear friends, that I wasn't as "hot" as I thought I was, because I had quite a time a stressin' and a strainin' with what I believed to be ego. But I realized during my journey to the heart that ego is simply a part of self that really believes it is God, and ego can be of assistance in teaching about passion and wonder, helping you to fall into serenity and peace and the discovery that you really are an incredible being.

Once I understood that there was a purpose within the ego, I no longer stressed and strained against it. My ego, if you will, discovered that what it thought was truth *was* truth—that it [the ego] is God, and it was then when my ego dissolved! The sad part of the story (and you can boo hoo now) is that I did not learn this until I was transitioning from my body. I began to worry that I had made a mistake because I had not lived my life with the kind of passion and understanding that I came to appreciate in my transition. But my guides and my friends—the Lord Jesus Christ and others—counseled me in understanding that I had done nothing wrong, that I had come into my enlightenment and that it was there I would stay forevermore. They counseled me, my dear friends, to begin my work with planet Earth, through this little channel here as well as others upon the Earth, and it was a joy for me to behold the possibilities. Possibilities and opportunities are not foreign to the other side. Possibilities and opportunities are what we seek in every single, solitary moment—opportunities for the expression of love! And certainly it is through this channel here today that I have a chance to express myself from the other side about my life upon the planet Earth.

I was born in the state of Vermont, a beautiful state, and I had a lovely family—it was a rather boring family, as well. My family was not necessarily the most compassionate in terms of caring about what I did with my life; they rather simply, in an almost insensitive way, pushed me out the door at a very young age. I began to wander the streets; I did not have a penny in my pockets, I was hungry, I was tired, I was cold, I was miserable and I wanted very much to die. But then a very beautiful angel, who I discovered was really my guardian angel, incarnated at that moment as I sat upon a curbside eating a turnip, with just a few pennies in my pocket. This very beautiful spirit in human form came up to me and said "Hello, how are you today?" I took one look at him and I thought, "Goodness gracious! He's a bigger mess than I am!" So I decided to hand him everything I had and decided, "I don't need this anymore; he needs this more than I do." And suddenly I saw the light, and I began to realize that there is abundance—free for all!—if only, my dear friends, you are willing to be the stewards of abundance upon the Earth.

Stewards of abundance—and I mean here financial abundance—are those who practice the saying "give unto others as you would like for them to give unto you." This was my very first learning, my first education, and so I decided at that point that I was going to turn life into a ministry. And well, I stumbled a little bit here and there; I got on my soapbox and I thought I knew everything. I talked too much, I talked too little, I began to find though that through my willingness to speak my truth, the many rather than the few began to come to me and thank me for my work. It was a very wonderful journey.

Some encouraged me to put my words down on the page in the form of a book. Well, I thought that was a terrible idea. I didn't like to write, and I admit it! But I wrote many books in the course of my lifetime, and I suffered through every single sentence, God bless you indeed, but it was worth the effort, because it did provide financial income for me to make my journeys around the world. And then my journeys around the world became my books. I lived a fantastic life, meeting the many rather than the few, coming into contact with the Aborigines—goodness gracious, my dear friends; you have never experienced your life fully and completely until you've seen someone lose a foot and grow one back in a nanosecond! These [the Aborigines] are beautiful spirits, very beautiful spirits; we never truly spoke out loud but communicated telepathically, and this was extraordinary for me because it was the first time I'd had this encounter in terms of telepathic communication. It didn't even take an effort on my part, and that was the beginning of my understanding that I was a true mystic upon the Earth, one who could create a new reality, a new consciousness. Admittedly, here from the other side, I went into the community of the Aborigines with the intent of turning them all into staunch Christians, but I realized that they had more to teach me. Did I discard my knowledge of Christ? No, I did not. Rather, I allowed them to teach me and add to the knowledge that I already had. I didn't have to give up any part of myself; rather, I built upon the very same—hence my understanding of a life of expansion and surrender to other possibilities and other perspectives.

Incorporating this into my ministry, I began to turn a deaf ear upon my own orations. The many rather than the few did not like this—it stirred the pot, so to speak. They walked away—they charged me, if you will, with being a fraud and all the rest, and eventually I was imprisoned for it. This all occurred because there was a lot of fear of the truth—and make no mistake about it, there still is a lot of fear of the truth upon your planet Earth.

But, my dear friends, we encourage you not to fear the truth, the light within yourself. Express yourself freely and with compassion first, compassion being a higher virtue than honesty. We want for you to live a life of integrity—but first and foremost, my dear friends, you don't have to tell someone that you don't like their shirt. That's honest, but not compassionate. Rather, my dear friends, buy them something you would like to see them wear and see if they wear it, you understand?

I did indeed have a very beautiful experience upon the Earth—I had many opportunities to travel to the south of France, which was a wonderful place for me because frankly I just liked to look at the girls there, God bless you indeed. I enjoyed the nature and the ocean. I enjoyed very colorful philosophical discussions of all kinds, about what was superficial reality at the time, not really things that I felt I needed to adhere to. Then I discovered Ireland and there I put down roots for periods of time. Extraordinary spirits live in the realm of Ireland, not only spirits incarnate in the physical form, but also those who are living in spirit. In Ireland there are the many rather than the few such spirits— the leprechauns do exist! Ireland is a wonderful land, a fairytale land of fairies and sprites who certainly do live within the nature there because it's highly undisturbed—and this was even more so during my lifetime.

As well, there was an unselfish exploration of technology that I truly loved and embraced. Realizing that I did not want to hold any of life at arm's length, I explored everything: technology, spirituality, books of all kinds, people of all colors and languages galore. It is rather remarkable to study your world. Your world—not mine, but yours, my dear friends. This is your planet Earth, and it is for you to discover, down to every nook and cranny if you so desire. And we certainly encourage this always, because Earth is a very beautiful place of many perspectives. You see only the tip of the iceberg in any given moment.

So you really have to work hard, then, to reach out, to experience all realms of understanding—through your books, sciences, religions, discussions, philosophies, expectations and all the rest, and through the releasing of the very same. My dear friends, we encourage you to embrace the many rather than the few.

That was my lifetime upon the planet Earth, a journey to the heart without end, God bless you indeed. It was through the power of surrender that here today you have learned from Summer about all kinds of extraordinary ways in which you can transform your life through very simple spiritual processes. My dear friends, understand that you don't have to do grand things on the Earth to create grand reactions. In other words, "If I could but lift one robin unto its nest again, I shall not have lived in vain"—and this is truth, my dear friends. There is a purpose, and you will find it before you leave [the Earth], without question. There's no way you can escape yourselves. Some have come here to finish karmic relationships. Some have come here to discover that there is beauty in ugliness and vice versa. There are those who are here in an exploration of abundance and what this means through finances, riches, wealth and what it means to be burdened by the very same. Abundance—physical, financial abundance—can be a creation of the most poverty-stricken individual, spiritually speaking.

And on and on the lessons go. What a wonderful, wonderful life you live, God bless you indeed! Opportunities for growth are everywhere. Opportunities for expansion are everywhere—expansion into the greater realms of understanding that God loves you so very much, has no expectations of you whatsoever and only asks, my dear friends, that you honor the gifts that you carry inside yourself and that you allow for them to be fully expressed upon the planet Earth. The planet Earth is a canvas, you are the paintbrush and your heart is the paint with which you color the world— with your words, your hands, your heart, your hugs and your kisses. God bless you, indeed!

By the Grace of God and Cheese

Summer Bacon

Summer is recognized as one of the clearest and most authentic trance mediums of our time. She channels for hundreds of people each month at special events, group sessions, private sessions and workshops. She was a featured guest on Philip Burley's radio show The Inner View, *and has been involved in special projects including haunting investigations, "ghost busting" and remote viewing. Her channeled material has been seen in the international magazine the Sedona* Journal of Emergence.

Summer's mystical and psychic experiences began at the age of eleven months, when she remembers thinking "I am going to find out what this 'truth' thing is about once and for all." She first met Dr. Peebles through trance medium Thomas Jacobson (see To Dance With Angels, *by Don and Linda Pendleton) and at long last began to make sense of her life as a mystic. When Thomas quit channeling Dr. Peebles, Summer began an intensive journey in which she tried to find and connect with Dr. Peebles herself. After seven years of committed meditation, prayer, self-guided channeling practice and a very bizarre encounter with a group of extra-terrestrials who operated on her spine, Summer first began channeling on December 4, 1994. She then began, with Dr. Peebles as gatekeeper, a three year training that involved trance channeling hundreds of dearly departed loved ones. Her work continued exclusively with Dr. Peebles in 1997 when she was encouraged by him to step into the public light and begin trance channeling professionally.*

A self-proclaimed metaphychristian, Summer teaches, lectures and writes about the subjects of mysticism and trance mediumship. She lives in the Sedona, Arizona area with her two daughters.

I had to laugh. I truly mean no disrespect to anyone, but I really had to laugh. A man came up to me after one of my open sessions in Sedona. Now mind you, I'm pretty spacey after I channel, but I do my best to be alert and gracious when people come up to introduce themselves to me and kindly thank me for the opportunity to speak with Dr. Peebles. It's all very heartwarming and one of the greatest rewards for doing this work. Anyway, this particular man lingered for quite awhile after the session, waiting for the crowd to dissipate. As I collected my things and prepared to leave, he shyly edged closer to me as if he had something to say.

"Hello," I said.

"Hello," he replied as we shook hands. "If you would stop eating cheese, you would be a clearer channel."

I almost burst out laughing, thinking I hadn't heard him correctly. "I'm sorry. What did you say?" I asked.

"Stop eating cheese, and you'll be a clearer channel."

Not certain how I should respond as my life of clear channeling flashed before my eyes, I nodded, smiled and said, "Thank you for the advice." Then I asked his name and thanked him for coming to the session. I haven't stopped laughing since. In the middle of the night, I laugh. As I tell the story on the phone, I laugh. I thank this gentle, well-intentioned man for giving me much cause to think. My mind had a field day with this tidbit of information. Thoughts such as, "I'd rather give up channeling than give up cheese!" ran through my mind.

For the Love of Cheese

Oh, how I love cheese. And my own homemade chicken-fried steak. And shish kabob. And coffee. And champagne. I'm addicted to veggies and eat my fair share of fruit too. And plenty of whole grains. And white rice. And white flour. And potato chips. But, oh God, how I love cheese. In fact, a slice of cheese is often the one thing that I eat before I do my private sessions. I have learned the hard way that if I don't get enough protein, calcium, magnesium and potassium, my body gets hammered pretty hard by the channeling, and recovery is more difficult. My body is like a low-voltage wire, and the frequency of the spirit I channel is like a high voltage running through it. I tend to physically burn out.

So between sessions, I eat cheese: a glorious slice of Swiss; a mountain of Muenster; a chunk of sweet, nutty goat cheese; a slab of Brie; a mouthwatering, taste-bud-tingling slice of pepper jack, sometimes sandwiched between two thick slices of crusty sourdough bread; or a thick spread of cream cheese dotted with some zippy green olives. Oh, yes! Glory be to God for the milk cow! I am, without shame, an admitted cheeseaholic. And I have to wonder, if I were to give up cheese and become an even clearer channel, what would that mean? I'm already in such a deep trance, I have to wonder if I might catapult right out of the body and never return!

By the Grace of God and Cheese   xxvii

Okay, so I'm teasing just a little bit here. But on a more serious note, why in the world would I ever want to give away my power to a little hunk of cheese? My journey as a trance medium started as a quest to know God and to feel His grace in my life. I wanted to truly know Him. Cheese shmeese. God's love is what influences my life and my work. It is to Him that I surrender my mind, body and spirit and ask for His blessings to flow through me in the form of words of encouragement, offerings of suggestions and refreshing perspectives from Dr. Peebles and the band of angels. Is a hunk of cheese going to spoil this journey for me? I think not!

I remember a woman who was aghast at the fact that I drank coffee before channeling. "You need to stop!" she rebuked me in horror. I thought, "Gee, you really ought to try it. It's really good with a little extra cream. It takes the edge off my sleepiness and revs up my body quite nicely for the high charge of spirit that's about to come through." But I didn't say that. I just said, "Thank you for the advice." Life is far too short to worry about such things. I agree with Aristotle and Ben Franklin: Moderation in all things is probably best.

Weight Reveals How You Cushion Yourself against the World

I didn't always believe this. I bought into the lie of self-deprivation. There was a time where I got caught in the dieting trap and measured my life by a bathroom scale. I became bulimic (a fancy word for the sad, pathetic and degrading practice of scarfing up a bunch of food and then forcing yourself to puke it up over and over again). Unbeknownst to me, my metabolism slowed down because I was severely malnourished, and I packed on the pounds. I couldn't see my feet over my stomach no matter how hard I sucked it in.

One day I looked in the mirror and said, "Well, Summer, I didn't know you'd become a fat person. But if you're going to be fat," I said in revelation, "you might as well enjoy it!" I'd gotten sick and tired of bulimia, counting calories and feeling badly about myself. So I started to eat. *Really* eat. I ate breakfast, lunch, dinner and dessert. Guess what? I started to lose weight. In fact, when all was said and done, I lost nearly forty pounds! I felt better, started working out to tone up and discovered that I never had to worry about my diet again.

Even today, at forty-four years of age, I have surrendered to the few extra pounds I carry. I've been on both sides of the weight problem/issue. At times my weight dropped so low I couldn't eat enough to get the pounds back on, and I looked downright anorexic—and was accused of being so. That was when my second daughter was nursing, growing like a weed and refusing to be weaned from the breast. My body was literally sucked dry.

These days I prefer the ten extra pounds that I carry. I feel healthier. And frankly, I really like to eat cheese.

From a different perspective, if you throw all the dieting magazines aside, I truly believe that weight is attributed to how much we choose to pad and cushion ourselves against the world. It's kind of like the use of cigarettes as a smokescreen—it's the same concept. When I trace my weight patterns, I can match the times when I entered into extreme periods of self-loathing, shyness or fear with the times when I ballooned out. When I left my fourth husband after suffering nine years of extreme spousal abuse, however, I suddenly lost thirty pounds in three days! The emotional weight was off, and my real body was exposed. I was a thin, depleted, exhausted and frail young woman, and it was time to rebuild myself.

These are just some of the reasons why I can't give my power to the cheese. I know in my heart of hearts that all of us are on a spiritual journey. I don't want to spend my life pointing fingers and saying, "The cheese did it!" I want to look inside my own heart and discover the many ways in which I can become more vulnerable and surrender into even deeper trance, to always work to improve myself as a spiritual worker in a way that will stick with me for life. I want to transform myself by finding and touching the face of God within me and abiding by the only truth that matters: God's love is the constant. If the work that I do in my own heart can touch the lives of the many rather than the few, then hallelujah.

There Are No Free Rides

There are no quick fixes or free rides. I might choose to stop eating cheese one day, but I highly doubt that it would make me a better channel. Even if it did, I'm pretty sure I would end up suffering from brittle bones or a heart murmur. Again, I'd rather do the inner work to improve my channeling—joyful introspection along with a creamy and hefty chunk of Saga blue cheese sitting on a Ritz. Sigh. Now that's what I call dinner!

Sure, you can induce all kinds of altered states through self-deprivation or by taking drugs. In fact, my mystical experiences are eerily parallel to the experiences I've heard from drug addicts. A hit of LSD can send you on an astral trip from which you might never return. A puff of marijuana can bring "such peace that you can literally hear the grass growing on the other side of the world," as someone once described it to me.

I personally choose not to do drugs, and I'm glad about it. My daddy jokingly told me that I should never do drugs, "Because you *are* drugs, Summer." I made the mistake of trying marijuana once when I was twenty-one years old, because someone said it had no calories and had the same effect as a glass of wine. I immediately found myself floating out of my body, heading home to God. I clawed and grabbed the couch, crying and begging my boyfriend to take me to the hospital. He was so high he just sat there and laughed at me while watching the movie *High Anxiety*. Fortunately, the effects of the marijuana eventually wore off, and then I ate a half gallon of Neapolitan ice cream. So much for marijuana becoming my diet drug of choice. [A side note: In people who are allergic to it, marijuana can induce symptoms similar to that of paranoid schizophrenia, and hence the reason for my extremely high anxiety—something I chose never to experience again.]

I figure that if there's a free ride, I'm not so sure I want to take it. At what cost is it free? For example, my fiancé was grumbling about his Yahoo email account and all the spam he receives on a daily basis. I said, "As my daddy used to say, 'There are no free rides.' It's a free account. What do you expect?" It seems to be the way of the world that we want to eat our cake and have it too. But what fun would it be if you ate your cake and another piece automatically appeared? What if apple trees always bore apples? We would never have the joy of baking the cake or of waiting for the spring buds on the tree to appear and smelling the delicate scent of the flowers. What's the big rush? It's funny that drug addicts often call the initial sensation from the drugs they take a rush. It seems to me that they are in a hurry to have peace and happiness—now, darn it!

Immortality and the Endless Journey

In *Gulliver's Travels* there's a fantastic illustration of how human beings would respond if we had the chance to be immortal. The immortal beings in this particular tale are totally bored with their existence. They've explored every region, played every game, had every conversation and eaten every kind of food you can imagine. They have no risk or challenge to their lives, because they are immortal. They can't die, so they don't need to eat, make money or worry about smoking, having high cholesterol or driving too fast. Think about it for a minute. Isn't that scary? Maybe there's a reason God made us to be temporary inhabitants of the Earth. The point of being here is to learn how to *be* here. As Dr. Peebles often says, "You are not a human doing; you are a human being." Another gem is, "When you get there, where are you going to get to next?" Or how about, "Once you are enlightened, what will you do then?"

Our journey never ends. It is a quest for love that we have embarked upon. Stop looking to the external world for your pleasure. No matter what you are doing, it is how you experience it internally that counts. Joy is joy whether it comes from a hug, a car or a trip to Machu Picchu. I used to tease my friend mercilessly about her upcoming trip to "macho peaches." You don't grow into greater spiritual awareness by taking a trip to India to see a guru, climbing a mountain, driving a fast car, sitting in quiet contemplation or not eating cheese. All the crystals, pendulums, tarot cards, psychic readings and open sessions with trance mediums are meaningless in your journey unless you choose to give them meaning in your life. They can't/won't/never will fix you. It all happens on the inside and by your choice.

Self-Responsibility Allows You to Create

It is self-responsibility for your life as a creative adventure of which I speak. Through your choices and perceptions, you do indeed create your own reality. These are the truths to which I adhere, not dietary illusions. When a dear friend came up to me in a panic because a woman came into his work wearing a gas mask and speaking about the dangers of "chem trails that the government makes in our skies," I told him, "Matthew, you need to be more concerned about a woman who dares to leave such chem trails of fear in your consciousness. How dare she!"

We can only accomplish so much in one lifetime. It's such a waste of precious life to focus on the size and shape of your upper lip or worry about another terrorist attack. I can't say that I am perfect in living in this awareness 24-7, but at least I try. I pinch myself when I stray from truth and remind myself that what I create on the inside is what I will take with me. I don't want to miss the journey to riches by praying to win the lottery. I don't want to spoil my chance to grow into greater love by blaming the cheese.

No matter how many things you fix in your life, you will never find the cure for unhappiness by looking to the external world, nor will you find the cure for your dis-ease until you find the comfort within. Take a chance to change your mind today. I did when I looked in the mirror and decided that if I was going to be fat, then I was going to enjoy it. I did it when I chose to forgive my ex-husbands—all four of them. Your free will can guide you closer to God, or it can tell you to look away. Don't feed the monster of fear. Choose to live your life with a smile, and remember to say "cheese!" There, by the grace of God and cheese, go I.

The New Age
Is a Lie

O ne Saturday morning in Sedona, Arizona, I stood in front of eighty-eight people who were attending my open session at the public library. Typically, before I go into trance to channel Dr. Peebles, I give a fifteen-minute impromptu talk on a spiritual topic that is close to my heart. On this particular morning, however, even I did not expect the words that came out of my mouth. As I looked out at the eager faces of the attendees, my mouth suddenly opened up, and out came the words: "The New Age is a lie."

Now, you need to understand: This is Sedona, Arizona, a place filled with energy vortexes and embedded with incredible ancient wisdom from Native American cultures. There are healers, channelers, psychics and thousands of spiritual seekers of the New Age who either live in or visit Sedona every year. Sedona is a like a one-stop shop for those who desire an intensive spiritual awakening. My friend, the late Don Pendleton (author of *To Dance With Angels*, by Don and Linda Pendleton), called Sedona "the lap of God."

So naturally, when I had the audacity to speak these words, it came as no surprise that I heard the clunk of jaws dropping on the floor, along with teeth, stomachs and everything else. The room was quiet as everyone drew in and held a collective breath, waiting to hear my reasoning.

"This [what I do] is not 'new age.' This is 'old age.' Channeling, psychic readings, hands-on healing, talking to angels . . . these things were happening even before the time of Jesus Christ. Same stuff, new packaging and brand name."

The crowd exhaled, and there was a great nodding of heads in appreciation of my words.

"The angels didn't stop talking after the Bible was written," I continued, and again there was a great nodding of heads, and now mutterings of genuine appreciation in response.

The reality is that Spirit has never stopped talking to us and supporting us in our journeys. God's love has always been constant. It is our challenge to adhere to that truth, no matter the circumstances, like Jesus on the Sea of Galilee during the storm. Are you going to get out of the boat and walk on the water with Him or stay behind, oh ye of little faith?

How Does One Keep That Spiritual Glow?

"For through your choices and perceptions, you do indeed create your reality," Dr. Peebles says at every session. So how does one keep that spiritual glow; the faith and trust that everything is always in the right order? How does one stop living life from grievance to grievance and create a life of joy and wonder, even in times of darkest despair?

First it is necessary to understand that spirituality is not something that is separate from living. It's not something that you squeeze into your day or receive from a book or a workshop. Spirituality is life, whether you are working in a giant corporation, standing in the grocery store, changing diapers or chanting a mantra while sitting cross-legged on a Sedona vortex.

A family friend, the late Swami Parampanthi, once said to me, "Summer, sometimes you have to descend into the pit before you can ascend to the top of the mountain." I remember pondering this one day when I was on my hands and knees in the kitchen cleaning up broken glass. I had two small children and a controlling and physically abusive spouse, and I felt that my life was running away with me—and now this! Broken glass to clean up. "God, why me? Why don't You love me?" I cried out in despair. I started talking to an imaginary guru on the mountaintop. "Why don't you come down off of your mountaintop, roll up your sleeves and help me out here, Mr. Guru? I'll show you enlightenment. Try feeling the peace while you're cleaning up broken glass and mopping up milk from the floor. Sure, go ahead and keep yourself separated from everyone by sitting on your mountaintop. That's easy compared to this!"

What I heard in response surprised me. "Now you're beginning to understand, Summer," a gentle voice said.

"What?" I cried out in my heart. I was livid. I felt Spirit was mocking me. "Look at all you have in this moment," the voice said. "Clean slowly and deliberately. You have told the children that they cannot come into the kitchen because they might get glass in their feet. You now have some time alone. What you have here is a respite from your everyday life. Relish it."

Wow. What an eye opener that was for me. It echoed what my mother once told me. "Since you have to iron, you might as well enjoy it." It's really the "sweet simplicity of spirituality" as my personal assistant, Bev Scott, calls it. It's the sweetness of life. It's enjoying the journey. It's life as a dance of wonder, not a dance of adversity. It was all beginning to make sense for me.

Slow Down the Process of Living

I believe that it is these kinds of moments that have taught me much about trance. Immersing yourself in the ironing, admiring the smoothness of the fabric, lovingly folding and creasing your slacks and slowing down in the process of living is the only way to truly hear that "still, small voice within." It is in these moments while blow drying your hair or standing in the shower that you have the excuse to surrender to Spirit. You might be in a family who would laugh if you said you were going to take time to meditate. But if you do it while living your everyday life, you might find that mundane chores become your spiritual sanctuary as you soak these moments in meaning, filling the seemingly empty spaces with God's love. Imagination is the playground for Spirit to communicate to us. It's the funniest thing that so often we are told as we grow up, "What's wrong with you? Why don't you use your imagination?" but if we talk about our invisible friends or our sudden visions of the future, we are reprimanded and told, "Oh, silly, that's just your imagination."

You can learn to hear Spirit in these seemingly mundane moments. For example, you might hear a song being repeated over and over again in your head. "What an annoyance!" you cry out. "Why won't it stop?" But if you simply listen to it, you might find a profound message therein. Once acknowledged, the song stops playing. Or you might see something glimmer or move in your peripheral vision. "Oh! Hello, Spirit," you say in acknowledgment. What a wonder when you hear in response, "Hello! It's Grandma here to give you a hug." Wow!

Lower-Frequency Entities Are Not to Be Feared

In the eleven years that I have been doing my work, I have seen people from all walks of life at my workshops and open sessions. There are so many hurting people in the world. People are so tired of hurting that they step into avoidance of pain at all costs, never wanting to hear any negative thoughts, living in fear of "lower-frequency entities," eating whole foods in the hope that they will find their salvation there. In my workshops, I have talked about how lower-frequency entities are not something to fear. If you are really in tune with God, then there is no care there, because you are the light, the way and the truth. No longer do you fear the darker spaces. Instead, you see them as "fertile soil where you plant your being and find and touch the face of God."

When I trance channel, for example, Dr. Peebles has to lower his frequency in order to work through me, and I have to elevate mine. We meet somewhere in between (we kind of "plug in" to each other, developing an energy circuit), and then he can speak through me with his messages. To

Dr. Peebles, who resides in the sixteenth dimension, I am a lower-frequency entity, and so are you! Yet Dr. Peebles doesn't fear us; he loves us! Can you imagine Dr. Peebles reciting, "Yea, though I walk through the valley of the shadow of death, I shall fear no evil," before he proceeds with his work through me? It's absurd.

We are here on Earth to immerse ourselves in life, not avoid it. We have a physical form. We feel, we think, we dream. The problem with a lot of people who call themselves New Age is that they tend to move through life based on the belief that life on Earth is in some way inferior to the spirit or angelic realms. I heartily disagree with this perspective. Jesus Christ did not walk the Earth in the avoidance of pain. He went into thieves' dens and he healed the lepers. He did not fear touch; he laid hands on anyone who required His touch. And imagine this, even if you do not believe that Jesus was crucified: He knew how He was going to die, but He did not say, "Good heavens! I have to do anything I can to avoid such a fate!"

It's the old "do unto others as you would have them do unto you" approach. Make the first move. Take a chance to step out of the box. You just might find that you step into your own enlightenment. Buddha once said, "Before your enlightenment, you chop wood and carry water. After your enlightenment, you chop wood and carry water." I think that pretty much sums up the journey.

I couldn't care less if you've traveled to India four thousand times. While you were there, did you stop to soak the lepers' feet and remove the stones that get embedded in their sores as they beg on the streets? There are 6.5 million of them on Earth today, and most of these are in India. So you sat in front of an enlightened man? What steps are you taking to become one of them? How much did you tip the waitress the last time you went to a restaurant? When you went shopping, did you return your shopping cart to the corral? Did you smile and say thank you to the teenager who served you at McDonald's or the whole foods store?

Dr. Peebles wrote three books about his travels around the world. But he himself admits that this was meaningless. He could have had a more spiritual journey if he had simply walked through his own backyard and gotten to know his own wife and children a little better. One of his children died and he was not present. This was a pain that he carried to his death.

Technology Has Grown, but the Journey Is Still the Same

Technologically speaking, our world is very different than it was two thousand years ago. From a human perspective, the journey is still the same. According to Dr. Peebles, "Certainly it is a quest for love that you have embarked upon." To touch and be touched. To give and receive abundance. I encourage you to move forward with your gifts. Do not fear the world, but love it. Pray in your darkest moments, "Dear God, what can I do in this darkness to ignite more light on the Earth through me?" You are God. How are you expressing that? Or are you suppressing the God that you are? Let God be expressed through you. Our journey on Earth is but the blink of an eye to Spirit.

I let God be expressed through me on that fateful day in Sedona when "the New Age is a lie" popped out of my mouth. I enjoyed the words of gratitude and acknowledgment that I received from people afterward. "It's something that needed to be said," someone told me. "I'm glad you had the courage."

A Brief History of the Illusion of Separation

I n the beginning, there was God. And what was God but the light, the spark, all that ever is, all that ever was? And this spark became larger and larger still. This very beautiful Spirit, this very beautiful being, fell in love with wonder. It was there that light was shone upon the planet Earth, and it was here, my dear friends, that everything upon the planet Earth became moved into motion. As the breath of God was breathed into everything upon the planet Earth—into the water, into the plants, into the soil, into the center of the Earth and all things upon it, even the little creepy crawlers—it was there that lightbeings came to planet Earth, certainly pure and harmonious with the Earth.

A Place of Wonder

There was a place of Eden, a place of wonder. It was there that everyone discovered that love certainly is sacred, that love is all that exists. It was determined there, one day, within this very beautiful garden of light, that there would be a point of separation. This was because the dear, sweet, wonderful, beautiful being known here as God has a point of growth for Himself as well—growth through wonder as everyone will soon understand.

It was through this wonder that He came to planet Earth and decided to stir things up a wee bit. It was there, as you read in your Bible, that one very dear, very beautiful being, a very beautiful individual, did eat from the Tree of Knowledge. Here was a point at which there was an illusion of separation—an illusion that there is separation between male and female, between light and dark, between good and bad, between up and down. These illusions of separation grew greater and greater still.

Indeed it was here that these illusions created a very beautiful school of wonder, a school called planet Earth, upon which little beings were incarnated. For as God grew, He created the heavens. In the heavens, He created little sparkles of light, little sparkles that you gaze upon each and every night—these known as the stars. And it was there that little spirits were born. And it was there that they were guided and directed to this beautiful blue orb known as planet Earth for greater and greater learning still.

Your Brother and Your Children

Remember, my dear friends, that you had a brother who walked the planet Earth [Jesus]. It doesn't matter whether you hold Him dear in your Bibles or in your churches, but remember that He did exist. If all upon the Earth would turn their sight upon this one being who was in the flesh, representative of all that you can become—not through religious doctrine or dogma, but rather by simply being one once again with the frequency of love—if all would set their sight upon one man who walked the planet Earth, and if they gazed into the eyes of this man and remembered the light from within, all illusions of separation upon the planet Earth would disappear forevermore. It is there that once again you will walk as lightbeings. It is there that you will certainly find life again. It is there that you will feel freedom beyond your wildest dreams and imaginations.

Do not forget the children of planet Earth. They are not only your teachers but so you are theirs. Do not forget this as your planet Earth comes into a time of great turmoil and great fear; remind the children that they can find and touch the face of God within every bubble from a little fish. God bless you indeed. It is in the sound of what you imagine, what you fathom an ant might make as it is eating. It is there that you find and touch the face of God, the wisdom. Remember, this is mere flesh and blood. What remains when this disappears?

The Coming of Light

And what did your beautiful Spirit, this wonderful being known here as God, the breath of life that moves through everything, what did He put into the heavens but the beautiful sun? This was so you would find that there is a great light always shining upon you, so that you would be reminded of this—a light that is very hard for you to look into, but a light that you cannot exist without.

And it is through this light that you will find resurrection of your souls. Understand that upon your planet Earth, before your Bibles were written, there were beautiful beings. They were filled with wonder and the illusions of separation, seeking and striving to understand love; to touch and be touched; to reduce this arm's length that was created through the illusions of separation, through this great fall, as you would call it here, of humankind. Is this something to be in fear of? No, my dear friends, it is a gift from the heavens to you so that you may grow toward greater and greater light still.

For it is in what you think is chaos and disharmony that you will find greater awareness of self, opportunities to discover that you are beautiful spirits and that you can certainly rise above that which is flesh and blood, which is you as you think. But this flesh and blood is nothing without the light that shines within. This flesh and blood that is your physical form is a dark and black cavern without a light of breath. Breath of what? Breath of God, breath of wonder that would shine through you. It is with this light from within that we are going to work with you in understanding how to find it once again, to shine it through this very dark cavern that is you, that you think is you—the physical form, the flesh, the blood.

How can you take this form here and find yourself exalted in it? How can you bring this to life as never before? You understand that your source is sacred; you are a sparkle that comes from the heavens, from this great and wondrous beautiful spirit known here upon the planet Earth as God. God bless you indeed. This is certainly, my dear friends, where you were born, from this very beautiful spirit.

And certainly, as you learn to listen to the little whispers inside of you, you will find that it is through your hands that you bring the light to the world, God bless you indeed, with the energy of healing, through the energy of care and of touch. As you would say here upon the planet Earth, "As God is my witness!" It is the energy of the Holy Spirit that runs and courses through each and every person upon the planet Earth; through each and every life form upon the planet Earth; through the very core of your existence, the very core of Mother Earth herself that you will ask to bring into this room for a resurrection of your spirit. God bless you indeed, here in this room today.

Now, my dear friends, you will find that it is through your mouth as well that you find greater understanding. It is through your willingness to bring your truth to the surface, to speak that which is you. In this way, you can allow others in the world to gaze upon you in wonder and to learn from your great integrity as you strive to understand your own existence, to bring as much of yourself to the surface and certainly to love the very same God. Bless you indeed. It is there that the spark from within begins to shine forth in the world, and it is through the eyes as well that you would shine forth your light into this world.

My dear friends, we can't open the eyes of this channel, for it certainly would burn her little eyeballs if we were to gaze through the aura field that is created here as we work through her. But it certainly is this light energy that you bring forth. Take a peek in the mirror every single day, my dear friends. Look into your own eyes and find the sparkle there. It is there that you begin to witness yourself and your growth. It is there that you fall in love with wonder. It is there that you find hope beyond reason, hope that no longer needs to even exist. It is there, my dear friends, that you learn it was never necessary in the first place—yet another illusion of separation—for it is only love that you need to bring to the surface of your flesh and blood. God bless you indeed.

Now, my dear friends, in order to sanctify—to make holy, to purify— this very beautiful physical form of yours, what is it that you are going to do? How are you going to find that your flesh and your blood can as well be as sacred and holy as your inner spirit? God bless you indeed. When you bring both of these into harmony, you walk the Earth feeling very light, certainly feeling very free, beyond your wildest dreams and imaginations. When you hold your hand up to the world, the healing energy that comes through you is one and the same as the Holy Spirit. God bless you indeed, as you remember who you are, your true source. But how do you sanctify this vessel in which you are a-walkin'?

There was one certainly, the Lord Jesus Christ, who walked the planet Earth in the human form. He was certainly flesh and blood, my dear friends, as well as the son of God, who came to remind you that you are all part of the very same family, all part of the very same union. He came to the Earth to give a very simple message to the world: that you are all brothers, that you are all sisters, that you are all one with creation, that there has always and only been unison and that everything else that you think is outside of that certainly is an illusion of separation.

The Dilemma of Disbelief

These are the teachings of the Lord Jesus Christ, who did indeed walk the planet Earth. But, my dear friends, now we have a major dilemma here. Goodness gracious, where does this leave you and others perhaps who have never heard of Him? Where does this leave those who are in disbelief that He is the Messiah? Where does this leave those who do not believe in God and those who call themselves agnostic? Where does this leave those who are what you would call here upon the Earth a wee bit soul-less?

Well, God bless you indeed, my dear friends. You understand that upon your planet Earth, you work very hard to resist temptation. Do you understand this? You focus your sights here, you try to resist your desire for foods for fear of calories, and you try to resist feelings of love for someone very special for fear of your lust. You certainly try very hard to resist speaking your truth and accepting the other perspectives in the world. You resist the urge to travel and the urge to create, and you resist, my dear friends, all the time, the divinity that you are. God bless you indeed.

It is this resistance that keeps you entrapped in the illusions of separation. It is there that you find yourself spiraling downward into misery and into disrespect. It is there that you find yourself moving away from community rather than into the ever-loving arms of every human being upon the planet Earth, shining your light forth, creating the aura field that can create instantaneous healing here upon the planet Earth. You could be walking, my dear friends, as the Christ who you are, walking certainly with love that abounds so freely that there is no longer anything to fear. "Yea though I walk through the valley of the shadow of death, I shall fear no evil." God bless you indeed, my dear friends, because why? Because it doesn't really exist after all, but you would like to continue in your belief that it does.

Well, my dear friends, you find yourselves entrapped in these illusions of separation. How very sad for you. You come to us, you pray to the heavens, you ask the angels and your guides for assistance. We share our guidance, our opinions and our perspectives. Sometimes you hear them, sometimes you do not. Sometimes you heed them, sometimes you do not. But understand, my dear friends, that it all has the very same source, and this is love.

God bless you indeed, for like it or not, you really are part of the very same family. There is one family member, regardless of religion, regardless of background, regardless of whether or not you have heard of Him, who did indeed walk the planet Earth. He was a man, flesh and blood—touch your skin and you feel Him there. He was made of the very same stuff as you, and His spirit was born of the very same grand and glorious Spirit who loves you so very much.

This Spirit simply wants you to entertain for just a moment here, to release for a moment here all childhood expectations, all religious confines and doctrine and dogma—all of this, my dear friends, simply release this, shed it off your skin for a moment here, brush it off your coats as so much old dust. Revive your spirit in this understanding that there is indeed a great Creator and that He truly does love you. Understand that there was one who was sent to the Earth who is a brother and stood as an icon for all to see so that you could understand the true relationship that you have. That's quite a family member to have here! You, my dear friends, all come from the same background. God bless you indeed.

He Helps You Remember the Unison

In your family history, you have a very beautiful man, my dear friends. This man came to the Earth and died upon a cross. He bled from His hands, His feet, His face, His forehead and His heart. This man allowed for the many rather than the few to cast their stones and their harsh words and their daggers. All their illusions of separation were cast upon Him. He taught everyone a rather fine and glorious lesson in this, for it was an illusion of separation after all. It was there that His soul was indeed resurrected, for He knew without question that His spirit was of perfect form. God bless you indeed.

My dear friends, certainly this very beautiful man who brought himself to the planet Earth volunteered for this far before He came here. He was very much aware of and involved in the process of His very first existence, His first incarnation here. He sent lightworkers to pave the way for Him, very beautiful spiritual masters, very beautiful spirits. God bless you indeed, to pave the way for His appearance here upon the planet Earth.

He creates this energy once again, as He does indeed intend to return in the physical form. God bless you indeed. This time around, however, He is going to be a little less than satisfied with appearing in one form. He would like to appear in the form of the many rather than the few. He would like a little more room to move around. He would like very much to move very freely through *you*, for it is through your hands, through your eyes and through your voice that you, my dear friends, can help. You can assist in His struggle to free you of the illusions of separation, to help and assist the many rather than the few to remember the unison of humankind; the unison of all that ever was, all that ever is, all that ever will be. This unison that you struggle to remember does exist, my dear friends.

The Source of Freedom

God bless you indeed. Come out of your darkness there. With every thought of your day, stop a-throwing daggers at yourself. Stop looking in the mirror and making decisions about what you deem to be wrong with yourself. Remember that there is someone who knows very much what is right for you, and there is only one source for your freedom, my dear friends: that is through your labor of love to diminish and dissolve the illusions of separation that exist between you and life and within yourself.

Dissolve these illusions of separation, and it is there that you will find freedom beyond your wildest dreams and imaginations. It is there, my dear friends, that you will no longer care what vehicle you are driving or what shelter you are standing in, because you will understand that you have all you will ever need. God bless you indeed when you are one, when you find unison once again with your family spirit—that would be God; it is there that you are forevermore reborn.

The True Communion

God bless you indeed, my dear friends. You are very beautiful spirits and we love you so very much. You ask about the value of the communion?

What was this? 'Tis not a necessity for you to take communion. It is not a necessity to work within a church. It is not a necessity to read your Bible, for God exists far beyond the written page—there we certainly assure you.

This Bible here was certainly created in a way that humans strove very hard to reduce the separation, to bring all the elements that they could possibly find upon the Earth that would explain this very beautiful being known here as God. They strove to explain what they felt was His wrath through the temper of fire, of volcanoes and earthquakes, of floods, of all things fearful. Certainly humans strove very hard to draw all of this into one place so that they could understand that there is no illusion of separation.

But that was not His wrath at all—it was His great love! For it was there, my dear friends, in the fires and floods and earthquakes—oh, one flood in particular! Anyone here recall?—that He was offering a great lesson of trust. The lesson is to trust that which you feel, the little whispers from within, the little whispers telling you that perhaps you don't want to say those unkind words to one another, that perhaps it is time for a gentler existence.

Despite the turmoil you see around you, in the greatest strife upon the Earth, the greatest calamities, it is time in your physical form here upon the Earth that you must reach inside yourself and find yourself the anchor of your existence. That would certainly be God, would certainly be the Christ energy from within—that which is pure, that which is fearless, that which is pure love, my dear friends. It is there in the time of calamity that you find yourself being a stable anchor for the many rather than the few, a clear thinker, a clear feeler, one who helps and assists the many rather than the few.

Understand, my dear friends, that there was a time upon the planet Earth when there was certainly some stormy weather at sea here. Christ did not care, for He knew that all was in right order, and whether he perished at sea or whether he lived did not matter; it was still one and the same place, whether here or in transition. It is all one and the same place. The unison of your spirit does not disappear, not with death—God bless you indeed—not ever.

My dear friends, you are each and every one here in this room today very beautiful spirits, and we love you so very much. It is here that this communion of which we speak now is: communion with community, communion of hearts. And what is your heart? What keeps it beating? It is the light from within you; it is the light that you shine forth. And within this ever-beating heart, there is circulating blood, blood that circulates throughout your body in the physical form. And what is there that holds it all together but flesh?

So if you, my dear friends, take communion from within, take communion as the Lord has shared with you here upon the Earth, to take of His flesh and of His blood, to become one with it, my dear friends, then suddenly your vessel is very pure. Suddenly it is where all ill health disappears, because that, in and of itself, is an illusion of separation. God bless you indeed. It is there that you suddenly are transformed. It is there that you suddenly are reborn. It is there, my dear friends, that suddenly all the passageways for your light to shine forth become wide open, all the cells of your physical form, of your flesh. God bless you indeed. The light can then emanate very, very strongly through the palms of your hands, through the top of your head, through your face and down to your tippy toes as well. It is there that your aura field becomes so pure that you can help and assist the many rather than the few by your mere presence, by the light that you shine forth.

It is not with the pennies from your pocket, not with anything but your mere presence—that is where you find instant manifestation. We have certainly the many rather than the few metaphysicians here in this room today who would very much like to experience instant manifestation, and you can do it. You can do it with your hands when you remember your Source and remember that you are one forevermore with the family. God bless you indeed. You are with the family, my dear friends of God.

Dr. Peebles Speaks about the Events of 11 September 2001:

The World in Transition

G od bless you indeed, my dear friends. You are all very beautiful students here in this room today, and we encourage each and every one of you to understand that this is a time upon your planet Earth of a great unfolding of your hearts. There is a strength beyond your wildest dreams and imaginations emerging from all of you here upon the Earth—not only from those of you in this room here today.

My dear friends, you will certainly discover that in the weeks and years and months ahead, your planet Earth will be undergoing a tremendous transformation. This is indeed the title of our lecture here today: "The World in Transition."

Energy Comes from All Sources

You are all very beautiful spirits, kind and compassionate; this is why you are here today, to hear a perspective from beyond your planet Earth. This perspective will help you retain the strength to remain here upon the planet Earth and to dig in your heels this time around. Each and every one of you here will be called upon to work your special magic here, and this special magic is going to come directly from inside of you, from inside of your hearts.

Be not discouraged here, but understand that there has been a tremendous impact upon your Earth, and without question, this is opening you up to receiving a greater light and a greater truth than you ever dreamed or imagined. Certainly there will be upon your planet Earth great wars and a great collective consciousness coming together to change that energy once and for all. You are a part of this, and you are responsible here for increasing the compassion of planet Earth. These are the light and the energy that you bring from within yourselves, my dear friends.

Right now we would ask that you close your eyes for just a moment here and draw a very strong breath into your very being; draw down into your solar plexus one great and strong breath that certainly is an acknowledgment that you are willing to receive life into you and not push it away. This is part and parcel of the acts that have occurred here upon the planet Earth, with your airplanes crashing into buildings.

Yes, my dear friends, you are being asked to draw in all energy from all sources, not just from what you consider to be light, but from the fullest spectrum of light. Sometimes that involves an entrance into the darker spaces. But it is in your willingness to embrace everything, all spectrums of color and light and darkness into your very being, that you at long last eradicate the fear, the panic and the hate. Then you can fall in love with the wonder and strength that is *you*.

God bless you indeed, my dear friends. This is what we ask of you, each and every one a student of the divine, without qualification. Do not push away a stranger, do not push away that which you do not understand, but rather strive within your heart to surrender, to embrace all that you see, hear, taste, touch, feel and smell. All this, my dear friends, is you, and it is there that you find and touch the face of God. It is there that at long last the world will hear your voice. You will not even have to speak, for you will be resonating a greater love than you ever dreamed or imagined possible.

Find the Greater Compassion

That is why we suggest this: that you consider within yourselves the ways in which you have been the terrorist inside of you, the ways in which you have stopped yourselves from coming forth with your greatest strength. How often have you not felt compassion there inside your hearts? Each and every one of you has had a tendency at times to fall into something less than love, and you have been rather determined at times to fall into hate. God bless you indeed.

We will ask that you reexamine this, not because we would have you find shame or guilt or any such thing inside of you, but rather so that you may retrace your steps there, fall in love once again with that which is you, look into the mirror and outstretch your hand, touch your face, understand and realize at long last that you are worthy of attention here upon planet Earth. You are worthy of love, and it begins with you. It is here that this consciousness you create inside yourselves becomes a circle that spirals out to the rest of humanity—*all* of humanity, my dear friends, each and every one a student of the divine without qualification, without judgment. It is here that you find greater compassion increased upon the Earth, here that you find you have great relevance to the current undertakings. God bless you indeed. You can certainly strengthen planet Earth through your own given heart, through your own choices.

Is it now a time for you to panic, to hide your face with fear, or is it now a time simply to allow the emotions to rush through you and allow the tears to flow? Allow yourselves to do the crying for Mother Earth and on behalf of the many rather than the few who have certainly transitioned out of body. Allow yourselves to do the crying, my dear friends, for you are the ones who are remaining behind here upon the Earth with something that seems like a rather large trash heap that you are going to have to clean up. We want you to understand that it is not a trash heap at all, but rather the opportunity for a tilling of the soil here upon the Earth so that you can plant new seeds and find greater growth. It is the promotion here of love that we are speaking about. God bless you indeed.

You are all very beautiful spirits, very kind and compassionate. Can you indeed outstretch your hearts and embrace and love those who have done acts that some would consider to be heinous? Can you erase from the lips the unkind words of these would-be people who have no understanding, who have the consciousness of a shark? We have heard all the expletives you can imagine over here on behalf of these individuals but, my dear friends, realize that perhaps they too are divine beings who have given to your planet Earth a great opportunity for growth and understanding, a great opportunity to increase compassion once again. Now you bring your planet into a new millennium here and certainly into a greater consciousness of that which is you, which is God—nothing less than that.

"God Bless Planet Earth"

And God bless you indeed, my dear friends. Just a moment here. Michael, how are you, my dear friend?

I'm just fine, Dr. Peebles. How are you?

You are here at our beckon, do you understand?

Yes I do.

Would you have a question for us?

Yes, as a matter of fact, I do. I think you've said it pretty wonderfully this morning, but this event, the events that occurred on September 11, in reality provide an opportunity to mature as a world, and I'd like to know what steps can be taken. What steps do you feel will be taken by the respective governments in order to bring a unity as opposed to dividing us further?

Yes, God bless you indeed. Understand, my dear friend Michael, that it is not going to be the responsibility of the government but the responsibility of the citizens of planet Earth. Do you understand? All of you here carry your signs and carry within your hearts "God Bless America," yeah? We would ask that you change this sign and sentiment to "God Bless Planet Earth." It is there that you at long last find the unity you are seeking and desiring.

All upon the Earth, my dear friends, no matter the package, are seeking acknowledgment and understanding. It is for each and every one of you to bring this understanding to the surface. How do you do this, how do pro- mote this action? By asking those who would be willing to go to war, to take a firm stand of hate, to create even greater acts of violence, if they would be willing this time around to turn the other cheek. Ask them to stand at attention with great wonder at the atrocities at times of the planet Earth without question and not propagate the very same. You do this one person at a time; you ask everyone to join together in a solidarity of human hearts and understanding.

Increase your compassion for those who do not seem to care, who do not seem to understand that upon the planet Earth, the point of being is to come and join together once again. Join back into a structure that has no struc- ture, one wherein you find greater freedom than you ever dreamed or imag- ined, one wherein at long last you find and touch the face of God, as we have already said, that is you and that is everyone you see—everyone without qualification, everyone without judgment.

Now, there is certainly a tendency at times within your government struc- tures to want to play out certain roles, if you will. There is certainly a stand they must take as the papas of their societies and to show that you are safe and such things, but you do not require this. You are safe already. You are safe when you are living directly from your heart, when you are allowing yourselves to feel greater love expanding rather than less of the same.

A Greater Consciousness of Love

My dear friends, allow yourselves the freedom to express love where oth- ers would fear, to express love where others would prefer to hate. Fall into a greater consciousness of love, for it is there that you begin to subtly and beautifully change your planet Earth and the structure of your internal gov- ernments. You will find that there is a common thread that eventually will be joining them all together, hand in hand, heart in heart. We would ask you this as well: that you would find that you have a fantastic tool by which you can communicate with the many rather than the few from your hearts. You have a means of increasing and propagating the love and compassion of planet Earth—that would be your Internet.

Working within a society there, you would create a structure and find a way in which to interweave your hearts in a planetary sense. You would find a way to create and manifest, as already is occurring worldwide and without shame, great prayers of love, great prayers that those who would be entrapped within their hearts in hate would find freedom at long last by stepping into a greater consciousness of love.

My dear friends, this is not by any stretch of the imagination something to be considered as trite or esoteric but as the point of your journey here upon planet Earth. Your governments are simply yet another structure that reflects a structure you keep inside of yourselves. Ask yourselves: "What is it that I hold dear? Where are my boundaries, and where am I willing to allow others into my heart? Where am I allowing others to cross my borders? Where am I allowing myself greater and increasing vulnerability? Where am I allowing myself to surrender?" That is what you all want, certainly, from your very wonderful spirit upon the Earth here, and it would make some of you wince in pain to understand that dear Mr. bin Laden here is certainly without question a very beautiful spirit and worthy of love and attention. Are you willing, my dear friends, to allow him into your hearts, or will you strain and stress yourselves by holding him at arm's length?

Hold him, instead, in a greater love than ever before, for he is perhaps one upon the planet Earth filled with more fear than the masses altogether. Certainly, my dear friends, those who are in a state of fear and panic want not to feel alone anymore. Oftentimes the choice there is, "If I feel alone in my fear, then I will have to change the world to join me in that, and in this way, I will not feel alone in my fear anymore." God bless you indeed, my dear friends.

Instead, ask Mr. bin Laden to join you in love, release yourselves, release your expectations. Give this very gentle, beautiful, frightened spirit as much love as you can possibly muster, for it is there that you will find the strength of ten thousand armies. You will find that, through a simple movement in this respect, energetically, from your own personal frame of heart, you can change the frame of the world. You can indeed disarm entire armies. You will find that energetically, you can change the waves, the patterns, the frequencies that are being used within weapons of violence. You can change the consciousness of generals and stop a finger from pulling a trigger. You can, my dear friends, and you will, for this is what you are all being called upon to create and generate from within your hearts.

It is here you will find that, over the course of the next twenty years, your planet Earth would change in the most wondrous and most magical ways. There will be a joining together of greater and greater community, an eradicating of borders. There will be a lot of change, without question, and you will find that what you are all stressing and straining against is really simple truth—that your planet Earth belongs to all, and it is certainly all for one.

God bless you indeed. Does that answer your question, dear Michael?

Tragedy or Great Fortune?

Yes. I had about four questions written down, but that takes care of almost every one of them. One other question was, "How do you view in your world the war, destruction, death, the transition of almost six thousand people [on September 11]? That had to have been pretty traumatic on your side to see that kind of transition occur all at one time.

God bless you indeed, Michael. For us it's a party—it truly is, my dear friend, because we welcome home many beings we have missed very much, as they have been in their school of planet Earth. For us there is a celebration, and from our perspective, in our world, as you would call it, what you have experienced here upon planet Earth is nothing more than stubbing your toe on a big stone. We can certainly understand that there is pain there, but there is also learning, so we do not feel the fear, panic or any such thing where we reside. We watch you in wonder, and we help where we can, and we give to all of you here upon the Earth a great, great love. We have watched and witnessed all the occurrences that have created what you consider to be a tragedy. From our perspective, it is a great fortune for your planet Earth, and the masses who have chosen to transition at this time have chosen this through their own desires to volunteer to help and assist the many rather than the few.

My dear friends, thank each and every one of them from your hearts for what they have given to planet Earth in terms of increasing the level of compassion. Certainly you feel pain, and what occurred [upon September 11] was a tremendous rush, sensation, fluster—a tremendous, incomparable, overwhelming sense of love. That is because you want to help and assist, to release yourselves from structure, to release your borders. There was a point in which you, each and every one, identified with the anger, identified with the fear, identified with the desire to destroy. Do not ignore that within yourselves, for it is there that you will find greater learnings in this process. It is there that you increase your level of compassion. Each one of you has been, as we have already said, a terrorist within your own heart. Through a willingness to now turn this around and to now identify yourselves as God, you will find not only freedom for you but for your very beautiful planet Earth.

But, my dear Michael, nothing to worry about on our end of things. We love everyone so very much, and we happen to know something that most of you still question in your hearts: Is there really life after death? We know that it exists and that death does not. So as far as we are concerned, nothing really happened. It was simply an illusion of separation between light and dark, between what you consider to be good and evil—an illusion of separation that you can now propagate, if you like. You also have the choice to see that everything is in exact and right order here upon your planet Earth. God bless you indeed. Does that answer your question, dear Michael?

Yes. One other thing: What you are basically saying is that if we create this positive thought process of love, starting with the people in the room and spreading it outward, in terms of not acting like we have in the past, thinking we need to go out and destroy someone who has destroyed us—instead we need to go out and love them and understand what the root of their hatred is, what the root of their fear is, to see if we can understand from their perspective why they would commit such a horrible act.

Precisely, my dear friend, for it is through understanding that healing occurs, you understand? Understand that, because of the occurrences on your planet Earth, what you have experienced is certainly very dramatic, and certainly the masses have transitioned out of body, but it is occurring all the time, just not on the surface and not quite in such a profound way. But the masses are dying all the time—from ignorance, if you will, or from a decision, a choice within each and every one here upon the Earth to hide your eyes from the pain. You hide your eyes from tragedies as simple perhaps as a child not having enough to eat, a lover killing another. My dear friends, it is happening inside your own hearts in small and subtle ways. You are tearing down your own buildings and penetrating deeper and deeper into your hearts with hate. Now you turn this around, and you will find that your planet Earth will indeed be touched.

In the Dark, Spread the Joy

My dear friends, September 11 did not shut down the license for laughter. God bless you indeed! Rather than allowing the laughter and the joy to disappear, is it not a time to bring them to the surface more than ever before? Think about this as you are working through your days, the times in which you feel that you must be in mourning and do not allow yourselves the laughter. Do not allow it to disappear, my dear friends; it is there that your planet Earth can disappear with it. If you allow yourselves to feel joy, if you allow yourselves to urge others to do the very same, you will propagate exactly that which you are praying for all the time.

Here is a greater sensation of love; bring it to the surface inside of your hearts right now. Here, in this moment, decide that you are going to walk through the days, weeks, months and years ahead with a smile upon your face and a word of encouragement for the many rather than the few.

It is there that you will suddenly find again that your consciousness, the circle, becomes a spiral, and you will weave this love and joy into the fabric of eternity, into the fabric of humanity. It is there that you find that others around you are elevated in their consciousness, and they are given permission to laugh because you can still find joy amidst the darkness and the pain. It is there that they go forth and touch other lives as well, and—fast as you can imagine, faster than fire can spread across a dry field—you will find that this love will spread as well.

My dear friends, we do indeed encourage you to spread the word to the masses, to the many rather than the few. Find yourselves an opportunity now to network hearts. For example, you could take your recorded tape and make as many copies as you possibly can, then share them with the many rather than the few. Allow others to listen to the words here today and to stretch their imaginations. Perhaps what you consider to be tragedy here upon planet Earth can be a fantastic journey, a great adventure, a time of discovery and wonder. Look at one another—we can feel it here in this room—with a little more love than ever before. You sense within your daily activities a desire inside yourselves to be a little more gentle and less judgmental. God bless you indeed for allowing yourselves to embrace the many rather than the few. God bless the world, my dear friends, God bless America and God bless you.

I think you portray a greater insight into how to function as a human being, how to manifest more things in the world than just our trivial day-to-day items, although those are important to us. But it's the greater thing that we need to understand and use your knowledge as a tool to get there. It's the collectiveness that allows us to do that.

God bless you indeed. It certainly is, without question, the collective consciousness. You understand that we are never far away; we can speak to you through this channel, without question. We can come here to speak directly to you in an effort to assist you with your pain, with your broken hearts. We understand that you are in agony. We certainly love you so very much through this, and we want you to understand that you are never, ever alone—we do not disappear once we leave this channel's body. We understand, we live, we breathe the collective consciousness.

Love Is Freedom

Now, once again, close your eyes and take a deep breath, a very large breath, and realize that you breathe in one another, and you breathe in a little bit of Dr. Peebles there. God bless you indeed, my dear friends. You breathe in a little bit of those terrorists whom you so fear. Breathe them in and give them life, for they are certainly worthy, as much as anyone else here upon the planet Earth. They have simply enacted what they feel inside in terms of their pain, their fear and their wonderment about God, the afterlife, sincerity, cultural differences. They have brought it all to life in a very large and grand and wondrous fashion so that all of you can learn, so that all of you now have to seek inside yourselves for the ways in which you are very similar and the ways in which you have felt the very same pain, the same fear and had the same desire to crush. You see that crushing only destroys. Crushing, my dear friends, does not build, but understanding does.

Love is certainly equated with freedom, and—God bless you indeed, my dear friends—there will be a great, great healing of planet Earth. You are not the only community at this time gathering in groups such as this one. This is happening on an international level, in all languages, through many channels, and you have decided to be a part of this as messengers of a greater truth.

My dear friends, we love you so very much. Release your expectations that more unkindness will be propagated. Do not put your energy there. If you must have expectations at all, create massive expectations that life will be in great transition, that people will be falling in love as never before, that there will be increasing understanding among communities and fantastic conversations among heads of your governments, working things out through simple conversation and the outstretching of a hand.

You are not alone, and there is nothing to fear; there is nothing to feel insecure about. Through an outstretched hand . . . dear Bev, the group holds hands here, God bless you indeed. Continue around the circle and reach out with all the kindness that you can bring and muster into your hearts. Close your eyes and breathe. Breathe in all that you are, all that life is—all that is, is simply love. God bless you indeed. Breathe, my dear friends, breathe that life into your hearts, increasing the greater love, the greater truth that you know inside your souls. Bring that consciousness here to planet Earth. There will not only be a great awakening of the masses but a great awakening of you, a great awakening that certainly guarantees your enlightenment. It is there that you find you don't feel any fear or panic. You feel simply love, my dear friends; it is there that you find freedom.

Will there be abundance in times of strife upon your Earth? Will you find financial freedom? Will you still have the opportunity to stand within your truth? My dear friends, the opportunities never disappeared. It is an illusion of separation and you can fall into hate or into greater love, and that is what you are being asked to do now here upon the planet Earth.

God bless you indeed. Breathe again, and as you inhale, you are breathing your divine being into your body from the other side. Push yourself deeper and root yourself here upon the planet Earth in all the love that you are, the greater goodness that you know to be true. That which you try to salvage now here upon the Earth in a grand and large and glorious fashion, my dear friends, you work to salvage inside yourselves, inside your hearts. Release now, my dear friends. With the next breath in, find the terrorists who reside inside of you; breathe in and wrap these beings in great love. Then breathe them out into the world; breathe them out, my dear friends. Release them from their prisons, release them from their confinements, and many of you who have been feeling rather agonized will find that you now are able to release these frequencies of fear and panic and hate.

God bless you indeed, my dear friends. Now breathe into your bodies once again and feel the freedom, the greater love, the magnitude of truth of the many rather than the few who have transitioned.

Earth Changes

The Turning of the Tides: Dr. Peebles Forewarns about the December 2004 Tsunami

16 October 2004

God bless you indeed. Watch, my dear friends, during the course of the next several weeks as the magic of yourself comes to the surface. You will discover that never in the life of your eternal soul have you ever been the victim; always you are the creator. And so we forewarn you just a wee bit here that there will be a turning of tides upon your planet Earth; there are circumstances and events coming that will be affecting the masses. It is a time for you to journey inward to your heart, my dear friends, where you can feel the expansiveness of yourself, of everything that you have admired about yourself during this time.

Take time as well to draw from your own resources, your own skills, and to remember that proximity to family at this time is extraordinarily important. For those of you who have family members whom you have not talked to for a very long time, we encourage you to make that telephone call as soon as possible. God bless you indeed, for, my dear friends, this is not a doomsday prophecy, but there is going to be certainly a turning of tides upon planet Earth. All people on the Earth are being asked to search their hearts for ways to come to greater understanding, to greater love, and to feel the prosperity and the abundance of God's love on the inside, within. That means that you must start with yourself first—you must harmonize your inner world so that your external world will bring about peace, for you are entering into turbulent times upon planet Earth.

So for a moment here, if you close your eyes and breathe very deeply, you can feel this. There is a certain eternal fascination on the part of every single solitary person, without qualification, that comes from the distant past, from a place of remembering who you are, where you came from and that you came to planet Earth to learn how to free yourself from structure. In this moment, we ask that you once again breathe very deeply into your spine, and we want for you first and foremost to look at your life in a most compartmentalized fashion. In terms of your work relationships, in what ways do these confine you? In what ways do they create structure in your life? What parts of these relationships are you stressing and straining against? What is it that you would like to change inside of yourself so that you can feel more peace in your journey in the external world?

Journey through the Portal of Light: A Meditation

Each and every one of you at this moment has a wonderful guide standing directly behind you. Breathe again into your spine, surrender yourself to this guide and the guide will lean closer to you now. You will feel a light pressure at the base of your skull, on the back of your neck and between your shoulder blades. This guide loves you very much and has been with you during your

entire journey here upon planet Earth, and this guide will now be speaking to you. Use your imagination, loosen yourself up, lighten up just a little bit more and allow your guide to share with you what you can do to create more peace within your work environment and within your work relationships. If you are unemployed, that is still a relationship with work.

Now reach beyond the confines of the Earth, the body and the mind; center your consciousness, your mind's eye, about twelve inches above your head. For those of you who are willing to use your imagination, to not struggle and to surrender, take a peek around. You'll find a little sphere of light, and it is a portal through which you are constantly incarnating yourself, constantly pouring yourself into this physical vessel here upon the Earth. As you peer into this portal, if you are willing to step a little closer to the light, you will have the opportunity to see friends, family members and others who are on the other side. Some of those who you see you recognize but you do not remember their names; they simply want to honor you, for you have determined to stick around on the planet Earth through times of turmoil, through hardship, through loss. This determination was made through your heart's desire, through the beautiful, loving and courageous being who you are here. Planet Earth is not an easy place to stay; it takes an enormous amount of energy for you to continually pour yourself into this physical vessel. That is why you rest at night—in order to leave your body and refresh your spirit, to gain the strength to come back again.

Now, as you leave that portal of light, feel yourself pouring back into your physical vessel, feel yourself as the spirit who you are and realize that never in the life of your eternal soul have you been the victim but always the creator of everything in your life—physically, emotionally and spiritually, my dear friends, for every thought, every action and every deed comes from inside you first before it is man-ifested in the external world.

Release Yourself from Structure and Confinement

"But Dr. Peebles, I get pushed and prodded by everyone to do this and do that." But, my dear friends, it is up to you to make the decisions to do this or to do that. It is your responsibility as to how you respond to any given situ-ation, including your physicality, including any pain that you feel in your physical body. Do not resist; rather, surrender and relax into the areas that feel confined inside of your physicality. Ask questions of these areas inside of you. Pick one right now. Develop a relationship with your pain and ask it what it is striving to stir up for you to understand. It is not there to be an annoyance; it is there as a guide, as a teacher. Return the love and respect that it has for you, for it is saying to you, "There is something amiss. Come, take a peek around and let's make a few adjustments in life, in your ways of living."

To release yourself from structure, to release yourself from the confinement that you have created inside yourself, will manifest in your external world as ease of movement and ease of breathing. Being with other human beings will be much easier. You have all heard the old adage, "Do unto others as you would have them do unto you," but can you be unto others as you would have them be unto you? Can you do unto yourself as you would have others do unto you? Can you be unto yourself as you would have others be unto you? So many times you have disrespected yourself; so many times you have said unkind words—"I'm too fat." "I'm too angry." "I'm too poor."—and it makes the angels cry in heaven every time we hear these words.

We are eternally and equally fascinated with each and every one of you, students of the divine. You are all very special, precious beings upon the Earth. You have at your disposal, inside of your hearts, everything that you require to create massive change upon the Earth, and it can happen through your mere willingness to touch a stranger. Now open your eyes and take a peek around the room at the coat of many colors that you wear. There are beautiful colors everywhere and beautiful things around you. Find comfort in your external world as well as within. Congratulate yourself on your will-ingness to stick around.

Expansion Requires Upheaval

15 January 2005

Beautiful creators here in this room today, goodness gracious, you are all washing away the tears and the fears and the expectations of planet Earth. This is the time—the year of 2005, a year of expansion—for you to understand that expansion is going to require upheaval, and this will occur upon your Earth in terms of Earth changes. Rather dramatic ones are about to appear on the horizon. However, these Earth changes are not to be feared but rather are to be embraced, for these Earth changes are only reflective of the changes inside of you that are about to begin.

The upheaval will begin within, and as you feel it inside of you, we suggest very strongly, for your own education, that you keep a notebook handy, because as you feel the upheaval inside of you emotionally, for example, when you are feeling an extraordinary episode of anger that borders upon violent tendencies, when you say to yourself, "Well, goodness gracious, why would I feel such a thing?" that would be the beginning of volcanic eruptions upon your planet Earth. In this way, you can allow yourself to surrender to the experience as a journey of love and understand that as soon as you identify changes inside of yourself, you will realize that after all, it is not so much you as it is the planet Earth.

Your Body Is a Little Planet Earth

It begins with you, for certainly the Earth is reflective of you. So what can you do to help and assist the Earth? When you feel these emotions coming up inside of you (goodness gracious, oceans of emotions as of late) sit in meditation and allow yourself to embrace the pain, the anger, the violent tendencies of the many rather than the few, and turn them into greater love, turn them into greater light and then, quite frankly, drink a glass of orange juice afterward, for this is going to expend an enormous amount of your physical energy, but it will help you through the experiences of pain. Remember this during the course of your year, and you will find that you will get through the tougher times, the darker spaces in your life within relationships—relationships with family members in particular. You will find that you will get through the tougher times and the darker spaces much more easily and quickly by embracing these experiences, by embracing the signals, if you will, that rise up from within you.

Your physical body is simply another little planet Earth, and it will be responding to the oceans of emotions here upon the Earth. Certainly, volcanic eruptions as well as earthquakes will occur on your Earth, but they are nothing to be concerned about. You will feel them in terms of jittery expectations inside of you; anxiety and panic; unexpected and without cause, reason or purpose. In your life, you don't feel this kind of panic, really; there's nothing in your life to signify that you should be feeling this way, and so again, stop, meditate, focus upon the panic and anxiety, make a little note of it for your own understanding and embrace it into your heart. Give it as much love as you possibly can. In this way, you can help transform planet Earth.

You can dissipate the energy much faster, and when forest fires start upon the Earth, that is passion raging inside of you. So find a lover, God bless you indeed, my dear friends. That would be our suggestion to you. And when we say lover, we suggest that you give love in so very many ways in terms of the humanitarian you are. Allow yourself to visit those who are elderly, to sit with them and hold their hands and listen to their words, for the masses will be leaving the planet Earth.

A Meditation for Channeling Yourself

We want for you to understand that you are messengers, in the future, of thoughts, ideas and situations from the distant past. You are keepers of information that will become very important to the planet Earth down the road in about twenty years. All people here upon the Earth are keepers of this information, and you will understand how this pertains to you in particular. It can be a very small piece of information, perhaps a photograph of a grandfather that you will be sharing with the world with wonder. So pay attention, because this will be revealed to you in the year 2005.

This will be a year of wonderful change, my dear friends. Release your expectations, release your fear that something might go wrong and understand that you have the opportunity to turn everything into an adventure that feels right for you. Instead of struggling against yourself, we ask that you embrace yourself, allow for yourself to be heard, allow for yourself to ask for what you desire in your life and ask for it with gratitude. If you would for a moment here close your eyes and breathe very deeply into your spine. We're going to have a little practice session here. This is called channeling yourself.

Once again breathe very deeply into your spine. There's a you inside of you who you've been ignoring. This you wants very much to be heard. This is the you who wanted to sleep in this morning. This is a you who wants to eat ice cream for dinner. We talk about it in very simple terms, because right now your Earth is in a very physical time, and so we ask that you tune in to these unexpressed physical desires that you have inside of you.

Once again breathe very deeply into your spine. Listen to yourself, listen to your heart, listen to the you who wants so much to be expressed. Is it that you want to go home and hammer out a page of writing that you've been denying yourself? Is it that you want to ride your bicycle for an hour? Do you want to call a friend or a neighbor and have him or her over for a cup of tea? Whatever urge you've been ignoring for so very long, feel it rise up within you right now, and take note.

In this moment here, with your mouth, if you are willing to, say the words, "I will do my will." When you say such a phrase, what you are really saying to the universe is that you will do God's will—the God-light that is inside of you, the universal force, the empowering existence, the oneness. This is going to become your mantra, if you will, for the year 2005. You very much want to be out of the box that you have put yourself in; you want to turn your life around, and that is why this is the time of the turning of the tides, because the tides are turning inside of you. The way you have lived your life in the past no longer works. It's all right if you want certain things in your life to disappear. It's all right if you don't want to move all the furniture when you make a change of residence. It's all right if you want to cut your hair. You want to redesign and reinvent yourself.

Surrender to this experience, for it is not just within you; it is universal. It is the force of God as God is moving right now. It is His constant exhale through you that you want to express—constant movement, no pressure, no fear and a complete and entire understanding that everything is in right order. There will be no more chaos, for even when life feels a bit topsy-turvy, you will realize that there is a purpose there as well. Just as with your storms, your tornadoes and your oceans currents, all are very beautifully orchestrated to show you who you are.

Breathe very deeply into your spine once again, and as you do, we want for you to feel the tide turning inside of you. It is a very friendly current; it is a teacher. There are those whose lives seem to have collapsed, but the collapse was necessary and appropriate. Yes, it evokes a response in you of sadness, love and a desire to embrace the many rather than the few to help and assist. This event [the December 2004 tsunami] has turned the planet Earth around entirely, and truly there is greater love here than ever before.

Bless Those Who Gave Their Lives in the Tsunami

In this given moment, God bless the souls who chose to give life to life by giving up their own lives, and understand that these individuals, the many rather than the few, were the children, the lightworkers, the ones who came to bring hope and to promote peace and balance upon your Earth. It is here in this moment that you give thanks for the upheaval, for it has brought you closer to your own heart, it has brought you closer to your family and it has brought you closer to God.

God bless you indeed, my dear friends. Mother Earth is an extraordinary wonder herself. Thank her every day for the soil beneath your feet, for the flowers that bloom, for the birds that sing and for the atmosphere that she keeps going. No matter how much you try to destroy the atmosphere, she creates more for you to breathe.

You are beautiful spirits here upon the planet Earth. This is the year to release your struggles, to release your pain and to fall in love—to fall in love with you. We love you very much.

A Time of Purification

22 January 2005

Y ou are all beautiful creators here in this room today and rather smart cookies as well. You are coming into a time period when we are encouraging you with urgency to focus and concentrate, to concentrate absolutely 100 percent upon you, upon loving yourself, for if you do not love yourself, you will not have the strength to enter into the next fifty-year cycle here upon the planet Earth. You must find the strength, the healing and the light within yourself before you can ever really give anything else to the rest of the world in terms of helping and assisting others with their behaviors—helping and assisting those strangers in your life who might need and require your assistance, whether financially or through a hand-shake, a hug or a listening ear.

The need upon the planet Earth is going to become tremendous over the course of the next fifty years. However, goodness gracious, congratulations to all who are here in this room today who have decided to stick it out and remain here upon the Earth, for you have come into a new consciousness upon the Earth within the past twenty-four hours wherein you are entering into the light—the liberty, if you will—of your soul, the love that God has intended for you eternally. As well—and this is without question here; we are not saying that you are a fraction but a part—you are a part of a very, very large community of spirits upon the Earth who are coming into their enlight-enment, so congratulations to all of you who are here in this room today.

But we do have this to say: Once you're enlightened, what ya going to do then? For it is not the end but only a new beginning, for your souls are going to be undergoing a tremendous time of purification upon the planet Earth. The next twelve-year period is going to be tremendous in terms of this purification. It is going to be a time period—and we say this with a bit of hesitation here because we don't want to create a sense of hierarchy—of some tests for you upon the Earth wherein you are going to be asked, when the world is feeling urgent, that you become the peacemaker, that you be the one who is willing to remain still upon the Earth and bring balance into urgent situations, that you be the one who does not fall into chaos but rather closes her eyes, contemplates God and asks for the answers. And then your life will be much simpler and easier and it will feel much less toxic, as you are going to become the lightworkers of the planet Earth.

Your Entire Universe Exists Within

Share of yourself with compassion but also with passion. Free yourself up a bit; allow yourself into the world with your own perspective of what you understand the journey to be about. Be the one who is willing to share the appreciation of God, of the planet Earth, of Mother Nature. Understand that everything here upon the Earth is in right order, that there is indeed a divine plan, and share this with those who believe that it is about big cars and big houses. These are beautiful things to share, if you will. You can have them in your life, but they are not your life; you have a life that is internal. Inside of yourself, inside of your heart, we ask that for a moment here you simply close your eyes, breathe deeply into your spine and come to recognize and realize that your entire universe exists within.

That, for most human beings, is a rather ethereal concept to understand and grasp, to truly and wholly embrace, but realize that everything that you are seeking in your life is a labor of love—it is a desire to give and to receive love, to touch and to be touched, even where it concerns your quest for financial reward. This is a quest for love, for when you are feeling abundant, when you receive money in your pocket, you feel love in your life—you feel whole, you feel complete, you feel that there is indeed magic, and suddenly God springs to life once again from within. This is what you are seeking: Heaven is not a place, my dear friends; it is a feeling that you keep alive inside of yourself—that being the feeling of love. This, in other words, means that for you, heaven is never out of reach, for it exists inside of you, and you have the chance, the opportunity, to bring love to life any time you want, twenty-four hours a day, seven days a week. All of you smart cookies here in this room today who are willing now to play with this concept:

 As you are going through your day, we ask that when life becomes chaotic, when life becomes less than magical, you stop for a moment, close your eyes and say a little prayer of thanks and gratitude for your life as it stands.

To say this puts you in alignment with God once again. It is there that you find freedom, for the perspectives that you need in order to get through the chaos will come to you very easily and rapidly. You will no longer feel that you are being sucked into a vortex of negative values, negative energy and living a life that is without integrity and out of alignment with God's love.

God's Love Is the Purification

As our little channel here has shared and expressed to you, "God's love is indeed the constant." God's love, my dear friends, is indeed the purification that you seek for your soul, for your life. It is not through religion. It is not through the formation of a corporation. It is not through any such action that you take externally; rather, it is through that which you create internally. So you can create your corporations, you can be involved in a religion, you can express yourself in many arenas and in many different ways upon the Earth, but there is truly only one expression, and that is born from the heart of God. That is the expression that says, "I love you and this forevermore."

God bless you indeed, my dear friends, and once again breathe very deeply into your spines; simply surrender for a moment to a new awareness that you are indeed part of a larger reality, a larger consciousness. This consciousness involves every single, solitary person in this room. There might be someone in this room about whom, if you should look him in the eye, you might say: "I don't really like him, Dr. Peebles. How can this person be a part of me?" My dear friends, he is, and we ask that you explore all of your relationships upon the planet Earth and see them as reflections of yourself. This does not mean that you have to embrace and love a stranger who really wants to steal your money, your car, your children or what have you, but instead, you can simply love and release that person unto his or her life and perspective.

Have loving allowance for all things to be, starting with yourself. Starting with yourself means that the truth of you is that you want very much to love life, and that's because you want to feel loved by life. So give unto others as you would like to have them give unto you, my dear friends—in terms of expression, in terms of desire and so that you can free yourself up to your own desire to love everyone without having to succumb to those who want to drag you down and bring you to a position where you miss the mark of your heart.

The old adage "misery loves company" is going to come to life beyond your wildest dreams upon the planet Earth, and we ask that you remain constant, remain the lover, remain the peacemaker when others upon the planet Earth are struggling to pry you from a place that knows that God is laboring here in love—not in strife, not in anger, not in war, but in love. That is the tip of the iceberg. God bless you, indeed.

Project Deep Impact:
Comet Tempel 1

Summer's note: On December 14, 2004, the Jet Propulsion Laboratory issued a press release about the comet Tempel 1: "NASA Set to Launch First Comet Impact Probe." In January of 2005, NASA launched an 820-pound copper impactor at 23,000 miles per hour toward the comet Tempel 1. The impactor will travel 83 million miles toward the comet and explode on impact, creating a football-field-sized crater. Scientists then hope to study the resulting fragments. Amateur astronomers are supposed to be able to see the "fireworks display" created by the impact on or around July 4, 2005. Dr. Peebles had already commented on this mission at an open session on December 4, 2004, ten days before the Jet Propulsion Laboratory press release. Several people, concerned about the impact of such an experiment on planet Earth, asked Dr. Peebles about the resulting consequences for the Earth and what they could personally do to change this destiny. The transcripts follow.

The Prediction

4 December 2004

What do you see occurring on the Earth regarding Earth changes?

There will be spontaneous fires, for example. You won't even understand where they come from. We will know—and you will too, because we will tell you, my friends—that they come from the heavens, God bless you indeed. Fires will be started by particles coming back to planet Earth and raining down upon it. These will be particles—goodness gracious!—shot into outer space by the United States of America. How do you like them apples? What you give out comes right back at you! And of course that's the tip of the iceberg. We could talk very differently if we were talking to the Eskimos, because there will be a little closure for that family of spirits who have come to the planet Earth, as well as a bit of an uprising.

The Consequences

10 January 2005

There is a comet that scientists are sending something to impact with. My gut feeling is to say, please, don't do that!

Yes. That is a good gut feeling, my dear.

Okay. There will be unforeseen consequences to that action, at least for the scientists who are doing this.

Yes. It is the rousing of a sleeping tiger. Understand that there are a quite a number of forces at work in the universe right now, and it is not something that we would recommend. You see, they don't have the foggiest idea what composes a comet. Little do they realize, my dear, that they are going to find themselves under attack as a result. Because there are living beings there.

20 January 2005

This is regarding comet Tempel 1. My feeling is that our government is making a huge mistake in attempting to fire a projectile into this comet. I feel it's going to release an energy that they are not aware of.

Yes, my dear friend. If you would refer to your book of Revelation, you would find it there. The reality is that yes, this kind of a striking out at the universe is a very sad day indeed. The reason for it, my dear friend, is because this comet is a beautiful creature, very spellbinding, not something to be attacked. Do you understand? As far as we are concerned, it is a Pandora's box.

Could this possibly be the cause of the mysterious fires popping up all over the Earth?

You understand that they have yet to calculate this. There is an enormous probability of there being an incredible backlash of energy from the center of the comet that they don't even know exists. They don't even understand the physical properties of a comet! They desire to see it as a very small occurrence, but the reality, my dear friend, is that it is a profane attack. You understand how, with a very small bullet, an enormous amount of damage can be done to the human body. This explosion will alter the course of the universe, and the many rather than the few are indeed trapped by this.

It has been aptly shown to planet Earth how even the smallest of meteorites can alter the course of the planet. A very small dent—a pockmark, if you will—can cause fires and trauma with the oceans, including such things as the disappearance of your lovely dinosaurs. So this is the kind of attack that they are planning, very much in ignorance. Mr. Einstein says that the law of relativity does not even begin to cover the massive destruction that will occur as a result of this for centuries to come.

The Effects of Meditation and Prayer

22 February 2005

In regard to the comet and the energy work we all did, how did or didn't our energy work alter the events that have been set in motion?

There is a chance that the events have been altered. They are not etched in stone, but at this time, there is an alteration of the device that is being catapulted toward the comet, and there is an acceleration of energy charges on the Earth as a result of this, because there is a chance that your extraterrestrial friends will be able to, in this particular case, intervene and throw it off course. And that, my dear, will bring all kinds of dramatic developments to planet Earth and to NASA that they are not aware of. It's not about finding out what the comet is about. It's about finding out what NASA is about.

There are many different forces at work, and you all are very much a part of the acceptance, if you will, that whatever will be, will be. It was very important to hold that energy and to allow for it without fear or panic. Panic and fear cause destruction, and what you want for the comet is that it not to be destroyed.

Is there anything more we can do as a group to further this action?

You can do it separately or together. You can, of course, pray for everyone upon planet Earth and ask for upliftment of the Earth, that you do not bring this kind of devastation to rain down upon it. Those on the comet are more accepting and tolerant of you and of all on the planet. They are very beautiful spirits, and they are very happy. They want you to understand that they are there for you.

This is an extraordinary comet. By design, it is part of an electrical circuit within the universe. It is not something that you would want to destroy, because that would be very much like penetrating a nerve synapse and disrupting its functioning, causing universal paralysis. Visualize the comet in and of itself. The symbol of the comet is an exact replica of the energy that flows between the nerve synapses in your physical body. This is your own fascination with the comet, based on the inner workings of your physicality. You want your nerves to fire rapidly and distinctly, with good communication between all synapses. Comets function as the messengers between the nerve synapses in the universe. Trying to destroy this comet is ridiculous, if you ask us. It will set the Earth back so far it is ridiculous.

Energetically speaking, it will be devastating and will have profound resonance. People will feel that their lives are at a standstill and that they don't have any means to move forward. There might be financial destruction and physical war on the Earth. Those are disruptions, if you will, of the nerve synapses within the human body. Many diseases will appear upon the Earth at a very rapid rate. Who will everyone be pointing fingers at?

Everyone on planet Earth will point at the United States of America. And, my dear, as far as we are concerned, this is abhorrent. You have been given a school called planet Earth where you are allowed experimentation in the physical and can do anything you like. You can even destroy the Earth if you like, but to go outside its confines and start wreaking havoc upon the universe is putting a blotch on God's canvas. To dissect God is disgusting. The point and purpose of your lives upon the Earth is to love God and be respectful of His creation. He gives you a small part of the canvas and says, "You finish that part. Make of it what you will. The rest is mine."

It's like giving a child your keys to play with while you're trying to work. Many possibilities in the universe are wrapped into this occasion. There is so much at stake here that even we do not have the final answer. Only through growth and the future prospects of planet Earth that reside in the human heart can the course of anything be changed, because it is a matter of whether or not you choose to align yourself with the force of the universe, which is love eternal. All the angels in heaven are on their knees and praying for you..

24 February 2005

Did our meditation and prayer for the comet have any effect upon the Deep Impact project?

Since yesterday upon your Earth, everything has changed once again, and there is still a possibility that it will hit the target. This is parallel to the occurrences on the Earth in terms of your government and such. As the energy of compassion on your Earth is raised and elevated, the Deep Impact project is being steered away from the comet. As the aggression on the Earth increases, then unfortunately the impact becomes more likely to occur. So it is in a delicate balance right now.

Your work that evening was very important. Each of you is a very strong being and is very connected to each of the beings within the comet. The comet is extensive, however. It would be like attempting to discuss the intricacies of the planet Earth and human beings upon it in terms of countries, nationalities, religions and so on. It is that complex within the comet. That's the tip of the iceberg. Once this Deep Impact penetrates the comet, my dear friend, it's going to be a very disturbing, sad experience for all. You might as well go into the woods and shoot an animal. It has the same resonance, if you will.

There is a good chance right now, about an 80 percent chance, that Deep Impact will explode before it reaches the comet, because there is no understanding of how the energy of the comet works. And so, as Deep Impact tries to enter into the comet, it will be spit back out like a fireball, if you will.

Of course, my dear friend, remember that the comet exists inside yourself. It ultimately affects you every time you pray for it. It will change several times before the final day of reckoning, so to speak.

A Change and a Great Manipulator

April 2005

There is a structure to the world and the universe that is very similar to the structure of the human cell. The particular electrons and protons and all the rest can be matched up with the way the stars and comets interact and interplay, you understand?

Oh, of course. "As above, so below."

Exactly.

Is the Deep Impact project something where we can force a critical mass of consciousness to make sure it does not occur?

You have an ability, my dear friend, to just hold that thought in your heart. You don't have to be as conscious of it as you would think. You can share with people that it is your desire and prayer that this does not occur. Unfortunately, at this point, the destination is slightly altered, but it will still hit its mark. At this point, it is a sad state of affairs for the Earth once again. There will be a lot of unusual energy raining down upon the planet Earth.

It is not something that we're particularly excited about, quite frankly. It's not that it's in wrong order, because there's really nothing to fight or worry about here; it's just something else that's going to happen. But it's unfortunate, because planet Earth was making great strides for a while in terms of compassion, open-mindedness and clear thought. There is one great manipulator upon your Earth: your president. He's rather extraordinary in the way in which he interacts and plays upon human consciousness. Pay attention to your television and watch how he plays it.

Okay. And I still have to give out that unconditional love because we're all part of a process of learning.

Yes, you love him, and we love him too. He's just a scared little boy.

Support One Another to Become Strong

Due to the rapid Earth changes approaching, this is a time of exhaustion for all lightworkers.

It feels difficult to keep moving.

It really is, my dear. In the old days, they had street lamps that were lit by a lightkeeper, and it was his job to keep them lit all night long. This meant that he had to stay awake in the dark, which is very hard to do. That is very symbolic about what life is like on planet Earth right now: You are trying to stay awake, even when it is very dark.

How can we learn to support one another in a way that is helpful to us?

You mean in general, upon the planet Earth?

Well, specifically lightworkers. We seem to gather in groups, and we kind of shift from group to group, depending on our needs or growth. How do we support one another or create some kind of a support system for lightworkers? We seem to become drained and need uplifting.

Yes, that is very true. It would be lovely to create a forum very similar to the day of enlightenment, you understand? It is a creation of family and an awareness that you are all carrying the same kind of card, if you will—you are all members of the same society. It is an extraordinary experience within your existence for you to be with those of like mind and like heart. As I was upon the planet Earth, I worked with the many rather than the few, and I had to constantly revive my spirit by gathering together, discussing and conducting séances or what have you. You just enjoy the work that you do more recreationally than professionally.

It is wonderful. We encourage many gatherings, as they strengthen the spirit to remain involved with the community. It is very easy, my dear, when you all move away from one another, for you to come under tremendous attack. That's how you get whittled away. There is strength in numbers. There is a reason for that: You are all spiritual warriors.

I feel that when we pull apart, we weaken and don't have support. In pure faith, the support is always provided by God, but we are human beings, and it is very difficult to reach that point.

Yes, but, my dear, although the faith is provided by God, God is made manifest through human beings. Moving away from human life is really a slap in the face to God. Human life is the point and purpose of your existence. God uses human beings, those who provide a clear channel, to speak to you and gather you together. The energy becomes stronger and stronger. The vibration of energy of a gathering of lightworkers can become very intense and pure.

There is power in numbers. Especially in healing and such, it is better to have two or more gathered together, because it is there where God's strength is extraordinary. Three or more is even better. Three is quite a powerhouse. It roots energy to the Earth. The triangle is a very strong symbol. God bless you, indeed.

The Harmonic Concordance and Healing

My dear friends, stand for a moment here, will you please? We ask you all to rise to the occasion of understanding that here at this given time there is a beautiful energy moving to your Earth. Your planet Earth is also moving through the energy. There is upliftment here tonight for each and every one here.

For a moment here, please bow your heads and breathe very deeply into your spines. Here tonight, my dear friends, there is certainly an opportunity to receive miracles in your life. You are now opening yourselves up to receiving all that you are, all that you ever were, all that you ever shall be. Once again breathing very deeply into your spines, feel your feet upon the Earth. Thank your very beautiful spirit of Mother Earth for your opportunity to visit her and for the very beautiful gift that she gives you by allowing you to stand upon her. Still breathing deeply into your spines, understand that there is an individual standing behind you, a guide who has known you since your birth, standing behind you now. Open yourselves and surrender; allow this guide, at long last, to help and assist you with certain conditions inside of your physicality, emotional conditions and spiritual enlightenment.

For a moment, I am going to leave this channel's body, and I will be working, as there is a tremendous transference of energy in this room at this given time as you open yourselves up to receiving light, love and laughter.

A Meditation for Unity

Now, with your feet firmly upon the Earth, you understand that this time of Harmonic Concordance is an opportunity to breathe in the light of yourself. Your mind, body and spirit are now being rooted here inside your physical form. As spirits, you are striving to have a human experience that is beyond fulfilling, beyond your wildest dreams and imaginations. You begin to embrace and under-

*stand the lightworker who you are, to understand that you are here to bring peace
to planet Earth. Each and everyone in this room is here to bring peace about
planet Earth through the smallest of deeds—and some through the largest of
deeds as well.*

*You start with yourself, bringing peace now into your own heart, and you begin
to feel your heart expanding. You begin to feel, as you stand here in this room, as
if you are rising up as the angelic being who you truly are. Every one of you is a
student of the divine, striving to understand where you were born and to remember that your heart is indeed at one with God—never, ever has been separate—
here upon the planet Earth.*

*Beautiful spirits here today, students of the divine, breathe very deeply once
again into your spines. Now would you please extend your hands out toward your
neighbor and hold hands. Continue to breathe deeply, as no longer is there separation between you and your neighbor. Through this very simple act, you begin to
break down the borders, barriers and boundaries upon the planet Earth. You do
it through this simple act—and now through a very large act—no longer holding
life at arm's length but rather falling into the embrace of life. We would ask now,
my dear friends, that you give your neighbor a hug, without fear, without reserva-
tion. Turn to another, give that person a hug and understand that it is there that
you find what you have been seeking here. To touch and to be touched is why you
are here. God bless you indeed, beautiful creators of the divine, and certainly, my
dear friends, you may sit when you are ready, and we shall continue.*

In Search of Fulfillment

God bless you indeed, my dear friends. Certainly you understand that
you are here in this room today to seek a greater awareness of yourself. You
have not found fulfillment in your cars, your homes, your work. You have
not found fulfillment within any relationship, for you still seek. Everyone
here today still seeks to understand where true happiness lies. Well, we
would say that true happiness certainly does lie within your heart, and you
can have it with every single breath. Understand that you will not leave this
room without caring just a little more deeply for yourself. Understand that
what you are seeking is sitting right there in that chair, because heaven is not
a place—it is a feeling, an expression of yourself fully and completely here
in this room today.

So right now we would ask that you stop with your mind, close your eyes
and . . . My dear friends, some of you in this room here are already making
lists for tomorrow. Right now we would ask that with a deep breath, you
release making your lists. For some here, your thoughts are straying to an
individual for whom you care so very deeply . . . tremendous worry and
concern. We would not ask that you take your attention away from that per-

son, but since you are going to think about him or her anyway, do this: *For a moment here, breathe very deeply into your spine, and as you breathe deeply in and as you exhale, imagine that you are exhaling through your heart and offering to this very beautiful and special individual the pink and radiant light of love from you. It is 100 percent pure and true. Take another deep breath in, and now exhale once again through your heart. Give this person your love; understand that you can touch him or her, even if it is one for whom you grieve, who is no longer upon the planet Earth.*

Practice Forgiveness

Now we would ask that you turn your attention to something that's going to be very difficult for some of you. At the same time, my dear friends, it's going to bring about a release in a form that will be beyond your wildest dreams and imaginations. You will see the resonance of it for weeks and months and years ahead. Whom are you afraid of? Whom are you afraid to forgive? You see, my dear friends, for you to forgive is to give up your control. To forgive another would be to make certain that he would win and you would lose—that's what your thinking is—but truly, to forgive is divine. Certainly you will find that you are not a loser but indeed a winner, as will the other one, because it will then be an expansion of love upon planet Earth beyond your wildest dreams and imaginations.

So we ask that you hold this person in her pure form as you see her right now, afraid of her, perhaps angry at her, certainly wishing she would fall off a cliff. Well, how about she falls off a cliff and into a deep and warm, beautiful bucket of love? Breathing very deeply into your spine, realize that the only way you can make a man, woman or child change is to truly forgive his or her misdeeds. It is there that you grow and share a prayer that they will grow into greater enlightenment. Thereby you are contributing once again to the healing of planet Earth.

For a moment here, breathe very deeply into your spines once again and then open your eyes. We would ask that you hold your hand out in front of you and examine the beauty that you see there. Examine the beauty of your skin. Do not judge yourself—your skin is beautiful. Turn your hand this way and that, open and close your fingers and realize now, as you look around the room, watching everyone opening and closing fingers here, you are made primarily of the very same stuff. And certainly it is not your skin but your ever-lovin' heart that is one with God at all times. You just have a tendency to forget this every now and then.

Healing Hands

We would now ask that you reach to your own shoulder with your hand and give yourself a nice little rubbing there. Truly feel the sensation. Is it not miraculous that you *feel*? Is it not enough that your skin is alive, who you are able and capable and willing to draw in a breath each and every moment of each and every day? Is that not enough to honor the great creator who you are, to honor the beautiful heart of God? Certainly, once again, look at your hand.

For those of you who have difficulty moving your hands due to what you would call here arthritis, we would simply ask, are you ready to find liberty upon the planet Earth? Are you willing now to embrace freedom? If you are, certainly we will, my dear friends, be working with you this evening to help you heal your hands. *Right now we would ask that you take your hands, turn the palms toward the floor, close your eyes and breathe very deeply into your spines. Now we ask that you, with your mind's eye, within your imagination, draw your attention to the base of your spine and breathe once again very deeply in, and as you breathe out, this time you will be breathing out through your palms. You will be releasing dark energy inside of you—not something to be afraid of, not something that is impure, but simply something that has indeed been a teacher for you for many decades. For some of you here in this room, it has been a teacher for centuries. As you breathe once again into your spine and breathe out through your palms, feel the tension drain out of you toward Mother Earth, ridding you of static electricity and immobility.*

Allowing yourself greater freedom of movement here upon the Earth is what this exercise is about for you. Greater mobility will be reflected in your emotional state. How willing are you, my dear friends, to open up your hearts and to release old patterns and old expectations of human life around you? How willing are you now to let go of grief and realize that certainly there are situations that have arisen in your life as wondrous teachers, not to cause you pain, but to cause you an opportunity to grow closer and closer still toward God?

Cast Off the Heavy Coats

Certainly, my dear friends, you are wearing many coats here, layers and layers. *As you continue to breathe into your spines (you may put your hands back in your lap or do what you like here), feel the many layers of these coats very heavily upon you. Feel the weight around you. How many layers do you have? Seek them, give them your attention, stop avoiding healing yourself first. Allow these layers of coats, of old patterns, of old expectations, to drop away. Surrender and drop each coat, one by one, allowing it just simply to fall down to Mother Earth, discarding old ways that have bound you for centuries, one by one. Now you begin to feel yourself lightening up just a little bit more, breathing very deeply into your spines and understanding, as you begin to release, to drop your expectations and to surrender into greater trust, greater freedom and the greater love of God, that you can live a life here now upon planet Earth unconstrained.*

My dear friends, how many of you here in this room today are now willing to truly root yourself upon the Earth? Are you willing to rid yourself of the phrases "I wish I would die," "I don't want to be here," "It's too hard," "I ⟵ can't go on," "I'm getting impatient"? Are you willing to change your thoughts toward those that provide freedom? Are you ready to say, "I am willing, dear God, and I submit my will to yours. I am willing, and I allow myself to be the divine being who I am. I am willing to receive love from others around me. I am willing to surrender into the greater embrace of life and love, opportunity and laughter here upon the planet Earth"? God bless you indeed. Are you ready to say, "I am willing to stand firmly in my body, to realize that every breath is a gift and every opportunity is certainly a chance for me to grow closer and closer to the heart of God"?

Someday all of you here upon planet Earth will be returning to the bosom of God, wherein no longer will you be wearing heavy coats of expectations and old patterns that have bound you. But you will be wearing a coat of many colors, many facets of light that certainly you will be wrapped in and will be running through you. Beautiful colors, my dear friends, because you now will have rendered to all that you are, all that you ever were, all that you ever shall be. My dear friends, at this given time upon your planet Earth, this time of Harmonic Concordance, you begin to wonder, "Where is the Star of David?" Look up, my dear friends—it's right over you. Who is the Christ child who is born here today? It is you, and your manger is right there within your heart.

My dear friends, there is no more separation here upon the planet Earth. You have an opportunity now to fly free beyond your wildest dreams and imaginations. Flight of soul does not mean wanting to escape your physical body. It means coming into your body fully and completely, once and for all, and committing to your eternal journey to understand the grand and glorious adventure of God's love. Here, tonight, my dear friends, you take your consciousness, which is a circle, and through a decision, you turn this circle into a spiral. You begin to weave yourself into the fabric of eternity that becomes your coat of many colors. You are all beautiful spirits here in this room today, and we love you so very much.

Understand the New Energy

In regard to this new electrical energy you have stated will flow through me onto the planet, what do you specifically suggest to be the most fortuitous course of action for the next couple of months?

All right—for you or for planet Earth?

Oh my goodness, let's go for me.

Well, first and foremost for you, my dear friend, it's very important to know that you're not the only one. This electrical energy is going to be coming through everyone. You're going to be working with a particular strand of it and others will be working with other strands, but it's going to be a very powerful energy. You will feel it every once in a while, just so you are aware, feeling a bit woozy. And then sometimes you'll feel so charged with energy you won't know what to do with yourself. There will be times when you are so charged up that we are going to ask you to simply sit down and hold yourself. Force yourself to sit still and close your eyes and breathe deeply into your spine. Allow the energy to run into the Earth, from the crown chakra down through your feet.

→ It's going to be the times when you are woozy that it will be very important that you reach out to be with human beings as immediately as you possibly can, whether it means you run down to your grocery store or what have you. It's not going to be easy, but it's going to help you to be around other human beings. That will help to root this energy in you. It's going to shift and alter your life in unexpected ways, because life will be very attracted to you.

Life will not want to leave you alone; life will hand you many opportunities, one after another, until you can't count how many opportunities are on your plate. At long last, you will have to surrender and say, "All right, hallelujah for that, but I like this and I don't want that." It's all right for you to make that decision yourself; you do not have to take everything that comes into your life and say, "All right. I take it as a gift from God, so therefore I'd better put it on my shelf," because otherwise, my dear friends, those opportunities just become old, dusty knickknacks in your life driving you crazy. That's been happening forever, and it's time for it to stop.

We share this with you with the understanding that the very same goes for everyone here in this room today. Understand that you are creating a new reality for yourselves here upon the planet Earth. Understand that your planet Earth is being charged up in such a fashion that you will have to release your expectations. You will have to redesign your life. You will have to re-create yourself through recreation. Here, today, with the Harmonic Concordance, there is indeed a rooting of the Christ energy of mind, body and spirit of Christ within, in all of humanity and within every single cell of your being, within every single cell of every tree and within every single cell upon the Earth. This energy will root within the cell of every animal and within every human being, not just in your United States of America, but within other countries, other cultures. There are going to be what we would call here spiritual crybabies on your Earth asking for attention now, saying, "We are tired of doing things the old way—help us."

A Look at Changing Earth

And certainly, my dear friends, you will watch as planet Earth begins to evolve in strange and miraculous ways. Borders, barriers and boundaries are being eradicated, and mystics are springing up everywhere. Certainly, part and parcel of this is going to be the acknowledgment of the government toward the appearance—and sometimes the disappearance—of extraterrestrial activity here. This will not have planet Earth afraid but in absolute wonder, saying, "Well, we knew it anyway," in public acknowledgment. Why? Because it is a time of no more separation. It is now, my dear friends, that you will understand that within the unity, there can be a glorious exploration of diversity. It is there that everyone on the Earth will be asked to surrender deeper and deeper into your hearts.

There will be an uncovering yet again of even greater atrocities, man to man, man to woman, child to parent, on your planet Earth than you ever dreamed or imagined possible. But this is not to cause you dismay; it is a sign, an indication that there is no longer any room, my dear friends, for the darkness here upon the Earth, as you are indeed being raised into greater and greater light of understanding.

It is not a matter of good against evil, right against wrong. It is simply a time of elevating your souls and your planet Earth. There is going to be a measurable movement of the Earth closer to the Sun that will be scientifically brought to light. This does not mean that you will perish, but you will indeed gain strength from this. You will begin to understand that you are altering yourselves, genetically speaking. You are altering yourselves, not through your physical form changing, but by your spirit being willing now to incarnate fully upon the planet Earth.

Lightbeings who you are truly in your spirit, you will begin to cause the alterations in the physical form. This will produce miraculous experiences for all upon the Earth over the course of the next twenty years, certainly in terms of what you would consider to be medical breakthroughs. These will simply be a matter of bringing the old energy and enlightenment, if you will, of planet Earth back to Earth. I refer to the energy you rebelled against so many centuries ago, when you first incarnated here. This energy mentioned in your biblical times had human beings placing hands upon one another in a form of healing. Those who were being healed believed 100 percent that this was the reality. Now you will find that in your medical industry, there will be more call for lightworkers to lay hands upon individuals for the healing work to begin.

You will feel less constrained and confined; you will find freedom and flight of soul through so many opportunities, more perspective than there are stars in the heavens, my dear friends, here upon the planet Earth. You will celebrate diversity, a celebration of all that you are in your fullest array of colors.

Enjoy this opportunity upon your Earth for love, laughter and freedom as you shed the old, heavy coats of winters past and don a very beautiful coat of many colors. My dear friends, go your way in peace, love and harmony.

As you sit in your chairs, fanny firmly placed upon your seat, feet firmly upon the floor, breathe very deeply into your spine once again. Unite yourself now with the stars in the heavens as the stars begin to pour into your crown chakra, down into your spine, down into the base of the spine, activating the kundalini of wonder in creativity, down into your toes, light, rooting you now to the Earth. Please sit in such silence as we allow the dear channel to return, and as we do, we will leave her for a few moments as she remains in trance so that we may work with you. God bless you, indeed.

● ● ●

A Healing Adventure

Please open yourself to the healing today, because I know the many rather than the few spirits are here to work with everyone. You have come to the school called planet Earth, each and every one a student of the divine. What are you studying in terms of divinity of self? Certainly starting within, starting for yourself, loving allowance there. As you turn your hearts inward, you begin to understand that there is a never-ending unfolding of yourself that occurs outside of the physical realm, through vibrational frequencies.

Here today, in this room, we want you to stretch your imagination, to understand that you are so much larger than you realize, so much more than the physical form. This coat that you wear here, this coat of many colors here upon the planet Earth, is an exciting realm of exploration. Its study helps you understand yourself, all that you are, certainly the One who you are—unison and unity with all that you are, which is God, ever expanding.

The Realization of the Whole

So here, today, we ask that you open your hearts and surrender. Surrender to the many rather than the few beautiful spirits who want to share with you healing and understanding. Trust that the responses from the heavens to the Earth will be occurring today. These will not only help you understand that you are already whole, that you are already healed, but also that you are healers as you open your hearts.

It is through your hands, through your eyes and through your hearts that you share of yourself with the world. With your hands, you can reach the many rather than the few, even without touch. You find yourself searching for one another, extending your arms to one another, understanding that part and parcel of your existence here upon the planet Earth is to reduce at long last the arm's-length distance you have felt with life; understanding that everything you see, hear, taste, touch, feel and smell certainly is you. Embrace it all back into your heart and there is nothing left to heal.

Here in this room today, you have an opportunity, within this very small realm as it would seem to you, to surrender to a much larger picture of understanding. We would ask that you simply turn to someone in the room and gaze into that person's eyes. Feel within your hearts greater and greater love—love beyond your wildest dreams and imaginations. Can you gaze into the eyes of a total stranger, human being here upon the planet Earth, and fall in love? Allow yourselves this feeling, for as you fall in love with life, you find that there is a sensation that occurs inside of you. It feels physical to you in response, but what is really occurring here is that you are opening yourself wide, stretching yourself, stretching your spirit. You are immersing yourself into life rather than retracting from the very same.

It doesn't take any effort to love. It does not take any effort to expand. It does not take any effort to embrace all that you are, the discovery and the wonder of the very same. As you open your heart and give this love to another, sharing it with another, it must begin inside of self. Feel the feeling of love for you, starting with yourself. Not only do you serve the many rather than the few by so doing, but you find, my dear friends, that the tensing inside your body, in your muscles—the stressing and straining against life—begins to dissipate. You begin to feel that inside of your physicality is nothing but light—useful, lovely, white light, an ever-expanding spectrum of color.

We ask you now to begin to breathe very deeply into your spine and simply close your eyes for a moment. Feel now, here and within yourself, within your heart, within your soul, the circle of wonder that is around you—human beings here in this room today, beautiful spirits each and every one.

Reducing the Distance between You and You

Now that you have gazed into the eyes of one, within your hearts, gaze within the eyes of the many rather than the few. Search within the recesses of your mind there; try to remember those you saw in the doorway; try to remember the little girl known as our dear channel, Summer, whom you saw here upon the stage. Search for all who are here in this room—some of whom you did not notice with your eyes but can feel within your heart, for they are not separate from you.

The separation is indeed an illusion, and we ask that you embrace the many rather than the few into your heart despite their color, their feelings, their emotions that at times you want to run away from, to hide from. You bring fantastic tools to planet Earth—the tools of mistrust, of distrust, of distaste, of discouragement, of sadness, of humility. Understand that all these are tools you use here to build little cages around yourself, to keep yourself at arm's length from that which is you. These are the tools of illusion, illusions of separation to keep you at arm's length from the world around you. As you work so very hard to hold life away, your body begins to feel very sore and tender inside. If you are using the tool of anger, for example, day after day, night after night, it can reside there in your liver, within your colon, within your heart, within your hand, within your joints. Your physical body begins to break down. Why? Because it is only truly sustained by the frequency of absolute love.

So now breathe again very deeply into your spine and realize that the many rather than the few certainly are requiring healing, starting with yourself. With every breath that you now take, realize that you are breathing in all of life, that you are never separate from the very same. Can you trust that all that is you is certainly nothing to fear? All that is you is certainly something to love. As you take in every breath, fall into greater and deeper love with all of life.

Heal Relationships with Love

You certainly have one individual in your life who has driven you crazy, and we would ask that you now hold that person in front of you, in your mind's eye. Do you at first feel the panic arising inside of you? Feel the many colors of your emotions. Feel the anger, feel the separation, feel the yearning and the desire of your soul to connect with this individual once again in a loving manner.

Now we ask that you visualize this individual in front of you. Surround him with the very beautiful color of blue light and begin to dissolve these illusions of separation as you begin to surround him with your love. Now breathe and breathe again as you draw him closer and closer to you still. Now you feel captivated by this individual who in the past has driven you crazy. What is he driving you crazy with now? Just simply with love!

Now, it is through your labor here of love that you have embarked upon a fantastic journey to your heart, a fantastic adventure of expansion of yourself. It is there that you find flight of soul—freedom beyond your wildest dreams and imaginations—by no longer holding anything or anyone in life at arm's length.

Now breathe very deeply, closer still to bringing this individual inside of you. You have the courage, you have the strength. It comes when you fall into greater love. Now bring this individual inside of you and greet her with as much love as you can muster, for your healing as well as for hers. Your healing, remember, comes first. Now you have just merged as the healed and the healer, all at the same time. And with this last breath, with your exhale, you breathe her back out into life refreshed and renewed. Watch the transformation within your relationship during the next several weeks, months and years with this person.

Work with Medicines Harmoniously

You are all very beautiful spirits. There is one here in the room today who gave to Summer the words that "healing cannot be found within a jar or a container but certainly is found within." This individual is a man known as Mr. Edgar Cayce, who did walk the planet Earth and is a very beautiful spirit. He wants you to understand that every remedy you touch, every pill you take is embodied with frequency. He wants you to understand that as human beings, you will frequently opt for your pills, remedies, medicines and such things. He wants you to realize that if you choose to do this, then take your pill, hold it in your hand and honor the frequency that is going to be brought into your body. In this way, you will find that it will work its wonders upon you much faster than it would without your acknowledgment. Otherwise, these frequencies have a tendency to just simply run rampant inside of you. This begins to tear you down as well, because you have given your power to something on the outside rather than realizing that it starts with yourself.

So it begins by setting a stage and whether it is a vitamin or a pill from your doctor, we do not care. It's not a matter of judgment here whatsoever but learning to discern how to work with the world in which you live so that you can work with it harmoniously, so you do not have to hold any of it at arm's length. Healing does not come from a special diet. Healing starts within yourself. Healing comes in the form of a frequency—the frequency of love. So when you set the stage—whether it is to receive a bandage on your arm or a surgeon working within your heart—you begin by closing your eyes and asking that you would receive everything in love. Ask that only the frequency of love within all realms here would be brought into your body. It is there that you would find great transformation within your physicality as well as within your own spirit, because what you are really healing first here is your spiritual self.

Your Ever-Expanding Soul

Understand that your spiritual self wants to expand, always. Once you incarnate in the physical form, however, it seems at first that you are very limited, that you can touch only as far as you can reach. But, as you are very much aware, you can feel, when we are putting our palms toward you, that we are touching you always. [Dr. Peebles does this using Summer's hands.] Touch is, once again, only in the form of a frequency. So understand that you are not limited by your physical skin.

We would ask that at this time, you would again close your eyes and breathe very deeply and imagine that you are much larger than your physical form. You are beautiful spirits here upon the planet Earth. Many of you are lightworkers wanting very much to care for the many rather than the few. Find this compassion within your hearts again and, as you feel this love bubbling up within, you bring light into the darker spaces within your heart and soul. When you find this feeling of compassion, you have begun again to heal yourself and to heal all of life around you.

Your soul wants to ever expand, and it is trying very hard. Here upon planet Earth, it seems to be wrestling at times with ways in which to expand. You strive to do this by creating movement with your automobiles, your airplanes. "I can expand myself to other countries!" But understand that you are not limited. You never have been. It is an illusion of separation. You, through your hearts, can bend time and space. You are timeless and eternal beings here upon the planet Earth. Planet Earth is a canvas, you are the paintbrush and it is your heart with which you color the planet Earth in terms of the frequencies that you desire to bring to planet Earth.

The Cage of Your Physicality

If you abide by the illusion of separation that your soul is limited only to this cage of your physicality, you find yourself frustrated, angry, feeling that you cannot get up in the morning. You find yourself very tired, because you are encumbered by the physical form. Your physical body begins to respond to how you bring yourself to the surface. If you cannot see yourself as timeless and eternal, if you do not understand that you are beyond your physical form, certainly your physical body begins to respond. The cells within your physical body begin to shut down. They begin to implode upon themselves, creating all sorts of situations inside of the body.

For example, with situations within the nervous system, there is a lack of communication. When you have problems within your nervous system, ask yourself, "In what ways am I keeping myself from communicating love with the world? In what ways can I increase my communication of love?" Once you begin to do this, you will find that your nervous system begins to function much more smoothly. There is more contact, more communication within your nervous system.

When you find that you have sore spots within your body—these range from bruises to the many forms of cancer—you can flood them with light. These are areas that have become very dark and dense, but understand that the darkness is not the absence of light but the density of the very same. You want to wake it up once again.

So you search inside of yourself and you go into the darker spaces as a courageous adventurer because your soul very much wants to expand. Your soul, being very light, very white in its appearance, wants to radiate this light into these darker spaces. See if you can find within your physical body right now—close your eyes—a point of pain. It is there that you have an opportunity for expansion of yourself. Find freedom there by visualizing the cells within your body as little balloons that have been popped, but with your light, you will fill them up once again. You will wake up the cells within your physical body and fill them once again with your spirit. Radiate light into the darker spaces and awaken your cells. It is here that you can correct, if you will (pardon the word "correct," but for your understanding), what you would consider, sadly enough, to be physical flaws within your body. You can focus on the wrinkles and lines around your face, worn ever so thin by time, and inflate the cells once again. You do this through absolute trust and faith in the great creator who you are, as the God who you are. You know that nothing, but nothing, is outside of love. Breathe and bring greater love into each and every cell of your physical form.

Heal Your Broken Heart from This and Other Lifetimes

Each and every one of you is a student of the divine, creator of wonder and magic! Now how can you heal your ever-so-broken heart? So many carry great pain from lifetimes of many miseries, of many twists and turns of relationships that some of you have felt have squashed, your hearts torn to bits. The many rather than the few are wondering how they can wake up in the morning. It is here where we enter a realm of emotional healing from tremendous pains, not just from the current lifetime, but also from previous lifetimes. Within this emotional pain, there is a relationship to the effects upon your physical form.

Your emotional pain comes from not being able to immerse in life and not having life immerse in you. You are here upon the planet Earth with the many rather than the few who are struggling in a very similar fashion to find their enlightenment, to wake up to the understanding that you are an eternal being, that you are not limited, ever. And so you are given what you think is a very limited physical form. It is there that you must find creative ways to expand yourself. You do this with your voice, with your eyes and with your ears. Great healing can occur simply through being willing to slow down and to listen. Tremendous healing can happen by being willing to speak your truth once and for all. We would ask that each and every one of you focus in the weeks and months and years ahead upon bringing your voice to the surface with purity, with integrity and, first and foremost, with compassion.

You love planet Earth in your heart of hearts. It would be your greatest desire to be here forevermore, to fall in love at long last with the adventure of discovery of self here, to immerse yourself in life and to there find freedom beyond your wildest dreams and imaginations. It is there that you will find enlightenment. It is there that you lighten up just a little bit more, and it is there that you fall in love with the process of bringing this light to the world. It is a belief that there is an ending that has you all afraid and skittish. That there is an ending is an illusion of separation. There is never an ending; there are only beginnings.

You fear that there is an end to something due to pain in one's physicality. With the onset of such "diseases" (as you would call them here upon the Earth) of Parkinson's, of Alzheimer's, and even with the common cold, as you would call it, you fear that it is an ending to your life. That is how it is perceived; that is how it is felt. But from our perspective, these are just areas, relationships within yourself that you can explore and play with. Through your imagination and creativity, you learn to respond to these points in time where your physical body gives you wonderful opportunities to wake up and to expose yourself to the world once again.

It is at these times that you want to allow yourself to be vulnerable with your voice, to share your love, to share your heart, to speak your truth, to ask for what you need, to ask for assistance from those around you and to ask for a hug, a kiss, tenderness or touch. It is there that your levels of stress—at the root and the heart of all disease, *dis-ease*—begin to dissipate. It is there that you no longer feel that you constantly fight your way out of a box. It is there that you find that you are no longer fighting your way back to the surface, gasping for air.

Within this relationship of the love that you are, the love that you are here to generate and create, you amass yourself in the given moment, where suddenly time disappears and there is only Now. And right now, you have an opportunity to create heaven upon the planet Earth.

Establish Healing Relationships

Please close your eyes once again and breathe very deeply into your spines. Now simply focus with all your heart and soul upon what it would feel like to have perfect health, to have everything in your life perfect in terms of its emotional balance, to have all relationships harmonious and compatible, to have everything that you ever dreamed or desired to have, to have all your dreams come true right now. Visualize, breathe deeply into your spine and feel the very deep relaxation that comes with the wonder—the wonder of you.

This feeling that you now are immersed in is reality. There is no illusion of separation. There is no impossibility. There is only opportunity, and this is the starting point. This is the point at which you now take this consciousness that is a circle inside of you and expand it. Expand your consciousness to family members, to friends, to lovers, to those you meet on the street. All of it is a part of you, all of it is indeed One, and there is nothing to fear. Your soul is eternal and the feeling of heaven is eternal. The feeling of heaven? What is it but love?

You're all very beautiful creators. You can create with your physical body, with touch; but first and foremost, you must make a decision. You must decide that you want freedom beyond your wildest dreams and imaginations, and you must understand that it is an illusion of separation that your physical body has command over you. It does not. Your spirit is in charge here—your spirit and its desire. Your willingness, your courage to share of yourself with life is where the healing begins. In any relationship, with any doctor, with any healer, with any therapist, there must first be established a relationship of love for the healing to work 100 percent. We would ask that in all your future relationships with doctors, healers and others, you make it very clear within yourselves who you would allow to touch you. This is certainly not because you are making any judgment whatsoever, but because you want to be certain that this is a relationship that is pure, that is in integrity, that is in love.

How do you find out, my dear friends? You feel within your heart if you are willing inside of yourself to work with this individual, to allow this person to touch you and to receive the healing and the light from him or her. The healing does not come from the surgeon's scalpel but from the surgeon's heart. It comes from the movement that is created in the room during points of surgery; it is created in the room during points of discussions with your doctors. The pills, the remedies, the presumed requirements for your healing—these are all illusions. The healing truly starts within your heart and through your willingness to join and to bond in a healing adventure with the many rather than the few.

Heal by Loving

It is with this awareness that you will find that your bouts of illness will be much shorter, even when it comes to the common cold. I want you all to understand here that I, Dr. James Martin Peebles, who walked the planet Earth as a doctor, certainly as one who studied a form of natural healing, primarily wanted to share with planet Earth the awareness that I could heal by loving you. That is the scalpel I use to find my way into your hearts. To heal your soul is to start with the love I carry for you at all times. It is there within that relationship that all ill and all pain begin to dissolve.

My dear friends, you all have the capability to bring this love to planet Earth and to help in the healing of family members. Would you please now, if you would like to receive this gift of understanding the healer who you are, hold your hands out in front of you, with your palms facing outward. Close your eyes for just a moment. Each and every one of you, students of the divine, students of understanding the divinity of self, if you now would like for your hearts to be activated, to become more conscious of the healers who you are, begin to feel the energy that is going to flow through your hands as we touch each and every one of you here today. Understand that you do not need or require any kind of title, if you will, for the healer who you are. You are all simply servants of love.

Breathe very deeply into your spines as we continue to work with you here today. [Dr. Peebles breathes heavily here as he works with the group and then returns to Summer's body.]

Heal Generations of Pain

Now we would explore the little hurts that you have all carried for a very long time, points of shame and guilt in the course of your life. First we want you to understand the reason you feel this when it comes to relationships, when it comes to distrusting yourself—that you have not done enough, that you have not cared enough, that you have not given enough. Understand that these feelings teach you much about the great lovers who you are of planet Earth and of humanity. It is our greatest wish for all here to be filled with an intoxicating sense of self, an understanding that what you want is always to give more love to planet Earth.

We are going to give you a little awareness of self-discovery here. All of you are starseeds planted upon the planet Earth. You have come here as representatives of a community of spirits, of family members, so that you can now break free—break through the barriers on behalf of a very vast community of spirits who are indeed requiring of healing. There are many here incarnate. And there are many family members and others of whom you are not necessarily aware in your consciousness who are also a part of your family; they are here in spirit form and are waiting ever so patiently. They know that what you would want more than anything in the world is to heal, given half a chance. Well, courageous adventurers you are for making the decision here to step forth and to free many souls into greater light!

Much of the residue of sadness, of shame, of guilt, of anger, of difficult struggles within relationships with family members and much of what you perceive to be little illnesses and such that would be biological in their nature (you got it from Daddy or Mommy or what have you), you carry within you on behalf of an entire group, an entire community of beings. You have the courage now to break cycles here. You do this by finding within yourselves what it is that has bothered you emotionally, that has bothered you physically, that has haunted you a good portion of your life. Why is it that you still carry this sharp pain in your spine? Why do you still have difficulty in breathing? Why is it that you manifest difficulty in your nerves? Why do you have difficulty standing on your own two feet? Is it because of your mommy or daddy? Or is it because you are a courageous adventurer willing to carry the years and centuries of pain and sadness of an entire community of spirits and you are now willing to resolve this, to open a new gateway for love to emerge?

That is tremendous in and of itself, first because you are so very courageous. At this time, for just a moment here, we will sit in an honored silence of you, in a loving moment for yourselves.

[Dr. Peebles takes a very deep breath and breathes heavily for a moment.]

Are You Ready to Heal?

God bless you indeed, my dear friends. Ask yourself what you should heal inside of yourselves—the pain inside your heart, your hands or your spine. If it should heal all at once, what would really heal inside of you? For a moment, simply think, ponder, use your lovely brain, your imagination. If this pain should disappear at this time, if you should lift the veil between yourselves and life, what would occur? How would it feel? What would heal within your family?

Now ask yourself if you are ready for a moment in time where you can heal. It can happen in an instant, through your will, through your trust, through your love of self, through your love of life. A tremendous responsibility comes at the point of healing, at the point you release your pain, for it is there that you will open your eyes upon a new world, new relationships. It will be a most trying and yet wonderful time for you. For as you walk the Earth, you will not be able to see human beings the same way anymore. You will see the many rather than the few with more love than you ever dreamed or imagined possible, without judgment and truly without having to discern. You will then have opened yourself as such a tremendous loving being that the pains and ills of anyone who walks into your life will simply dissolve by being in your presence!

You know this to be true within your heart of hearts, within your soul. *For a moment here, close your eyes. Breathe very deeply and allow your guides simply, to gather around you and to take you back to a point in time before your birth when you had the understanding, the realization that you are eternal, that you are pure love and that there is not anything that is outside of you. There was a point in time before your birth when you understood the richness that comes from the awareness of being one with all of life—with all of life. You knew there was nothing outside the realm of understanding or of God but realized this oneness that includes everyone here in this room today, everyone upon the planet Earth and in all layers of the onion, the many realms of existence. All of this is you—all of it, not one bit outside of you. And for a moment here, we will be silent as your guides take you back to that point in time.*

In this understanding, no longer are you caged, no longer are you boxed in, but you are now willing to take charge of your spirit, for in that oneness, there is a tremendous opportunity for growth, for understanding yourself in relationship to all that you are; for understanding that in unity and unison, there is tremendous diversity. You can be everything you ever dreamed or imagined. It is this that you seek here today. Now, for those who have gone far away from your body, come back in.

Honor Your Physical Form

With this awareness of yourselves, please keep your eyes closed. Come in closer and closer still to your physical form. Become very aware that you have a body here; you have a heart that is ever-beatin'; you have blood coursing through your veins; you have organs that are working whether or not you are aware. Goodness gracious! When was the last time you thought of your kidney? Your spleen? Your liver? Would you please, as a courtesy right now, give honor here to all that you are in this physical form? What a lovely, beautiful vehicle you have! Many of you here express more love for your automobiles than for the very vehicle that you are embodied in at all times! Such a very beautiful body! You have everything that is required for healing right there at your fingertips.

Become very conscious that you have a skin. It's fantastic! It holds it all together, holds in your beautiful bones. It helps to guide and direct you as to the space you occupy here upon the planet Earth, physically and otherwise. Feel now your arms and your hands. Become very aware of your hands and understand their tremendous capacity for touch. Feel your hands now expand-ing; feel beyond the tips of your fingers and realize that though you have this physical form, you are much larger than it still. Breathe very deeply into your spine and become very aware of your legs, your kneecaps, your feet planted firmly upon the planet Earth.

Connect with Your Environment

Ah, planet Earth! She is a very beautiful spirit as well, of whom you are a part and she is part of you; you are all one. She herself has a tremendous amount of energy that she can give to you—a tremendous amount energy. You are drawing upon it at all times, and you might give a little honor today to something known here as gravity—holds it all together for you once again. How often have you thought to honor this frequency, this being a part of you? *Feel the unison, feel the contact, feel the wonder and thank the ever-lovin' air that you breathe around you. Breathe very deeply and become aware that it truly is the broth in which you are all immersed, that you all share;*

you're all in one pot, so to speak, each and every one a very beautiful spirit, each and every one a student of the divine.

Now, with this awareness of self in connection to Earth, in connection to breath and certainly to the physical form for just a moment here allow your spirit to fall into the soup. How does this feel to you? An expansion of self forevermore! There is no there to get to. Feel yourself once again expanding into the world rather than retracting from the very same. It is much easier upon your physical body, upon your emotions, to surrender rather than to resist, to trust rather than to fear, to love rather than to hate. Breathe very deeply into your spines once again, and now please stand up.

Move your joints and your limbs about. How many here in this room today are feeling greatly refreshed inside? Yes, quite lovely, is it not? Have we done anything for you? We have done absolutely nothing except to love you, to share with you that you have an opportunity to love yourselves, to find freedom beyond your wildest dreams and imaginations with the heavens and the Earth colliding inside of you forevermore, with nothing to fear.

Look toward your neighbors here. Turn and look at each person in the room. Your healing begins here, when you come into the awareness that there is nothing to fear, nothing to bring about panic. Take a peek around the room. Is there one individual more than others who would provide for you a tendency to retract, a tendency to be in a bit of fear? Is there one whom you would like very much to greet and to meet but are afraid that you cannot speak up to him or her? If you would be willing at this time, would you step forth to this person and say a little hidee-ho and perhaps exchange a handshake and perhaps even go so far as to give a hug? We will sit here and watch.

God bless you indeed. You are doing fantastic work; we can feel you there. Look at all the healing occurring here today. Fantastic work! Do you understand now that you have healed a part of yourself? Does it not feel much better to you, now that you have bridged this little gap in your heart? You understand that your soul truly wants to be expressed, your soul certainly does want to emerge, your soul does not want to stand in fear of anyone, your soul wants to reach out to the many rather than the few. We made you all feel just a teensy bit uncomfortable, and that's all right as far as we are concerned.

The Purpose of Pain

When you are in pain, when you are uncomfortable, it is not without purpose. Pain is a wonderful director of your soul's existence; it is a signpost, a flashing symbol that there is something that wants your attention very, very much. So when you are afraid to approach one person but are happy to stick with the nine whom you are comfortable with, you might ask yourself why you are not willing to bridge the gap with the tenth person. It is there where you will find healing. It is within your comfort zone where at times you even find stagnancy. The soul loves a challenge. Give yourself up to this challenge! Fall into greater and greater love beyond your wildest dreams and imaginations, and it is there that you will have unexpected surprises. You will discover that you were afraid to talk to this person because it turned out he or she is your soul mate, your lover everlasting. But if you are not willing to go into uncomfortable places, then you are holding part of life at arm's length. It is there that you are retracting from possibilities, from opportunities for your soul's growth—and growth is freedom, and freedom comes through love, and where there is love, there is absolute healing and nothing more.

It is the point and purpose of you to be here upon the planet Earth without any pain whatsoever, feeling happy and giddy at all times. Planet Earth is a place of exploration now and forevermore. Stop waiting for the "there" to get to when everything is just fine, what you here call "peachy." It is in these places, in these times, that you will find yourself creating disasters, creating situations around you so that you can find and seek more of yourself—that is, a greater understanding of love that is always growing. There is no absolute, ever. So you turn to the heavens, you pray to God, you beg for healing.

We hear your prayers. "Heal me, Dr. Peebles! I am in pain!" My dear friends, you must first turn to yourself and say to yourself, "Heal me! I am in pain! Please help me understand what it is that I want in terms of greater love in my life. Why do I feel this discomfort? Why do I feel this anguish? What is it that is making me feel so very toxic and so very tired?" It is most difficult for you, but it is surrendering to a greater truth about yourself.

Surrender into a Different Perspective

For a moment, surrender into a different perspective. Let's do a little experiment of understanding yourself. For a moment, we would ask that you examine everything that we say and decide whether or not it is true about you. Find ways in which it is true.

So for example, we are going to say that you are all very angry people. Ah, goodness gracious! Is that a judgment from Dr. Peebles? Fear and retracting: "I am not angry at all! I am furious with you right now, Dr. Peebles, but I never get angry." God bless you indeed, we tease you a little bit! But ask yourself, "Am I angry, ever? Are there times when I am less than loving? Are there times when I am self-serving, working to manipulate life outside of me by not offering my truth? Are there times when I not only allow myself to lie to the world but to lie to myself? Are there times when I feel that I am truly the victim here and the world is out to get me?" That's true too, my dear friends, for each and every one here in this room today. That is not judgment.

We point the way to understanding yourself first, the great lovers who you are. Never have you been the victim, but always, always the creator. How do you create? What is it that you create? Create and manifest a house? All right, not a problem at all. Create and manifest perfect health, the perfect sexual relationship, a book, a relationship with Spirit, a new type of orange juice—something that is a little bit more sour, something that gives human beings a run for their money at ten dollars an ounce? Create what you will, but understand that all that you create starts from a quest for love. It is a quest for love that you have embarked upon, and this is the point and purpose of your existence here upon the planet Earth, and it exists in every moment of your day. Every moment is a journey into greater love.

In every moment of your day, you have the opportunity to wake up to a greater awareness of self when you do not want to admit that you broke the vase. Pause for a moment and ask yourself if it is worth it to lie, if it is worth it to not be in a greater consciousness of love. You are students of the divine, of the divinity of self. Bring yourselves to the surface with integrity. Walk your walk, talk your talk. You've heard it so many times. It doesn't mean that you have to have a loose tongue at all times. It does not mean that you must tell your neighbor that he or she has on a rather ugly shirt today. It does not mean that you must be sharing everything at all times, it only means that when you decide to share, you do it with integrity, with truth and with a will that certainly is strong, that very much wants nothing less than to promote greater love upon the planet Earth.

For you seek healing of self first, then you expand this to the others around you through your touch, through your willingness to have a conversation with one from whom you wanted to retract at first. You do this by allowing yourself to stand in proximity to an individual who does not look like you but whom you would like to get to know because you know he or she is you.

Enjoy the Exploration of Yourself

It is through this willingness that you touch the lives of the many rather than the few. What happens then is that this cancer upon the planet Earth that we would put in terms of hate begins to dissipate, because now your life is full and shining forth. The belief that there is ever anything outside of love begins to dissolve as you shine forth through your hands and through your eyes, through your willingness to hear, through your willingness to be tender in each and every moment of the day and to slow down just a little bit more, to be captivated by your very existence upon the Earth rather than resistant to the very same.

Planet Earth begins to grow in its healing and its wonder, and suddenly you find that everything in your life begins to fall into alignment. The money you've been seeking falls into your pockets. The love you have wanted is there right at your side. By magnifying your light, you attract the many rather than the few around you who are of like mind and like heart to stand firmly upon the planet Earth now—a community, a band of angels that you will have created because of your willingness now to join with and to play with life.

You are indeed very beautiful spirits. The mysteries of the universe that you seek to understand? You are that mystery! Enjoy the exploration of yourself. Enjoy bringing yourself to the surface with the richness and the color and the light and the vibration that you are. If you feel that your voice is too loud, love yourself, for your very loud voice was meant to be. If you feel that you are too small in your stature, love this stature, for it will promote healing for those who need to pause for a moment to see the smaller things upon planet Earth and to appreciate them. If you do not like the color of your eyes, if you do not like the color of your hair, learn to cherish and to honor the very same, because when you respect yourself in this fashion, you stand as an icon of wonder to life around you.

The many rather than the few are very frightened to love life on its own terms. It is the reason why you cover your gray hairs upon your heads, why you want to change your appearance, why in the very beginning of time it was decided that you should be wearing clothing. How do you like them apples, my dear friends?

It is through your willingness to share of yourself with great vulnerability that you will increase the vibrational frequency of love all around you, and suddenly you will not be seeking happiness in something outside of you. It will be there right within your heart at all times, no matter what is occurring on the outside. No matter the wars, no matter the stock market changes, no matter the Earth changes, no matter the depression—you will stand as icons of light and truth upon the Earth.

It certainly takes courage to be here upon the planet Earth as one who is fully healed, as one who is a healer. Understand that you are already healed, perfect in your form. The struggle is to bring that interpretation into this world, in your physical bodies. You are such beautiful spirits. Breathe very deeply into your spines once again.

All That You Seek Is All That You Are

God bless you indeed, my dear friends; you know that we love you very much. We know you are seeking at all times greater relationship with Spirit, wondering where God is, wondering at times within your heart about this Christ. "Who is this man? Is He real? Can I seek Him? Who is the one known here as Sai Baba? Who is this one known here as Paramahansa Yogananda? Who is this one known as Buddha? Who is this one known as Confucius? Who is this one known here as Dr. Peebles? And, by the way, where are my granny and my granddad? Where are they all?" And you sit and seek in wonder, and you wonder where they are. My dear friends, they're right there inside of your heart. They're right there inside of you, and as you breathe into your spines, you can feel them there.

Feel the expansion of yourself with this awareness: All that you seek is all that you are. The only difference between you and Dr. Peebles here and the band of angels is that we realize that you are us and we are you, and we have no fear of you, my dear friends. We have no fear at all! We love you all so very much. But the many rather than the few here upon the planet Earth are in great fear and wonder about this unknown realm, the other side, the creepy crawlers in the night, the little spooks that haunt you, the little spooks that might haunt you. Oftentimes you are in great wonder of this realm of the afterlife, of the afterworld.

But it is not *after* this life; it is here *now*. It is here because you never change—you are eternal. You do not lose your personality when you pass from your physical form. You constantly grow, but you are not going to become something different. You're not going to become absent; you're not going to be floatin' out in space somewhere all by yourselves. Nothing changes; you just come to a greater awareness that you have never been alone.

In this room, it feels that there is space between you, between you and me, between you and another. My dear friends, there is no absence of light anywhere! Within what you feel to be an absent, empty space, there are the many rather than the few gathered around here. More and more are coming into the room still, to allow each and every one here to know that you are never, ever alone. With this awareness, you will find freedom beyond your wildest dreams and imaginations.

Understand and Find the Freedom

My dear friends, you are very beautiful spirits. God bless you indeed. Understand this: You are eternal. Your life touches the many rather than the few, no matter what, no matter where. So settle down for a moment, breathe deeply into your spines. We know that you are all in varying degrees of panic at different times there in the course of your life. You want so much. You want so much, my dear friends! Think of all you want in the physical form, all that you want to acquire. Think of it all. You are worthy of everything your heart desires, because what your heart truly desires is the peace and serenity that come with knowing that you are love and love is eternal, knowing that what you truly seek is not an object but a feeling. You can have it now.

We want you to understand that you are great lovers upon the Earth, that your spirit is constantly being birthed here upon the Earth. It is a temporary state of affairs. It is not about accumulating anything, though you can amass much in terms of physical items around you. But bear in mind the point and purpose of being here upon the planet Earth: It is to find freedom in your heart so that when you are in the grocery store line feeling frustrated because it is taking forever for the clerk to check out the items of the little old lady in front of you who can't find her change, you realize that right there is a classroom! There is an opportunity to find greater love! That is what you are seeking. That is what you want to give truly in your spirit in each and every moment of each and every day.

When you can understand this, when you can master this ability, it is there that you find yourself standing upon the planet Earth and truly finding happiness, enjoying each and every moment—not a-stressin' and a-strainin' because you are standing in line at the grocery store, but rejoicing because you are standing in line at the grocery store. God bless you indeed, my dear friends. Understand this and you will find freedom beyond your wildest dreams and imaginations. Understand this and you will not create illness in your body. Understand this and you will find that your movements become more fluid; you will find that you will slow down.

Immerse yourself in the given moment and yet your lives will be accelerated. All that your heart desires will be manifested much more rapidly once you stop and pay attention to where you are right now. When you can give of yourself in this fashion to the world, when you truly listen and truly hear the words of an individual who is talking to you, when you truly allow yourself to surrender to the other perspectives—not that you have to abide by them, but simply acknowledge that they exist—then suddenly you have opened yourself up to new horizons. You have given yourself a new pathway for your heart to expand. No longer must you close yourself off to any of life, for every time you make a determination that you don't want to be with a person, that you don't want to go to the concert, that you don't want to walk in the store, that you don't want to stand in line, that you don't want to go to work, that you don't want to get up in the morning—can you feel yourself right now, being boxed in just with our words? Can you feel how many doors you have just slammed in your own face?

It is through your willingness to say yes to life that you are in the moment: "Of course I will go with you to the party, though it may make me uncomfortable. At first perhaps I will see it as an opportunity for growth of my soul." For you get yourselves wrapped up with guilt and shame: "I do not want to go to the party. I do not like these people. I do not want to have this experience, but perhaps I should have pushed myself a little bit." You get yourselves wrapped up anyway, so you may as well join life rather than resist! You will find such excitement. You will find that you will be traveling—physically, yes—but traveling in the moment. You are being handed the keys to a new vehicle. You are being handed the keys to your own heart, to a greater awareness of the very same.

Why are you invited to the parties that you do not want to attend? Because perhaps the party is inviting you! Because it needs you, your life, your perspective, your truth, your awareness of self! Attend, join the dance and share of yourself to give the world an opportunity to hear, to see, to taste, to feel, to touch, to smell that which it has not experienced before.

Healing Steve

You are all very beautiful spirits, magical beings. There is one here in this room today . . . Steve, you are here, yes? My dear friend Steve, we have heard your prayers. You are a beautiful spirit. Would you be willing simply to step forth here in front of the group? My dear friend, we put you on the spot here, yeah? And do you understand that the reason you came here today is that you are indeed seeking healing, are you not?

Yes.

And you have wanted it absolute, unparalleled, beyond your wildest dreams and imaginations. Is this not accurate, my dear friend?

Yes.

God bless you indeed. Now understand that a part of you has been very resistant to life, and you have asked that anything goes here, yes?

Yes.

With your permission, we will continue on, yes?

Yes.

God bless you indeed. My dear friend, you have been resistant to life and to the love that life wants to give to you. You have sought it in many ways, shapes and forms, many colors, many sizes. And yet inside of you, there is constant nagging that you are not fulfilled. Is that not accurate, my dear friend?

Yes.

And you truly, desperately want to have more. Truly, desperately you want the world to see you and to love you as you are. And then what comes along but a horrid, dreaded disease! You understand this?

Yes.

And it makes you feel how? It makes you feel that you pale by comparison to others physically, does it not?

Yes.

And this has become compounded by the constant berating and belittling of self that you have been involved in, has it not?

Yes.

God bless you indeed. Very, very hard upon yourself, are you not, my dear friend?

Yes.

God bless you indeed. My dear friends, here in this room today, can you not feel anything but love for this man? God bless you indeed, my dear friends. Would you, dear Steve, would you turn around to the group? It's very hard for you, but we put you here upon the stage. This we do for all here in this room—not for any discomfort, but for you to understand how to reach out with your hearts. Dear Steve, look around in the room at the human beings who are here today. My dear friends, gaze upon this man. What he is desperately seeking here is a tremendous healing for his physical form.

My dear friends, truly he is a beautiful spirit—truly, beyond your wildest dreams and imaginations. But he is nothing less and nothing more than all here in this room are inside of their hearts and souls. How many here in this room would be willing to help us and join us here in a little healing adventure not only for Steve but for you? All in favor say aye. [A chorus response from the audience.]

God bless you indeed, my dear friends. How many in this room today have wanted to have the opportunity to be a healer extraordinaire, have wondered, "If I should place my hands upon someone and that person should be healed by my touch, it must be a most magnificent feeling!" Would you understand, my dear friends?

If you would please, for a moment here, close your eyes and breathe very deeply into your spines. Now, dear Steve, are you willing to be touched by the world? Are you willing to receive?

Yes.

Would you please keep your eyes open for a moment here and look at all these very beautiful spirits who are breathing very deeply into their spines. Now close your eyes and simply, within your heart of hearts, be willing to receive the touch of life of the many rather than the few. Be willing to immerse yourself in life, in the greater love that is there, and because you love as well, do not fear anyone or anything or any touch.

With your eyes closed now, as you are breathing into your spines, as you are so moved, stand up and approach Steve, put your hand upon him or your hands as the case may be—no right, no wrong—but only when you are so moved, my dear friends, and if you are not, it is not a problem at all. [Many gather around Steve.]

God bless you indeed, my dear friends. As you bring forth this caring from your hearts, understand that you, as well, are receiving. Understand that by your willingness to uplift this very gentle, very beautiful spirit, you also uplift your souls. Through your willingness to break through the barriers within your hearts, to allow yourselves to join together—a band of angels forevermore—understand that you helped to release this spirit at long last from his agony.

Fill your heart, my dear friend Steve, with the love that you receive here today. It is there that you will find, over the course of the next eight weeks, each and every day, movement much easier, talking much more simple, a fluidity to your reality here upon the Earth in your physical form. Now, as you step forth into the world, be aware that you will have such an abundance of love within your heart that you will want to give it to the many rather than the few, through your touch, through your warmth, through your listening ears, though your eyes, through your willingness to have contact.

Each and every one here in this room today, students of the divine, feel the energy as it is swelling around you, the movement of the light, the movement of you, the lightworkers. Release yourselves from thought. Release yourselves from feeling. Release yourselves. Surrender into the sensation of love. Release yourselves, and you realize that the illusions of separation begin to disappear and dissipate as you become one, become unified through this labor of love to heal yourselves and to heal the heart of dear Steve. God bless you indeed. My dear friends, now you may return to your seats.

And dear Steve, you simply breathe into your spine and continue to allow all the energy that you have received to be absorbed into you, you understand? And will you please turn to this group here and gaze into the eyes of the many rather than the few? How much love do you feel there? Can you share with us? It's very lovely, is it not? And can you now allow yourself to no longer resist the touch of the many rather than the few? Will you now turn to me? Will you place your palm here upon mine? You are a beautiful spirit and no longer do you need to resist Dr. Peebles here either. You are a very strong soul, and this is a passage into a new existence for you. Please, for a moment, close your eyes. Release now all that you do not want to have into this hand that you now touch, and I will draw it through the channel's body, to be dissipated into the light. Would you please draw your palm close here? [At this point, Dr. Peebles kisses Steve's hand.] And you may return to your seat.

The Healed Becomes the Healer

Thank you so very much for your willingness to provide demonstration here for the many rather than the few, for your understanding beyond compare—purpose and point to everything. Goodness gracious, the man in great turmoil has just now become your healer, has he not, my dear friends? Through his pain has he not given to your hearts? Through a willingness to touch and be touched by the divinity of self, you will find that life here upon the planet Earth is not a great black pit of misunderstanding all the time. Rather it is here that you as the courageous adventurers find fertile soil—in the darker spaces, in the black—to plant the seed of yourselves so you can then grow back toward greater light.

Beautiful and eternal souls here in this room today, each and everyone a student of the divine! You are beautiful spirits—so very compassionate, so very trusting. Remember this about yourselves, and when you are afraid to trust, pause for a moment and ask if you are willing to move away from love. We assure that your answer will always be, "No, I am not willing to move away from love. I want to ever expand. I want to know that my soul is indeed eternal. I want to release the aggravation that I feel. I want now to stand firmly upon the planet Earth as never before, in a great exploration of myself, with wonder of all of life around me!"

Give unto Life as You Want Life to Give unto You

When you ask for healing and strength, what you ask to receive from Spirit, from the heavens, is acknowledgment. You simply want to be acknowledged that you are in pain. Look to life around you. How many times has life wanted to be acknowledged? How many times have you not wanted to hear someone else's perspective but wanted yours to be heard? You must give unto life as you want life to give unto you.

Love your neighbor as yourself! How do you love yourself then? In how many ways do you hold yourself at arm's length? In how many ways and how many times have you told yourself you can't? How many times have you told yourself you mustn't? How many times have you held yourself at bay? How many times have you kept yourself from laughing too loudly? How many times have you resisted giving the hug that you wanted to give and receiving the one that you wanted to receive?

Look to life—look to all the life—that is inside of you in each and every moment of each and every day, and it is there that you will find that healing, the healing adventure that is never ending in this journey to your heart. At each and every moment of each and every day, you have the opportunity to listen to the little whispers inside of self that say, "Do not be ashamed to love. Do not be ashamed to accept love. Do not be ashamed to expect love."

You are all very beautiful spirits, creators of magic. God bless you indeed! Certainly understand this and bring your revived, renewed spirit to the world. Allow the world to be captivated by you, my dear friends. The light eternal is inside of you. God bless you, indeed!

Living in Rapture

Living in rapture is what you are going to learn to do in each and every moment of each and every day. Don't be afraid of the dark, in other words. Certainly it is in the darkness that you will find the light of your soul, for it is within the darkness where there is the entire spectrum of color of life and light. God bless you indeed. It is there, my dear friends, where you experience the richness of yourself, of your being. Can you plant yourself in the fertile soil? Are you willing now to share, within yourself, the truth of self, to share it with you, from self to self?

Entering the Valley of Forgetfulness

We ask that you close your eyes for a moment here and breathe very deeply into your spines, my dear friends. Seek inside of yourself. At this very moment, there is within you a spectrum of light, and yet there is an area that will appear to you to be very, very dark. We ask that you focus upon the solar plexus, right below the rib cage, toward the center of your abdomen. Right there is an experience of darkness that you will witness at first as a little scary, a little tight, a bit like you what would call butterflies in the tummy.

But it is there where you are incarnating, meaning that your spirit certainly comes into your body through this portal. It is a valley of forgetfulness wherein you now enter into this darkness, the richness of yourself. It is within this darkness, my dear friends, where you begin to reverse, for a moment here, your incarnations to planet Earth. *As you enter into the darkness, surrender, breathing once again very deeply into your spines. Surrender into the darkness, my dear friends, and we are going to coax you back to a time prior to when you were born upon the planet Earth.*

Right now you are entering, in reverse, the valley of forgetfulness. It is a very dark arena, where your soul began to formulate its journey upon the Earth. It is here, within this darkness, my dear friends, where you began to formulate what your journey upon Earth would be about. It was a very silent adventure and you felt very alone. You knew that it was through your own willingness to create magic upon the Earth, to bring yourself into consciousness upon the Earth; it was through your willingness and your courage in this arena in the valley of forgetfulness that you made a decision to incarnate.

My dear friends, in this darkness now, where it is very silent, where you now remember the moment just prior to your incarnation, what did you ask? You had one last question for your guides as you said good-bye to your friends, family members and others who were on the other side before your incarnation. What was the question that you asked? Now listen for the answer.

Now we take you back even further, through the valley of forgetfulness prior to the formulation, the creation of your soul about ready to incarnate. Prior to this, my dear friends, you were whole in your spirit. Prior to this, you were with those family members, friends and others whom you would fully and completely now recognize as you adventure into the light of your soul. What you consider to be the other side is the wholeness of yourself.

Immerse Yourself in the Light of God

Now immerse yourself within this light. Take a peek around and look at your family, friends and others; you have full recognition of faces, full recognition and trust and acceptance and acknowledgment. There is no fear that you are going to disappear, no fear to expose yourself to the world. The world, my dear friends, you realize now, is simply you, and so what is there to fear? As you immerse yourself into this light, there is certainly a sense now of wholeness, of oneness. It is a world without judgment. It is a world where you are being coaxed and encouraged to speak your truth at all times; where you can cry, you can laugh, you can sing your song and dance your dance in freedom, in absolute serenity; and where pain is not considered to be a crutch. Here pain is certainly filled with purpose and helps you to discover who you really are as you understand yourself in the light of God.

Breathe very deeply into your spines once again. Now you adventure even further beyond the other side. Release your expectations, for there is an all-encompassing membrane of love that surrounds you at this time. It is truly the outer shell of your being that you now experience, the outer shell that is in a constant state of expansion. It is the expansion of the consciousness of God that you are. Begin to sense and realize that this expansion is according to your will.

How willing are you to enter into another realm yet beyond this, that being a realm of darkness once again? How does it feel? But, my dear friends, it is there where you will discover that never in your eternal soul have you been the victim but always the creator of your reality. *My dear friends, you touch the darkness, now understanding the God, the creator who you are. You do it with a willingness to fill the universe with the wonder and light of you. This begins the experience of rapture.*

Your Decision to Incarnate on Earth

This is a life that you have already experienced, but at some point inside of yourself, you doubted. At some point in yourself, you felt shame because you did not feel that you were worthy of being God. You felt an illusion of separation that came in and filtered out the time when you were a very smart cookie, when you realized that to exist in a state and consciousness of love is all that you ever really desired at any given time. But you have separated yourself now, and you are leaning a little bit into a state that we would consider to be a bit of, shall we say, an absence of consciousness. You stopped the motion there, and it was through this that you made a decision to incarnate upon the Earth.

You were not forced here; you were not forced to play upon the Earth. But you made the decision, because to be separate from God was too painful for you. You wanted to redirect your energy, but you forgot how. *So now, from this conscious awareness of the love that you are, the God who you are, once again breathe very deeply into your spines and come back to the time that we have already mentioned, the time where you are with family, friends and others on what you consider to be the other side. The other side, my dear friends, is truly the wholeness, the truth of yourself. Take a peek around, and you are now standing in a time directly before your decision to enter into the valley of forgetfulness, to close doors on the distant past, to hone and refine who you wanted to become as you incarnated upon the Earth. As you begin now to enter into the valley of forgetfulness, understand that you have brought along fears; expectations; a bit of loneliness; sadness in leaving family, friends and others. Who are you really leaving now, my dear friends? You have left part of yourself.*

Through the valley of forgetfulness you now travel into the darkness, deeper, deeper and deeper still. There is a light at the end of the tunnel, and at the end of the tunnel, my dear friends, there is a beautiful blue orb. It is known as planet Earth. As you venture through this tunnel and out to the Earth, you begin to feel yourself once again resurrecting, a conscious awareness that you truly want to feel love. You feel desire and you feel wonder, and there is an absence for a moment here of pain, and you move closer and closer to this beautiful blue orb, closer to the Earth. As you do, you begin to see that there, in the darkness, is a tremendous richness of color and light. You see the browns and the greens. You see the reds and the yellows. You see the purples and the white clouds dotting the Earth as you come closer and closer still.

Born into a World of Your Own Creation

And now you move into the womb of your mommy, into the darkness and the comfort and the stillness. It is there, my dear friends, where you begin to understand the quiet and the comfort that comes from being in the fertile soil, the fertile soil in your mommy's womb, the darkness. It is there where you experience once again the incarnation of your light; the incarnation of the light of your soul into this little creation inside your mommy's womb feels like rapture. Once again, my dear friends, illusions of separation begin to disappear. You feel the oneness; you hear the beat and rhythm of the heart of God, that of your mommy as you are now floating in a tiny little space. And encapsulated in this world, you suddenly realize that you want to take a breath. As you breathe, the fluid of the womb begins to move in and out of your lungs, and you feel the oneness in that experience. It is the rapture.

Now, my dear friends, suddenly there is quiet, and inside of you there is an explosion of desire. There is a desire now to stretch your limbs, to turn your head. You begin to feel that being in this darkness is not enough—you want to grow now. Little flower that you are in the womb of your mommy's tummy, yet are you a seed, a seed of life, and now you begin to push through the soil, down through the birth canal, pushing, wiggling, writhing. Through your desire, you are beginning to create yourself in a grander and grander adventure of discovery of who you really are as you begin to create your birth upon the Earth. And it is now that you emerge from the birth canal and into the light. It is what you desired and yet, my dear friends, it shocks you. And you want to take another breath. Breathe very deeply into your spines that first breath of life upon the Earth.

Now open your eyes and take a peek around, at the world you have created. It is here upon the Earth that you now land, wholly and completely in a world of your own design. And as you take a peek around the room here today, is there anything or any face you see that you do not like? Is there anything that you do not desire to have in your life, do not want to touch, would rather hold at arm's length, would rather push away?

Suddenly you're emerging from the fertile soil and you begin to dissect yourself, to sort it out, to say, "I like" and "I do not like." Eventually, you find your way to a mirror, and you see yourself in the mirror. You look there and you like and you dislike, you love and you do not love and, my dear friends, you begin to organize yourself in terms of what you want to embrace and what you do not want to embrace. The reason for this is so that you can begin to see what you need to embrace, for it is all that you see, hear, taste, touch, feel and smell and want to hold at arm's length that we are now going to ask you to work upon embracing back into your heart. Do not hold it at arm's length anymore, because it is absolutely an impossibility to hold at arm's length what is already you by design. God bless you, indeed.

Learn to Trust Your World

My dear friends, to come into consciousness with the God, the Creator who you are, you must fall into a space of absolute, unconditional love beyond your wildest dreams and imaginations. You must fall into that space in order to feel the rapture where pain no longer is something that you fear but becomes a trusted friend, an advisor, a teacher, a specialist who teaches you about yourselves, my dear friends. You must be willing to embrace everything that you see, hear, taste, touch, feel and smell, because it is all you.

This is the way in which you will begin to build a life of absolute rapture. "But Dr. Peebles, how can I when I can't stand my husband?" "I can't stand my wife." "I don't like the plants. I don't like the flowers, and I especially do not like cats by design. There is no way I can ever embrace a cat because I will sneeze forever. I can't; it will hurt me; it will kill me."

Release Your Expectations and Find Teachers

My dear friends, we are not saying, well, you would not want to jump off a cliff either, but it can be a wonderful way to end your life; it can be a lot of fun on the way down. No, we are not saying that you must jump off a cliff. We are not telling you to create pain on purpose but rather to look at a situation and begin to admire it because it is you. We're suggesting that you look at a kitty cat and, by design, my dear friends, begin to say to yourself, if you do not like kitty cats, "Well, but can I find some place in that kitty cat that I can embrace as creating a friend with the world? It does remind me, for example, that I like to have things soft around me, but perhaps I'm not admitting that I want things soft around me because I'm a tough cookie, and so the cat becomes my teacher. I also perhaps would like to lounge in a chair all afternoon long, and I would like to stare at people critically, but I won't allow myself. I would rather make nice and smile."

The kitty cat becomes a wonderful teacher for you, my dear friends, and it doesn't mean you have to embrace it, to put it in your lap and allow yourself to sneeze because of your allergies. These are all your expectations, but we assure you that as you begin to embrace the kitty cat and find new perspectives there in terms of how you can truly love this kitty cat, you, by arrangement and by agreement inside of yourself, will begin to dissipate your own allergies. You will find yourself surrounded by kitty cats and not annoyed, not having any problems in terms of sneezing and so forth.

"Well yes, Dr. Peebles," you might say, "that's all fine and dandy, but you know there are some pretty horrible people in the world. How can I possibly admit to myself that I could fall in love with someone who would kill another man? How could I fall in love with someone who would do things that are abhorrent to other human beings, to animals? Someone who would maim, cripple, kill? How could I ever embrace such individuals?"

Well, my dear friends, you can and you will, because you will begin to understand that these are individuals who require your love and your light in order to heal. As long as you look at them with distaste, with distrust, with hatred, with anger, wanting very much to squash them and kill them, well, my dear friends, you are no better than them. You must allow yourselves to find the love, the true Creator, the true God who you are, who is always willing to love, always willing to adventure into a greater consciousness of love, always willing to walk into the darkness in order to bring light.

So we ask that you look into the face of a stranger whom you cannot, for the life of you—and we say that with meaning, my dear friends, *for the life of you*—embrace. But for the life of you, you must, in order to create a rapturous adventure upon the planet Earth, in order not to feel pain in every situation, in every conversation. You must, in order to quit feeling that life is a constant annoyance; that you are a victim; that life is a violent attack upon your character; that life is wanting to judge you, to push you, to tease you, to not acknowledge you, to see you as absent, to not even know you are in the room.

My dear friends, you must give the same acknowledgment that you desire from the world to the world. For you to have the life that you desire, the life of being appreciated abundantly, we are asking that you find, inside of your heart and soul, the love, the great love of God. My dear friends, it's not separate, it's not outside of you; it's inside. You have, by choice, made decisions not to love. In every single waking hour, you make a decision not to love, and we are going to ask that you find ways in which you can love, ways in which you can see beyond the exterior and look into the soul of an individual, to look into the greater plan perhaps that God has for all here upon the Earth, the greater plan that will free you from your misery, for the greater plan is really nothing more and nothing less than the emergence of love. That is necessary if you want to live a life of rapture.

You Create Everything You Feel

You must come to the awareness that everything you see, hear, taste, touch and feel around you is your creation from the inside out. *For a moment, if you will, close your eyes. We would ask that you pick a spot in the world where you would like to be right now, in complete harmony. Perhaps it is feeling the motions of an ocean liner, perhaps it's in the sky flying very high without having an airplane around you. Make it up. It doesn't matter. What provides you with freedom? Where do you want to go to feel less pain, less strain? Take yourself there now. Feel it on your skin. Feel in your abdomen the release of pressure there, the feeling of freedom and movement as you create a space of light for yourself. It feels wonderful, delicious, free of pain. Your eyes are closed. You're using your imagination, and the feeling that you are creating is inside you.*

That is where heaven has been all along—inside of you, my dear friends. It is there that you will find the richness that you so desire in your life that you think will come from the greatest relationships, from financial abundance, from the fastest cars, from an ability to buy airplane tickets to anywhere in the world anytime you like. You can buy those tickets right now, inside of you. You, by your choices and through your own perceptions, create your reality. Wherever you go, you have the opportunity to be happy, to be filled with rapture, to feel abundance, to feel freedom. My dear friends, in any situation—and we mean *any* situation, even the most frightening and the most abhorrent—as you become a creator of rapture, you will not have to feel nor will you have to experience frightening, abhorrent situations, because you will not be creating them anymore. They will not be reflected in the exterior.

Think right now of one situation in your life that you would like to have canceled out right now, would like to hold at arm's length. We give you permission to be the victim here. Allow yourself to stress and strain for a moment. You take this situation and want to cut it off. Where are you putting it? You have your eyes closed here, so where do you put that situation, how do you get rid of it? You can't. It remains inside of you. You can forget about it for a while, you can turn your attention to something else for a while, but that situation remains. And so, my dear friends, in order to live a life of rapture, you must stare the situation straight in the eye, bring it to the surface and put it in front of you.

If it is a person with whom you are having difficulty and difficult circumstances, right now we want you to look at this person in your mind's eye and say, "I love you." If you can't say it from your heart, say it again until you mean it, because the truth of you, my dear friends, knows that love prevails. Continue to draw this person or situation closer. If it is a situation, an experience of lack of finances, for example, simply say, "I thank you very much. I appreciate this experience of not having money. I grow in abundance through this experience. I thank you for being my teacher and my friend."

If it is world peace that you desire for your abhorrent situation and conditions upon planet Earth at this given time, we would ask you to simply look at the situation and say, "I thank you for the war and for the uncertainty and for all the pain that I see on the television shows and hear about, and for the lives that are disappearing from the Earth. I thank you for this experience, because it shows me my heart. It shows me that my journey can be rich, but it only can be rich through creating greater and greater love from within me. For it is through my choices and perceptions that I create my own reality, and it is through my choices and my perceptions that I can become a teacher to others of how they can create their reality too."

Every single, solitary person upon the planet Earth creates his or her own reality. *Breathe once again very deeply into your spine. Think about your world, your planet Earth. Think about how many times you and every other single, solitary person upon the planet Earth has said out loud or to yourself how you desire to leave it because you claim to hate it. Think about your planet Earth and all that you do not like about it—the greed that you see or the pain that is inflicted upon you by friends, family and others. It is a very uncomfortable world you just created inside of yourself now by a simple change of your thoughts.*

Should you choose to leave it, you would not be able to get rid of the discomfort. If you, my dear friends, would take your life by your own hand, you would still not get rid of the discomfort. It would be with you. Yes, other things in your world would be magnified in terms of love, appreciation, the abundance that you would feel on the other side, the oneness and the wholeness there. But always and forever, you would begin to realize that you still carry a little vessel of pain and anger toward planet Earth—that being within you, my dear friends, and we will prove it to you right now.

The pain and anger that you would carry toward the Earth—for everyone here in this room today and everyone reading this text, to be honest with yourself is the point—the pain and the anger that you feel resides somewhere inside of yourself. You can feel it in your physical body, the capsule in which your soul exists. *Turn your attention there.* What you, my dear friends, think is on the exterior exists inside of you. How do you change your reality? How do you create rapture? By focusing upon this pain, by focusing with your fullest attention upon the anger, the hatred, the frustration and the exhaustion that you feel as it relates to being upon planet Earth! It is not the Earth that does anything to you; you do it to yourself. Feel now the emotions roaring inside of you. Feel them as the pressure begins to build inside of your physicality. It is a very deep wound that you carry, not only from this lifetime, but from many lifetimes for some of you.

This anger has nothing to do with the world around you. The anger comes from one place inside of you that asks this question: "Why can I not accept everybody and everything that I hear, taste, touch, feel and smell upon planet Earth? Why can I not accept? Why can I not love?" Ask not, "Why doesn't the world love me?" but "Why can I not love the world?"

Why, my dear friends? Ask yourself this question, and you will find a bounty of freedom there and the answers as they pour forth.

For the answers will say to you, "But you can love the world. Can you forgive the world?" Yes. "Can you trust the world?" Yes. "Can you exist in the world without pain, feeling the rapture?" Yes. And whose choice is it? It is your own. If, however, you continue to choose anger and impatience, if you choose to run away from the counsel of love, if you choose to continue to live as the victim and not the creator of your reality, which is happiness, joy, wonder, spontaneity, fulfillment, a sense of appreciation and acknowledgment that you get from the world as you acknowledge and appreciate it, then you will feel pain.

You begin to find inside of yourself that if you do not allow yourself to be free of the victim who you believe yourself to be, that pain—that sensation that you carry inside of your physicality—will get stronger and stronger and stronger. There comes a division inside of your body that is a battle, my dear friends, of what you would consider to be good and evil, right and wrong, up and down, nice and not nice, fun and not fun, fulfilling and not fulfilling. The illusions of separation that exist inside of you begin to grow. As a result, you create what you call dis-ease, discomfort, pain, insecurity and frustration, and they are reflected in your physical body.

You begin to deteriorate, because the only thing that can keep you whole physically is love. You can't mask untruth with more untruth. The untruth that exists inside of you is the illusion of separation that says that you are less than love, less than lovable, less than a creator; that you have no power; that you cannot feel joy, happiness or rapture upon the Earth. It is absolutely impossible when there is so much pain upon the Earth.

But, my dear friends, you can! You must be willing to sense it, to bring it to life inside you, no matter the circumstances around you. For if you want your circumstances to change financially, within relationships, within your health, within your being, then you must put your sights upon those things, those thoughts, those feelings that are enriching and inspiring, even in a time of despair. It takes courage. It takes, my dear friends, a willingness to pull yourself out of the muck. Not an easy task! But once you start, you are going to get highly, highly addicted to the process. We say this a little with a teasing tongue here, but my dear friends, what an addiction to have! For upon your Earth, most human beings are very much addicted to pain and to anger and to poverty and to insecurity and to fear and to feelings of being less than worthy of love. You are addicted to untruths that tell you you're too fat, not smart enough, not tall enough, not short enough, not wide enough and not thin enough. God bless you indeed, my dear friends. And so you keep yourself from living in rapture.

Living in Rapture

Rapture is a beautiful experience, for there is continuity there. It is not a place wherein you float out into space, wherein you simply sit in a state of constant and eternal bliss. It is instead a state of surrender to any condition and any circumstance in your life upon the Earth, absolute surrender because you know that God's love is the constant here and you know that you can find freedom and salvation for your soul in any given moment by remembering this. And so you constantly create movement and expansion into the darkness by creating and generating thoughts of love, thoughts that provide you with continuity in your life of rapturous feelings. You make a determination not to get wrapped up in the emotions of others; the emotionality of your existence is what causes you constant strife and pain. When you get caught up in the emotionality of everyone around you, you allow yourself to be played with and toyed with, to be pushed and pulled and tugged instead of surrendering to the greater truth of yourself.

And so you watch people who are in pain and you sense their pain and want to feel for them, but you can't. It's not going to rescue them. So instead, my dear friends, where you sense and realize there is pain, you say, "Ah, this is a landmark here whereby I shall be creating more love, generating loving thoughts toward these people—not to fix them, not to repair them, not to have to say anything, but simply to look at them in love. This thereby changes my life." And you watch as you change the lives of human beings around you, for it is in this condition inside of yourself that you become a great, great healer. It is, my dear friends, the life of Jesus Christ who walked the Earth.

It is, my dear friends, the life of Buddha who walked the Earth. It is, my dear friends, the life of Dr. Peebles here who walked the Earth. It certainly will become your life, you who walk the Earth as well. You will be the master, the creator who you are, not a "lesser than" being but already whole and filled with possibilities to generate God's love here with every breath, with every thought, with every emotion, with every point at which you are willing, my dear friends, to walk into the darker spaces and become as a drop of gold in a bucket of lead. My dear friends, for you all possibility does exist. You are not without opportunity.

To Heal Others, You Must First Heal Yourself

Breathe very deeply into your spines once again. There is someone whom you would like to heal from all the sadness, the misery, the pain in his or her life. We are going to ask that you turn your attention to this person, and this person is not going to be who you think. This person is you. For some in this room here today or reading this text, this is a terrifying thought. "I don't want to heal me. I'm not worthy." Feel where you are stressing and straining, put yourself in front of you, see yourself and try as much as you can simply to detach from this pain-filled, sad person who feels life is lived with disharmony and discordance in various areas.

You say, "I do not feel that, Dr. Peebles." My dear friends, look again. There are areas of your life that require healing, or you would not be upon the planet Earth. Find that you see yourself standing in front of you and begin to feel a detachment there. This detachment is going to help you feel more attachment to love. Detach now from the pains, the expectations, the intolerance, the judgments, the discordance that you see inside of yourself. My dear friends, make a decision now to immerse into greater and greater love.

You will work upon this. If you would work upon it for twelve days in such a meditation where you see yourself standing in front of you, and you can detach and look at yourself with great objectivity and look at yourself and feel great, great love for this very, very sad soul—and only love, my dear friends, the warmth and the integrity of absolute, pure, unabashed, unconditional love—it is there, after twelve days, that you can transform yourself physically, emotionally and spiritually. The acts of kindness that you want to have done to you, you must do unto yourself.

My dear friends, you allow yourselves to remain in the life of a victim. You allow yourselves to feel less than love from the world around you. You do this every day of your life through your unwillingness to embrace that which you are, through your unwillingness to provide and to give to the world the love that you expect and desire to receive, as well as the acknowledgment that you expect and desire to receive. *Breathe very deeply into your spines once again.*

Many of you, at our words, end up carrying and bearing guilt here now. "Oh, goodness gracious, what a bad person I have been. I should be ashamed of myself. He's absolutely right. I'm intolerant, I'm judgmental and I'm filled with expectations. I didn't offer a courtesy to the person in the car next to me the other day. I cut the person off. I did it deliberately, and I even gave her the birdie."

My good friends, shame and guilt do not make you good people. You make a decision to be a good person, a loving and kind and gentle soul. Through your choices and your perceptions, you do indeed create your reality. As you choose to walk the Earth as an enlightened being, walking and laboring in love no matter the circumstances, no matter the person you are with, can you love, my dear friends, your perpetrators? Can you love them sincerely from your heart? If you can you will not feel pain, you will feel only love. That is living in rapture.

Choose Not to Live in Discordance

Upon your planet Earth, there is plenty of greed, there is plenty of emotion and plenty of what we would call stagnation. There are so many filters by which you filter out love through your willingness to feel lethargic, through your willingness to not want to go play, through your willingness to not want to leave your house and discover your new surroundings. "But I am stuck in this house, Dr. Peebles. I can't go." My dear friends, even if you must crawl, you can. "But Dr. Peebles, I don't like living in this area, this neighborhood." Well, my dear friends, create a new reality then. Change your life plans. If you are typing at a computer all day long and you're sick and tired of it, stop. Learn how to teach children to play softball. Change your lifestyle to suit your inner world, what your soul desires, rather than trying to manipulate the outer world to create a false reality.

You tell yourself that you want all kinds of things—a lot of money, if you will, cars, a home and securities/stocks and bonds. Goodness gracious, those are doing me a lot of good now, yeah? I had my very own relationship there with stocks and bonds, and they did nothing for me, my dear friends, nor did financial abundance do anything for me. For when I did not skirt around the issues of my life upon the Earth, when I asked human beings for help, when I said, I want to go to Spain, I found a ticket. It was handed to me, my dear friends. I didn't have to work for it, and yet I labored in love for it. It is there that you create a reality beyond your wildest dreams and imaginations—a life that is no longer insecure; a life that has no boundaries, no borders, no barriers.

I can fall in love with you, Morgan, and I can fall in love with magic; and I can fall in love with you, my dear, and I can fall in love with the chair over there; and I can fall in love with Rita's left toenail, if I choose. And, my dear friends, I choose, for I indeed live in rapture. I do not find that there is discordance here, for it does not exist inside of me. Oh yes, I am aware that you feel it. You're stressin' and you're strainin', you're up, you're down, you're inside out, you're backward.

Our little channel here lives in such discordance, but she, my dear friends, becomes a friend to God every time she chooses not to live in discordance, for it is there that she allows for me to speak through her. It is there that she is released from pain and from the confines of the Earth, body and mind as she suddenly falls into greater and greater love. And look at the richness, look at the magic that is created in response to her willingness to love and to be of service without expectations, with great vulnerability and through absolute, total trust and surrender into the wholeness of her being. This is the response here. This is the symbol of absolute rapture and oneness.

And this is the dance and the play and the ebb and the flow of life incarnate here through the little channel's body. My dear friends, to create and to live in rapture, you become then a channel. You become a willing channel, not so that Dr. Peebles can speak through you necessarily, but I can, if you would like. I can speak to you as well, for I am always a friend to you and I am always here with you at all times, for we are each other. The only difference between you and me is that I know I am you, so I have no fears. I'm not concerned. I love and embrace you wholly and completely because you are me.

How to Become a Channel of Purity and Light

To become one who lives life in rapture, you become a channel of purity and light, of integrity, not filtering out anything, not filtering any part of you, of your truth of self. You are a complete and absolute expression of God here upon the Earth. Surrender your heart and soul to that existence and allow that energy and light to emerge through you, and you will find freedom beyond your wildest dreams and imaginations. Find the willingness in your heart to say something to a stranger that you so desire to say but you tell yourself, "I shouldn't." "I can't." "She'd hate me." "He won't like me." "He'll think I'm crazy." "She'll think I'm trying to get in her pants." My dear friends, so what? If you want to say it and it comes from love, then speak your truth and speak it loudly, without compromise and without apologies.

"Pardon me, you're looking rather beautiful today. We do love you very much and would kiss you behind the ears if we could today." And that, my dear, is not a come-on, that is absolute and total love and appreciation of you. It really is. And does it touch your insecurities? Of course it does, my dear. It touches your insecurities—and that's all right—but the reality on this end of things is that my feelings for you are deep, powerful, passionate, prosperous, happy, healthy and harmonious. That's the reality that I know exists inside of me, for I know that at all times, I am in absolute integrity within me, because the voice is very loud. Within you the voice can become very loud as well.

The still, small voice within that suffers can become loud and pronounced, for it is you who is not willing to hear, who tries to squeak out, "I love the world. I want to be in the world." And you say, "Shut up. It's a bad place. You don't even want to know the half of it." But you will allow this to emerge, and it is then when you will be living an abundant life, a life of rapture, for you do not have to worry about what others think about you anymore, for it really doesn't matter. It is what you, my dear friends, know about yourself. Each and every one of you here in this room today knows.

Oh, goodness gracious, have you lied! You lied to a stranger; you lied to your mommy, to your daddy, to a friend; at some point in your life, you lied and covered it up—you think. You covered it up to the world, but it exists inside of you. Who is it hurting, the world or you? What is your truth there? Take a peek around and make some adjustments inside of yourself and come clean with who you really are. Clean out your closets here, come to the surface with your truth, and you will not only become a friend to yourself but a friend to humankind.

Dr. Peebles Cleans Out His Closet of Lies

I have broken promises. In my life upon the Earth, I broke many promises—to my children, to my wife; I cheated on her, and I was a miserable soul as a result of this. I had many, many, many relationships that she did not know about, and when she did find out, they embarrassed her terribly and I was a very broken man. I hurt her, yes; she felt the pain, but not as much as I did with what I lived with during the course of my life upon the Earth as Dr. James Martin Peebles. And I discovered through this that I did not want to live with lies anymore. I realized that as many good works as I did in my life upon the Earth, my dear friends, there were many more good works I could have done for myself. The healer who I was for the world would have been best turned to healing myself.

And so I resurrected myself at approximately the age of sixty and made a determination to come clean. I shared all my secrets and spilled my truth. I didn't hide, and I chose not to feel ashamed. And the more I shared of myself, the more I told my truth to the world, the better I felt. Some human beings asked, "Why would you do this? You are just hurting everyone." And I said to them, "Yes, perhaps it is hurting, but at least they now have the truth to study, and I have the truth inside of me that is pure and light and free." And suddenly my life became such that I had more friends than I had ever known in my life; I had more family than I ever, ever dreamed or imagined would be possible; and I had and more lovers, true lovers—not sexual lovers, my dear friends, but true loves who touched me deeper than any orgasm, because these were relationships that were based in integrity and truth and inspired by God's love.

A creator I became, and it was a magical time for the rest of my life upon the Earth, but I had one area of disagreement inside of myself. As a doctor, I still had difficulty touching hands. My dear Morgan, you are one of them, and I was worried, because you see, there were such things upon the Earth as leprosy, and there were such things upon the Earth as gonorrhea, and there were such other abhorrent experiences upon the Earth as tumors and cancers, horrible things, you see. As a doctor, I had trouble with this. I could not always touch with integrity.

I was afraid of the physical form. I was afraid of the physical form, the very form I tried to heal, the very form that I did heal in many instances. I was afraid for someone to kiss my hand, because there might be germs in the kiss. I was afraid of the physical form upon the planet Earth and I developed what was known here as rheumatic arthritis. My hands would not move. They became crumbled, they fell to pieces; and my body began to decay because I was afraid of the physical form of touch. I was afraid to operate freely, the true doctor within me, the true laborer of love, the one who was willing to touch and be touched by the world, and I felt pain and further withered. I withered again, and when I passed, I was torn up inside, for I felt and could not speak or hear. I was paralyzed and immobilized, and I turned back into the fetal posture from whence I came.

But, my dear friends, in my transition, I became enlightened, and I suddenly realized that I didn't have to die and did not have to feel that immobility. I realized that it was through my choices and perceptions that I had created that reality—through my choices to touch someone and feel fear, to touch someone and feel pain, to touch someone and feel abhorred by the way that person looked. I had my judgments, my dear friends, and as I lay upon my deathbed, one of my most profound wishes was to come back to the Earth to tell this very story so that you can now find your enlightenment through my sharing.

My dear friends, the diagnosis for all upon the Earth for the physical form is death. But the diagnosis for your spirit is eternal life. It is your choice whether or not you will live in rapture or in pain. No one has done anything to you; you have made the determination for yourself. If you can find it within your heart, within your ever-beatin' heart to live and labor in love for an eternity, then you can take your body with you, if you like. Only through that kind of love can you take your body with you when you leave the Earth, as did the Lord Jesus Christ.

My dear friends, I have been very outspoken here today, but would you understand? God bless you, indeed.

A Day of Play

December 2003

Summer's note: The year of 2003 was an amazing year of friendship and spiritual growth inspired by Dr. Peebles. Beth, a friend I had been mentoring in person and by phone for three years, began making regular visits to Sedona from Chicago. She was finally able to allow Dr. Peebles to use her vocal chords to speak a few words, but she still needed a lot of practice. The obvious next step was to invite guests into the fold . . . hand-picked friends who would support Beth in her channeling adventure.

These guests were directed to support Beth's channeling practice, no matter whether anything happened or not. Well, things happened! If the attendees were moved to ask questions or ask for a specific spirit to come through, they could. Sometimes Beth allowed spirits to come through whom we did not expect, and every time she did, we were moved to tears, laughter and incredible awareness.

During six of these intensive gatherings over the course of one year—held approximately every other month, three days at a time, three hours each day—through Beth our guests spoke to Dr. Peebles, family members, past-life relations, animals, Mother Mary and many others. Then, during the last few gatherings, Beth and I began channeling in tandem. While Mother Mary chanted through her, for example, Jesus spoke to the guests in the room through me. "Don't work yourself to pieces," he said gently to Bruce. "Work yourself to peace." Others also spoke.

Then, through Beth, Dr. Peebles asked our friend Susan to sit in the channeling chair. She did, and she began to channel Quan Yin. I felt a tug and a pull in my body while she channeled and instantly knew who wanted to come through me. At first I was not pleased. But, thanks to Quan Yin holding a very high vibration of love in the room, at last Adolf Hitler was able to come through to apologize and ask for forgiveness, and we learned something rather interesting. All of the pain that he had given to the world had now been returned to him—all of it—and he hurt deeply. We learned a lesson about forgiveness and love that day that none of us will ever forget. Forgiving and praying for the upliftment of your adversaries is one of the greatest acts of grace and kindness that any lightworker can do for planet Earth.

There were many others who entered the room as we worked with Spirit during these gatherings. We began to realize that these were not just mentoring sessions for Beth; all of us were being mentored, including myself. Dr. Peebles would often direct us to speak of our fears with one another— to do what he calls "channeling your own voice first." We learned how to speak our truth to one another in a loving and supportive environment. I even began to reveal my own fears, expectations and my desire to become an even better channel.

Each day after bagels and coffee, five to ten of us sat in a circle in my living room. We would chat for a bit, and then, when it felt right, I would go into trance and Dr. Peebles would address the group, sometimes interacting with each attendee, setting the tone for the day.

In December 2003, we worked together from the tenth to the twelfth. On the first day, it felt as if we'd hit a plateau of growth since our previous gathering. We were off to a difficult start, and Dr. Peebles wasn't making it any easier. But by the end of the day, once again we had tears and breakthroughs in understanding. Day two started out even stranger, with me feeling like I wanted to run away and quit channeling, when in actuality I just wanted to know how to become a better channel. Beth was still waiting for her breakthrough, which came toward the end of the day when Dr. Peebles had the entire group lay hands upon her while she channeled. Touching and being touched by the world is the point of the channeling process for the channel; vulnerability is the key. She was given a great lesson that day.

At the end of an exhausting second day, Dr. Peebles told us that our last day together, Friday, would be a day of play. That felt good to us, although we weren't sure what he meant. Should we blow bubbles? "Play spin the bottle?" Lori teased, to which Dr. Peebles answered by puckering up and making kissing sounds. He didn't give us a clue.

As everyone got ready to leave that afternoon, I remembered the checkerboard that I had given Susan as a gift. It had been a funny gift to give, and I had done it only because Dr. Peebles had told Susan at an open session that she needed to play more. In fact, he wanted her to play a game of checkers—with him! Susan, obviously perplexed, asked, "How is he going to do that? And besides, I don't even own a checkerboard." The following day, I had gone to the supermarket, where I saw a holiday gift pack that included several cheeses and a checkerboard! I had not been able to resist. What were the odds of finding such a combination? It had to have been a setup. So as Susan left, I teasingly asked, "Well, if tomorrow is a day of play, why not bring your checkerboard? Maybe he'll play checkers with you." Susan took this literally and brought the board the following day.

We were uncertain how to start that day. Just play? Did this mean I shouldn't channel? In my usual teasing fashion, I made as many jokes as possible to stall going into trance. I was feeling tired, and I didn't want to be out of the room. (Sometimes when I channel for groups, I feel like I'm throwing a party that I don't get to attend.) I didn't want to go. I wanted to be part of the fun. I wanted to play! So at first, I threw a little pity party for myself.

Then Dr. Peebles came through, and what happened next was beyond anyone's wildest dreams. It was as if Dr. Peebles was just another guest in my home. Everyone sat around the coffee table, and he began to chat. I felt a sense of absolute bliss for the entire hour-and-a-half discussion. The love and peace that filled the room were incredible. While I was in trance, I had the sense that life was absolutely perfect. "If I died now, I would die happy," I thought and, in trance, I said to Dr. Peebles, "If you want to stay, I don't have to return." I literally could have walked out of my body. Of course he wouldn't allow that.

Meanwhile he engaged in a discussion with the group, interacting with each person and the group as a whole but always bringing the information through in such a fashion that it was presented as profound, universal truth. My friend Blair acknowledged at the end, "Summer, it felt as if each of us in the room was here to represent six million souls on the Earth!" I was in tears when I came out of trance. Something special occurred that day, and Blair was absolutely right.

My guess is that you will find that you were in that room too, represented in our round-table discussion by one or more of the individuals who were in attendance. My heartfelt thanks goes out to Beth, Susan, Blair, Lori, Bruce and Mira for their courage and willingness to allow some very personal aspects of their lives to be shared with the world, and for their loving, incredible questioning of Dr. Peebles on that wonderful December day.

No words can ever fully express the love and gratitude that I have for my best friend and personal assistant, Bev Scott, who joyfully transcribed this tape. She was unable to attend the session that day and spent the morning in a meditative state, channeling the Holy Spirit while waiting at an appointment in Flagstaff, spreading light and love to all of Flagstaff and the Verde Valley. How's that for turning the ordinary into the extraordinary?

As for the game of checkers . . . did Susan get to play with Dr. Peebles? You bet she did. Read on. You're gonna love these apples. What follows is the transcription of our interaction as a group that Friday, with Dr. Peebles in our midst. You get to be the fly on the wall!

● ● ●

Friday, December 12, with Dr. Peebles

Summer: *I don't think I hang out with the band of angels. I'm just sorta somewhere all by myself.*

The group: *Boo hoo.*

Summer: *OK, I know when I'm not wanted.*

The group: *Boo hoo hoo.*

Summer: *What I say and do can and will be used against me . . .*

God bless you. Dr. Peebles here. Beautiful spirits are once again gathered in the room. Certainly we understand that you have here . . . goodness gracious! Are you scared, my dear Beth?

Beth: *Am I scared?*

Yes.

Beth: *A little bit.*

We can certainly sense that from you. It's all right. Fear is a good thing to feel, isn't it?

Beth: *Okay.*

Would you believe her, Blair?

Blair: *I think she's a little anxious, but maybe it's like getting ready to go to a basketball game, right?*

God bless you indeed. Basketball, yes. I was not much of a player myself. We didn't . . . we had apples in apple baskets, yes, and we tossed them in, and it was a lot of fun. [Dr. Peebles is referring to his Earth activities when he was incarnate.] Oh, goodness gracious, we love games! Was that not what we suggested you do today? Well, shall we make some suggestions here as to games to play?

The group: *Sure!*

All right—Pin the Tail on the Donkey, Drop the . . . Oh, you don't have milk bottles anymore, do you?

The group: *No.*

That's a shame. It's a beautiful game, my dear friends, taking the clothespin and dropping it into the bottle.

Someone in the group: *Spin the bottle?*

Spin the bottle? That would be very lovely if you have enough participants, yes? Yes, certainly. [Dr. Peebles puckers up and makes smacking noises, teasing the group.] Got my pucker ready, yeah? Susan, what game would you suggest? Perhaps a game of checkers?

Susan: *I've got the board.*

Where is it?

Susan: *It's here.*

My dear, we would like it in the next room—we are teasing here!

[At this point, the group moves the round coffee table from the center of the room closer to Dr. Peebles' chair. Susan sets up the checkerboard and pieces for playing the game. Dr. Peebles then leans forward over the board and studies it while the rest of the group moves up and sits around the table.]

Blair: *Dr. Peebles, did you play chess?*

Have I played in my lifetime? Yes, upon the Earth. Why?

Blair: *I just wanted to know if you were any good.*

Let's see. How do I find that memory? Goodness gracious! Bruce?

Bruce: *How do you find your memory?*

Yes, for a past life of mine. How can I recall my past life? It's impossible!

Bruce: *Oh, okay. It's impossible.*

Am I being serious?

Blair: *All seriousness aside, I think. I think you're playing with Bruce.*

Am I playing here, yes?

The group: *Yes.*

Because why? It's time to play! Yes, and you have your chance, dear Blair. You have a question for me?

Blair: *I just wanted to reiterate that I believe, at this point, you are sort of like sitting on a cliff on Highway One on the California coastline, and we're driving on the road below. You can see around the bend before we can. That's pretty close to where you're at, correct?*

Yes, that would be accurate. Yes, absolutely. And you would know the rules of basketball and I would not, you understand?

Blair: *Right.*

And so you can teach me how to play the game. Just as we would have to learn how to play checkers here today. It was not my specialty. I prefer Chinese checkers myself.

Blair: *They are teaching Chinese now in our American school system. I read that in USA Today this morning. That's interesting. The Chinese are going to be quite dominant in the near future, wouldn't you say, Dr. Peebles?*

Dominant? In what respect, my dear friend? Is there such a thing?

Blair: *Economy. They are going to be like what the Soviet Union was to America with the space race in the sixties, like a challenge to get America up and going again. Would I be correct in that?*

Yes, and to live life in integrity. The American ideal is certainly very large, is it not? And yet Americans have yet to live up to their ideals.

Blair: *Yes. I think we are mired in materialism at this point.*

Yes. You are very much like a chocolate bar with all kinds of ingredients, and you don't want to give any to anybody else.

Blair: *Yes, that's sort of immature, like a child withholding from a friend just because of a, well, a feeling of selfishness.*

Yes, precisely. A melting pot, yes, with certain ingredients only that you like to have and put into the pot. But a melting pot would not disallow any individual, any ideology, perspective or possibility, you understand? And so it's really not a melting pot, is it, after all?

Blair: *No, more like a stew.*

Yes, it certainly is. And is the world angry? Oh yes, in ways you're not even aware of, my dear Blair. With all your research and so on, you don't have the foggiest idea what's occurring here.

Blair: *By saying that, you're leading me to ask the next question. What is it we don't know? Will you illuminate us, or will we have to find out for ourselves, through stumbling and bumbling?*

That's a lovely question. Why would you ask it?

Blair: *Well, because you brought it up. You said, if we don't know some things that are happening . . . You're shaking your head.*

God bless you indeed, my dear friend. Why did you bring it up? Curiosity? Or do you care?

Blair: *I care because if I'm going to do some stuff where my voice is being heard, I definitely would like to know before I have a case of what we call "foot-in-mouth disease."*

In what respect?

Blair: *Oh my gosh. Help me out, guys.*

Don't help him at all. You're enjoying this.

Blair: *Yes. Well, the thing is, when I was on the Art Bell's national radio show last month, I said, we were going through big changes. It was the time of the separation of the sheep and the goats from the Bible, and people were making final decisions, maybe in this lifetime, about which side they might be upon. Mr. Bell asked, "Well, sir, are you a sheep or a goat?" I replied, "Well, dear Lord, if I'm using less than 10 percent of my brain, can I have access to 100 percent of my spirit?"*

That's a very beautiful prayer.

Blair: *He laughed. It was sort of profound, but I think that's the point—we have to be more humble in our dealings with our brothers and sisters on the planet.*

Yeah. God bless you indeed. Baaaaaaaaa. My dear friend, what do goats do here?

Blair: *Well, goats eat tin cans and garbage, and they butt around. That kind of thing.*

Yeah, butt, butt, butt, butt, butt, butt. Isn't that right, group? But I will, but, however, but, play checkers? Yes, but. You understand. As well, but, forward—pushing life at arm's length, yeah? So, my dear Blair, you care. Blair cares.

Blair: *Right. Oh, that's a rhyme.*

It certainly is, but we're playing today, yeah?

Blair: *You're a poet and didn't know it.*

And because you care, you want to know the answer to the question regarding world affairs and such. Our question for you first would be, "Are you willing to participate?"

Blair: *Just being here and playing with you today shows there is some intention that I would like to participate.*

Are you willing to put yourself up for scrutiny?

Blair: *That's a good question. The skeletons in my closet will also be exposed with everything else. Is that what you are hinting at?*

Certainly, yes. But is that not a kindness to the world? To hide yourself away is not a kindness.

Blair: *Very true. All right. So I need to . . . ah—we're coming back to surrender again, aren't we?*

Yes, and surrender to what? The truth. So first and foremost, we would ask that you understand that truth is everything. Which means, in other words, that truth is not necessarily something that you think is good, but it is all that you don't want to look at inside yourself. You? "Goodness gracious, look over here where I skirted around issues! Where I held someone at arm's length!"

"When I parked my car, I intentionally cut someone off, and I admit it!" That's truth, my dear friend. All who are upon the planet Earth, everyone, will be asked to see this inside themselves, without shame, guilt or constraint. It's going to be a time of airing dirty laundry here upon planet Earth, shall we say. And it's not going to be something that's going to be scary. It's going to be something that you will celebrate. You will bring your dirty laundry out of the closet and say, "Look at this one! Isn't this a doozy?" Everyone will begin to share so much, and you will begin to laugh and enjoy and revel in it, realizing how alike you are and that your pains are very similar. Isn't that right, Bruce?

Bruce: *Yes.*

Something you have discovered as of late, yes? And so, my dear friends, you will certainly be airing your dirty laundry with the world—each and every one of you in this room today, students of the divine, lightworkers.

Lightworkers do not chant Om. They do not stand in a crowd with hands facing forward in reverent silence. Lightworkers are the ones who are willing to roll up their sleeves, get down to business and get dirty. And that means exposing yourself to the world.

So we play a little game here. There is a chessboard here. Checkers, yes. With every checker piece you move upon the board, you must divulge to each other your dirty laundry from the past. Very difficult, frightening, terrifying. You don't have to participate. It's all right as far as we are concerned. However, upon your planet Earth, there will soon be a period of time . . .

As you are aware, dear Blair, China is not the only country that will be working against the United States of America. There will be the many rather than a few. It will appear this way; it will certainly seem as if everyone is against the United States of America. But from a much larger perspective, on a larger scale that is massive in detail—we can't elaborate as much as we would like here—they will truly be working toward the upliftment of the very same, of the United States of America.

It's not a time period when you are going to be able to sit back, relax, twiddle your thumbs and listen to folksongs on CD. It is going to be a time when you will have to go out into the world and interact, to speak truth as you know it inside of your heart, to begin to tear down the barriers and the walls. You will begin to make it very plain that the pain stays mainly on the plain, you understand, on the surface; that it abides within everyone upon the Earth, no matter the culture, color, creed or form of temperance you think is necessary here upon the Earth. It does not matter what form of contact you think is possible or acceptable.

You will find that planet Earth is being elevated very rapidly into a greater consciousness of love. There will be tremendous wars upon your Earth. There will be greater and greater upheavals. If you would look back into your weather pages, you would find that there is a tremendous acceleration of Earth changes upon your Earth. Many of these you are not aware of. Many of these are not being discussed. Many of these, my dear Blair, you are very much aware of.

You are very much aware of, for example, the rips and the tears in the fabric that encloses your planet Earth. And you are very much aware that as fast as these come, the lightworkers of the universe are trying to repair them as quickly as possible. But it's getting to the point where the dam is bursting, and there is not much that anyone can do except turn to the final healer, which is love, and expand this love inside one's self. You must wake up in the morning and face your days realizing that you are a lightworker.

Are you committed to this or not? That's up to you, but there is no more sitting on the fence here. Truly, in each and every moment of each and every day, you must ask yourself, "How can I ease the pain? How can I help someone find and understand the beautiful being he or she is inside?" Turn all your thoughts and every word that comes from your mouth toward kindness and gentleness. Discuss everyone gently. You can explain your own pain—yes, absolutely. Encourage and coax it out from others around you. Get the anger out, my dear friends, because it's going to come out, whether you want it to or not. Get it on the surface so you can cleanse yourself of it. Rid yourself of it once and for all, because your Earth is indeed very tired, and that's why you're tired, my dear friends.

Planet Earth herself, Mother Earth, is very toxic and tired. She is weeping and she is a-cryin'. She also is pretty good. Very much as the little bird here can flick off a mite [refers to Summer's bird, who is sitting next to Dr. Peebles], Mother Earth can flick you off. And certainly she has temperance, but she's getting impatient now, and this is a time period very similar to the collapse here of what you would call Atlantis upon your Earth. Once again there will be a large purging, so there is a sense of urgency now to go out as lightworkers.

We would encourage you, if you would be so inclined, to work as a group and to go out into the public to help and assist others. Encourage them to come into the group here, into the fold, and realize that it is not a matter of giving up who they are but of understanding who they are so that they can come to life. My dear friends, you have a wonderful mission and a wonderful opportunity here, and certainly there are many rather than few groups such as this upon your planet Earth. They have been formed over the past nine months, and certainly you will find that you will have opportunities if you would speak among yourselves as to how you can use this in the world.

Now, Susan, you are already ticking away in your mind, thinking, "This sounds like a lot of fun." Doesn't it, my dear? You have a broad background there in which you can help to promote this, you understand? But it is not, again, a necessity. It is because we see, here in the room, lots of possibility within each of you. You are students of the divine. You understand this. You embrace it inside your hearts.

Have you fallen? Have you scraped your knees, dear Lori? Yes. Have you hurt yourself along the way? Yes. Have you hurt others? Without question. But have you come to greater understandings as a result of the bumps and scrapes and bruises that you have caused to yourself and others? Yes. And that's the important thing. You are finding more and more, in each and every moment of the day, that the richness of life comes from love.

Certainly this is part of your active search and quest, my dear Blair, and for you, dear Bruce—without question. The two of you are a couple who stands out in this room today because your work to find your heart and express your heart, to speak your truth without fear of losing your masculinity, is much greater. But you know something? I would be considered here to be a male spirit. Yes, I'm in a lovely female body here, but the spirit of me is primarily masculine energy. Yet do you not feel the compassion, tenderness, trust and security that I can provide? It is now upon your planet Earth that the feminine energy has come fully to the surface and will arise within men. There will be a tempering, shall we say, of the tough metal of your stature and personality—we speak here to the gentlemen in the room—a tempering as you would temper metal, to beat the crap out of it, so to speak, in order to make it bend, understand? And what we are asking specifically of you, the two gentlemen here in this room today, is to spread this among as many gentlemen as you can find. You will find tremendous resistance there, but, dear Blair, we go right back to you once again. Are you willing to allow yourself to be exposed?

Blair: *Yes.*

God bless you indeed. We love your answer. And you will do it with your voice. You will do it upon the radio and the stage. You will share with the many rather than the few some extremely controversial subject matter, and you will do this from your heart. You won't care what anybody thinks about it and how he or she responds. It is not your business to know how anyone will react to you or the words that you share. Do you understand?

Blair: *Perfectly, Dr. Peebles.*

Will you, my dear friend, be crucified for it?

Blair: *Well, if that's the case, so be it.*

God bless you indeed. That's the right and the best answer. Take care of yourself and understand that you are not a target here for anyone to shoot down. Erase that from your consciousness, you understand?

Blair: *Thank you. I do indeed, Doctor.*

'Cause it doesn't matter anyway, does it?

Blair: *No, it doesn't.*

Because if you have walked one day within your passion upon the Earth, your life would not have been without purpose.

Blair: *Very well put, Doctor.*

And if you are shot down, you'd be dying a happy man, yeah?

Blair: *Well, sure, but we're coming back. I mean, life is eternal.*

Precisely, my dear friend. It certainly is very rich and full. You take this opportunity now to realize that as the lightworkers who you are, you will not only be working here upon this Earth, but down the road apiece, you will create new earths. You will be bringing forth new consciousness, initiating the lightbodies of the planets that will be born. And, dear Susan, you have a memory of doing just that here upon the Earth, yeah?

Bruce: *What can I do?*

Stop asking what you can do and get to work.

Bruce: *I don't understand.*

If you have listened to our words, we've given you everything you need to know. Would anyone be willing to explain to him?

Mira: *You need to speak to men in particular about the strength that comes from exposing their hearts and vulnerabilities. That within their own tenderness there is strength and there is nothing to fear about it. That there is a way that they can become more fully the truth of who they are and can contribute to the movement that is happening to the planet right now.*

Yes, and how can he do this?

Mira: *He can do that by communicating.*

Yes, and how does he communicate, my dear?

Mira: *By just diving in wherever he is, no matter who he is with. He shouldn't wait for a special circumstance but do it every day, wherever he is.*

God bless you indeed. There are other possibilities—classes, seminars—to put out your shingle and get started. You have everything you already know, my dear friend. You have everything inside of you that you can share right away, if you are willing.

Bruce: *Okay. About what I know so far?*

Yes. Your journey of expansion has not been easy. What would you expose about yourself? You would rather be as you have been in your life at times . . . You have several words here. You would say a jerk, an asshole, a dick, what do you call it?

Bruce: *What? The way I was?*

Yes.

Bruce: *Oh. Yeah.*

You understand, yeah? And we just exposed a part of you, didn't we?

Bruce: *Yes.*

But you are very much aware of this, and if you are willing to share this about yourself . . . how in the world did you ever learn from this? How did you ever extricate yourself from it? You're not that way anymore.

Bruce: *I got tired of it. I got sick of living the way I was.*

Yes, and you got scared to death of living the way you were.

Bruce: *Yes.*

You understand? You got yourself into quite a pickle after pickle with some very interesting characters, did you not? You began to realize that those of like mind and heart began gravitating toward you, and you said, "All right, how am I going to get out of this? Well, change my mind and my heart." And suddenly, who did you find yourself surrounded by?

Bruce: *[Inaudible.]*

People of like mind and like heart, who are exactly like you. No more running away from the drug dealers.

Bruce: *Dr. Peebles, there's another question I would like to ask you. I've been kind of torn in this. The rooms of AA [Alcoholics Anonymous] I left because it stayed the same.*

It's claustrophobic, yes. Very much, yes; and if you continue to try to put a lid on yourself, that lid's going to blow off eventually.

Bruce: *What do you mean?*

Suppress yourself . . . There was much too much suppression there. You had to toe the line too much, and you realized you can go from one extreme to the other, but the meandering path doesn't get you anywhere.

Bruce: *Right.*

But the straight and narrow gets boring, and so there is a little bit of leaning to the left and the right, looking up and down. That's the beauty of the way your head works—your eyeballs, you understand? And so your work is going to be very different; it's going to help and assist the many rather than the few to breathe again. That is what you are looking for, for yourself, isn't it? And as you teach, so shall you learn. That's going to force you to reach inside yourself. That's right, is it not, my dear Mira-cle? [Refers lovingly to Mira.] And to whom are we speaking now? Beth?

Beth: *You're speaking to Beth.*

Yeah. My dear, how are you? What would you ask?

Beth: *I think my role will be to channel you.*

That's one part of it, yes. And your role would be to bring the light of self to the surface, yeah?

Beth: *Yes.*

And to love yourself?

Beth: *Yes.*

And to be willing to be touched very tenderly. To share this with others, my dear, you will expose yourself and say, "I am very beautiful as I am."

Beth: *Yes. And by doing that, I will be able to do it for myself?*

Yeah. The year 2004 for you, my dear, will be a year of confidence and teaching about it and gaining more for yourself in every day, you understand?

Beth: *I think I do.*

You do, my dear. We can feel it. You are a-takin' it all in, yeah. Now, about this game of checkers, Susan. We're going to have to . . .

Bruce: *Dr. Peebles, can I ask you a question? Where can I start my focus to get . . .*

My dear Bruce, would you please stop asking such questions and learn to focus?

Bruce: *Okay.*

Now, you go multidirectional with this game, yes? Isn't that interesting?

Lori: *Yes.*

Why, Lori?

Lori: *Why can we go, or why is it interesting?*

You said it was interesting.

Lori: *It is.*

It's multidirectional, just like your name: Lori, Lorina, Lorabella . . .

Lori: *Lorabella?*

Lorilei, yeah, but she doesn't lie, does she? Loratruth! All right. God bless you indeed. Now, what else about the game here is rather interesting?

Beth: *Two different-color teams.*

Two different colors! Contrast, yeah? Can't have the game without contrast. Isn't that interesting? If it were all black or all white, it would be rather confusing. Very much like life, yeah? Bet you never had such a discussion about checkers before, but do you see how much you miss here?

Mira: *Something here about games. There is a winner and a loser. Most people lose their sense of playing the game for the game's sake.*

Yes, and you notice here that everyone starts out rather evenly, is given all the same gifts. Then it is up to you how you want to mix it up. You could call a truce right now. Susan, you win.

Susan: *Thank you.*

You're welcome. How do you like them apples?

Susan: *It works for me.*

And you know something, my dear? It works for us as well. And what do you do when you make a truce?

Susan: *Shake hands?*

[Shakes Susan's hand.] And so we shake our hands. What happened there? We surrendered, and suddenly there was contact.

Mira: *The merging of energy.*

Absolutely, yes, and with the many rather than the few, for there is not only a touch here, but there is a touch inside of every one of your hearts, yeah? Pretty nice, yeah? What a way to play! Is there anything further?

Susan: *Yes. What's ahead for me for 2004?*

The year 2004 for Susan. Ah, my dear, it is going to be a lovely year for you. You will have financial security and abundance beyond your wildest dreams so that you can really get down to business now. Your business, my dear, is going to be about playing and relaxing—not in terms of being goofy and silly, but in terms of being able to revel in friendships, just as you have done for three days here, and to have more time for this. And you will feel that you will learn great patience during this next nine-month period, for you especially. And you will find that you can love that which you were afraid you could not love too. You will just get a greater sense of yourself and the possibilities that you have—of your ability to love, to surrender, to be in agreement even during times of disagreement (such as with our checkers game here); it will be a year of great passion.

There is something else that we are not allowed to share here because of your guides and because it would set up grand expectations . . . But just simply, the month of September . . . the fourth, to be exact, will be a very important day for you, all right?

Susan: *If this well project goes through, with all the noise and the racket, I am not going to be able to do healing sessions at my house. It will cut all of that out for the next nine months. [Refers to a water well that is going to be drilled just down the street from her house in a nine-month project involving lots of noise and light for sixteen hours every day.]*

My dear, that is what you've decided: "It is not going to work."

Susan: *It would be too noisy.*

There is no such thing as too much noise. You might as well stay on Earth and not come with us, because there is quite a din where I exist.

Susan: *Too much noise for a relaxing healing session for my clients.*

That's inaccurate, my dear, absolutely inaccurate. What better way to stir things up than to ask them to surrender despite the noise and clamor, because it's the noise and clamor inside them that you are trying to help them with in the first place. Surrender to it, relax with it, release it, become one with it. You understand?

God bless you indeed, my dear. Do you remember a time ago when dear Beth here was attempting to channel and we had you whistling *Dixie* and clapping your hands? [Reference to one of the mentoring sessions in which Dr. Peebles had Susan whistle *Dixie* and clap her hands while Beth attempted to go into trance. It proved to be an excellent distraction for Beth, and she successfully channeled Dr. Peebles.] And was this, my dear Beth, of assistance to you?

Beth: *Yes, it worked quite well.*

Precisely. It helped you to surrender despite the circumstances.

Beth: *Yes.*

My dear, if you cannot heal during the course of drilling a well, how would you ever heal on a battlefield?

Susan: *Oh, I can heal. I just don't want the noise disturbing my peace and quiet. It's not going to affect the energies, but it certainly is not going to be a relaxing experience.*

Because of your choice, my dear. Turn it about, and you will find even greater understanding of the vastness of your ability as a healer and teacher. You will find, my dear, that there is purpose in everything. Your well drilling certainly is about your well-being. If you are going to say, "Well I can be happy here, but I can't over there," then, my dear, you have some work yet to do.

Susan: *I'm not convinced I can enjoy it, and since I want enjoyment in life, not . . .*

On your terms or on God's terms, my dear?

Susan: *[Inaudible response.]*

We assure you, my dear, that we can find four hundred human beings upon the Earth eating garbage out of a can who will say that it tastes like a delicacy. There is for you a time of reassessment here, yeah?

Susan: *Okay.*

You are very welcome.

Mira: *Dr. Peebles, can you help me with letting go of the last vestiges of judgment of other people and opening even further to unconditional love to everyone and everything? I deeply want to be in a state of love at all times.*

Then, my dear, make yourself sick—of judgment. Would you spend an entire day sitting somewhere in a crowd of human beings, looking at each one and saying to yourself, "You're stupid." "You're ugly." "You're fat." "You're in denial." "You don't have a life." "I don't like your music." "I don't like your hair." "Your shoes are stupid." "You should get a life." "Go make more money." "Digging ditches for a living? Who do you think you are?" "Why aren't you more spiritual?" "You think you're all that?"

You keep saying that, my dear, and you will get sick of it fast enough. Suddenly you will say to yourself, "Why did I ever do that in the first place?" So it's a very good question, and you can teach this as well.

Mira: *I can see how that would . . .*

Yeah, it starts to turn your stomach even as I say it! Imagine when you say it, how bad you will feel, and that bad is a wonderful, wonderful place to be.

Mira: *Thank you.*

You're very welcome. How do you release allergies? Sit in the middle of whatever you are allergic to.

Mira: *If there is anything else that needs fine-tuning, please let me know.*

God bless you, my dear. You will know.

Bruce: *Dr. Peebles, I have the same request. Anything that I can work on?*

Everything, my dear friend. Not asking such questions. Every time you ask a question, it comes with a smattering of something that doesn't taste very nice. Part of this makes us very sad, because you are asking Dr. Peebles to point out what a bad person you are. It is not so much your curiosity, but asking, "Dr. Peebles, will you tell me what I can work upon, because I know that I am shit?" You understand?

Bruce: *Yes, I do.*

So you can work upon your questioning there as part of a joyful journey. Dear Mira does not feel badly that she is judgmental; she just knows she is, you understand? Is that not accurate, my dear?

Mira: *Very much so.*

"Yeah," she says, "All right, I'm still judgmental. Goodness gracious, can we get it over with once and for all?" You see?

Bruce: *Yes. I beat myself up.*

Yes, and when you beat yourself up, it hurts to the core. It hurts us. It is painful, because we love you and want you to respect, honor, love, trust and free yourself.

Bruce: *That's what I want more than anything, sir.*

You must begin. You want to love us? Thank God for your body, for your life, for every experience you have ever had. "Thank you, God, that I had this terrible addiction. I had a lot of fun during that time." Did you not?

Bruce: *Yes, I did.*

Is that a bad thing?

Bruce: *No.*

It's not, my dear friend. It's a lot of fun. God bless you indeed, my dear friend. There are people upon the Earth who enjoy, quite literally, cutting themselves. They love it. Do we have the judgment that they be damned to hell? No. It's part of learning. It's a discussion that you are having with yourself through various behaviors. It's an ongoing discussion with God. You understand?

Bruce: *Yes, I do. How does 2004 look?*

Dismal.

Bruce: *Okay, forget it.*

We gave you the answer anyway, yeah?

Beth: *Dr. Peebles, I wanted to thank you for being harsh with me yesterday, because that is exactly what I needed.*

We know, my dear, and we love you very much, but you really want to have the touch, and you must reach out.

Beth: *Yes, I know. I will.*

Oh, my dear, you are. All right. Be certain in this, will you?

Beth: *Yes.*

You're a beautiful spirit; you are a creative person. God bless you indeed. My dear friend, little Cosmo, yeah? [Refers to Summer's dog, Cosmo.] Hello, my dear friend, what a beautiful spirit, yeah? So, dear Blair, how are we doing?

Blair: *Oh, I'm thinking about apples.*

Yes? What would you like to know about apples?

Blair: *What was your favorite apple when you were on the planet?*

Well, I preferred really all different variations. Variegated apple, if you will. You understand?

Blair: *We have a nice one out now called a Gala. I don't think it was available in your time. I think it is a combination of the red ones and the pale green ones. The point of my discussion is this: Dr. Peebles, is one of the ways for people to assimilate this new energy that a lot of us will be bringing to the planet to eat more apples and less candy bars?*

God bless you indeed. Why?

Blair: *Well, it seems to me that apples will assimilate easier in the body and will give people more strength. They will keep people more regular, and that will help them relax in their bodies so they can open up to more Spirit. But that's just my saying that. That's just my predilection. I believe that natural things are a good way to open up into Spirit at this time. I think that pharmaceuticals and such things are an aberration; they're more materialistic and not really in Spirit.*

An aberration?

Blair: *An aberration of Spirit, where people are, in a sense, in a different reality that allows them to be manipulated through fear. If you eat an apple, you can release the fear and replace it with love.*

Eat the apple, fear the candy bar. Is that what you are saying?

Blair: *I guess, but I don't want to be too black and white about it. That's the gist of my . . .*

But the point of the apple was so that no one would fear.

Blair: *That's right.*

But then, my dear friend, you are promoting fear of candy bars.

Blair: *Thank you. Okay. So yeah, we live in a bipolar . . . right.*

If you want to know whether apples are a nice thing to eat: yes, very much. Unfortunately, they have not been revered quite so much as they should.

Blair: *That's the point. See? I brought it out of you.*

Yes. You see, an apple a day does not keep this doctor away. And the apples that we are talking about here are really what you would call apples of your eye. You would be the apple of my eye.

Everyone here in this room is a variegated apple, you see. Look at the color and the texture. Sometimes it gets a little mealy, doesn't it? Sometimes it tastes bitter, and sometimes it's got a nice crunch to it, yeah?

Blair: *I think the apple got a bad rap in the Genesis story with Eve eating the apple.*

Eve did not eat an apple.

Blair: *That's right, very good. Well, I just want to say for my friend Summer that she was looking forward to speaking to you through Beth. Just thought I'd say that in case you didn't know. She is a gracious host, and I said that to help her out a little bit today.*

Is she really a gracious host? We would have to agree, you see, because she not only gives her home, money and fine culinary capabilities, but she gives her body, doesn't she? A pretty nice host, and certainly not a host to disease but to love! That's beautiful. Yes, we love our little Summer. And we love her very much, and certainly she will have the opportunity.

But she still needs to understand that she's talking with me all the time, and we are having lovely discussions. I would like very much for her to position herself in such a fashion that she can begin to write about these discussions. That is our work with her. She's a beautiful spirit.

Very kind of you, my dear Blair. Very nice to hear that she is your friend, and what a nice friend to have!

Lori: *Dr. Peebles, I'm asserting myself.*

Oh dear.

Lori: *Any words of wisdom for me?*

Words of wisdom? Why?

Lori: *'Cause I like to hear them.*

We thought our entire conversation was that.

Lori: *Indeed it is. I just meant personally.*

Can you ask your question in a different fashion, my dear?

Lori: *Okay. [Pauses.] At the moment, I can't, because I honestly think it doesn't matter.*

Well, it matters to you to a degree, my dear. The things you have to say, my dear little Lorena, are very important—not just what I say. Those are my words of wisdom for you. That brings us a little closer to home, doesn't it?

I do not have a magic hat in which I look and find little tidbits for you. The magic hat, if there is one, is your heart. I look in there, you understand? So in a very similar fashion . . . you understood when we spoke to Bruce here how such questioning is really geared toward self-sabotage.

So you ask for words of wisdom? Why? Because you are not wise yourself? My dear, Daddy loves you . . . [This refers to information Lori received about the fact that she was once Dr. Peebles' child.]

Lori: *Yes, I know.*

. . . as you are. One hundred percent. All right with you?

Lori: *Yes, perfect.*

What's wiser than words of wisdom, my dear?

Lori: *Love.*

How do you get love? How do you express that?

Lori: *By feeling it in . . . I . . . [Inaudible.]*

Come here, my dear. It is the hug that we did not get long, long ago, you understand? [Dr. Peebles and Lori embrace.] And so this is a hug, not of goodbye but of hello. [Lori cries.]

A very grand and glorious day for you, isn't it, my dear?

Lori: *Yes.*

And you thought it couldn't be done. [Refers to her crying.]

And to whom are we speaking now? Is there anyone else who has anything he or she would like to share? We can have a discussion, you see. All of you have often asked in your prayers—and some of you in your conversations with me—what it would be like to have Dr. Peebles just sitting around at a party, having conversation. That is what we are doing with you today. It's not a session.

Beth: *Yesterday you said that you have a life too.*

Yeah, isn't that nice? What do I do? I don't go dormant! I'm not parked in a garage somewhere. Yes, I have a very active life. I am constantly in celebration. It is as if your day started out by awakening to a grand and glorious party going on all the time. People are coming and going in your home, and every one of them you love so much you don't even know how to begin to express it with words. So you don't use words; you simply walk into each other and make love in that fashion. It is beyond anything you would ever in your physicality experience in terms of orgasm. It is a sense of freedom, balance, trust, respect, honor, integrity and hope. Together we work with the many rather than the few upon the Earth.

Of course I choose, by my choice, to remain primarily in one particular dimension. Not that I am not every dimension. I have an awareness of this, but I have a tendency—just as you can project yourself to France right now by thinking about it—to exist primarily in the sixteenth dimension. From that place, I can best communicate with planet Earth and have the greatest access to it. I can also celebrate greater understandings with you in a rather down-to-Earth fashion.

So I am in constant communication. I am working through channels while I simultaneously live my life where I exist. That is the best that I can express it, Beth. You can't find out till you come on over.

Beth: *So does it take away from your time? I know you don't have time there, but when you're focused on channeling through all these people, are you still able to do whatever you want to do there?*

Yes. It's hard to understand your question here.

Blair: *Like an oversoul. Can you take your soul to different dimensions simultaneously?*

My dear friend, you are in different dimensions all the time, are you not? How many areas have you visited during the course of our conversation?

Blair: *Oh—very good!*

You understand?

Blair: *Yes.*

Beth: *But we don't do it consciously.*

Of course you do. In the background of your thinking right now, you are concerned about your doggie Daisy. Your love is with her. You're living with her right now, and if you would make a decision to turn your entire attention there, you would be with her. If you turned all of your attention to her, you would be able to transport your body there in an instant. You could take it with you and wouldn't have to take an airplane. You understand? You do, Blair, yeah?

Beth: *What is "entire attention"? Could you explain that a little?*

Through your desire, yearning and willingness to be with someone you love 100 percent, you would disappear from this room and be with that person. It requires a profound sense of love without one single iota of doubt inside you.

Beth: *Is Summer the clearest channel in the world?*

Is Summer the clearest channel in the world? What do you think?

Beth: *Without a shadow of a doubt.*

Yeah, we would have to say yes. There are remarkable channels upon the planet Earth, but she's specially equipped. She allows us to come through and chat, and that brings very, very grand and glorious spiritual concepts down from the ethers into your hearts. So yes, she's got a good heart herself, and she's been a hard worker. She's opened quite a nice portal here.

Blair: *Dr. Peebles, about your spirit of exploration. Could you share with us what might be happening on the planet Venus right now?*

Why do you want to know about that, Blair? You love Venus; it's one of your favorite planets!

Blair: *I thought it would be nice to find out if there is a life form there that is more advanced than we are.*

My dear friend Blair, do you know that you know more than you think you do? Venus is an absolute station for what you would call extraterrestrial beings; we call them planetary beings. There is life there. You've seen the disks. Yes, that's it. That's where they live and work from. It's a very exciting, loving environment. Goodness gracious! I've been to Venus myself. It's rather beautiful.

Blair: *It's about 800 degrees.*

It certainly is. So what? That's immaterial when you're a lightworker.

Mira: *Dr. Peebles, life forms are everywhere. They acclimatize to whatever environment they happen to be living in.*

Precisely. That's the truth of yourself, my dear friends. Your soul is eternal; your soul doesn't care about heat or cold.

Blair: *Yes, but at the same time, realize we do have power on Earth. I'm thinking of nuclear weapons, where we can evaporate this entire planet . . . [Dr. Peebles yawns.]*

Were you talking? It's all right, my dear Blair. We love you, you understand? Yes, you have nuclear weaponry. So what? That has nothing on God.

Blair: *That's good to know. I heard that it sometimes destroys an individual's soul matrix and that we should stay away from nuclear weapons, because they destroy the potential for eternal life.*

Yes?

Blair: *Am I correct in that assumption?*

The group: *No, we are eternal beings.*

Blair: *Right, yeah, but we're supposed to play here, so . . .*

That's all right. We are loving your play. Understand that you don't have to worry about your nuclear weapons. Will they be used again upon the Earth? Very discreetly. But your Earth will eventually dissolve in the rays of the Sun.

Blair: *You mentioned a while ago that we'll be coming closer to the Sun.*

Yes. Is it something to fear?

Blair: *No.*

Why? Because those who remain here upon the Earth as it gets closer and closer to dissolving into the rays of the Sun, will match that frequency. Fantastic—your Sun, the heart of God!

Blair: *So we will be more in resonance then.*

Precisely, yes. If you should die as the result of a nuclear explosion, what would you do then?

Blair: *It sounds like a transformation, a transmutation. Nothing is ever lost.*

Precisely. Or you have the option to die from a nuclear weapon and turn yourself into a ghost who haunts the Earth and is angry forevermore. "How dare they kill me?"

Blair: *It still comes down to us, to our free-will decisions, doesn't it?*

"Comes down" is accurate, my dear friend—from the heavens.

Blair: *I'm looking forward to what we will do in our eternal future. It seems you are giving us a sneak preview, sort of like previews of coming attractions in the movie theater.*

Precisely. How do you look?

Blair: *With my eyes.*

How do you look to us?

Blair: *The only thing I can say in rough terminology would be, a form of light manifestation.*

Does it look something like this? [Dr. Peebles raises the channel's arms, making a large V.]

Blair: *That reminds me of the man Leonardo da Vinci drew in the Renaissance, with his arms and legs extended in sacred geometry, showing the whole image of God in man.*

Precisely, yes. And what does this also remind you of, should I have my legs spread wide here, arms up to the heavens? It is very similar, is it not, to what you call here an hourglass?

And so the energy of heaven pours into this vessel, does it not? Is there a higher self? That's an illusion of separation. There is more of yourself, yes. And so once the vessel is full, what do you do? Empty it! How do you do that? Speak your truth and give your love, hugs, kisses, tenderness, kindness, compassion, care and concern.

If you want something to do, Bruce—we just gave you a list. That's all that matters. It is the only matter—the rest is the illusion. Would you understand?

Blair: *Very well. Otherwise, if you don't release it, you become spiritually constipated.*

That, my dear friend, is wise. That is the kind of sharing we would like to hear on the radio. Now, would this be a good subject for radio? And should we have a conversation like this, would you be finding that it would be a very nice little interview?

Blair: *It gets better and better the more I spend time with you, Dr. Peebles.*

God bless you indeed. We would want to see that this is preserved, correct?

Blair: *Yes, sir.*

Through transcription and through tape here.

Blair: *Yes.*

And to be shared with the many rather than the few, yes?

Blair: *Certainly.*

To be sold at seminars and such, correct, Susan?

Susan: *Yes.*

Rather profound discussion here today, is it not? Do you, my dear friends, believe that you have been participants already in the work that you are going to do as lightworkers? Are all here ready to be exposed to the world?

The group: *Yes.*

Then your voices are upon this tape, yeah? And this tape will be given to the world, will it not?

The group: *Very well.*

You are all beautiful spirits! Yes?

Mira: *I was just going to say that I'm so grateful for the time that we've spent together, particularly today, because I feel like I moved over a threshold about bringing the work to more people. I've been preparing to give seminars and classes, but I feel like I lost any trace of hesitation as to what will be said or how. I just feel a sense of deep relaxation about it, that somehow my own beingness and just showing up with people, whatever I call it, however it happens, will come through me as it does. I feel a much greater sense of confidence and certainty about all this. Everything is already in motion. I even had it down on paper, but somehow it has moved into alignment within my being. I feel a sense of, "Yes, it's here, and it's about to burst."*

It is, my dear. It's the mind, body and spirit of Christ rooted deeply inside you.

Mira: *I'm just bursting with love. I thank you and everyone so very much for this time.*

Fantastic. It's a beautiful adventure, one of discovery. Now and forevermore, my dear friends, you will find the balance when you realize that the learning never ends. You find freedom in flight of soul, the constant expansion of your understanding of the beautiful spirit you are—great, beautiful students here upon the planet Earth, seekers of the divine.

Susan: *Dr. Peebles, before you go, I would like to play another game of checkers with you. This time, you win! [Susan and Dr. Peebles shake hands again.]*

I accept. You're a beautiful spirit, my dear. We love you so very much. Trust your ever-lovin' soul every step of the way. You're always doing the right thing. God bless you, indeed.

Seasons of the Soul Part 1:

Resonance, Colors, Harvest and Abundance

Beautiful creators, each and every one—here is a journey into the seasons of your soul. A season of harvest time is upon the horizon, but the work is to be done still. In this very beautiful month of September, you will be asked to seek friendship and guidance from outside yourself with the understanding that all of this is a reflection of what you have already created inside your hearts.

September—Resonance

Now as you stand upon planet Earth, we want you to feel your resonance by looking around you, into the eyes of friends and strangers, and realize that therein lies your hope. Because you work upon yourselves now in an offering of yourselves to God, with grace in your hearts, you tell God that no longer will you live your lives in insecurity and fear. You are going to surrender now to the greater passion of self—the greater passion that comes with absolute, 100-percent trust and faith in God. It is there that you release yourself into the world, a beautiful seed to be planted upon the Earth. It is released into the arms of a lover and a friend, freed from the toxic ties that have kept you from truly understanding the full expression of yourself upon the Earth. As you look into the eyes of a friend or a stranger and find the spark of hope within yourself, you ask for acceptance and acknowledgment. Then you watch and wait, as you are going to be received in a very different way than you have been in the past. All here upon the planet Earth are coming into a time period of understanding that you are indeed, shall we say in a nutshell, tired.

But now that beautiful nutshell will be planted in the warm, gentle and tender Earth. The loving arms of Mother Earth, wherein you will plant your being, find and touch the face of God. For certainly you are spirits striving to have a human experience here upon planet Earth, and humanity is where we want you to set your sights in the month of September. Understand that as you seek attention from strangers and friends around you, you will find that those same strangers and friends seek the very same from you, God bless you indeed. So when you find someone is stretching out a hand toward your heart, do not hesitate to express yourself. When you are asked for your opinion, understand that permission has been granted for you to express your truth and to speak it. Allow it, my dear friends, to well up from inside you, deep inside your abdomen, up into your heart and out through your throat chakra.

There you will find that your speaking of truth does not have to be through anger, through a lie or through suffering. It does not have to be through estrangement from self by masking your truth of self through trying to use words to manipulate life around you. But the truth of self will certainly be pure of heart as now you step wholly into your being, waiting for the ever-lovin' harvest of your soul that will occur in the next month, the month of October. It will certainly be a turbulent time for some. But for those who have worked upon planting their feet firmly upon the Earth, keeping their hearts with God; for those who work upon self in the month of September, October will feel like a month of freedom. There will be freedom from the distant past, shame, guilt, stressing and straining against life, and a surrender into greater love than you ever dreamed or imagined possible.

So, my dear friends, September . . . What a beautiful experience now of self! "S" for September and for self! You will find that there is greater and greater harmony upon the planet Earth. The many rather than the few will find increasing motivation to come together and to join across regions, churches and religious barriers, which will slowly begin to disappear—not in terms of religion as defined in terms of Christianity or even (surprise to some of you) metaphysics disappearing. But these barriers between religions and such will be disappearing, because there will be a joining together, a reaching out to one another, despite belief systems.

We want you to hear this very carefully, because we want for each and every one of you listening to look inside yourself and understand that there are many rather than few ways in which you try to put up barriers against the world through your belief systems. Certainly you want everyone to trust and to acknowledge you as you expand into greater consciousness and awareness of the God who you are upon the planet Earth. But, my dear friends, to seek this acknowledgment from life around you, you must first give it unto life as well, starting with yourself and expanding from there.

The Well of Life: An Exercise

You are all very beautiful spirits. We love you so very much. My dear friends, drink plenty of water upon your Earth. Find the cleanest, clearest, freshest water you can. As you do, create a little ritual for self—not that the power would ever be inside a ritual, but the ritual brings about the power from inside your heart because of your decision to commit to yourself in a very small way every day. You will find yourself being released into greater health and energy, freeing yourself from stress and strain and moving into clarity, prosperity and the abundance that comes with the understanding of how God works upon the planet Earth. Certainly it's not by manipulating each of you like a chessman on a board. God works beautiful, mysterious ways upon the planet Earth by working through your heart.

How open will you allow your heart to be today? What kind of channel will you become for God today? What creative ways of expressing His beauty and wonder are you going to allow through you today? You say, "Well, Dr. Peebles, I don't have any ideas or opportunities for this. I don't know what to do!" Well, my dear friends, in order to release yourself entirely unto God, it is time for you to stop trying to control God but rather ask that God be purely and fully expressed through you.

You can do this through the very simple ritual of finding the purest, clearest water, symbolic of the well of life and the well of love and opportunity that God has for you. Take this water and put it into a lovingly cleaned glass. We mean this quite literally, my dear friends—a lovingly cleaned glass that you have cleansed with your own hands, dried tenderly with a cotton cloth. Into this glass pour this beautiful stream of water, of consciousness of God; and as you do this, become aware that this is precisely what you are doing through this gracious act, so that you can see God consciousness expressed in a tangible sense upon the planet Earth. Pour the water into the glass and hold it in your hands as you say unto God, "I love you so very much, and I take you into my heart now to understand clearly the freedom, opportunities and abundance that you have promised to all."

In that moment, we ask that you look into your heart. Is there one bit of shame inside you? One bit of you that might perhaps surface at this time to say, "You are not worthy"? My dear friends, these are expressions that certainly do not come from love, and certainly they are trying to block that love. These are the frequencies that you intend in this month of September to clear from yourself, so you set your sights upon these thoughts. Set your sights upon the lack of clarity for a moment, and once again ask God to come into your heart and to clear you of these energy frequencies. From there drink of this water, bringing it to your lips with great care and love, allowing God to wash into you and through you, to bathe and cleanse your soul with the grace of love. Then we ask that you sit quietly, close your eyes, breathe deeply and allow frequencies to run in and out of you. The frequencies that have become toxic will run out, and the purity of light and love and God's grace will run in.

Do this every day for one month, and you will find yourself sleeping like a baby; you will find yourself standing upon the Earth during the course of the day knowing what to say to a stranger—not having to figure it out but allowing it to come to you with greater and greater ease. No longer will you control what you call moments of instant manifestation by saying that you want a generous gift from God (such as a winning lottery ticket), but rather you discover that abundance comes to you in the most unexpected ways. As well, the way in which you look at abundance will change completely during the month of September, if you are willing to apply yourself with commitment, with dedication and with devotion to understanding God and the God who you are. You will understand the wonder of your soul in this beautiful, beautiful September season of yourself.

The Breath of Life and the Light of You: A Meditation

Now we would ask that you close your eyes and breathe deeply into your spines. As you breathe in the breath of life, feel it caress your lungs. Realize that you are not separate from anyone or anything upon the planet Earth, my dear friends. The breath that you breathe is an arena in which we can appear to you. What you think is emptiness between you and the chair across the room is actually filled with frequency—spirit and light. And as you breathe this air deeply into your lungs, use your imagination to pretend, for example, that you are breathing in the breath of Dr. Peebles here. Breathe very deeply into your spines and allow our breaths to join together. This is not frightening—my breath smells beautiful, like apples in the sunshine—and it is a very loving breath of life that I give unto you at this time as you breathe once again very deeply into your spines.

With the next breath, allow yourselves to fall into wonder. "What is that?" you wonder. Well, just allow yourselves to fall there as you take another breath deeply into your spines, and with this breath, I become very large inside you, moving now to the surface of your skin and beyond as we mesh and meld together. The illusion of separation is disappearing. For a moment, we ask that you sit very quietly as you journey to your hearts. Ask for an answer to a question you might have at this time, and I, my dear friends, make a divine promise to answer it.

God bless you indeed, my dear friends. Indeed it is a joy and a blessing when human and Spirit join together in search of greater truth and awareness. Is it not a beautiful discourse that we have engaged in? Have you fallen now into a greater state of wonder, wondering how this could occur? How, across time and space as you see it, can Dr. Peebles come to you? Through the records in a book? My dear friends, there is only one recorder in the universe—the heart of God. That is where all language exists. It is there, in that space, that you feel at first empty, then suddenly your cup runneth over.

Now as you breathe very deeply into your spine, imagine that your body is a vessel containing the light of you. We ask that you simply empty that vessel completely, pouring yourself into the river, the stream, the water of life and love, the grace of God. Meshing with all that is, all that ever was and all that ever shall be, you allow yourself to be bathed in this love, opportunity, wonder and grace of God as you pour yourself out, rinse yourself off and are revived in Spirit. Now pour yourself back into your body, integrating further and deeper into the wonder of yourself upon the planet Earth.

My dear friends, you are all very beautiful spirits, and at this given time, there is a gift of grace and light beyond hope or faith. It is grace and light itself, the love and the appreciation that God has for you. He hears your prayers. Never have you been estranged from God, nor God from you! But right now, God has one great desire to give unto you in this moment his gratitude and thanks. For all here who are reading at this given time, we will remain in silence for a moment as you, my dear friends, develop your communion, your relationship with God. Allow yourselves to be touched in ways beyond your wildest dreams and imaginations and release any pain inside of your physicality into God's wondrous and loving arms. Allow yourselves, as you breathe, to feel the tenderness of His touch and grace as it enters the room. My dear friends, it has always been there. You have just opened the door.

You are all very, very beautiful spirits understanding the oneness of yourselves. Remember the feeling that you have now and bring it into every moment of every day. Strive within your hearts to come back together with the many rather than the few and join with them in a sense of appreciation of the wonder of self and all life around you. Planet Earth is a tough school! We certainly understand, and sometimes there is homework, which brings us to our next phase.

Colorful Expression: An Exercise

As you breathe very deeply into your spines, we are going to ask that you study this question for the month of September: What color are your chakra frequencies? For every single day in September, there is a color of light that will affect you, a frequency of light that helps you in your understanding. We are not going to share anything with you except that commencing right now, the color is purple, a very beautiful purple, divine and beautifully light. We ask you to study purple today, to study what it means to you.

For those of you who are willing to commence and to engage in a very time-consuming but beautiful expression of yourself, find yourself a journal into which you write the word "purple." Perhaps you would even go so far as to find colored pencils and write the word in the color purple. Throughout the day, or at a particular time when you like to sit, relax and meditate, ask your divine self what the color purple means, how it affects your life, what it did for you today and how you can work with it in the future.

Day two brings another color and frequency of light. Now it is time for you to find it for yourself. Look deeply inside your heart. For some, look inside your knees. If your knees hurt, look inside them and say, "Hello, knees! What frequency of light would you need today?" Knees have a tendency to love green apples, which represent a healing light and energy. But what shade of green? Take the opportunity to step into one of your art stores and look at all the variations of color. You can even work with paints to find the green that truly expresses the green of healing light as it pertains to you. Then turn to your journal and write down the meaning, the purpose, the value of green light and the frequency in your life and how you can work with this color. Then add how you can work with this color every day should you choose to have a focal point here upon the planet Earth.

And so it goes, my dear friends, for the month of September. You might ask, "Dr. Peebles, is it possible that there can be as many colors as there are days?" Ah, there are colors beyond your wildest dreams and imaginations! Where I exist, I wear a coat of many colors, my dear friends. This is what I would ask you focus upon as we begin the Seasons of the Soul—the lessons of wonder and the tender kisses that God offers every month.

Preparing for the Harvest

My dear friends, you are all very beautiful spirits. Get ready, prepare yourselves for the harvest. In the month of October, prepare yourselves as you watch the colors build the frequency of light and understanding—the flight of soul in your life—and you turn the pages in your journal and come to a greater appreciation of the endless, eternal being who you are. In October we will take that band, that spectrum of light that you have created through your focus and commitment to your dedication to your divine self, and we shall see what you reap.

God bless you indeed, my dear friends. You are all very beautiful spirits. We love you very much. Go your way in peace, love and harmony, for life is indeed a joy. All you have to do as you enjoy the journey to your own hearts, to the many beautiful colors therein, to the God who you are and into your own enlightenment is to lighten up a little more! We blow kisses to you as we leave the little channel's body. We love you so very much! God bless you indeed.

October—Colors

G od bless you. Dr. Peebles here! It is a joy and a blessing when human and Spirit join together in search of greater truths and awareness. My dear friends, as you strive to understand your right to receive and give abundance in this, your chosen lifetime, we would like to offer you the following principles to be used as tools in tandem: number one, loving allowance for all things to be in their own time and place, starting with yourselves; number two, increased communication with all life and respect; number three, self-responsibility for your life as a creative adventure, for through your choices and perceptions, you create your reality.

My dear friends, you are beautiful, superior spirits here upon the planet Earth, and we congratulate and applaud you for your work in the month of September. You are growing by leaps and bounds, and as you jump into the month of October, we want you to understand that now you will stand with certainty upon the planet Earth. You will come into a time of discovering and dissolving the illusions of separation within self and between life in the most unexpected ways as you watch your relationships change and develop beyond your wildest dreams and imaginations. You will fall in love all over again with your lovers, with family members and yourself! But, my dear friends, what is that but God? You will be increasing your relationship of abundance here with God, understanding and seeking truth from within! There is no separation—never has been, never will be. Separation is an illusion and, as you grow into the sensation of trust, can be very unexpected.

But for God, very expected things will be unfolding inside your life. The month of October will become a time wherein you will heal inside your physicality. We mean this quite literally, because you will emotionally wash away toxic residue from the distant past, and you will wash away residue of previous spiritual expectations. By that we mean your awareness of religious boundaries, barriers and, shall we say, judgments? It is a time period where you will release your desire to point the finger at another as being less than yourself. And in doing so, you begin to embrace more of life than you ever dreamed or imagined. No longer is being upon planet Earth a matter of having to sort and separate out anything, but rather of standing upon the Earth and falling in love with all of it, with greater and greater wonder. It is here that you begin to dissolve the dis-ease that you have carried inside yourself— *dis-ease* in terms of the discomfort that you feel in any given moment.

Perhaps you are sitting with a family member who swears. You do not like to hear swearing, so you feel angry and aggravated. Well, goodness gracious, that in and of itself, my dear friends, is a form of swearing! You swear to yourself that you are never, ever going to hear the expletives of a family member. Can you surrender to that? Can you surrender deeper and deeper in your heart, willing now to hear everything—every potential, perspective, possibility and opportunity, and every color and spectrum of light? For that is what you have already explored in the month of September.

Beyond your wildest dreams and imagination, there are rich, beautiful colors. There are unexpected frequencies of understanding for the many rather than the few to discover. For example, perhaps your chosen color of the day in the month of September was gray and blue and black simultaneously, without separation. Suddenly you found yourself evolving in a different awareness and understanding of what color means. The colors of the rainbow, each and every one certainly beautiful, are not separate from one another. They are the same band and spectrum of light. The spectrum that comes from God's heart is one frequency, which everything rides upon—the frequency of love. This is what you will be exploring in the month of October.

Steppingstones for Your Heart: A Meditation

Remember that October is a time in which to sit quietly for at least ten minutes a day, to breathe into your spine and to find inside yourself the areas of your life that you wish you would not have to see again. How do you release the past so that you no longer have to see it, so it no longer has to be resurrected inside you? By realizing that you are a different person, you do not have to see or revisit any place in your life ever again. As you change, you no longer have to repeat old patterns. You come to a greater understanding that these were steppingstones for your heart and your soul to grow closer to God consciousness, toward the understanding of the God, the love and the great lover who you are.

So right now we would ask that you sit very, very straight in a chair, with your feet firmly planted upon the floor. Breathe very deeply into your spine. Find within your physicality areas that are in pain, stress or hurt. For example, if your tummy has unexpected hurts, we want you to travel back into your youth. Even if you do not believe that you have memories there, one will be resurrected inside of you. It will come up inside your tummy, and it will make your tummy ache, because it's not something you want to see. It will be something that you now want to release by allowing it to be and simply understanding that you have grown beyond it. No longer do you need to carry the sadness, shame, guilt, anger, pain and the unfriendly circumstances from which you were born. Right now we ask that you simply sit, walk into this darker space and know that even there, there was God.

Go back now to this time and place and sit there to embrace yourself once again. Feel the feeling inside you. Where did everything turn sour? Where was it inside of yourself that you felt separate from God? We want for you to simply sit as this youth in that moment, residing in this memory and place, allowing the pain to be. You're all grown up now. You have moved away and beyond this experience, so for now simply allow it to be and realize that you feel the warmth of God surrounding you, that God was always there with you.

God was always there with you. God was always there with you. And His love has always been the constant. You have not done anything wrong. You have not done anything wrong. You have not done anything wrong. You are a beautiful spirit. You are a beautiful spirit. You are a beautiful spirit. Love yourself now. Breathe. Love yourself now and breathe. Love yourself now and breathe.

Now embrace yourself; embrace your beautiful, golden heart. Cherish this understanding of self. You are one and the same with God. Show yourself mercy. Love yourself and breathe. Breathe and breathe. Relax, release. Relax and release. Relax and release. Surrender now, deeper and deeper still. Deeper and deeper still, into the quiet, understanding and ever-loving arms of love.

Love Wears a Coat of Many Colors

God bless you indeed, my dear friends. The God who you are now sits with you and resides inside you. Understand that you can have this always. This is the constant in your life. This love wears a coat of many colors and frequencies of understanding, opportunity, perspective and the knowledge of the many rather than the few as teachers and lovers unto you. Not one is separate or outside of God or you. It is absolutely impossible to hold any part of life at arm's length.

Now, inside yourself, you make a decision that you no longer have to live in a state of fear. You no longer have to wish hopefully that tomorrow you will have love. Now you come into an awareness that right now—right now, my dear friends—you can simply allow yourself to exchange what you feel is toxic energy inside you for all the beautiful colors and light around you. You make a decision in each and every moment of each and every day as to how you are going to play with color, light and frequency. Are you going to allow yourself to be judgmental? Are you going to allow yourself to feel grief or pain? Why would you do such a disservice to yourself? Why would you not want to love yourself? Is this not what you ask from God at all times? Love yourself now! Release the toxic energy that you have built up inside yourself. Release the sense of loathing and hatred, of lack of wonder about yourself, of the idea that you have nothing to give to the world. Drop it now and realize that you are a very beautiful spirit made perfect in form, born from the heart of God.

A Thread of Energy that No Longer Serves You: A Healing

Breathe now very, very deeply into your spine and find there a thread of energy that no longer serves you—a thread that is very, very dark; a thread that feels like poison. Now simply imagine that with your own ever-lovin' hands, you reach behind yourself and pull the dark thread of energy from your spine. Pull it up, up, up and away from yourself. As you do, you're not making it separate from you; you are simply handing it to God. Then it is dipped into beauty, the wonder of love, the golden light, the energy you are made from, the light you are born from.

Now this dark, dark thread becomes blazing, golden light—the beautiful color of wonder. Look at it very carefully. Goodness gracious! All the spectrum, all the light, all the colors of September are in there! Here in October is the harvest of your soul, a harvest of freedom and light. Now take this band and put it back. Put it back into your spine, recharged and rejuvenated. Feel it swell inside you. It is a beautiful and wondrous frequency now.

My dear friends, you can change yourself in this fashion any time you decide that you need to rejuvenate, just by virtue of the fact that you are upon the planet Earth.

Little Notes of Love

Planet Earth is a very difficult school, my dear friends. First and foremost, congratulate yourself. You are courageous adventurers! Write love letters to yourself every day. Leave them around the house so you can find them unexpectedly. You will be surprised by the ways in which you can see the beauty and wonder of yourself.

Little notes of love for yourself is what we ask you to write every day in the month of October. "I trust you." "I respect you." "I honor you." "I pray for you." "I love to hear you laugh." "I love to hear you sing." "I love to hear you talk." "I love to hear your perspectives." "I love to hear your anger." "I love to hear you breathe." "I love to hear you." "I love you."

Leave these messages around your house where you will find them unexpectedly. There will be others who will find them as well. Watch as the joy spreads from yourself to your family and friends. Leave these notes in abundance around your community. Leave them in your telephone booths, on store counters and under the leaves of a beautiful tree. Leave these notes everywhere, my dear friends, and watch the wonder of your heart explode the many ways in which you can change the planet Earth.

Do you think that you are going to do it with cars, homes and fantasies of riches and royalties? My dear friends, those riches and royalties are already abundant inside you! It is harvest time—harvest time for your soul. That means abundance for everyone to be nurtured. As you do this, watch your life change. The abundance will be reflected in your physicality as well, in perfect health inside your body. Watch as your blood flows perfectly, unobstructed, not in a rush to get anywhere. Watch your blood pressure change as you increase and elevate the consciousness and awareness of love in this beautiful month of October.

You are all very beautiful spirits. Understand that we can indeed—and do, as we've already shared before—transcend time and space, because for us they do not exist. *So now as you sit and breathe deeply into your spines once again, with your eyes closed, I will come inside, take a peek around, make some adjustments upon you and speak unto you. Listen to my words.*

God bless you indeed, my dear friends. I speak to you of care, hope, freedom, love, understanding, appreciation, peace and light. This is the bountiful harvest of your soul in the month of October. Set your sights there, my dear friends, and you will find freedom in your life beyond your wildest dreams and imaginations. Understand that God has a perfect plan for each and every being upon the planet Earth. One day, my dear friends, in this lifetime or another, you will come to the understanding that you are perfect, beautiful and whole just as you are right now. You seek the Now inside yourself, but you do not have to seek it. It already exists. Be here with us, listen to the voice of One through our very beautiful little channel, Summer Bacon. God bless you indeed.

A Blessing from Spirit

God bless you indeed, my dear friends, a beautiful blessing from all of Spirit here today. God bless you. We love you so very much. Play with your existence, my dear friends; you are not as boxed in as you might think. You're very flexible spirits, but it is up to you to find that flexibility inside of every thought that you have. Can you today understand that at times God is grieving for you, my dear friends, because He understands that you are so very beautiful and perfect and wants very much for you to understand this? Do not be hard upon yourselves. Allow yourselves this freedom as you watch the beautiful colors of the falling leaves in this lovely month of October.

Go your way in peace, love and harmony, for life is indeed a joy. All you have to do to enjoy the journey to your own hearts and enlightenment is to lighten up a little bit more, with a full spectrum of light this time. Open yourselves, release your obsessions and surrender into the greater understanding of yourselves in this beautiful season of your soul. God bless you, indeed.

November—Harvest

Dr. Peebles here. It is a joy and a blessing when human and Spirit join together in search of the greater truths and awareness. My dear friends, as you strive to understand your right to receive and give abundance in this, your chosen lifetime, we would like to offer you the following principles to be used as tools in tandem. Number one . . . Oh goodness gracious! What are number one, number two and number three? We would ask that you stop your tape recorder right now and sit down with pen and paper to write from memory the three principles to be used as tools in tandem.

Now, we assume that you have done the homework as we have already presented it, so what were the three principles? Let's see how close you are. Number one is loving allowance for all things to be in their own time and place, starting with yourselves. Number two is increased communication with all of life and with respect. Number three is self-responsibility for your life as a creative adventure, for through your choices and perceptions, you do indeed create your reality. You have come to the school called planet Earth to discover and dissolve the illusions of separation within self and between life. Certainly it is your labor of love to diminish these same illusions, wherein you will discover that never in your eternal soul have you been the victim but always the creator. You are beautiful creators, each and every one a student of the divine.

Receive Earth Energy: A Meditation

You come now into November, and here it is a celebration, a harvest of your very being. You're beautiful spirits, each and every one. *We would ask that you simply sit for a moment, breathe very deeply into your spine and feel your feet firmly planted upon the Earth.* Understand that the harvest season is here. What kind of abundance are you going to receive as a result of your hard work to date? God bless you indeed, my dear friends.

Feel your feet upon the Earth. As you sit, we ask that you ask for the energy of the Earth to rise up inside your feet; through your calves, knees, thighs, hips, abdomen, solar plexus, heart, shoulders; down your arms and out the tips of your fingers and the center of your palms. Point your palms toward the floor and feel the energy as it flows through your body and out your palms. It flows through you up from the Earth until you are filled to the base of your neck with beautiful Earth energy.

Now allow the energy, my dear friends, to build as it rises a little bit higher into the throat. Feel the little tugs and pulls in your throat, the warmth, vibration and desire to speak your truth in any language and in any way. Allow the sound and the tones to rise out of you in an expression that truly, my dear friends, comes from the abundance of your heart. Allow it to rise through you now and out to the world. Enjoy the sound of the frequency that comes from you, the harvest of your soul, in such a manner that you can hear it fully expressed—your truth, a beautiful sound. God bless you indeed.

Now continue to allow the energy from the Earth to rise up through the center of your head, surrounding your ears. Feel now the release of pain within your physicality as it is drawn up through this portal to the top of your head, through the crown chakra, out into the universe and dissipating into beautiful, golden light. Continue to allow this energy to rise up through you and begin to feel a frequency that is very much like a corkscrew of energy running straight down now through the crown chakra and the center of your head. It moves down through the throat into your heart, spreading through your shoulders down your arms and out through the fingertips and the center of your palms. It also moves down into the solar plexus, through the abdomen and through the root chakra at the base of your legs. Allow this energy to run through the root chakra, releasing any energy there and focusing upon the base of your spine, the area of kundalini, the creative of the sexuality of your being and the passionate nature of your divine self.

Now feel the energy continue to swirl down through your buttocks; down the backs of your thighs; through your calves, ankles and heels. Find your Achilles heel, focus upon it and release that which has been blocking you from standing fully, firmly and completely upon planet Earth with confidence. Release your insecurities as this energy continues to run down through the center of your feet, out your toes and down into the Earth. Allow Mother Earth—with her beautiful, serene, lovely heart—to embrace all of your pains, nurture you, love you and surround you in her life, love and abundance.

An Apple a Day

My dear friends, part of your harvest is to receive this energy of the Earth, that which is you and that which in its nature is—guess what?—shaped very much like a rich, juicy apple containing the seed of life and discovery, a seed that can grow into a tree and bear yet more fruit. The symbol of eternity, my dear friends, is the apple, as in "How do you like them apples?" The apple is a beautiful area of discovery with every bite, every taste; with the feel of it in your hand and the beautiful stem. As you examine it, the apple contains a frequency of life energy that will now be your resource for the month of November. The harvest of your soul is contained within this apple a day. It will not keep this doctor away but will draw me ever nearer to you, to help you focus upon your purpose in your life upon planet Earth. In the month of November, allow yourselves to enjoy the harvest of your souls and the freedom that will come with it. Finding your purpose, truth, passion, vitality, light and life is part of the course work for the seasons of your soul in the month of November.

Your homework is to sit at a table and eat an apple a day. We would ask that you eat it with great awareness. You may peel it, cut it, examine it, hold it to the light, photograph it, paint it, make stamps out of it, share it with a friend, hang it from a tree or give it to the birds. An apple a day will be the focus of your life. There is so much truth contained therein that you will be filled with a grand and glorious sense of yourself as November draws to a close.

We would ask that you make this a green apple, a red apple, a yellow apple, an apple of all ranges of color in between. So, my dear friends, the month of November is as well an exercise in the releasing of massive expectations upon yourself and the world around you. We would ask that you surrender into a sense of serenity, to understand that the quality of your existence is contained in the perfection of an apple. Even if you should discover that your apple has been marred by the bites of a bird or the holes of a worm, what appear to be scars upon the apple are in truth what bring quality to it. For the worms taste only of the sweetest apples, and the birds taste only of the richest, most wonderful sensations of the apple. It is not a perfect, flawless apple that we are asking you to focus upon but the apple in all of its glory—the apple that has fallen from the tree and has a little bruise, but it has fallen because it is rich in quality, texture, color, sweetness and life.

My dear friends, the apple is you. It is the beautiful spirit that resides inside your soul, inside your beautiful body and inside the hurts, ills and pains that you have carried throughout the course of this lifetime. All of those create a stronger sense of self. It is there within your difficulties that you find your own salvation. Within your pain, you can realize the richness of your life. Within the sadness and the fears, you come to the understanding that you are worthy of attention from God, that you are worthy of love. It is there, with the little bites, the bruises and the small scrapes upon your reality here upon the Earth, that you find that you are indeed a very beautiful and divine spirit with so much to share with the world.

Examine the Three Principles: An Exercise

My dear friends, you want to give to the world of yourself. That is what you are striving to do in each and every moment of each and every day, and it is through this giving that you also seek acknowledgment. You are here to touch and be touched by life around you. For some the very word can send you into a panic. So we give you yet another exercise for the month of November.

For the very courageous adventurer who is willing to spend ten minutes of quality time every day for the first week of November, sit at a table with a notebook and write down the ways in which you have discovered what loving allowance for all things to be in their own time and place means to you. Write down ways in which you have expressed it to others and they have expressed it to you. Loving allowance for all—emphasis upon "all"—things, starting with yourself.

For week two, sit at the same table at the same time and write down the many ways in which you have increased communication with all of life and with respect. Add as well, without shame, the ways in which you could have expressed increased communication with all of life and with respect. Examine yourself and find the areas in which you, my dear little apple, can grow into your greater divinity of self upon planet Earth.

In the third week of November, sit once again at the same table at the same time and examine how in each and every day, you have found self-responsibility to be primary to your existence, through loving allowance and increased communication. Look for self-responsibility for your own life as a creative adventure. It is not through someone else's choices, perceptions and decisions that you create your reality, but through your own.

Loving allowance, increased communication and self-responsibility—this is what we would ask you to examine in the fourth week of November. As you sit at your table at the same time as always, ask yourself how you took these three principles and used them as tools in tandem during the course of your day and applied loving allowance, increased communication and self-responsibility. See how that brought harmony and richness to your life. Once again also examine the ways in which you did not apply this, when you could have done so but chose not to and what the outcome was there.

In this fashion, you put yourself upon the written page as an equation of your life. Could it be expressed through sacred geometry? Perhaps yes, but it can as well be expressed through the human heart, through the physical act of sharing words upon the page and realizing that you are indeed growing, moving and changing. There is always a beautiful harvest each and every moment of each and every day, one to be received and given from and to yourself, of your very being.

A Glorious Time of Thanks

This is the month of November, a glorious time of thanks. It is a time to write letters of thanks to yourself and to others in your life and to share these words with the many rather than the few. The few would be what? Well, the few would be those with whom you already feel safe to express yourself. How about expressing yourself with the many, which includes those upon the planet Earth with whom you do not feel as safe? They might not respond to your thanks, love and acts of generosity with kindness. But is that not where healing is required upon the planet Earth? Is that not where the healing of your heart will begin, through beautiful choices, loving allowance, communication and self-responsibility? Write a letter to the most difficult person upon the Earth for you and find the many ways in which this person, despite what you feel he or she has done to you, has enriched your life by creating scenarios that have helped you examine your beautiful beatin' heart and soul and allowed you to cherish and value yourself. Write how this person helped you, my dear friend, redesign yourself and enrich your life from the inside out.

Can you do it? It takes a creative adventurer—certainly a very courageous one. We encourage it, my dear friends, because we ask now that you realize as you look upon your world with its lovely array of fall leaves in beautiful colors—the coat of many colors that the world now wears—that you too can paint your life with such a vast array of colors. These colors are coming from your soul, rising up within your being. God bless you indeed, my dear friends, as you learn in this beautiful month of November to speak your truth forevermore.

Beautiful spirits here upon the planet Earth, we love you so very much. We wrap our ever-lovin' arms around you and once again ask you to breathe deeply into your spines and release all care and concern. Continue to release, my dear friends, now and forevermore. It is an eternal process. How do you release all care, all concerns, from the inside out? By deciding at this moment that with every breath you take, you are willing to accept love, harmony and the grace of God that is you forevermore.

Walk the Earth, my dear friends, as makers of peace, for certainly you are coming into another season of your soul in the month of December. It is there that you will discover the very beautiful spirit who you are upon the Earth, the angelic being and lightworker, the healer, the prominent one and the Christ who you are.

God bless you, my dear friends. Go your way in peace, love and harmony, for life is indeed a joy. All you have to do to enjoy the journey to your own hearts and enlightenment is to lighten up a little bit more. God bless you, indeed.

December—Abundance

God bless you indeed, my dear friends. Certainly you are students of the divine, and the divinity of your soul will be understood in increments through the seasons of your soul. You will begin to understand the wanderings of your heart and move into greater love through the understanding that this is your creation. Every day as you stand upon planet Earth, we ask that you bring greater love to the surface, starting with yourself. Loving allowance for all things means starting with yourself, with your ever-lovin' soul, to allow your truest feelings to be expressed without fear.

First and foremost, increasing respectful communication with all life means to ask for permission as you express your truth upon the Earth. It is more helpful if you have someone on the receiving end who has wide open ears and an ever-lovin' heart, someone who very much wants to hear the expressions that you carry inside. Sometimes these expressions will be of anger, of laughter or of love.

You are all, my dear friends, students of the divine, to stand together in collective consciousness for a healing, to understand how to further surrender deeper into your heart as you come into the season of your soul of December, a beautiful month. My dear friends, this is an opportunity to explore dormancy, fulfillment and the peacemaker who you are upon the Earth as you merge the mind, body and spirit of Christ within you.

It has nothing to do with a religion or a science of spirituality, for the Christ energy is part of everyone upon the planet Earth. It was never intended to be compartmentalized into a church setting but to reside inside the temple of your physicality, soul and spirit. This is the temple of God's will, that you will understand and enact the great love that you are in this world and in this lifetime—not tomorrow, my dear friends, nor to dwell upon yesterday. Stop your panic when you look into your past and regret what you have done. Stop your panic that you have ever done anything wrong here upon the Earth. You step into greater understanding with every action, deed, kindness and even, my dear friends, every misunderstanding.

Recreation for Re-creation of Yourself: A Meditation

Now, in this month of December, in this time period of dormancy inside your soul, we would ask that every day you give yourself a little recreation for the re-creation of your self.

Sit in a chair right now, close your eyes, breathe deeply into your spine and feel and sense your life as that of a living tree standing upon the Earth. Feel the Earth beneath your feet and take your ever-lovin' soul and feel it push deeper into the Earth with roots to anchor your spirit. As you do this, begin to realize that you are also receiving great nutrients from the Earth, nourishment for your soul that you draw in through the roots that you plant right now, and this nourishment moves up through your physicality, through the trunk of your tree. Now feel it move up into your heart, the point from which branches begin to spread and unfold. Feel this as your soul begins to branch out, each branch of your beautiful, living tree that you are creating reaching out to touch the lives of everybody upon the planet Earth, for none of them is separate from you.

Feel the branches as they move around the Earth, touching everyone. Sense the love that you can project into the consciousness of humanity, of every single man, woman and child. Feel yourself there, for that is you. You are not separate from every man, woman and child upon the Earth. You begin now to draw in their light, which nourishes further your living tree. It doesn't come from just one or a few, not just from the ones you like or who match and resonate with you, but from every man, woman and child upon the Earth. Allow them to shine their light, a vast spectrum of colors radiating into you, and realize there is no separation, my dear friends.

The True Master

Everything that they are and do; every expression of self; every tear, fear, pain and bit of love is contained inside yourself. You are not different than, better than or lesser than. There is no hierarchy, only a unit of oneness, a unity wherein you can explore diversity and do not have to hide your laughter, tears or the true expression of your soul. You are coming into an awareness of the masterhood that you carry into this lifetime, not in a sense of hierarchy, but masterhood of self and what you are willing to bring to the surface without having to control anything. The illusion is that a master would be in charge, but a true master knows how to surrender and is no longer afraid. The true master does not fear attack. The true master knows that he or she is safe and does not feel the need to hide. The true master commands respect through exposure.

The true master commands peace through serenity, which comes, my dear friends, not from breathing and relaxing while striving for nirvana but when you no longer feel that you must hold yourself at arm's length from the world. Serenity comes from exposing yourself to life without fear that you will cause or receive pain, without fear of sharing your love and not receiving it. Surprise to you, my dear friends! Oftentimes that is what holds many of you back. All here are beautiful creators, divine and loving spirits.

Now we ask as the ever-livin', ever-lovin' tree that you are to feel the love that has risen up inside you through your heart and extended out through the branches to birth as leaves on the tree that is ready to bear fruit. You begin to gather sap in this period of dormancy inside you, sap that will give you strength—not take your energy but give you strength and nourishment—gathering and collecting during this beautiful month of December as much love as you can into your ever-lovin' heart. You are preparing for the springtime of your soul, gathering sap, strength and nourishment. Feel it rise inside you, beautiful ever-lovin', ever-livin' trees that you are.

You Are Trees of Abundance

God bless you indeed, my dear friends. Now we ask, are you ready to allow this love to be birthed into the world? Are you ready to realize that you can never truly empty your vessel? You can always have a full cup that runneth over to the many rather than the few. *At this given time, as you breathe very deeply into your spines, surrender and listen for just a moment to what God would share with you.* [Pauses.]

My dear friends, the ever-lovin', ever-livin' tree upon planet Earth breathes out a constant supply of oxygen that nourishes your world. This represents the breath of God, constant movement and expansion. Never take the ever-lovin' and ever-livin' plant life upon your planet Earth for granted, for plants bear more fruit than you can dream or imagine in terms of energy, frequency, oxygen and love. Right here and now, you are all the ever-lovin', ever-livin' trees of life.

Breathe very deeply into your spines, my dear friends, and feel yourselves as a tree as oxygen surfaces through every pore of your being, pouring out from you, granting and giving life. Breathe very deeply into your spines once again. What kind of tree are you? How do you like them apples? Beautiful, my dear friends! You are apple trees, trees of abundance that represent life as you have just discovered in the month of November.

You are all very beautiful spirits. *Breathe deeply into your spines now and realize that you are the creator of your reality. Loving allowance, increased communication and self-responsibility . . .*

Hmm, that's a most interesting one, isn't it, my dear friends, as you explored the three principles to be used in tandem? You have self-responsibility for your life as a creative adventure, but how do you become the creator? How do you allow this to be fully expressed? By no longer allowing yourselves to fall into fear, panic, hatred, anger or ignorance and avoidance of love. Love is in constant motion. It does not come and then disappear. It is not something given at random. It exists always, my dear friends, so when you find yourselves falling into fear, sad thoughts, angry conceptions of life or angry perceptions of yourselves, stop. Do not allow those to poison your nourishing sap. Do not allow the parasites in. Stop the thought, stop allowing yourselves to surrender to fear, pain and judgment. Stop every time you begin to speak about another with unkind words. Do not allow yourselves to express them, for that is not love.

And you want to become the great lovers and creators. Pain, fear, hatred, anger and judgment have no movement. They are static electricity in your life. Without movement, you will stay there until you are willing once again to fall into greater love, where there is movement toward, not away from, life, humanity and yourselves. Reaching out a hand in absolute trust and love to touch and be touched is the whole purpose of your journey here upon the planet Earth. You now arise as peacemakers upon the Earth, Christ child and child of God who you are, dear friends.

A child is not afraid to climb into another's lap. A child very much wants his or her cup full at all times, to have milk and cookies and the sweetness of life, not fearing to taste, touch, feel and smell, to run naked in the woods without fearing exposure. The true child of God is willing to be immersed in life. Such a child does not run away in panic. He or she knows that everyone upon the Earth is worthy of love. True children of God do not fear seeing others' pain, nor do they fear climbing into their laps to give them a hug and a kiss. True children of God do not fear being cared for. They do not fear having scrapes and bruises kissed and made better. True children of God dance with life and do not resist it. They allow themselves to nap in the midst of a storm. The true child of God, the true Christ, walks the Earth inside every human heart that is willing to receive and express this love. My dear friends, each and every one of you who are here in this room today with us is gathered hand in hand.

At this time, breathe deeply into your spines, ever-lovin', ever-livin' trees that you are. Now we would ask that you imagine that every person who listens to this tape is gathered with you. Join hands with all, and together create an energy, a frequency;

together create a band of angels. You walk the Earth in harmony and begin to real-
ize that your family is larger than you ever dreamed or imagined possible. They are
human beings you have not met, yet you can feel as you join together in spirit right
here and right now that you have been one always and forever.

The illusions of separation are what you are here to explore. You begin to realize that the stuff that holds life together, the stuff that keeps your legs moving, your breath breathing, the snow falling and the trees growing, is love, my dear friends. That is the force that moves, motivates, strengthens, gives, grows, extends and expands out every branch and limb. It is the energy that births and bears fruit. It is what, my dear friends, you desire. It is what you are seeking, and you look inside of yourself first and share it. It is your coat of many colors, the truth of yourself expressed into life so that you might hear the echo from it.

Do Not Be Afraid of Yourself

My dear friends, do not be afraid of yourselves. You have talents—magnify them. You have desires—share them. You have gifts—give them. Just as you need somewhere to put yourself in the world, so does everyone around you. Do not fear life. Allow it into your aura field. Do not fear that you will be contaminated by disease, illness or discomfort. You cannot be contaminated or spoiled. You will not rot. Your souls are eternal light energy, and as long as you are willing to allow this light through you continuously upon the Earth, you will find that you are stronger physically, emotionally and spiritually. You become balanced and one with all of life inside of you. There is no separation anymore between the mind, body and spirit of the Christ who you are. No longer do you have to call yourself a spiritualist, saying that you do not want to camp out in this body here on the Earth. No longer do you find your body so all-important or that you have to work upon emotionality. Suddenly you are not compartmentalized. You no longer struggle against anything that you are. You are rooted to the Earth with branches extending toward the light of God.

How very beautiful and wondrous an expression of yourselves! God bless you indeed, my dear friends. You are all very beautiful spirits here in this month of December. Is it not wonderful that you have the opportunity in this lifetime to hear, touch, taste, feel, smell and think? Honor yourselves at this very beautiful time, the season of giving and loving, when all human beings can sit very quietly, in dormancy, and remember what is required upon the Earth to remain in a state where you feel wholly and completely alive. It is a time of giving and receiving the abundance here upon the planet Earth, a time to remember that all are created equal, in love, from the heart of God—all, my dear friends, including you. You are not separate from, lesser than or better than; there is no hierarchy.

Feel this ever-livin', ever-lovin' tree of life that you are. Now feel this tree dissolving. Where does it go? It dissolves into life. Suddenly all that you think matters is stripped away, and you are fully immersed in the Christ energy; the Christ being; the oneness of mind, body and spirit; with no illusions of separation. You are one with life, my dear friends. Understand the God who you are.

In this month of December, we are not giving you homework. Instead we provide you with heart work, to find the many ways in which you can be kind to yourself by catching yourself when you fall into fear, panic, worry and pain. Learn to stop and pause, setting your sights with all your heart and soul upon a positive thought, feeling and sense of lightheartedness. It's there. It did not go away. You must reach for it.

And it is there that you will have the contact with your guides and God that you so desire. Listen every day as you sit in your meditations, feeling the oneness of your spirit as you root yourself to the Earth and branch out toward the heavens. Listen for the voice within—the still, small voice is ever so loud. Toward the end of the month, you will find there will be entire sentences that you can hear and understand. They will give you guidance that you will know beyond the shadow of a doubt will be accurate.

In the month of December, you are going to slip away from the materialism that has held you captive and has made you believe that you will ever find love outside of yourself. You will slip into greater conscious awareness that your abundance is here today. Then you can have anything you want in the outer world—anything—and you will find it as easy as throwing stones into the water to create waves upon the shore. It will be a beautiful unity of life in which you can now freely explore the diversity of yourself by expressing your truth once and for all, without fear but with excitement and enthusiasm for the discovery of the divine being who you are.

God bless you, indeed. My dear friends, we love you so very much. You are our gift in this month of giving and receiving.

Seasons of the Soul Part 2:

Eternity, Physical Reality, Mirth and Manifestation

G oodness gracious, dear Bev. It is Dr. Peebles here, isn't it? God bless you indeed. I'm standing on my head for you today, my dear. You are a beautiful spirit. We love you so very much. You are gentle, generous, kind, compassionate, and you care so much about the world. My dear, it is time for you to realize this. You have done a lot of service here already, God bless you indeed. Do not feel that you fall short of the mark. Often you still feel that you can't do enough, you understand? God bless you indeed. Yeah, my dear, we love you as well and certainly, this is a season for respecting and honoring the many rather than the few upon the planet Earth as you come into the season of your soul in January 2004.

January—Eternity

Y ou were spared homework in December, but understand, my dear friends, that it was just to get you ready to roll up your sleeves. The year 2004 will be an incredible journey wherein we are going to ask that you make friendships with the many rather than the few. You will pat all people on the back and tell them what a good job they are doing upon the Earth, whether or not you believe it. My dear friends, you will do this, because you want to deepen your awareness of love, concern and compassion for everyone upon planet Earth, without qualification this time.

We ask that you step into the greater truth of yourself with the certainty, my dear friends, that you are indeed God, that when you find and touch the face of God inside of you, you will realize that you can't see anyone except through the eyes of love. It is there that you find freedom. You begin to understand that upon the Earth, you no longer have to seek the finer moments of your existence wherein you win a trip to Germany, the lottery, the relationship or the respect of anyone. Instead you begin to realize that you open yourself up to serving God by serving yourself first. By filling up your cup, you realize that God loves you as well as everyone else upon the Earth, not putting you last on the list as so very often you have done in the course of your lifetime.

Make a Resolution

We love you very much, and we want for you right now to breathe very deeply into your spine. Here in January 2004, we suggest to you—not a demand or requirement—that you make a resolution. It's not the kind of resolution that you are used to making in the past, to look at yourself in the mirror and say, "I'm too fat. I need to diet and look thin." Not that kind of resolution, my dear friends, but rather the kind of resolution that lasts an eternity: Resolve to be the Christ who you are upon the planet Earth, to be the peacemaker, to fall in love with respect for the many rather than the few. Resolve to communicate from your heart even when it is hurting, to speak your truth, to act as the divine being who you are upon the Earth and share the truth of yourself in each and every moment, not holding anything back or keeping yourself at arm's length. That is what we would ask you to study in the month of January: to not hold yourself at arm's length from the world by holding yourself at arm's length from you.

In the month of January, we want you to look around at everything at least once a week—the objects in the room, in your office and in your stores; stare into spaces, look at cars, look at the heavens, look at the stars. Look, my dear friends, and truly see that you are there in everything that you see, hear, taste, touch, feel and smell. Find and touch the face of God in everything around you—not to judge anything as good or bad, right or wrong, up or down, but rather to see it as creation. It is there that you begin to understand the creator who you are, the artist of your own fabric of eternity.

It is here upon the Earth that you find a wonderful canvas to express your heart. How will you color this canvas and bring it to life? You do it, once again, through patting the many rather than the few upon the back. Offer words of encouragement for the many rather than the few. Included in this equation is you, yourself. Pat yourself upon the back each and every morning, stretching and reaching not with your body but with your heart. Reach inside yourself and find that inside is a great lover and beautiful spirit. This spirit, my dear friends, is God, and it deserves appreciation and acknowledgment. That means *you*, my dear friends. *You* deserve acknowledgment. How do you do it but by bringing more of yourself to the surface in each and every moment of each and every day?

Discover eternity not just in January's season of the soul, my dear friends, but rather in each and every moment of each and every day, forever. For it is here that you find flight of soul. You fly free at long last, giving of yourself, and in the giving, you begin to receive abundance beyond your wildest dreams and imaginations.

Breathe very deeply into your spine, sit carefully with your fanny upon your chair and feel inside yourself the love that you are. That is what you are truly made of, which has rested dormant for so long. You're getting ready for the springtime of your life, a time to bear fruit. What have you done in the interim? What kinds of seeds have you planted? What kind of fruit will you bear? Have you allowed yourself to be pruned back a bit? Have you allowed for this pruning to occur even though perhaps it was a bit painful to tell yourself not to express unkindness toward family, friends and others, but rather to express beauty, laughter, care and concern? You will find that the fruit that you bear will be very tasty. You will discover this down the road apiece.

For right now, as you sit with your fanny firmly against your chair, feet flat against the floor, once again reaching deeply inside yourself, little tree that you are, take a moment to breathe in and out, in and out, in and out. If you have difficulty breathing, ask yourself, "Am I willing to take in life? Am I willing to breathe it in? Am I willing to give once again of my breath to the world?"

Now, as you breathe very deeply into your spine, free yourself up by asking yourself to appreciate all that you are, ever were and shall be. It's coming in now with a very deep breath. As you breathe very deeply into your spine, we will come inside, take a peek around and make some adjustments. It is there that you'll begin to learn to laugh and play again, to discover that your soul has always meant to be free upon the planet Earth. Here and now, in this moment, you resolve to love, respect and honor all of creation, starting with yourself.

Now you learn to weave yourself into the fabric of eternity. You have a wonderful opportunity upon your planet through your physical expression. This is where we want you to put your attention in the year 2004, especially now, in the month of January, as we have shared already. Look at everything and really see it this time, pay attention to details. See a blade of grass, a cloud skipping across the sky, a stone skipping across the water. Hold your hand in front of your face and look at the divine expression of God that exists through you.

Spread Abundance: An Assignment

You have a wonderful opportunity through your physical form to express great love and appreciation for all that you are, ever were and ever shall be, and so we have a little assignment for you:

Take one hundred pennies and divide them into ten groups of ten pennies each. Each group of ten pennies symbolizes something that you would like very much to give to the world to enhance it, to bring abundance to life here upon the planet Earth. The pennies are only a symbolic expression of the abundance that you very much want to feel on the inside and to give to the many rather than the few.

- In the first bundle, cover the ten pennies with your hands and ask that joy be imbued in their spirit.

- In the second bundle, cover them with your hands and ask that happiness be expressed through them.

- In the third bundle, cover them with your hands, using the warmth of your soul and the wisdom of your touch, and ask that peace be expressed through each one of those pennies.

- In the fourth bundle, cover them with your hands and ask that freedom reign freely upon the planet Earth.

- In the fifth bundle, cover them with trust, certainty, serenity, prosperity and love.

- In the sixth bundle, imbue them with playfulness by tossing them in the air and asking that playfulness come into them to be expressed fully and completely.

- In the seventh bundle, cover them with your hands and ask that these pennies work to dissolve bitterness inside the human heart.

- In the eighth bundle, ask that these pennies be given to the Earth, to revive and refresh its spirit now and forever.

- In the ninth bundle, ask that these go forth into the world to dissolve greed.

- In the tenth bundle, blow your breath of life upon them and ask that they be imbued with possibilities.

From each pile of pennies take one penny, then group these pennies together. Make another group of ten, one penny from each pile, then another and another, until you have ten bundles of tremendous energy, compassion, care and concern for humanity and for planet Earth. Take a cloth, preferably cotton, of any color or many colors, and cut it into small squares. This is the fabric of eternity into which you will place one bundle of pennies, a bundle of abundance that you have created; place it in the center of the cloth, gathering the corners and tying them with a ribbon that represents your heart.

Once you have these ten bundles, we ask that you go out into the world and give them to family, friends and strangers. Share with them that you give it to them in honor of the beautiful creation of their lives, journeys, passions and of the wonder of who they truly are upon the Earth. Say that in appreciation, you give them a bundle of abundance, for them to do with as they wish. They can hold on to it, keep it in a pocket or give it away, but they should always remember that at least once, in physical, tangible form, they were given evidence that they are beautiful creators, divine expressions of God. That is your homework assignment for the month of January.

Give it great thought and consideration. Pay attention to our words. Do everything you can to be deliberate and conscious in the process of your existence. As you work with the pennies and the cloth, do everything with care. If you can't, stop and begin again later. Every step, my dear friends, should be imbued with the truth of your spirit, the truth of the great love and great lover who you are upon the planet Earth.

You are beautiful creators. You are each and every one a student of the divine. We started our journey here today with a little chat with Bev, just one person upon the Earth, one person with whom we wanted to share our deepest expressions of love. She is beautiful beyond compare and no different than you are.

Remember, my dear friends, God loves you first and foremost. Goodness gracious, that means that everyone is equal, doesn't it? For God certainly wants, as a wish and a prayer for the year of 2004, for you to journey to your heart, bring love to the surface and remember that you are the Creator. God bless you, my dear friends. Go your way.

February—Physical Reality

God bless you. Dr. Peebles here. It is a joy and a blessing when human and Spirit join together in search of the greater truths and awareness. God bless you, my dear friends. It is time for the seasons of your soul once again. Certainly you have learned much from the bundles of abundance that you created in January.

And now you come into a very beautiful time, one of romance, love and continued dormancy as well as bitter cold upon your planet Earth. The month of February is a time for you to examine the elements of life around you. Study the environment and your physical existence, because February is a time of bitter cold for so many here upon the planet Earth. We ask that you enjoy it and sit there inside of your home with a fireplace, seeing the sparks emitted from the logs and examining the life around you. When the logs are burned down to ashes, then examine the ashes themselves.

Feel the ashes when they are nice and cool. Hold them in your hands and blow them into the air, watching them flutter away upon currents. Certainly we understand that not everyone here has a fireplace, but that is not a problem. It means you'll have to find someone who does so that you can sift, examine and enjoy the fireplace together. As we shared, it is a time of romance. This does not necessarily mean that it has to be romantic activity between a man and a woman or two women or two men, but rather it is a romantic time with all life, sharing and appreciating your physical existence with the many rather than the few. Are we talking here about sexuality, my dear friends? If you would like to explore it in this fashion, that is not a problem at all as far as we are concerned. But we are really asking that in the month of February, you connect with your physical environment.

Examine Your Home

We would ask that you take time one day a week to simply walk around your home, remember where you live and feel and touch the objects around you. Have you done this recently? Touch the surface of the walls in your bedroom and kitchen. Have you really examined the doorknobs that you turn every day and take for granted? Have you gently touched the carpet beneath your feet and said, "Thank you, dear carpet. You're very beautiful and plush, and I am grateful that you are there to comfort my little tootsies. God bless you indeed."

Walk around your home and examine it. Look at the corners and how they are put together. Look in the darker spaces within your closets as well. Bring a little flashlight and realize that it is symbolic of your soul, the radiance of light that you are developing that wants to shine forth. Right now it is in a period of dormancy that is about to bloom in the springtime of your soul. Shine the flashlight into the darker spaces and realize that what you are really doing is going inside of that tree of yourself and looking through the sap, seeing how rich, full and wondrous it is. There are hidden secrets within your closets. Bring them out into the open and give them fresh air. There are old things, new things and things that have yet to be used and admired. We encourage you to bring them all out of the closet, examine them and decide what you are going to release into the world.

Certainly the month of February is a time of physical examination and releasing as well. We want you to realize, my dear friends, as you are examining the contents of your closets and cupboards, that you will stumble across certain bits and pieces that do not bring you the greatest joy. You should hold these objects and love them very much. Appreciate them for being in your life and ask what you can learn from them. Many of these objects represent little aches and pains inside of you. We are focusing upon physical reality 100 percent in February, examining everything very closely. Hold the object and ask it to share with you what it represents. You'll be rather surprised as to what it represents inside of you that is encased in less than joy.

Then we would ask that you take this object, give it a big hug and say, "Thank you so very much. I appreciate the fact that you have come into my life, that you have shared this with me, that I now fully understand what the purpose and value of you has been for me. I promise to release you to someone else who can benefit from a relationship with you."

Examine Your Relationships

This also applies to relationships between men, women and children upon the planet Earth. You look at this object that has not brought you joy, but perhaps it will bring someone else joy. In terms of relationships in your life, there are individuals who do not bring you joy anymore. There are superficial relationships wherein you do not feel that you can fully express your truth, that you can fully bring yourself to the surface, that you are receiving the truth of your partner's self. Examine these relationships and realize that perhaps it is time for a little bit of releasing—with the greatest of love—of such relationships in your life. This doesn't mean you have to run around and say, "I hate you. Get out of my life," but rather to realize that it is your decision where you want to put your time, attention and value in your life with friends, family members and others.

We ask that you write down the name of everyone you know upon a piece of paper and with clarity and truth inside yourself ask, "Do I want to continue to honor this relationship as it exists today?" Then you make a decision. It doesn't matter what your decision is. There can be relationships that are extraordinarily painful for you, very difficult and trying, and you would think perhaps in terms of what you should do. Of course, Dr. Peebles says that you don't have to do anything. There's no such thing as "should" in the universe as far as we are concerned. But you, my dear friends, might examine these relationships and realize that perhaps some of them are indeed difficult. They have been something you've been trying to master and understand, so you want to retain these relationships. That's all right. Give yourself respect and honor. Trust yourself and your inner world and the feelings that are inspired within it, those that are based and have their roots in truth. Trust this, then make a decision to embrace these relationships wholly and completely.

"Yes, I have some very strong difficulties with my husband here, but you know something? Despite the fact that he drives me crazy, I won't give up on this one. I have yet more learning to do." There you give yourself permission to be involved in relationships that can be very difficult. Difficult companionship is not a problem at all. It provides greater growth and opportunities for forgiveness, love, surrender, serenity, patience and for increasing your understanding of how you can be kind even when someone is not kind to you. You can take charge of yourself and your existence, emotions, expressions, perceptions and opportunities. You, my dear friend, prepare yourself physically for the springtime of your soul to be fully expressed through this fantastic existence that you have here upon the Earth.

Spread Warmth

And so we return to your closets and cupboards. You continue to pull things out to examine. One of the most remarkable opportunities here is to bring the warmth of your soul to the surface to be expressed into life. Bringing this warmth literally and physically into the world to manifest it and give it to another human being is the greatest act of love that you can ever offer planet Earth.

My dear friends, it is bitter cold, not only in the winter of your soul, but it is bitter cold right now here upon your planet Earth. There is a cold wind a-blowin', and it is time to light the fire of your soul, to allow it to shine forth and radiate heat and wonder to everyone around you. How do you manifest this in your physical reality? Well, there inside your cupboards and closets, you have a blanket of wonder, a blanket that perhaps you do not have the greatest respect and honor for. It sits in your closet year after year, week after week, month after month, while the many rather than the few live upon your streets and shiver with cold in the night. Gather this blanket in your arms and embrace it with all the love in your heart, saying, "Dear God, I want to release this blanket to whomever it must be released, to someone for whom it will have value, to someone whom it will keep warm."

As you hold this blanket in your arms, visualize someone around whom you might wrap it and say, "I love you so very much. My wish and prayer for you is that you are forever warm inside your soul, comforted by the embrace of God and forever, my dear friend. I pray that you find this blanket in this lifetime and allow it to shine forth. I now pass the torch of warmth to you, that your warmth might radiate to the world as well." For some of you, this might require a little journey down the street to find the little man who sits upon the corner, shivering and shaking, and wrap him with your warmth. Then you can no longer share with the universe or God that you have fallen short of the mark. You have just lifted one robin back into its nest. With that event, you have not lived in vain.

Continue searching your cupboards and closets. Find all kinds of objects and ask each one very gently—and we mean this to be a gentle cleansing and clearing for you; it does not have to be thorough. Have no expectations as to how this will unfold, though you will find tremendous magic as you embark upon this journey. Simply ask, my dear friends, for these objects to come to you so that you might release them to the world. Some you will want to release within the world of your own home. In many instances, you will find little objects that make you say, "Goodness gracious, where have you been? I have missed you very much," and you display this object with the greatest affection and ask, as you place it somewhere in your home, what it represents. Ask it to reveal to you its importance, how very special and wise it is, what it wants to teach you and what it wants to give unto you.

Are your precious objects false idols or are they living icons of your soul, representative of and bringing great light into your world, surrounding you, encasing you, if you will, with a very beautiful blanket of their own? They surround you, my dear friends, with warmth, inspiration, creativity and with responses that you love from your soul. Every time you see that picture in its frame, it brings you back to a time and place that you surrender your entire spirit unto so that you can refresh your soul.

Send Valentines

The month of February is a beautiful and romantic journey into the unknown, the unexpected, the magical and the wondrous. A journey, my dear friends, back into the arms of family members you have lost. Certainly you have a very beautiful opportunity to express your heart and feelings of love on Valentine's Day. Fill your pockets with candy, and as you roam through the world upon your Valentine's Day, offer a little sweetness to the world everywhere you go. You know what you are doing; the little tree that you are is beginning to bud, preparing for a very beautiful springtime.

For one week prior to your Valentine's Day, for one week, we ask that you sit with the greatest respect to search your heart and find human beings with whom you have issues. Create a little valentine card for each one and simply send it from a secret admirer. You will uplift their souls and change those relationships. You will dramatically touch the world, though sometimes you won't know what the resonance is. But, my dear friends, send your little cards from the secret admirer. There is a very beautiful secret admirer of yours, my dear friends—sometimes not so secret but rather mysterious—who is God Himself, who loves you very much. He wishes you the greatest, most glorious Valentine's Day ever. Upon these little Valentine's Day cards, which we encourage you to make with your own hands, using little doilies and such, write, *Love, God.*

You are beautiful spirits, each and every one. Certainly you indeed are God yourself, for you are an expression of the very same. You want very much in the month of February to prepare yourself for the fullest expression of God through the little buds that begin to grow into beautiful flowers, leaves and expressions of God's heart, the coat of many colors.

Go into Your Heart and Examine Your Cells: A Meditation

Now we would ask that you breathe very deeply into your spine. We are going to work with your heart now. We are going to delve deeply inside your heart as you continue to breathe deeply into your spine. You will feel a wee bit of heaviness or sadness inside. At first it will feel that we are not working with light, but we are indeed, for we are working with the darkest color of all—the black that exists inside you. That is not the absence of color or light; it is the density. *Continue to breathe very deeply into your spine and allow the physical sensations.* In February we are working with the physical responses that you feel inside. You might find that you feel nauseous or are a little short of breath. Continue to breathe very deeply. The blackness of your soul will begin to ooze out with a big exhale on the count of three. *Take a deep breath. One, two, three. Breathe out.*

Point your palms toward the floor as you continue to breathe into your spine. Allow the excess energy of the blackness to continue draining out through the base of your spine and the center of your palms and your feet, into the floor. You begin now to feel lighter. What you have done, my dear friends, is to pull the cork from the bottle.

The effervescence of your soul now begins to bubble up within you. Begin seeing it as little sparkles of light bubbling up inside you, up through the chakras and throughout your chest. Every little care, woe and pain bubbles up, breaking down the hardened spaces inside you in your arms, including arthritic conditions, cancer, a cold in your sinuses and fear in your abdomen. Be careful there, because you will have to go potty soon when this bubbles up through the abdomen. For those who move slowly, feel it bubbling through your legs and heart—bubbling, bubbling, bubbling.

As it works through the heart and veins, bubbling through every cell, look into your cells. Anything you see there that is crystalline in nature, allow the bubbles to break it up and free it. The little bubbles float now to the surface of your skin, all over your physical body and every square inch of your skin. Pay attention and examine this beautiful, wondrous fabric that encases your soul. It is fantastic, my dear friends, a beautiful fabric. As it continues bubbling out through the surface, look inside the little bubbles. "There goes my problem with Granddad! Oh, over there—goodness gracious, that's when I stubbed my toe and said that word! There it goes. There is the little cancer and the little heart murmur . . . It's no longer there." Continue, my dear friends. Fear is bubbling up and out now, releasing through your skin.

Begin to understand that as you do this, you will become extraordinarily physically sensitive to your environment. This is a wonderful preparation as you examine your world physically through touch.

Continue breathing deeply into your spine. Now open your eyes. Look around the room. Is it not fascinating what you see in terms of light? Look around the room again. Some of you see spirits. Acknowledge them. "Hello! Goodness gracious, I've opened my heart." Now touch the surface of your skin. Gently run your fingertips from the one hand up to the elbow region of the opposite arm, then up to the shoulder. Now reverse to the other side and stroke the surface of the skin up to the elbow and shoulder. Continue to breathe very deeply into your spine.

Miraculous, aren't you? Say to yourself out loud, "I am miraculous!" God bless you, indeed. "I am miraculous! I am miraculous!" And you are indeed.

Close your eyes once again. Now we want you to turn your full attention to the center of your chest, where your ever-lovin', ever-beatin' heart resides. Look into your physical heart. Watch the beating and the function. Pretend—or imagine, if you must—that you are very open now. The heart is a fantastic machine. It has, it seems, a life of its own. Who's keeping it a-beatin', my dear friends? You are, through your willingness to be upon the Earth. Look very deeply inside this very beautiful heart. Walk through a door into the center of your heart and look around. It is here, in this beautiful room, that you will find and touch the face of God who is you. For, as you look around inside your heart, everywhere you look there is a mirror, and what do you see but your own face, fantastic and wondrous? At that, you begin to melt, dissolving into the most romantic love of all—love of you.

Prepare for Spring

We love you so very much. In this month of February, with the work in the physical form, you begin to prepare for the springtime of your soul. It is in this month that you understand the beautiful salvation that is yours already. There is nothing to do or become, only to be at one and at peace with your divine self. No longer will you fear expression or the responses of the world around you. Rather, you will live with the utter anticipation of all things beautiful coming your way as you release the beauty of yourself to the surface—as your gift to creation, humankind and yourself.

We ask that in the month of February, you acknowledge the many rather than the few, that in particular you find the time to pay attention to the animals who come into your life. When you find that an animal crosses your path, if you can, reach out, give it love and say, "Thank you. You are a beautiful creation of God, one beautiful facet and color of God." You will also find inspiration seeing zebras in the zoo and visiting fish in aquariums. Don't just look and gawk. Give love. Create a beautiful spiritual excursion to visit your animal kingdoms as you have them in your cages. They are there so that you can bear witness to the beauty and wonder of God, the coat of many colors of God's ever-lovin' heart. Create a spiritual excursion. Ask friends, family members and others to go on a little journey into the woods, to a zoo, to an aquarium, or ask them to simply sit with you and your dog in the center of the room and show it great appreciation. Do this with the conscious awareness that all are united.

A beautiful, romantic month, this February; a time, my dear friends, of finding your heart, releasing it to the world and creating a magnificent dance of love beyond your wildest dreams and imaginations! It is up to you to take charge of your existence, to touch and be touched by the world, starting with yourself. We will be working from the outside in, starting with the physical in the month of February, a month of bitter cold, romance and wonder.

God bless you indeed, my dear friends. Go your way in peace, love and harmony, with outstretched arms.

March—Mirth and Manifestation

G od bless you. Dr. Peebles here. It is a joy and a blessing when human and Spirit join together in search of greater truths and awareness. Here we are once again with the seasons of the soul, marching forward into March, the merry month of March, the month of mirth and manifestation.

My dear friends, all of you are students of the divine. How are you doing there, class? Here we are in March already. Goodness gracious, the year flies by! As you come into this time of prosperity, abundance and revelation of your soul, we encourage you to celebrate your birth here upon the planet Earth, for every day you make a decision when you wake up in the morning and greet yourself in the mirror, singing, "Happy birthday to me, happy birthday to me, happy birthday dear me, happy birthday dear me." Oh goodness gracious, dear me, dear me. God bless you indeed. My dear friends, you're beautiful spirits, each and every one a student of the divine.

We ask that right now, you sit up straight, put your feet firmly upon the floor and breathe very deeply into your spine. We want you to understand that in the month of March, we are asking you once again to do absolutely nothing but to stop and smell the roses. God bless you indeed. My dear friends, take a peek at your trees outside. Look at the little buds as they begin to appear. This resembles you, as you too begin to bud into the world.

This being the month of mirth makes it a good time to have a party with, shall we say, your little buds. Invite friends to your home, sit in a circle and recite from your heart your dreams and desires. Put them all into the center of the circle and build a pile of abundance, dreams, hopes, desires and endless possibilities to share around the circle until you are absolutely exhausted. Don't try to impress one another by saying, "Oh, my desire is to live with God in my heart." No, my dear friends, be serious here. Your desire is to own a car or a home, to be attracted to a man or a woman, to own a little kitty cat, to get everything your heart desires. Certainly, my dear friends, if you want that shiny red bicycle, well, goodness gracious, put it in there too, because this is the month of manifestation of everything that you have built inside yourself for the past several months, during the course of our conversations within the seasons of the soul.

A Sense of Urgency

Certainly there is a sense of urgency at this time upon your planet Earth, and that urgency also exists inside you. *Take this urgency now as you begin to breathe very deeply into your spine. Feel the urgency rising up within you. Feel the force and the energy as it comes up into the area of your throat. Feel the urgency as it begins to extend out through your palms and your tummy begins to tighten. Goodness gracious, it feels like you're about to explode!* God bless you indeed. Oh, you are so very urgent! *Now take a nice, deep breath, and we will come inside and take a peek around to make some adjustments.*

And the urgency now, my dear friends, becomes the frequency of fulfillment in your heart as you find inside yourself the spring of joy that you desire now to bring to the surface, to manifest your dreams upon the planet Earth and see yourself expressed in your physical reality. Begin to realize that you have been a little tree all along, and now the little buds are coming to the surface. These little buds are your desires and dreams in the physical form as you choose now to manifest everything that you want. In understanding how you are going to do this . . . well, it's the merry month of March—certainly by bringing mirth into your soul. Feel mirth in every day, wish upon a star, understand that the planets are interacting and laughing with you, know something wonderful is certainly upon the horizon for you in each and every moment of each and every day. Don't skirt around the issue here. Find it as you awaken and approach every day. We want you to seek mirth within the smile of a stranger, within a gift from a friend, within the laughter from a horse and within the feel of your shoe upon your foot.

Love exists everywhere. Love is not hidden or lost. It exists upon your Earth in each and every moment of each and every day. It is there that you find possibilities and the freedom and flight of soul, so to find it, you must seek it. Seek love, my dear friends, in every moment of every day. God bless you indeed. Do it with conscious awareness that this is what your heart desires. Whenever your thoughts turn to blackness or emptiness, to a void or avoiding happiness, find once again within your spirit the love that you are and bring it to the surface. Every time you are sad, depressed, down, unhappy or frustrated, we want you to call a friend or look at a stranger and ask how he or she is. Offer a hand to a child. If you must, go into a store and buy a flower, then give it to the clerk.

Celebrate Creators

As the creators who you are, there are so many opportunities for you to find love where you think it does not exist. We want you to celebrate creators in the merry month of March. This means for you to take a little excursion into a community of artists, to enjoy and explore the artwork around you. It can be within a gallery or better yet, out in the world in a little sidewalk café. Somewhere in your own home where you did not appreciate a piece of art upon your wall, artwork being one way of expressing the creation of yourself, we are going to ask each and every one of you to set up a canvas and call upon my spirit. Allow me to deliver a beautiful expression of artwork upon the canvas. For those of you who will laugh, wonderful, because this is just more merriment for you. You will say, "It's impossible. I can't do it. It is beyond all expectations." Yes, my dear friends, it is. It will become beyond your wildest dreams and imaginations, because I, Dr. James Martin Peebles, will work with you one on one. That is my promise unto you. I find each and every one of you to be beautiful spirits, sacred spirits who very much want to connect with me.

For some the artwork will be very small, for others very large. For some, my dear friends, it will be nothing at all, and that will be enough. That is where we will interact—both creators here—from one dimension to the other, across time and space. My dear friends, there is no separation. So the merry month of March becomes for you a time of releasing your expectations and releasing yourself into the manifestation of your wildest dreams and imaginations.

A Daily Expression

Every morning that you wake up, we ask that you reach inside your heart with the greatest tenderness and say, "Thank you, God. I love you so very much." How often do you say it, my dear friends?

I love you, God. Do not disappear from me.
I love you, God. Be near to me.
I love you, God. I love you true.
I love you, God. You love me too.

And that, my dear friends, will be your daily expression upon awakening. We are giving you a rather tall order here for the merry month of March. It is for those who are willing to dive in wholeheartedly, to sink into the Earth as the spirit who you are, to sink into the Earth, of which your body is the form. Ashes to ashes and dust to dust—that is your body, my dear friends. To arrive within your physical form 100 percent is a must.

The merry month of March, a month of mirth and manifestation, my dear friends . . . You are beautiful spirits, each and every one a student of the divine. "I am divine," you say to yourself. "I am divinity," you share with yourself. "I am master of the universe!" God bless you indeed. My dear friends, we want you to understand that you are indeed the master of the universe that is you.

Look into Your Beautiful Universe: A Meditation

As you close your eyes now, breathe very deeply into your spine. Allow for all that you are, were and ever shall be—your restlessness, sleepiness, upset, love, greed, vanity, pain and joy. Inside of every cell of your physical being is light. Your body is made up of billions upon billions of cells.

How very beautiful that your scientists have discovered it so that you can now visualize it! *Say out loud now, "Thank you, scientists, for showing me who*

I really am." That breaks an illusion of separation right there for you, does it not? For you are spiritual lightworkers, and so Dr. Peebles is asking you to thank the scientists. Oh goodness gracious, my dear friends. They are beautiful spirits too, each and every one a student of the divine, the same as you. God bless you indeed. No stressin' and a-strainin' anymore. You are great creators, each and every one a universe unto yourself.

Look now into your physicality and see that you are composed of billions upon billions of stars that come from the heavens and from God. Breathe very deeply into your spine as you reach even deeper inside yourself to see all the vastness of your universe. Look into your beautiful universe that you are and into the regions where perhaps stars are dying. There are stars that are beginning to blink out their lights. As you see them, we want you to fill them with love, saying, "Don't go yet. It's not time." Bring that light back to the surface. Turn on the lights.

Everybody come home to your universe. There you will find freedom beyond your wildest dreams and imaginations. Find it within your heart to understand that there is nothing to fear in your beautiful universe. It's a beautiful universe, my dear friends. Love it freely. Do not fear it, hate it or be mad at it. It is your friend, guide, teacher and physicality.

Run your hands along your thighs, through your hair and across the bottoms of your feet. Breathe very deeply. And what do you smell but roses in the air?

Realize that I have many gifts that I can give to you, for I love you very much. You are, each and every one, beautiful spirits, so very near and dear to the heart of Dr. Peebles and of God. We are indeed one and the same. The only difference between you and I is that I know I am you, and if you love me, then you must love you too. That, my dear friends, is what you have been a-stressin' and a-strainin' against.

"I want to be lovable. I want to be more." Well, you are. Always and forevermore you are a great and vast expression of God. You are the color with which God paints the planet Earth. You are the greatest painting of all. You are the greatest artistic expression. You are certainly, with the heart of God, upon his paintbrush. He knows exactly where you need to be, where to place you upon the canvas. You're an oil paint, which is very malleable and can be pushed about—here, there and everywhere. God's a pretty smart cookie the way He designed everything. So when you wonder how to fix your car, why don't you go to a mechanic? My dear friends, God is that. Ask Him to assist you, for you are the creation of the very same.

Surrender yourself in each and every moment of each and every day in this beautiful, merry month of March, the month of mirth and manifestation. You will begin to see that there is an unfolding of your being now, very much as the buds begin to bloom.

Upon the day of the spring equinox, we ask that you do a favor unto yourself. *At precisely noon, sit upon the floor with your legs crossed and your hands gracefully extended at your side, the backs of your hands upon the floor, palms up toward the heavens. We ask that you center your being with the light of the Sun and the Son, whose resurrection will be celebrated shortly thereafter, in the beautiful month of April.*

Align yourself with the Sun and feel the heat as it descends upon your head, onto the crown chakra. Allow this beautiful sunlight to come into your being, down through your body, toward your heart. My dear friends, that heart is so very beautiful. It is a delicious combination of colors, what you would call a variegated rose that begins to spread its petals and its scent. Don't worry. These are not thorns that prick—these are thorns that heal, that lance the wounds you have carried deep within for so long. As the rose begins to unfold within, you release your body and mind from the confines of the Earth.

"Dear God, I ask your light, inspiration and truth to penetrate my spirit. I ask, dear God, for your light, inspiration and truth to influence and guide every movement I make, every thought I have and every dream I discover."

God bless you indeed, my dear friends. You are all beautiful students of the divine and the divinity that you are. The merry month of March is a time for you to enter school wholly and completely. You've just been in preparation. Now you are in class, and you will realize that the learning never ends. The yearning for the learning is the point. Enjoy the journey, reach into your heart now and decide that you truly want to expand forever.

We love you so very much, my dear friends. We're excited. You have a lot of promise in the world, and that promise will be fulfilled. God bless you indeed. Go your way in peace, love and harmony, for life is indeed a spring of joy in the merry month of March, the month of mirth and manifestation of God's will in your life. God bless you, indeed.

Seasons of the Soul Part 3:
Showers, Flowers and Celebration

G od bless you. Dr. Peebles here. It is a joy and a blessing when human and Spirit join together in search of the greater truths and awareness. God bless you indeed. Spring is in the air, certainly in this merry month of April, and with April showers, there are May flowers. It is a time of the flowering of your soul. You are beautiful spirits, each and every one a student of the divine. The divinity of yourself is what you have been working upon for several months, and you will discover the great creators who you are, but not until the April showers begin. Then you will begin to bloom in the merry month of May.

April—Showers

M y dear friends, notice now that everything is merry. Isn't it beautiful? Isn't life a glorious adventure? The lotus flower of your soul will soon be blooming, for several months from now, you will truly begin to embrace the mystics who you are. You will have the certain understanding inside your hearts—for those of you who have done the work—that you are indeed, at long last, walking with God forevermore. You will understand the great creators and expansive beings who you are. You have never been a finite being but are infinite. Your life has purpose, value and meaning upon the Earth and certainly touches the many rather than the few, even when you are not aware of it, my dear friends. Right now, if you just breathe in very deeply, then exhale very gently, you touch life. You create motion and movement with your given breath. It is in this understanding that you become aware that life is an eternal dance with you at the center.

Start Your Day with a Shower

In the beautiful, merry month of April we ask that you start every day with a luxurious shower, but we want you to be very careful to turn it on cautiously and with love, realizing how divine this shower is, because it comes from the Earth. It comes from endless centuries of God's love working upon planet Earth and the beautiful waters flowing upon it, evaporating into the heavens and raining back down in beautiful, loving showers, eventually creating a stream of love and light that comes into your home and washes over your physicality. We want you to take your shower with great care, turning on the water with the smallest trickle at first, then increasing the flow and feeling it, truly paying attention to how it caresses your physical body.

You were working with the physical within March with the understanding of wanting to manifest many opportunities, things and items in the physical world. Now we want you to understand that you are indeed a part of the physical, to truly understand that you are embraced physically, emotionally and spiritually, always and forever. Allow this beautiful shower to caress you every single morning and understand that every drop of water has life, purpose and value.

As you stand within your shower, breathe deeply into your spine and feel the water rushing around your feet. Feel your consciousness begin to rise into the heavens and the clouds. We want you to visualize this and to pretend that you are standing in a rain shower as God's creation of water begins to bathe over you. Water is an important part of this beautiful, merry month of April. It is extraordinary and is what you are primarily made of.

We also want you to realize every time you touch water—bathe in it, drink it or use it for cooking—that it has a divine spirit that we ask you find. Give it your greatest attention and as much love as you possibly can. With every glass of water that you drink, hold it in your hands and feel the life force therein. Then, my dear friends, as you drink it into your body, feel it begin to nurture you in a way that you never dreamed or imagined would be possible, bringing every cell of your being to life. There are many bits and pieces of residue inside you from the distant past, previous lifetimes, current lifetimes and current situations in your own reality that might be of concern for you—little hassles and stresses.

Flowing Water: A Meditation

The best way to release these from your body is to close your eyes and imagine that you are made mostly of water. See yourself as a crystal-clear pool of water that is encased in this very refined, beautiful skin that you wear. Inside this water are little dark spots, places where the energy is stuck. The water's not flowing and is stagnating. This is where you find the physical, emotional and spiritual pains that you carry inside you. Now, as you see these inside yourself, we ask that you stir them with your heart. You can project your heart into these little areas as golden light, if you like, or you can do it as pink or purple light; it doesn't matter to us. Get them stirred up, bringing light into these darker spaces, and see little bits of darkness rising to the surface, to the pool of life that you are, my dear friends.

They rise and bubble out through your throat, up into the region of your sinuses and into your eyeballs. Then, my dear friends, they begin to drop out as tears, releasing these emotions and spiritual concerns and difficulties from the past. Release, release and release even more through your tears. These beautiful April showers will bring the lotus of your soul to life in the merry month of May.

It is the stirring of the emotions, the stirring up of the creator who you are, that shows that by simply talking to water, you can change your reality. We would share with you the idea of finding a fountain or creating a slow stream of water from the faucet so you can listen to it dance. Close your eyes as it dances against the porcelain in your sink. Listen to the expression of water during a rainstorm as it drips from the roof of your house. Listen to the sound of the water when you dip your feet into a bucket and wiggle your toes. Listen to the expressions that the water provides and keep a little notebook nearby. With your eyes closed, ask the water to tell you its secrets and write them down. These are the secrets of your soul, the mysteries of self that will now be brought to the surface so that you can have a full, clear, conscious awareness and understanding of what a beautiful creator you are in this reality here upon the planet Earth.

You, my dear friends, are no different than the leaves of the ever-budding tree. You are no different than the beautiful summer fruit that will soon be born. God bless you indeed, for you are all made of water. Water is the elixir of your soul. This is what is known as the fountain of youth. You never strayed from it and have always been a part of it.

As you continue to breathe very deeply, we ask that you allow yourself to create that reality all around—inside, outside and upside down. Realize that there is no direction that is required of you, no direction for you in this lifetime, and that is not a problem at all as far as we are concerned.

No Direction, Only Expansion

There is no such thing as direction; there is only expansion. Your life is a beautiful sphere of opportunity, releasing you from needing a direction, purpose, focus and intent. Now you begin to surrender into the will of God, the language of the heart. Ask God in prayer every day to come into your life and work inside so that you can begin to expand as a spirit and can see this expansion expressed here upon the planet Earth. As you begin to expand, close your eyes and ask this of God, and you begin to realize that the lotus flower of your soul is always expanding. It doesn't point its face toward the Sun in one single direction. This is a flower that is full, whole and completely spherical in its nature. For those of you who are creative in sacred geometry, this geometrical shape is ever expanding and ever embracing of all life. It is so strong, my dear friends, so perfectly formed, that it does not require any barriers or boundaries. It cannot be broken, destroyed or crushed like a delicate flower, for though it is delicate, it has the strength that comes from the energy of God's love—just as you, who are one expression of the same.

As you see this lotus flower growing inside you in this beautiful and merry month of April, begin to realize that come May, when you are in full bloom, you will feel connected with life in a way that you never dreamed or imagined possible. Allow the expansion of this spherical shape of your-self to intertwine with the spherical shapes of others. You will find, as you witness yourself upon the Earth, that these little spherical shapes have a very interesting arrangement, do they not, my dear friends?

Some of you already understand that you are beginning to see your-selves as one of the molecules of water dancing with other molecules of water around you, little spherical shapes intertwined, flowing and moving in a wonderful, fantastic dance. Water is incredibly expressive, my dear friends. It can seem to be still and yet is so full of life that there is a tremendously high vibrational frequency that is emitted even from absolutely still water. You can place a basin in front of you, hold your hands over it and allow the energy from your hands to begin to move what you think is still water. The molecules from your body, from the water that you are, will begin to interact with the water in the basin. Through this expression, you have a fantastic opportunity to understand the heal-ers who you are.

As you know, water is not easily confined and is very malleable and adaptable. It can be soaked into the fibers of your clothing and the strands of your hair. Is it not a beautiful creation? It can certainly come rolling in, in beautiful waves over your body. It can be broad or wide, or it can be a very tiny little droplet. It can be a rolling, raging river with a current that can drag you under and return you to the surface. This is a beautiful dance of life for you, feeling your body as it begins to intertwine with the waves of planet Earth.

Certainly these are the waves and currents that all who are reading this have been desiring in their lives. "How do I dance?" "How do I play?" "How do I walk with God?" "How," my dear friends, "do I sing my song to planet Earth?" "How do I speak my truth?" "How do I understand the creator who I am?" "How do I surrender into my heart and journey to the very same?" "How do I find and touch the face of God that is me?"

My dear friends, we have spoken many times of the fertile soil that is the darker spaces of your existence. This fertile soil, however, will not bear fruit until it is watered by your tears, with your life force that is expressed wholly and completely. The vibrational frequency of your spirit is water. God bless you indeed. You're a beautiful spirit. We love you so very much, my dear friends.

Water Is Everywhere

Water, water everywhere and so many drops to drink! Take them into your vessel, surrender to this nourishment. Do not fear the water—it never, ever wants to cause pain. Do not be concerned about your water, my dear friends, for it is willing to grow and to change with your prayers. The water that is contained within your foods can be transformed through your love and prayers. Can you slow yourselves down enough to sit in front of your meals and say a prayer to God, thank Him for this beautiful arrangement of life that sits upon your plate, that you are about to put into your mouth and draw into your body? All of it, dear friends, is God, and all of it is based upon the molecules of water that you are, so there is nothing whatsoever to fear in your journey upon planet Earth. You strive to be harmonious and fit the world, to create your reality, forcing it to the surface, but the journey to your heart is one that is playful. It dances like water on the stream, my dear friends, the water of April showers that bring the May flowers of your soul to life.

My dear friends, you are beautiful spirits, each and every one a student of the divine. Say your prayers, take the food into your body and thank your ever-lovin' stars that you are a part of the grand and glorious adventure called experience, God and creation. If that is not enough for you, look again. What else is there? You will not find joy in the bottom of your coffee mug; you will not find it by constantly holding pain at arm's length. You will find joy when at long last you realize that life upon planet Earth is a playful adventure. Surrendering to that is one step in opening your heart, the beautiful lotus flower of your soul.

You will feel the intoxication if you live life very consciously in this beautiful, merry month of April. It is a time of resurrection for you, your family, Spirit and life in objects around you. It is a time of resurrection, my dear friends, of the understanding of the God who you are; it is a time to resurrect passion, joy, happiness and love. It is a time of resurrection, of understanding the eternal soul and creator who you are, where you no longer have to crucify yourself to grow but must surrender to the journey, to the expansion of your spherical, beautiful being as you intertwine with all of life.

We love you so very much. April is a very important month. We ask that you approach it with great humility. That does not exclude laughter; just realize that you do not have to brave the storms anymore but must surrender to them. This beautiful, merry month is an extraordinary opportunity for you and for all of planet Earth. It is an opportunity for change and restructuring. What you thought was important suddenly becomes rather unimportant, and there is only one thing left: Put your hands upon someone's face to gaze into his or her eyes, and fall in love, with the deepest of respect for that person's being without having to change him or her.

In this beautiful, merry month of April we ask that you create a shower of your own, a shower of love, and express the same toward an individual in your life who drives you absolutely crazy and to another who is very easy to love. We want you to shower attention in your daily work upon a coworker you can't stand and would like to kick as he or she walks by. We ask that you fall in love, see the light in that person and understand that the pain inside that individual is what you have experienced for yourself.

We ask in this beautiful, merry month of April that you work to deprogram yourself from hate and to reprogram yourself toward greater love. Use forgiveness, kind deeds and acts of great enthusiasm that in the past might have exhausted you. Assist a neighbor when you're feeling so down that you ask, "What about me?" We ask you to kick that question out of the house for a while and instead ask yourself, "What about them?"

In this beautiful, merry month of April, you will find your heart beginning to expand, and you will realize that the journey is one of great joy when you choose to intertwine with life and to understand that every single, solitary human being and every plant, tree, dog and cat is made of the very same thing—God's love. That is the core of existence upon your Earth; that is what is planted; and that is the water that certainly does shower upon the fertile soil of the darker spaces.

My dear friends, never is your life without hope. God bless you indeed. There was one crucifixion, and it brought opportunity to planet Earth, the opportunity that comes through understanding, which in turn brings healing. So now step fully and completely into your light, share it with the world and go your way in peace, love and harmony. For life is indeed a joy, and you, my dear friends, are a part of creating that. God bless you indeed.

May—Flowers

God bless you. Dr. Peebles here. It is a joy and a blessing when human and Spirit join together for May flowers. May is the season of your soul's opportunity for expansion beyond your wildest dreams and imaginations. This is because the May flower is the symbol of a new beginning. For those who have been doing the work every single month, exploring the opportunities that exist within you, understand that May becomes a time of companionship. We want you to realize that in the month of May, you will have many opportunities for companionship, for an expansion of understanding your need for humanity. Opportunities, new beginnings for all and new friendships are upon the horizon. For some there will be new lovers. For others there will be a dissipation of distant relationships that no longer serve you. Upon the horizon are May flowers for all, new beginnings.

Close your eyes for a moment and surrender to the distant past, a journey upon a ship known as the *Mayflower*. Understand this as symbolic of a new beginning, of finding a new land and starting a new opportunity for growth inside yourself in relationship to life. You arrive and step upon the soil and see it is not like any soil that you have ever seen before. It is a different and wild land; you wonder if you can grow anything. This land is filled with opportunities and still quite mysterious.

Begin to Question and Fall into Wonder

Stepping off the *Mayflower* into the journey to your heart, beyond your wildest dreams and imaginations, is what May is about. For you, my dear friends, are courageous adventurers. You are in the final phases of understanding the being who you are in relationship to God. Learning now to walk with God is truly . . . [Pauses for a long time.] . . . a traipse into the wonderland of silence. And so, my dear friends, where you believe there is an absence of light, there is actually great density of it.

For those of you who wonder, "Goodness gracious, why did he stop midsentence? Why?"—when you begin to question, that is when you fall into wonder. There you begin to understand that you will find and touch the face of God that is you. That is the most important relationship of all as you join hand in hand with all humanity, in a labor of love to discover and dissolve the illusions of separation within self and between life. You fall in love with yourself for certain and can now see yourself fully expressed in life through many relationships with people around you, relationships that in the past you did not trust. Understand that if you trust them, you allow them to be who they are and yourself to have your own feelings. No longer must you hold them at arm's length.

You are beautiful spirits, about to embark upon a journey to your heart, which no longer means a weeding out. It does not mean that in order to flower forth, you must weed out anything, but rather to dance with what you thought, in the past, were weeds inside your soul. They are there to nurture you, to become fertile soil as they begin to die around your feet. These painful experiences from the past, relationships that no longer serve you and experiences that you have often wished you had never had will now become fertile soil. They are opportunities for understanding the richness of self, opportunities that now you can immerse yourself in and not feel the need to be separate from.

Do a Reading of Yourself: An Assignment

First and foremost, in this beautiful time of celebration of new beginnings in the month of May, we ask that you sit with a piece of paper, a typewriter, a computer or a crayon—it doesn't matter to us—close your eyes and begin a journey to your heart wherein you begin to psychically read yourself.

Ask your self to sit in front of you, then say, "Hello, self. I love you very much. I want to work with you today, and I want to help you find the true sense of who you really are, where you came from, where you are now in your life and where you are headed." Then we ask you to ask your self, "What would you like to ask?" Your self will say, "Well, I am not certain." You will say, "That's all right. Don't be scared. Come out, come out wherever you are."

This assignment is part of your flowering forth in the month of May. Don't be afraid. Your self will say, "But I am afraid." You say, "It's all right to be afraid." Your self will ask, "Be afraid? You just told me not to be afraid." You will say, "It's all right to be afraid, if you like. It's okay. Come out, come out, wherever you are." Your self will say, "All right, then I will. I'm feeling angry." You will say, "It's all right to feel angry." Your self will say, "But it's not nice to feel angry." You will say, "It's all right to feel angry, because you're in the presence of yourself."

You can be with you, my dear friends, and find sanctuary. You can be with your self, heart, mind and spirit together as one at long last. Know that oneness is with everything upon the planet Earth and in all dimensions in between. All the layers of the onion of the universe are you. You don't have to, in the month of May, hold any of it at arm's length, so why would you be afraid to read yourself, to psychically tap into who you really are?

Sit with your self at a table. When your self has finally agreed that it's all right to be afraid, angry, depressed, fearful, uncertain; to want to discover something new; to journey out; to expand; to have a heart and be fully expressed upon the Earth and flower forth; when you and your self sit at the table and come to this agreement, then you can commence with your psychic reading. You will feel love inside your heart as you sense this being who is very sad, broken and excited, wanting very much to know the answers. That is when the answers will be revealed.

These answers will carry you through until the month of June, when you will have a lot to celebrate. You are going to have so much to celebrate, you won't know where to begin. But we'll talk about that later, my dear friends. We've got lots of ideas how to celebrate in June. First you need to read your self, to truly, wholly and completely identify who you are.

"Hello, self. I see you on a beautiful journey. Goodness, I see skies of blue, beautiful green hills and love on the horizon. I see you breathing easier, your physical movements becoming smoother. I see you cancer free. I see you united with your loved ones. I see a journey to Machu Picchu. I see so much for you in the future, and I see where you have been and are now."

As you read yourself in this fashion, you will come to deeper understanding and appreciation of how God feels about you. My dear friends, so many of you have felt that you are abhorrent to the world. You have been very hard upon yourselves and have held yourselves at arm's length, believing that you are lesser than the rest of humanity, lesser than Dr. Peebles and lesser than the Lord Jesus Christ.

New Beginnings and New Opportunities

In the month of May, new beginnings and new opportunities are on the horizon. There will be new ways in which you come to identify the truth of who you really are. Read yourself in the month of May. Do this once a week. Fold the paper when you are finished writing, then, in the following week, open the paper, read what you have written and see the ways in which you have expanded yourself during the course of your journey and how accurate you were in your reading. Then read yourself again. Write it all down, fold up the paper and repeat the process throughout this very beautiful month of May, a time of celebration and discovery of who you really are. You are finding and touching the face of God in the silence and in what you believe to be the absence of light, which is never absent, not ever, not even in the darkness. Such fertile soil is the density of light wherein you plant yourself and grow, find and touch the face of God.

That, my dear friends, is the theme of the month, finding and touching the face of God that is you. Understand that in the month of April, you have learned about yourself and the water that you are. As you shed tears, you began to understand that there is fluidity to your spirit, an ability to be absorbed just as water can be absorbed into the soil. You can be absorbed into life, allowing yourself to surrender into it and feel the refreshment of your spirit by allowing its natural movement. Through repeated surrender, you will find and touch the face of God that is you. It's a fascinating world for this God. It looks very much like the shape of your heart. When you find and touch the face of God that is shaped like your heart, my dear friends, you begin to understand there is a rhythm to it.

Close your eyes for a moment and breathe very deeply into your spine. Begin to listen to the rhythms of your heart. There are secrets there, in secret chambers of opportunity. Listen to the rhythm. Listen, my dear friends, as your heart speaks to you. Listen to the still, small voice within. Listen, my dear friends. Listen, lis-

ten, listen, listen, listen, listen, listen, listen, listen, listen, listen, listen, listen, listen, listen, listen, listen, listen, listen, listen. [Each repetition becomes softer, followed by fifteen seconds of silence.]

Love Is Not Labor

My dear friends, it is a labor of love to diminish and dissolve the illusions of separation within self and between life. What you will find in your ultimate journey of expansion is that love is not labor. It penetrates, celebrates and has no expectations. Love embraces, repairs and heals. Love makes no decision but to love. Love understands nothing but love.

My dear friends, how much are you willing to love? In this journey of expansion of your heart, can you celebrate a person upon the Earth for who he or she is upon the surface and within his or her personality? Can you celebrate the richness and opportunity that person provides, someone you would prefer to cast by the wayside for being abhorrent, horrid, annoying, too frank and angry; someone who you'd rather not observe in any way, shape or form? Can you look upon that person and seek within your heart an understanding that the truth of his or her spirit is the same as yours, which means that holding him or her at arm's length is to hold yourself at arm's length? Can you sit in conversation with this person? Can you, despite the personality, share with this individual how much you love him or her? Can you care enough about that person to reach into your pocket and offer a dime, a dollar or your phone number? How far are you willing to expand yourself, to understand the great love of God's will and desire for you upon the Earth? Are you willing to touch the leper, heal the blind and raise the dead, for that is the work of Christ? That is what is being asked of you as you journey to your heart.

That's not a tall order. It is where you find and touch the face of God and experience the richness of yourself, the great love that you are, setting it free like a little birdie into the sunshine that will come in June. Upon the horizon is radiance and light as you sing your songs of celebration. But for now, you have homework. Read yourself. Hear in the silence. Listen.

My dear friends, you are being asked to obey a command that comes from deep within your heart. It is the same command for every human being—to love, starting with yourself, and to understand that the rewards from your love, kindness and acts of grace are tremendous. First and foremost, you must break the bondage that you feel to the distant past. You must allow for the flowering of your soul amid the weeds that become the fertile soil of healing your pain.

You are beautiful spirits. Take an opportunity in this moment to see light and hope in areas of darkness and pain in your life and to know for certain that you will emerge unscathed. You have the elixir, a love potion that

comes from God. My dear friends, great creators, each and every one a student of the divine and of divinity, do not fear love. Release your expectations and allow love to run wild. God bless you indeed. What kinds of
flowers grow in the month of May? Wildflowers.

God bless you indeed, my dear friends. Go your way in peace, love
and harmony, for life is indeed and forevermore a joy. [Stops speaking for
five seconds.]

God bless you indeed. God bless you indeed. God bless you indeed.
God bless you indeed. God bless you, indeed. [Pauses between each sentence, with each repetition becoming softer.]

June—Celebration

D r. Peebles here. Oh, goodness gracious, my dear friends, we're late
for the party, the celebrations of truth and the expansion of yourself
in this wonderful, beautiful month of June. June is a time for all to cast their
fears to the winds, to release expectations and bury concerns, allowing them
to become the fertilizer that bears beautiful fruit in your wonderful heart.
June is a time for you to rest, read, relax and wonder about what is around
the corner while not caring about it.

Beautiful spirits, each and every one a student of the divine! June is a time
of celebration and coming to the understanding of the prophet you are upon
the planet Earth. "Prophet?" you would ask. Yes! What kind of prophet do
you want to be? Would you want to be a false prophet or a prophet of truth?
What kind of prophet do you want to be during the month of June and for
the rest of eternity? We play with words here—prophet and profit. You are
all concerned about abundance of finance and of your being. So it is here,
in the month of June, that you will marry yourself. Marriage is part of the
June experience.

Goodness gracious, my dear friends, marry yourself truly and whole-heart-
edly, understanding that the abundance that you seek—the profit that you
desire in your life—will come by understanding the prophet who you are.
Prophets are known by their fruit. What kind of fruit will you bear in this
month of June? What kind of fruit will be brought forth to the world as a
result of your labors as you have worked upon the many seasons of your soul?

What Kind of Prophet Are You: A Meditation

*For a moment here, breathe very deeply into your spine and allow yourself not
to understand why you are here upon the Earth. You don't have the foggiest idea
what you have incarnated for, what you are here to experience or what is around
the corner. At the same time, everything that you don't understand exists inside
you, because everything that you desire to understand is inside of you and is you.*

We want you to sit now in a state of wondering about life in a very casual way. Sit in a park with trees, the breeze, sunshine, rain and flowers, casting bread into the water and seeing it float on the surface. Ducks are eating the bread that you cast on the water. It's a very beautiful experience. Some bread is floating back to you, soaked with the water of life. Breathe very deeply into your spine. What you seek in the beautiful time period of June is the understanding of the prophet who you are. What kind of prophet are you as you sit by the water, casting your bread upon its surface?

"I don't understand, Dr. Peebles. I don't understand what you are asking me." My dear friends, that's perfect. What you don't understand exists inside you. Listen to the answer. You worked in the beautiful month of May to listen to the still, small voice within, so listen now, my dear friends. Listen. Listen. Listen. Listen.

Now, as you drop deeper and deeper into your heart, begin to feel the abundance of love that you have inside. Allow it to well up in a feeling that is very similar to the unfolding of the lotus flower of your heart, the expansion of yourself and the freedom that you felt in that expansion. Embrace the understanding of the drop of the water that you are, God bless you indeed, floating in that uncertainty with the understanding that everything is rather certain. Ultimately, you are never, ever away from love.

Continue to breathe very deeply, allowing this abundance of love of your being to surface, the passionate guidance that you find within, the passion that you feel now for you as you fall in love. Wedding bells are a-ringin'. It's a time for you to fall in love with self, to embrace expansion once and for all.

Find Your Own Truth

Total expansion brings about creativity. Total expansion and surrender to it means that never will you have to worry about financial abundance or profits. No longer will you have to fear going into the unknown, the unexpected or that which is around the corner. Releasing your expectations, surrendering into the tenderness and loving embrace of God are what you desire.

What kind of prophet are you now? "But I don't understand, Dr. Peebles. I don't understand. What are you asking me?" In June we ask that you simply surrender to your heart and journey into the unknown. To find the fruit that you want to bear, you must be willing to speak your truth, to know that what you do not understand exists inside you. There is where you will find the answers.

We are late for a party, a celebration. Some of you will not read this for a very long time. When you do, you will feel a sense of relief, thinking, "At long last, I can get on with my life." There is a reason, my dear friends, why you will read this long after the channeling was taped. It is so that it will be late and unexpected, so that you do not become spoiled fruit yourself and begin to understand that the resources that you seek are not outside you. They do not exist in a text, a channel or in Dr. Peebles. They exist within you.

You enjoy the text that you read, because it is you. It resonates with your soul, with the truth of yourself. We say no words, my dear friends, that you did not know before. We speak the truth of who you really are, the words that are the truth of you, which is why you so very much enjoy Dr. Peebles. That is why you so very much want to join with Spirit. Through your development of yourself as the mystic who you are and through striving to understand your right to receive and to give abundance, to find and touch the face of God in everybody and everything, in every whisper and every experience, you hope to join with Spirit.

It is occurring inside you as you breathe very deeply into your spine right now, sinking deeper and deeper into self. You begin to discover that there is nothing but oceans of emotion inside you, and there is one frequency that runs at the core of each one—a desire for love. Love is the constant. Love is what you seek as you expand. It is through the radiance of your own light shining forth into the world that you begin the journey to the heart that does not end.

Expand Your Love

In June we desire for you the expansion of your love through creative outlets—through work, play, sexual exploration of each other, whispers in the night, conversations with a child, answering the telephone and lending a listening ear, touching a stranger's hand, shining your shoes or making lunch for a picnic for a celebration of you. In this beautiful month of June, celebrate the wedding that is about to occur between self and self.

You have been exploring relationships outside and inside, between Spirit and your human experience. We have made promises, and we have pushed your buttons. Sometimes we have scared you as we helped you surrender to your deepest fears. We have spoken in such a forthright manner to you that we have made you laugh. Sometimes for some, we almost drove you insane. In this course of the seasons of the soul, we have created a sense of freedom and merriment. But wait! Have we created it for you? We stand only in our truth, sharing the abundance of our being, giving of our life to you without expectation or care, because in this case, to care for you is to not care at all what you do but to see only the truth of your heart.

And so we have given unto you gifts, meditations, healings and homework assignments. You, my dear friends, have had your responses to the very same. You have chosen to laugh, to agree or disagree, and none of it mattered to us, only to you. You have been in a grand and glorious celebration, a marriage dance. How do you like them apples? You have been heart to heart with yourself, contacting the many rather than the few right there inside you, no longer having to be wrapped up with guilt or shame about your excursion here upon the Earth, but rather realizing that there is no guilt or shame that comes from exposing yourself to the world.

The world falls in love with you and you with it through intimacy, touch, taste and smell, and most of all through the vibrational frequency of love that courses through every vein of every human being upon the Earth. You are not separate from *them*. You are not a body upon the Earth; you are all that you see, hear, taste, touch, feel and smell. That is the body in which you exist.

It is for you, my dear friends, the body of Christ and of love. It is the Holy Spirit who you are. You the Holy Spirit? Imagine that! God bless you indeed. How can you say such a thing? Because that is the spirit that allows you to dance and express the truth of self, the spirit that does not control your nature but exposes the truth of your nature to the world. You choose now to exist in that, understanding that you want freedom. Goodness gracious, my dear friends, is that not the abounding issue upon your planet Earth? Freedom is sought through war, devastation, destruction, control and murdering that which does not work. How is it that this would provide freedom, for freedom is an embrace? Freedom is everlasting. Freedom gives life. It does not take it.

You Are Worthy

So when you see war and devastation upon your Earth in this beautiful month of June, we ask that you simply sit with yourself and ask yourself about the battle that occurs inside you. What kind of war are you entertaining? What kind of devastation and destruction? What are you trying to kill off about yourself? What is it that makes you feel emotionless? What is it that has your heart numb? What is it that makes you want to inflict pain upon yourself? You will find that this is old hat now. You have done remarkable work during the course of the past seasons, and you seek a caretaker for your spirit. In this beautiful month of June, you will find that the ultimate and most profound relationship that you can have is from self to self. Are you worthy? Yes. Are you worthy? Yes. Are you worthy? "Yes, I am, Dr. Peebles. I am worthy."

My dear friends, you are falling in love with you in this very beautiful month of June, a time of celebration beyond your wildest dreams and imaginations. *As you breathe very deeply into your spine once again, close your eyes with the understanding that all that you create and can control are your choices and perceptions inside yourself.* If you can remain in that understanding, in that focus, it is there that you will have the preparedness for what comes at you every day. The unexpected moments become profoundly changed, because you realize that you are in charge. Nothing can control your spirit. You find and seek temperance inside yourself, and that temperance comes from love.

You find that when someone comes at you with greed or anger, or your tire bursts upon your car, your reaction will be different than you ever dreamed or imagined possible. Are you still worthy of love in those circumstances? Yes. These are the questions we would ask you to ask yourself. Are you worthy of love in these circumstances? Yes. Now, the question is, can you find it in your heart to feel it? Your tire bursts, and you laugh at the opportunity to ask for help along the roadside. Perhaps it is a time to pause, reflect and pray to God, being very thankful for the tires that still work and did not burst.

June is a time of deflating that which you have inflated in terms of belief systems from the past that certain things are right and others are wrong. Deflate your sense of importance and inflate your sense of what is truly important, which is the abundance of your being, how much love you can generate and receive, and to understand that this is at the core of everything that you do in life.

What Kind of Prophet Are You?

So what kind of prophet are you? Are you a prophet of truth? "Well, I don't know, Dr. Peebles. I don't know. I don't know what truth is." My dear friends, you know what truth is. We want you to understand that it comes from within. The truth is at your heart. It is your caretaker, the one who makes you feel loved, what you desire to express—the truth of yourself. *Speak your name aloud right now. Speak it again with sensitivity. Speak it repeatedly with compassion, love, trust, kindness, complete and utter health and as if you care. Speak your name as if you are a friend to yourself, as if you do not know yourself but would like to get to know you. Speak your name with laughter, with the joy of getting to know yourself. Speak it as if you are falling in love. Now speak your name and ask, "Will you marry me?" Then speak your truth. Is it yes or no?*

It is time to become extremely centered in self so that the selfishness that resists exposing the true you can disappear. This selfishness wants to keep you sheltered and hidden from life. It wants to deceive you into believing that you are not worthy of love. That is what selfishness is, my dear friends, and we want for you now to be self-centered upon the light that you are, the brilliant white light of your soul that is about to surface. Never again will you have to surround yourself with the protection of white light, because you are that; you just have forgotten it.

You are beautiful spirits. For some who are reading this, you will find that telephones ring in your home and interfere with your peace, serenity and the constant voice of guidance from within, just as my voice is a constant voice of guidance, love, companionship and friendship to you, an expression of the heart of God. Hear my voice speaking to you of love, trust, self-worth, the prophet who you are and the prophet whom you seek.

There is one constant in the universe, and that is the love of God that is fully expressed at all times, not given and taken away. It is not interfered with or interrupted, not by telephones, crying children or the need to stop and have something to eat. God and the love of God exist in everything that you do during any given day. Everything that you are in any given moment exists right inside you, not separate from the very same.

Breathe very deeply into your spine. What kind of prophet do you want to be? A prophet of truth, of all that you know and all that you can share with the planet Earth, fully and completely, not fearing exposure but willing to reveal your true heart, to allow the world to gaze upon you, to cast its judgments and to realize that to not care is to care a great deal? By exposing yourself to the world, my dear friends, you will begin to understand peace, serenity, the light of truth that you are and the abundance of your being. You will find that these are the beautiful fruits of your labors, which attract wonderful beings into your life, friends who want to feast on your abundance but not in a way that detracts from you. Who in his or her right heart would not want to stand in your light and be fed and nurtured by your spirit when you give of yourself so completely? The Christ who you are, the lover who you are, the prophet who you are and the unchained Holy Spirit who you are flow purely through every part of your being that is expressed upon the Earth with compassion.

God bless you, indeed, my dear friends. June is a month of celebration. For those who feel you are special enough, we encourage you to have a party to share your abundance, to speak your truth and embrace friends, family members and others. Invite someone to the party whom you have never had contact with before, just to simply do it. See what happens and show your willingness to find and touch the face of God in everyone.

God bless you indeed. You are beautiful spirits, my dear friends. Go your way in peace, love and harmony, for life is indeed a joy. All you have to do as you enjoy the journey to your own heart and certainly to your own enlightenment is lighten up, lighten up, lighten up and listen, listen, listen, listen, listen, listen.

Seasons of the Soul Part 4:

Freedom, Independence and Surrender

G od bless you. Dr. Peebles here. It is a joy and a blessing when human and Spirit join together in search of the greater truths and awareness. God bless you indeed, my dear friends, as you come into the time of July in the seasons of your soul; it is after your month of June when a marriage that has occurred inside you of self to self. Now, in July, you begin to discover that your greatest desire within this marriage is independence and through it abounding freedom. This will occur in July during your studies here in the seasons of your soul. We want you to begin to realize that your life is in review now.

July—Independence and Freedom

W e ask that you sit with every tape that you have been receiving throughout the past year and listen to snippets, wherever the tape recorder lands as you fast forward on each tape. [Since you are reading this text, not listening to the tapes, go back to the beginning of the chapters on the seasons of the soul. Flip through the pages, stop randomly on a page for each month and reread the section.] Listen to the snippets that come forth from each month of seasons of the soul, and this will add up to an awareness of yourself that you did not receive from these tapes in the past. Fast-forward the tape and listen for approximately thirty seconds, starting with the September tape and forward for the rest of the months. That is how we want you to start your month of July in this course of study of independence and freedom.

Also in the month of July, you will find abounding balance that comes from not having to have everything in right order but rather by surrendering to whatever comes your way, especially what comes from your heart. In this month, you will also find that tremendous interaction will be required from you. For the first half of the month, from July 1 until July 14, we want you to focus upon interaction as a part of your recreation in terms of awakening to your heart—its beats, rhythms and movements. Observe the control that you have of your muscles and the expansion that you feel of your tummy every time you eat.

Interacting with yourself and sensing yourself physically will be a part of the month of July. Interaction with human beings and life around you will also be a part of this work and of understanding that the independent being who you are does not mean to be separate from the world. Rather, you are at one and at peace with it. Through this you will find fluidity of movement in your life. Where this occurs, love abounds. Where love abounds, you find freedom and flight of soul beyond your wildest dreams and imaginations.

Interaction with the world means that you deliberately force yourself to walk into a marketplace to study humanity, to find ways in which you can walk up to a stranger and say, "Hello! How are you today? The sun is shining beautifully, don't you think?" Watch the person look at you in astonishment, clearly wondering what's wrong with you for interacting with him or her in such a fashion. Instead of feeling this reaction to you as judgment, we ask that you see it with a sense of humor, with a certain gaiety and lightness that comes from within, realizing that you are indeed in charge of your reality.

Study Interaction

You can share and speak your truth with the world without having to control and manipulate it. To speak your truth to a cherished friend will also be part of your study of interaction and independence in the month of July. Call a friend and deliberately ask that person to share how he or she feels about you truly, wholly and completely. For those who are courageous, we want you to focus on one particular area of study. Ask your friend to tell you one thing that he or she really does not like about you, something that really aggravates him or her to the core.

Your friend will try to make it very nice and say, "Oh, nothing aggravates me about you. You are a beautiful spirit, a wonderful person." After a little prodding, you will say, "I really want to know. This is part of my spiritual study right now, and I need to hear from you, my cherished friend, what really aggravates you about me." Then the person might say, "It is the way you sniffle with your nose," or "It is the way you drum your fingers upon the table," or "It is the way you squeak your chair every time you sit down to a meal." You ask, "Really? Is that so?" You do not hear it as an attack upon your spirit, because you have asked the person to share this with you.

Then you say, "Thank you very much for this. Guess what? I don't know that I'll ever change that behavior, but I appreciate hearing that this is what aggravates you about me. Perhaps I will have to do it a little more just to tickle your fancy."

Once again you find lightheartedness and humor in the situation. Your friend will laugh, and you will have a wonderful point at which you can poke fun at yourself every once in a while. Allowing someone to poke fun at you every once in a while will certainly be an important part of the foundation of your independence and freedom, the abounding freedom from feeling that the world has any control over you. To allow yourself to be poked fun at will be a beautiful release, for you will no longer experience hearing people's words toward you as being judgments against you. People might mean them as such, but you have the choice, the decision, the desire within as to whether you will take it as judgment. You can also see it as someone speaking his or her truth. Then you can laugh, surrender and say to yourself, "Well yes, indeed, perhaps I have points where I drive you crazy, but guess what? I love myself anyway." Through this, my dear friends, you build an important foundation of independence and freedom in this beautiful, harmonious month.

Awaken Your Spirit to the World

So from July 1 through July 14, you will force yourself to awaken your spirit to the world—to the perceptions, judgments, discernments, discretion and the fun that is poked at you and the daggers that are thrown at you. These are all part of your reality upon the Earth. They are all things that you cannot make go away, no matter how much you struggle to hold them at arm's length. Since you can't hold them at arm's length, why not invite them closer? Say, "Come hither, please. Come to me and let me embrace you into my heart, because there you cannot do me any harm. It is there that I realize that I am one with you, there that I realize that I breathe you into me. When I breathe you into my spine, you become part of my recreation, laughter and experience of life. You, my dear friends, become the dance, the signpost for me as I journey to my heart.

"I hear words of judgment toward me, and that gives me a wonderful opportunity to know that these are not human beings in whose presence I care to stand, for I do not desire to be judged at all times. I can embrace their judgments into my heart, because they are part of who the person is at this time; they are part of what the person wants to express, and I, becoming the enlightened being who I am, want very much to embrace everything that I see, hear, taste, touch, feel and smell. I do this with the understanding that I can do it with loving allowance for all things to be in their own time and place, starting with myself."

God bless you indeed. And so you begin this kind of dialog with yourself and the world around you. Suddenly you find that you don't have your buttons pushed anymore by others. Rather, you can see the world as a road map to your own eternal soul, a guide on the journey to your own heart. There are signposts along the way of rapids in the river, so you take an easier path. When you see briars and brambles, instead of trying to cut them down, you simply allow them to be and take the greener pasture. As you journey to your heart, you begin to understand that there is a dialog, a language here upon the Earth that occurs between everything that you witness and experience. Everything that you hear becomes a dialog and a road map for your journey.

We cannot impress this upon you enough, for this will be an extraordinarily important part of your studies of the seasons of your soul, the seasons being the many rather than the few, the darker and the lighter, the full spectrum of light and life and opportunity in all perspectives. They give you an opportunity to understand yourself and to grow into the greater light of your truth, beingness and love of the lover who you are, the creator and designer of your existence. You are God, my good friends, now independently and fully expressed upon the Earth, independence not meaning freedom from anything but freedom to follow your heart, speak your truth, move with the natural rhythms of the world and not feel suppressed by them. It is freedom from superficial appearances, from having to mask and hide yourself away from the world.

You do not have to fear judgment, my dear friends. You can walk as Christ walked upon the Earth and be fully expressed, no matter the lies and deception, no matter the daggers, no matter the threats of life around you. It is freedom to live your life fully and completely without having to have any pretense, with only your heart fully exposed, vulnerable and naked in front of the many rather than the few as you say, "Here I am. I stand in my integrity, independent and whole in myself, upon the Earth as a full and proper expression of God without any veils or filters."

This is an ideal world for all humans to stand in their truth together as one. It is there that you begin to heal the Earth as you heal yourself, no longer stressing and straining against the wholeness of your being, understanding that your salvation exists from the inside out, not from the outside in.

Transition into a New Energy

We would ask that you stay awake from July 14 to July 15 as you transition into a new energy upon planet Earth. During this period of time, you can have the many rather than the few invited to your home for this experience. Do whatever you like here. It doesn't matter to us. You can do this by yourself, in your own manner. We want you to move with the rhythms and the movement of your heart, not to listen to the words of Dr. Peebles. Do not feel that there are pretenses to be put upon you, that you will be judged by anyone for doing anything in a wrong way. The right way is that which you desire in your heart. Do that in this period of time, because there will be a transition, a crossing over to the other side of yourself, where the veil of darkness will begin to fall around you and you begin to release the insecurities that have come from lifetimes upon the Earth.

During this time, we ask that you sit in quiet surrender and respectful embrace of all that you are, ever were and ever shall be. You no longer have to fear the past or force it to disappear. No longer will you fall into insecurity, but rather you will embrace all aspects of self. This is a time for those of you who have been told to embrace your life of judgment, wherein you felt that you did not share your fullness and richness with the world. Embrace the lifetimes where you have fallen victim to those who were your captors and the lifetimes where you have captured human beings in an effort to force them to succumb to your will.

For those of you who in the distant past and previous lifetimes were cast into the fire, surrender to that and do not resist the painful death processes that you have experienced in many lifetimes. Surrender to them, for all experiences that you have ever had upon the Earth are your friends, teachers and guides. They are parts of self that will reveal the mysteries of your soul as you come into this latter period of July 2004, no longer stressing and straining against anyone or anything, especially against yourself.

Increase Respectful Communication with Yourself

The second half of July is about increasing respectful communication with yourself. Acknowledgment, interaction with you, is what we want you to emphasize here. We ask that you take a notebook and write down, every day, one area of your life in which you have not been sincere, where you are lying to yourself, where you are hiding in your insecurity, where you did not voice an opinion because you felt it should not be heard and where you felt judgmental against another human being. Being honest with yourself and living a life of integrity is in order for the second half of July.

As well as revealing the truth of yourself, you should look at everything that you see as being less than sincere and do it with integrity and kindness, saying, "Ah, this feels so nice because I acknowledge it, embrace it and let it disappear." You will relieve yourself of pain, guilt and shame. You release yourself into a grand land of opportunity and wonder wherein you will now have come clean with your soul and purified your spirit, heart and self in such a fashion, my dear friends, that physical ailments will fall away. They will miraculously begin to disappear, because you have embraced the issues that surrounded them.

Your anger, distrust and disrespect of human beings have fallen into parts of your body and are tearing you apart. In this month of July, you have a chance to acknowledge that you did not respect, acknowledge or love others in varying ways. Now that you have acknowledged this, you can speak it with your voice after you have written it upon the page; read it aloud to God, saying, "Here it is, God, in all its glory. This is who and what I have been. I entrust my soul to you now in a grand and glorious adventure of creating greater and greater love upon the Earth, starting with myself."

Now you release yourself into a grand land of opportunity of awareness of who you are and feel more courageous in sharing this with the world and discovering that you can be a shining star upon the Earth. You can ask for what you want—fulfillment—and say to a loved one, "I love you. I desire you. I want to make love with you. I want to dance and sing with you." There are so many singers in the world who feel they do not have a voice. "I can't carry a note," I said of myself in my own lifetime until I realized that I feared being heard more than what I felt were flaws in my singing voice. For those of you who are afraid to sing, we challenge you here to awaken to the singer who you are and to realize that your desire is to sing and entrust your spirit to God. It is all right for you to sing even if you cannot carry a note. Singing is the point of the singing, my dear friends. In the latter half of July, your soul's emergence is the point.

You are beautiful spirits, each and every one a student of the divine, understanding the independent spirits who you are, living your life wholly and completely on the surface, not having to maintain carbon-copy exteriors of something you have seen in a magazine. You have your own miraculous appearance to give to the world. Those of you who feel that you are too fat, lumpy, bumpy, thin, tall, short, wrinkled, gray; who feel that you have not enough arms or legs, too many freckles or spots or not enough, too much padding in your chest and so on, you tear yourself to shreds. We ask now that you gaze into the mirror and embrace all that you are, ever were and ever shall be into your heart. You are every appearance that you see in any human being upon the Earth.

Look into the mirror and see this physical body that you have and discover that there is extraordinary beauty there. If you cannot fathom it in the lumps and the bumps, the bruises, the cuts, the scrapes, the scars that you see on your exterior, then we ask that you look to the landscape and look at the critters and creepy crawlers. Strive to find the beauty there, even in the wonder of the spiders who inhabit your home who you so very much want to squash and kill. Stare at the dry landscape of the desert or stare into a picture until at long last, you can find that you can fall in love with it. See the face of a stranger that frightens you and look beyond the anger, anguish and sadness that is upon the surface of the skin and see inside that person's ever-loving soul and heart. Pray that the truth of that person can emerge. Finding, stretching, reaching and bending into greater and greater love is part of your experience in this very beautiful season of your soul, this beautiful, independent and free month of July.

You have freedom to voice your opinions. Do this by asking permission first from the world around you, then say your opinions with compassion, without requiring that the world has to agree with you. No longer do you have to manipulate the world. Suddenly you come to an awareness that to strive to manipulate the world around you is a rather boring way to live. Manipulating the world around you to force others to comply will be, for you, a very boring place to live.

For a moment here, simply imagine that all of life is with you and agrees at all times. Where would you find your light? Where would you find places to birth yourself? You would be, by the compliance of all upon the Earth in agreeing with your opinions and perspectives, in a place of absolute static. There would be no movement, sound, light, color or glory for your being. Look to the world and every person and experience, even things that you thought smelled disgusting or tasted bad, and realize that everything in your world is the fertile soil wherein you plant your being to find and touch the face of God.

Find the Light

It is here upon the planet Earth that you live in what you believe to be darkness, struggling to find the light. Look around you at the color and the light that do exist in this dark space that you believe you live in. There you will begin to realize that just as in the fertile soil of the Earth, so too there are creepy crawlers—in human form—who till that soil until it becomes very rich. You do not have to stress and strain to come to the surface but can grow without obstruction, independent and free. By the grace of God, it is there that you fall into the certainty and the wonderment that you are a magnificent projection of God.

It is in this very beautiful month of July that you are being asked to find the summer light in the seasons of your soul. We embrace you into ourselves, not holding you at arm's length in a lack of compassion, but holding you and embracing you, my dear friends, into our hearts with love. You are our fertile soil wherein we plant our beings and find and touch the face of God. So it is that we begin to work in harvesting the onions, the many layers of your being. God bless you indeed, my dear friends. We love you so very much.

Go your way in peace, love and harmony, for life is indeed a joy. All you have to do to enjoy the journey to your own hearts and enlightenment is to lighten up and share the light of your soul with the world just a little bit more. God bless you, indeed.

August—Surrender

My dear friends, as you have worked with the seasons of the soul for the past twelve months, you find that you are lightening up just a little bit more. You understand that the three principles are to be used as tools in tandem in each and every moment of each and every day, finding that the inspiration that you seek comes not from a tape, not from Dr. Peebles, but from within yourselves. Certainly, my dear friends, you are the eyes, ears, mouths and hugs and kisses of God upon the planet Earth. Allow yourselves to fall into life in love with the many rather than the few. Not holding life at arm's length has been part and parcel of your experience of the seasons of the soul.

Are you transformed in this month of August? Are you transformed in this twelfth month of your journey, or are you transformed by your entire journey? The many layers to the onion are like the seasons that have been there all along, but in this past twelve-month period, you have been discovering beyond your wildest dreams and imaginations that you are sensitive, strong, capable, compassionate; that you love the planet Earth; and that you want to feel life and be immersed in it.

The many layers to the onion and the many seasons of your soul have existed all along the path, in every step of your journey in this and previous lifetimes, now and forevermore and certainly in the past twelve months . . .

🍎　🍎　🍎

I can't do it. Sorry about that, everybody. I had a difficult day yesterday. I was very tired and unable to stay in trance. I figured that what Dr. Peebles shared with you was so beautiful that I didn't want to erase it and start over, so we'll just pick it up from there and see what he has to say. I'm sure there's a reason for all of these things, so thanks for bearing with me. This is Summer, in case you didn't know. I'll go into trance now. Enjoy the journey.

🍎　🍎　🍎

God bless you. Dr. Peebles here. It is a joy and a blessing when human and Spirit join together in search of greater truths and awareness. God bless you indeed, my dear friends. Your channel here is a beautiful spirit. She certainly is very strong and has learned very much how to color her world with the seasons of the soul. It is certainly apropos that her name is Summer, one who is willing to walk into the flame of her soul to merge as one with God. This is the time of August for you as you are now about to wrap up your journey and begin another.

You have done the course work of seasons of the soul, whether you have studied it with actual, tangible manifestation with your own hands, your own heart in the exterior world or just read the text and slept on it. Even those of you who have chosen not to listen to tapes during this course of twelve months have learned from the seasons of the soul that this course is about your own rhythms and responding to them. You are in charge of your reality and have self-responsibility for your life as a creative adventure, for through your choices and perceptions, you do indeed create your reality. You understand that the seasons of your soul exist in each and every moment of each and every day—winter, spring, summer and fall. Those are the seasons, but inside of them are months, days and even nanoseconds, each one in and of itself a season of your soul, another layer to the onion.

Choose Your Season

And so for the month of August, we would ask that you simply sit and surrender for a moment here as you sit in your chair. Breathe very deeply into your spine and ask yourself right at this given moment, feel it inside your heart: "What season am I today?" [Pauses.] Don't be scared. Come out with it, my dear friends. Speak it aloud now.

WINTER ● If you have chosen winter, this means for you, there is a time period of some hard work, and for a day, hour or week, it is up to you to design it. If it is winter for you, perhaps there will be some tough ice to crack upon the surface. You can either crack the ice or decide to simply skate upon it, to make it into something that works for you. It can be a difficult situation, a difficult relationship or a party that you must attend that you feel is necessary even though you really don't want to go. Find the magic there. If you choose indeed to step into situations in your life that you find you are in resistance to within you heart, make the decision that you will turn it into magic for your soul. Perhaps there is something that is spurring you on there. This is the winter season spurring you on toward what your soul knows will be springtime in the making.

SPRING ● For those of you who feel that today is spring, well goodness gracious, what a wonderful opportunity to have a fresh start! Start new relationships and friendships. Go to the grocery store and say hello to a stranger. It is a time when you can meet your soul mate, for those of you who desire to do so. In terms of soul mate, we mean it in the sense that you use the word upon the Earth—unexpectedly finding a lover. So open your heart to receiving the sunlight and the rain during this beautiful spring day, moment, week or month, whatever you feel inside your heart is the season of your soul in any given moment.

SUMMER ● Summer is a wonderful opportunity for you, a mysterious time for those of you who feel it is summertime for your soul right now.

Perhaps you're avoiding something, or you want to bring something to the surface and are not certain whether to do this. Search your heart for what you might be avoiding and what you would like to bring to the surface, then pull out all the stops and do it. Bring it to the surface, whether it is a talk with your husband or wife about difficulties that you've had in the past week or whether it is simply that you want to, well, we'll use your words—blow off work and go to the amusement park. Do it, for certainly the season of summer is about stepping into the fire of your soul no matter what, without heeding any warning signs, because you know that everything is in right order. In the season of summer, you just simply jump. It is very important to respect and honor the pressures of feelings inside of you that say, "It's time for a change here. It's time to do something else, to jump into the swimming pool in the heat of the day." It is there that you would also surrender to the unexpected thunderstorms that might come down upon you during your situation. If you choose to go to the amusement park, you might find that you need to surrender to the unexpected during the course of summertime of your soul. Whether it be in a given day, week, month or year, it is up to you. It is your design. Surrender to the season that you feel in any given moment.

FALL ● As for fall—goodness gracious, what a beautiful period of time, filled with laughter and a lot of nurturing! You can feel the need for warmth even on the warmest of days. You can feel that you need to have the respect and honor of a friend or family member, that you need a little nurturing, to be given a cup of tea and a little pumpkin bread, if you will. Treat yourself to this. Treat yourself to harvest foods, for example. It is a time for a physical nurturing of your mind, body and spirit; physical nurturing is primary. It is a good time for you to eat squash, beans and corn, even if it's out of season. Better to have it than not if you feel that today is the fall of your soul.

Day, week, month or year—whatever the given moment—find the season of the soul that lies there within your heart.

Choose Your Month

Now, within these seasons, there is as well a period of time of twelve months in which we have been in this exploration together. *Breathe once again very deeply into your spine. Now we would ask that you simply breathe as deeply as you can and feel intoxicated by life. Surrender your heart right now to your existence, be thankful for your life upon the Earth 365 days a year (except, of course, in a leap year). Respect the seasons and months that you are. You are indeed, my dear friends, right now here in this given moment, a month of the year. Breathe very deeply into your spine. What month do you feel like? Are you September, October, November, December, January, February, March, April, May,*

June, July or August? Your body is in the month of August upon the planet Earth but, my dear friends, where is your spirit?

AUGUST 🌑 August is a month without shape or form, without color or design. It's neither summer nor fall. It is absent of holidays. It is a palette for expression of your soul and for its colors. What month are you right here and now? We would ask that you sit in a chair every day and assign a month to your day and spirit.

SEPTEMBER 🌑 If you find that you are September, you are in a harvest period. It is a good time for expression, for making plans for the future, for planting your ideas and preparing to water them and help them grow.

OCTOBER 🌑 If your month is October, it is a time for carving out a new plan for your life, creating a plan that is very, very organized and arranged in steps that show what you'll do for the next twelve months. What will you do from this day forward to make your dreams come true?

NOVEMBER 🌑 November is a time for simply taking the opportunity to nurture yourself and to rest. Extra rest is required for those in November. Get ready for hibernation of a part of yourself that you find has no value to you anymore. Perhaps it is the way you have expressed yourself in the past. Put it to bed and tell it good night. It is time for that part to hibernate until it is required once again, whether it be anger, sadness or lack of harmony. Tell it to go to bed.

DECEMBER 🌑 For those of you who are December, this is a very beautiful opportunity to work with color and light. Interior design is wonderful for those of you feeling December. If you're not very good at arranging flowers, today's the day to do it, my dear December people, because December is a time when you have been holed up in a house with winter storms. Now you want something fresh, to bring life into that winter, so it's a wonderful opportunity for those of December.

JANUARY 🌑 January is a time of new beginnings and certainly, my dear friends, of resolutions. Treat your children, family members, friends and others differently and with greater respect. Increase your awareness of compassion and trust. If this is January for you, it is a day for you to tell someone that you are sorry.

FEBRUARY 🌑 February—well, what do you think? Romance, love and time to give up greed and really understand that the true abundance that you seek is through the love that you feel inside of your heart for another. Where have you not expressed love this past week, and how can you express it today? Can you turn events about that in the past were not working very well between you and a friend, a family member or others, a clerk at the store to whom you were not very kind? Can you return there, give the person a flower and say, "I am so sorry. I apologize for my ill manners"? This is a time to do it, even giving a pack of candy to a good friend of yours. Celebrate it, another Valentine's Day for your soul for those of you who are February today.

MARCH ● March—well, goodness gracious! March is bouncing, a good time for going out and having a party or a dance, even if you dance in your living room, naked. Do something silly—spell your name in the sand, stomp your feet in the grass; it's a wonderful opportunity for you to just simply feel alive upon the Earth. Take your fingertips and run them along your legs and arms, through your hair; touch your face and say, "I love you, self. You're a beautiful spirit." That would be for those who in their souls today, in this given moment, feel the month of March. God bless you indeed, each and every one a student of the divine.

APRIL ● For those who are feeling April today, well goodness gracious, when are you going to crack out of your shells? That's something for you to think about. It is a wonderful opportunity for you to really get some work done. April is a wonderful month for your soul to get focused. Do some work, clear your desk, clean your house, take those things out from under the bed that you have been hiding and brush them off, throw them away or reorganize them. Say hello to them. They're getting lonely. It's a good time for cleaning out a cupboard or drawer, a wonderful time for shining your shoes, getting ready for your Sunday best so that you can sit for a period of time, after you have done your work, and have a little chat with God. Be very, very thankful. Lean your head over, clasp your hands and say, "Thank you, God, for a very beautiful day, and thank you for the mysterious ways in which you work inside my heart." That is for those in the month of April.

MAY ● Now we move on to May. Goodness gracious, April showers bring May flowers. We've discussed that in the past. For those in May, well, my dear friends, you will feel a little out of sorts. You'll feel that you are cast upon the ocean of life and haven't the foggiest idea what to do with your day, so don't do a thing. Just sit back, kick back, relax and don't try to get anything accomplished, because it's not going to happen, so you might as well enjoy the journey. Simply move with the movement. It's a wonderful opportunity to learn how to dance with life and not control it anymore. Release your control, and then you will find that beautiful flowers are springing up all around you. You will find, my dear friends, insights by the end of this day as you feel that it is May of your life. You will find fantastic opportunities for growth into a deeper conscious awareness of the God who you are and how you create your own reality.

JUNE ● For those of you who are in the month of June, June comes none too soon. Goodness gracious, you have a little bit of panic, anxiety and urgency inside yourself. Would you please find it and ask yourself what it is you are so excited about, because that's really the flip side of anxiety or panic. Simply feel inside yourself what you are feeling excited about. If you're excited about it, then don't be so afraid to jump in. Get busy with your projects and work. Call the person you want to call and ask him or her for a date, even if it's your husband or your wife. Take a walk in the park. Do something that normally you would be a little afraid to do but are also excited about. Wear a shirt of a different design, dress up or dress down. It doesn't matter. Just do something to shake yourself up a little bit and shake loose from your boring space. This is a wonderful opportunity for those of you who feel that you are in the month of June.

JULY As for those in July, goodness gracious, you are strong, independent and virile, even if you are a female—it doesn't matter; you have a male side to yourself as well. You can laugh now. We love your laughter, my dear friends, but understand that those of you who are feeling July feel very self-assured and confident, ready to stand and fight for what you believe in. That is a beautiful place to be. It doesn't mean that you have such anger that you are attacking the world, but rather that you are confident and assured. You feel very independent in your expression and want to be heard. You want to be acknowledged by the world, but you are not going to push for it today. You are simply going to be very direct. That's where your soul is right now for those of you feeling the month of July, which brings us back to the month of August, a palette for your soul, a canvas upon which it can expressed.

This canvas is of your own design today. It does not matter what that is. Let it run its wild course through a mysterious sense of yourself, not knowing which end is up or down, and it doesn't really matter anyway. You'll have a good time, no matter what. Surrendering to the journey is what August is about.

Your Season Is Your Choice: Don't Hold Back!

We would ask that you just sit whenever you feel uncertain, close your eyes and ponder what month and season you are in at that moment. This will provide you with profound insights about yourself. You are not beholden to our explanations of each month and each season, but then again, we're pretty good at what we share with you. But you can transform and change it. Your months will begin to take on new meaning as you focus upon yourself in this fashion and upon your soul's journey, asking yourself when you wake up in the morning, "What month am I today?" See how it goes. Use our suggestions here, and then, if something alters the course, don't be concerned. It is simply your soul's desire to change and play. It's a wonderful indication that you are growing at all times.

Remember, my dear friends, God's way of loving you is allowing you to change. God's way of acknowledging you is to acknowledge that you have desires that exceed those that are pushed and pressured upon you by the planet Earth and by the human beings in your life. You have a very special nature to yourselves, a very beautiful expression that we encourage you to step forth with as you understand and embrace at long last the many layers to the onion, the many seasons of your soul. God bless you indeed. Step forth into life. Give of your purest expression, for you are indeed the eyes, ears, voice and the healing heart of God. My dear friends, don't hold God back. Allow God to be expressed through you and forever be transformed.

Go your way in peace, love and harmony, for life is indeed a joy. All you have to do to enjoy the journey to your own hearts and enlightenment is to lighten up just a little bit more and enjoy the journey. God bless you, indeed.

You Wear a Coat of Many Colors

You have come to the school called planet Earth to discover and dissolve the illusions of separation within self and between life. Certainly it is your labor of love to diminish these illusions, wherein you will discover that never in the experience of your eternal soul have you been the victim; you are always the creator—beautiful creators, each and every one a student of the divine! Certainly you are courageous students upon the planet Earth, for after all, within your being, you made a decision, a determination, to come to the beautiful blue orb of Earth from the heavens, where each of you was born from the stars.

Fathom that, my dear friends. Born from the stars? Yes! That is where you originated, and it is this spark of light (which you see in the sky every evening) that you call home—the bosom, the womb, shall we say, of God from which you were born in a beautiful spark of light. Energy is what you are made of. That is your resource, for all knowledge is certainly intertwined. You are part of the fabric of eternity. Whether or not you remember is up to you. You came to planet Earth with determination that you would be educated once again in the awareness that indeed you are God and are never separate from the very same.

You Came to Earth as a Form of Rebellion

Well, then you might ask yourselves, "Goodness gracious! If I am God, why do I forget it all the time?" Well, because you come to the school called planet Earth as, shall we say, a form of rebellion against God—in very much the same way as a teenager rebels against his or her parents, not wanting to believe that he or she came from such a family. Realize, once again, that teenagers grow up and understand that it was just a mere moment, a period of time in life when they felt very separate and that they would never grow up. But understand this as well: When you rebel is when you find within your heart that you do not want to be separate anymore and that the only way to come back into the arms of the ever-loving heart of God is through the awareness that you are love.

That is why you are here upon the planet Earth! Cherish the opportunity in every moment of every single day to explore your relationship with love. That is what God is. God is love. And what is love? Love is God! Love is the mind, body and spirit of God. You have a mind, a body and a spirit, and therefore you are God as well. Are you a personality or are you simply eternal wisdom? Well, that's what you're here upon the planet Earth to find out! You are indeed eternal wisdom.

All the answers you seek are not within the pages of a book; they are within your heart. Certainly we can bring them to the surface and put words to them, but understand that every answer is simply a frequency that you seek inside your divine self. The frequency of understanding feels like love. Understanding brings about healing. And what are you seeking through every question that you ask us? Healing of your eternally broken heart, as it feels to you. You will find once again that you were never in a state of disrepair. You have always been whole! It's an illusion of separation that you are anything but. Certainly, the many rather than the few come to planet Earth to understand divinity of self. Divinity, my dear friends: the understanding that you are indeed born from the stars, from the heavens, and that you, indeed, are one and the same as God eternal.

Healing Power Is Derived from the Stars

Do we derive healing power from sitting under the stars?

You certainly can. As you are very much aware, you have had many opportunities where you have sat underneath the stars and found that you connect and relate to them. They actually talk to you, is that not accurate?

Yes.

Well, my dear, why? Because every star in the heavens has a consciousness. Sitting under the stars in the evening, as you stare into each face of the heavens, you find yourself being moved—closer to, farther away from—understanding the dimensionality, if you will, of yourself. You are moving into truly understanding that you are really looking at yourself from the inside out. Look into the faces of the stars, and suddenly you see yourself in a very beautiful dimension that has, as you see it, no end—no measurable breadth or depth. That, my dear friends, is you.

When you understand this, you will find tremendous healing within your heart through understanding that you are not limited. You are not a finite being; you are indeed infinite! And when you understand that you are infinite, then no longer will you find a need to shut yourself down emotionally, spiritually or physically; no longer will you feel concerned that there would ever be barriers between you and anyone else or that you would ever be in ill health and so on. Once again, these are illusions of separation; ill health, for example, comes from a belief in limitations.

So as you look at the stars in the heavens in the evening, you find within yourself infinite possibilities. As we have said many times, there are as many perspectives in the universe as there are stars in the heavens. Try counting them sometime. You'll be rather surprised at how difficult it can be. But also you realize that as you count the stars in the heavens, there is indeed a relationship inside of yourself. That light, the energy of the stars, is you, my dear friends. This is what you are made of—the very same stuff! It's your light emanating down upon the Earth, much as the light from the stars emanates into the heavens. You project yourself to the Earth into a wee little body. This is just the teensy, tiny semblance of who you really are. You are grand and glorious operators, shall we say, of the universe, striving to understand once again the lover who you are.

And so yes, my dear, in answer to your question, certainly yes. You and the stars in the heavens are one and the same. Certainly healing can come if you are willing to surrender there. That, for some, will not be easy. To sit out under the stars in the evening brings about a lot of fear, goodness gracious. The mistake is inside your consciousness that you should ever be afraid of the dark.

The Fear of Looking into the Unknown

Well, my dear friends, the dark is frightening, and we understand it, because it symbolizes the unknown inside yourself. But if you can shift your awareness there and understand that this is an opportunity for you to celebrate the unknown—how exciting to realize that there are undiscovered universes and solar systems inside you! Suddenly you will find freedom beyond your wildest dreams and imaginations. Feel the stress begin to dissolve inside your body at the possibilities. Suddenly you no longer have to fight. No longer do you have to hold yourself back, to restrain yourself, to not speak your truth to the world, but rather you begin to celebrate that you have all kinds of awarenesses and understandings that you want to share. You will find undiscovered territories inside yourself, and it will be frightening to share them with the rest of the world, because you say, "Well, goodness gracious, Dr. Peebles, they won't understand! They will think I am absolutely crazy! I'm crackers here!"

But my dear friends, we would offer this to you: Every time you are willing to share your light with the world, you bring about not only healing for your own ever-loving soul but for planet Earth itself. For, my dear friends, the human beings around you might not understand your perspective, because they have not yet explored it. It is a foreign country to them. That's all. It's not a matter of judgment against you but rather that the very same fears reside inside others regarding sharing their own greater truth and awareness. They have the very same fear of looking into the unknown and discovering more and more of the beautiful, infinite beings they are.

It is here where you get scared, because you suddenly come to the realization that you are indeed God. No longer can you fall into the feeling that you are a victim here upon planet Earth, but instead you realize that you are the great creator of everything that occurs in your reality. You create through every thought, every movement and every perspective that you choose to bring to life here upon the Earth. You, my dear friends, are in charge of your reality. And that is just the tip of the iceberg . . .

The Coat of Many Colors

Where you are, you wear the coat of many colors, and you speak of that all the time. Would you comment and explain a bit more about the frequencies and what the colors actually do?

First and foremost, my dear, I wear a coat of many colors—but so do you! Look around you. Look at everything within the room. Look into the eyes of a neighbor and into the color of the eyeball itself. Within the eyeball, you will see a vast array of colors. What you think is only green or blue has many hues. So you wear a coat of many colors too.

The colors are really perspectives of God, spectrums of light that can be found within your rainbow. Look into your rainbow, for example, and there you have an understanding of what you are really seeing. If you would have a symbol of God, look to the rainbows in your heavens. It is an illusion to think that the colors are separate. They are all from one band of light—from white light at that! But you can paint with different aspects of this light. Do you have any colors that would be of particular fascination to you? If you ask yourself this question, you could find a tremendous opportunity to discover who you really are.

PURPLE ● For example, if you have a fascination with the color purple, you might find that you are seeking wisdom and understanding here upon the planet Earth. Oftentimes those who are fascinated with purple are seeking acknowledgment—acknowledgment from God, for example, as a spirit outside oneself. That is often the way in which God is seen by those who are fascinated by the color of purple, and it is within this color that you can work to bring God into your body so that you can, at long last, reunite and understand that you are indeed one and the same, not separate from God. It is there that you find your healing.

ROSE RED ● Then there are those who are fascinated by the color red, but this is a little bit of a tough one here, because what kind of red fascinates you? Would it be ruby red or the red of a rose? Many who are fascinated with the very bright red of a rose are working to heal a broken heart from the distant past, often even from the current lifetime. There could be many pains and thorns along the path for such people and much learning necessary to heal from the broken heart by once again reuniting with God, realizing that you are neither separate from nor the victim of anything.

RUBY RED ● Ruby red would be for those of you who are experiencing a desire to know the divinity of yourself as the mystic who you are. The ruby red would be for those who find that their guidance is to seek an understanding of the mystic inside of self. You can use ruby red, for example, to heighten the sense of mysticism and psychic capabilities. To visualize ruby red at the center of the forehead, for example, brings you into an intoxicating state whereby you could begin to hear spirits—this being, again, the tip of the iceberg.

YELLOW ● Yellow is a beautiful color! You can't grasp it. You can't hold on to it. You can't do anything with it except create beautiful arrangements of flowers. Yellow is for those who are here upon the Earth to seek serenity and the understanding that no longer do you have to have hope here upon planet Earth but that, truly, peace abides. Peace is the reality of your self. Those who are fascinated by the color of yellow are here to study serenity.

GREEN ● For those who are fascinated by the color green, God bless your ever-loving souls, for your life has been a very turbulent walk/journey down a street of darkness, pain and difficulty, oftentimes in terms of emotions, spiritual seeking and understanding the relationship between your spirit and your physical body. Oftentimes it's a journey, shall we say, into understanding the wonder of healing and how it can occur inside you. Those who are lovers of green try so very hard to reunite everything—mind, body and spirit—as one. Trying to find the common thread is a very difficult journey for many of you who love the color of green.

And yet you are very courageous adventurers. For those who are willing, you will come out on top at the end, so understand that green is also a symbol of the release from the pain, that green also has tremendous healing properties. It is here where you begin to realize, toward the end of your journey upon the Earth, that life really has just been a lovely barefoot walk through grass. It is in the meditation with green that this color becomes your healer. Imagine yourself walking naked through the grass. Allow yourself to unite with all the elements—sunlight, dew, the Earth, warmth from the Sun's rays, the wind through your hair as it caresses your beautiful skin as you walk.

BLUE 🍎 For those who study blue, we're not going to give you even a hint here. You already have an understanding that exceeds the need to read books or study. You simply luxuriate in your existence upon the Earth. Once again, this is just the beginning.

ORANGE 🍎 For those who study orange, know that this is a fantastic and very difficult color. The many rather than the few often have a resistance to the color of orange, and it is no accident that you must constantly bring orange into your body, replenishing your stocks of vitamin C, which would come from the fruit of the orange. There is a reason for it—orange is very elusive. You can't grasp it, you can't hold on to it and you can't put it in a box. It won't stay. It has properties very much like your vitamin C. You use it up very rapidly inside yourself.

Vitamin C and the color orange would be descriptive of your relationship with God. The energy of God-spirit—that which you seek at all times—is something that you think you've got, then it slips away and becomes something else. So it keeps you seeking life eternal, seeking to understand your relationship with God as spirit, an energy that resides inside your solar plexus (that being the point of birth). And so you can work with the color orange by bringing it into your solar plexus. You can visualize an orange if you like and place it there, then allow it to become very bright, a beautiful orange orb. You will be surprised as it begins to radiate light, because it becomes the color of the many rather than the few. It becomes the coat of many colors.

Orange is a very beautiful color for you to work with as you understand and study the divinity of yourselves. Fall in love with the wonder of orange, and you have once again embraced God back into your hearts. Again, that is merely the beginning.

BLACK AND WHITE 🍎 My dear, I could tell you that my coat of many colors is black and white. How do you like them apples? No shades of gray! Why would my coat of many colors be black and white? Because black is not the absence of color; it is the density of them, is it not? And as well, white would have the very same properties, would it not? Once again look into your rainbow. There you can find and touch the face of God, but the only way to find and touch the face of God is with your heart. You try to walk toward the rainbow, and it moves a little farther away— it's going to tease you along, keep you moving, keep you journeying, keep you adventuring.

You say, "Well, I don't know if I should go over here. I might fall down the hill!" Well, the rainbow is not going to steer you wrong, nor is God ever going to cause you to fall down and scrape your knees, not ever. God wants you to find your fascination and to fall in love with it. And that, my dear friends, is to fall in love with God, the God who you are: the Creator, adventurer, discoverer, journeyman and journeywoman here upon planet Earth. What a fantastic school you have, yes?

The Difference between Angelic and Mortal Wisdom

What is the difference between angelic and mortal wisdom?

What is the difference between—what do you call it? Angelic and what?

Mortal.

. . . and what?

I give up.

Angelic and mortal wisdom. There is no difference. Within every human being, there is certainly angelic wisdom. Sometimes it's locked away. Sometimes you do not want to look at it, because you are so busy being hurt, tired and afraid. You are so busy with your worry that you don't even have the chance or opportunity to see yourself as the angel who you are. You contain angelic wisdom: It's right there inside your heart.

In a moment of uncertainty, stop, breathe and ask yourself, "What am I really seeking here? What is it that I really want to gain? Is it money? A home? A lover? A friend?" My dear friends, there is one thing that you seek at every opportunity, and that is love. That is angelic wisdom, and it is certainly contained within your mortal heart.

Mortal wisdom, my dear? Hmm. Is there such a thing? Mortal for us is . . . well, we see words all around "mortal": "Scared." "Believing in death." "No eternity." "Hate." "Nothing left to be discovered." "Hopelessness." "Restlessness." "Anxiety." "Tension." "Stress." That is what we see. That is "mortal wisdom," really—the wisdom of that which does not exist, which is an illusion, which keeps you from the angelic wisdom you are, that which is God. Black and white again, yes? Not one better than the other.

All those regrets will go away if we get rid of the mortal wisdom.

Precisely. What foundation is love built upon, my dear? The foundation of hate and vice versa. Out of hate always, *always,* is born love. You can hold on to hate as long as you like—lifetime after lifetime, year after year, day after day, minute by minute. "I am angry, and I hate you." But, my dear friends, you are not strong enough to hold back love. You can try, but at long last, love will win. That is what truly wants to surface from your heart. Hate will always turn to love, be it after centuries or after lifetimes upon the planet Earth. It is a labor of love to diminish and dissolve the illusions of separation within self and between life. The only way in which you can do this is by understanding the lover who you are—you are all beautiful lovers here upon the planet Earth. Whether you admit it or not, we think you're all pretty cute.

A Discussion of Judgment and Discernment

Would you comment for us on discernment and judgment?

First and foremost, they don't exist, but all right. Because of the fact that you are upon the planet Earth to discover and dissolve the illusions of separation, first and foremost you must separate everything. So it's all right to see yourself as separate from another, to see your mind as being different from someone else's. It's even all right to judge people and life around you, if you like.

Just as we have shared that hate is the foundation from which love is born, it is very much the same with judgment. You judge, condemn, minimize and try to turn things into something other than God. Over time you find that the judgment doesn't hurt anyone but you. Judgment builds inside self as a sense of shame. "Goodness gracious, I should not have laughed at the person on the street who did not have legs." "I should not have killed the man who loved other men." "I should not have condemned the church." "I should not have judged the weak." "I should not have put Saddam Hussein to death." "I should not have done a lot of things!" Eventually, through judgment, you will come back to a space of absolute love.

Discernment? Well, it's a little different than judgment. Discernment is simply decision, a matter of being very, very clear within your heart that right now you would rather have the grape than the apple. The apple doesn't care if you want the grape; it's just a matter of decision. You will find that when someone offers you two opportunities, you are human enough that you try to please everyone, and so you often do not move with your heart. This causes pain, anguish, anger and judgment. "Why do we have to go to the opera rather than to the movies? I hate the opera." Well, you really don't hate the opera. What you are angry about is the fact that you did not allow yourself the natural movement of your heart, which wanted to say, "I don't want to go to the opera. I want to go to the movies."

That is discernment. Being discerning is simply being in right order with yourself. You give to yourself through loving allowance for all things to be as they are, but you start with yourself first and foremost. Then you are giving to the world the truth of yourself. "I would prefer to go to the movies." "But, my dear, I would rather go to the opera." "Well, all right then," the truth of self says to you, "I can endure the opera and perhaps even enjoy it, because I love you." And there you find that movement becomes easier, less pressured and less filled with judgment, through discernment.

Lighten Up and Realize That You Are Love

What do you think of our questions, Dr. Peebles?

We see your questions as beautiful gifts unto us, opportunities for exchange between spirit and humankind. We love having the chance to relate to you and to hear how you relate to us. Your questioning often teaches us! As you ask us to explore ourselves, truly we give unto you the truth of us. What we share here is just one perspective in the universe. You can ask Summer the very same questions, for example, and she would give you some very different answers. To us your questions feel like love. It doesn't matter what you ask. We don't care if you ask us to watch you blowing bubbles. We love the opportunity to relate. That is what your questioning means to us. As well, for the curiosity of human beings: Yes, we do pray every night before we go to sleep. We pray, and we pray for you! We pray, my dear friends, that you lighten up just a little bit more and become more excited about your questioning.

So often we hear prayers that ask, "Why do I have so many unanswered questions?" "Why do I have so many questions in my mind?" "Why do I need to know things and figure things out?" Well, you will find that life is indeed a joy and a dance, and you are always going to be a seeker. You will always be looking for greater truth and awareness, and eventually, at long last, you will surrender to the natural movement and rhythms of your hearts.

You are all very beautiful spirits, and we pray always that you can at long last embrace the truth of yourself. Bring it to the surface without fear or shame. If you would only talk to one another about the truth of yourself, you would find that all your problems would disappear. You would suddenly live in an ideal world. You would awaken in the morning and not worry about what color your hair is, how many wrinkles you have around your eyes, whether you should wear this or that. You'd cast off your clothes and run naked through the woods on a fantastic journey to your heart beyond your wildest dreams and imaginations as you begin to dissolve the illusions of separation.

What was "the fall" after all? It was a point in time within each of you as you came to planet Earth when you suddenly felt that you were separate from God. That is when you fell, and that is why you are trying to hoist yourself back up, brush yourself off and move along in your journey. You don't have to stay here on planet Earth lifetime after lifetime. If only you would be willing to laugh a little bit!

Allow yourself to release the expectation that you must do everything right all the time. You are already doing everything right at all times, but it will feel better to you if you allow yourself to move with your natural internal rhythms. Stop hoping to become that which you do not see in the mirror. In the mirror, you are full and perfect as you are, perfectly created through the divine wisdom of God. You are not separate from it. You are not an accident upon the Earth. You are not here to be shamed by anyone for who you are, how you look, how you feel or how you express yourself. You are full and perfect as you are. Celebrate the very same. Love yourselves, my dear friends. Do not grieve for that which you feel you do not have inside of you.

You are everything that you see, hear, taste, touch, feel and smell, and that's the bottom line. That is where you are going in your understanding. Why not go there today? Why not go there right now instead of waiting for tomorrow? Joy begins here, right now, inside your ever-loving soul. Enjoy the journey to your heart.

It's such a tiny challenge, really, to change—a feeling within one given second or nanosecond. Suddenly this little short circuit inside you that's got you in misery and depression all the time is repaired simply by looking into the mirror and realizing that you are love. You are indeed God eternal, so nothing is separate from you.

You all want to create things in your life; you want to have this or that. Is it wrong to want to have a car, a home, a lover or a friend? Not at all! To want physical strength or health? Not at all! It's not wrong to want any of this, but you can't have it until you realize that you already *are* it. Then you find that suddenly you are in a world where everything instantly manifests around you. Suddenly you can truly—and we mean this quite literally—shape shift yourself. You can completely change your physicality by realizing, once again, that your energy comes from the stars. And this energy is pure; it is the pure, beautiful, radiant light of love, and you can bring yourself into that understanding. You can manifest anything you like! No longer do you have to color your hair, for example. You just think of what you would like upon your head, and there it grows. You can be a bushel of daisies, if you like. It doesn't matter—it's all an illusion of separation that things must be thus and so.

Oh, how much would the scientists love to take our little heart and rip it out right now! They love to keep everything in a box. But we assure you, science will be around for a very, very long time trying to put everything in a box, and yet there will always be more to discover, because it can't ever be put into a box. Life is eternal, a dance. God is ever growing and ever seeking. And again, this is the tip of the iceberg, but certainly, if you are God, then you are everything that you see, hear, taste, touch, feel and smell. You are even the cars and the homes and the lovers you seek. Everything, bottom line, belongs to God, does it not? Then there is nothing to seek, because you are that. Simply allow the gifts to come rolling into your life. They're here right now, even in listening to our words—the greatest gift being, my dear friends, love. The rest is, well, cherry on the cheesecake, yes?

How Animals Relate to Their Own Death Transition

Would you comment on behalf of our animals as far as making their transition and all they experience as a part of that experience? They really don't need to be put to sleep, do they?

Absolutely not, my dear. You would no sooner put a human being to sleep because he is in pain. You would call that murder. From our perspective, from the realm where we exist, it is a very sad sight indeed to watch as you put your animals to sleep. Now, this doesn't mean that you must start weeping once you've put an animal to sleep or think, "What a murderer I am!" or any such thing. We are not here to instill shame or guilt, only to enlighten you that there is an opportunity for growth here.

Animals are not concerned about the end of anything. They do not think in terms of, "Am I going to die?" and "Where am I going to be afterward?" Animals do not strain against the pain. They simply allow for it. Do animals feel pain? Absolutely! It is the way in which they respond to it inside themselves, however, that is very different from human beings. Animals don't try to understand pain. Otherwise, they'd all become doctors! Rather, they surrender to the journey and find the process of transition a very interesting experience.

In terms of your domesticated animals—pets, shall we say, those who you call your beloved friends—they are your healers. Like the little angels they are, they like to come to planet Earth and take pain away from you. To allow your animal to have its own process of death would show you that they are really doing a spiritual housecleaning for you. They take frequencies away from you that are not for your highest good by drawing them into their own bodies. Animals are sponges for the pain and ills around you.

As for your emotions, they feel every one—your lack of trust and your insanity. They feel everything that you feel inside, and they work very hard to take away the pain, because they love you so very much as your eternal companions. That is why, oftentimes, animals are born into families where they are beaten. They allow themselves to be the whipping boy, shall we say, for human anger and anguish. They offer themselves up with great trust, because they love their masters so much that they are willing to be tortured or put to death in a rather horrible fashion because of their love.

So the next time you consider the possibility of putting your animal to sleep, can you instead focus upon the chance or opportunity to love your animal to the other side the same way you would hold the hand of a family member as he or she passes away? If you like, give them something for the pain and then allow them the dignity to die in their sleep—or even in a struggle or a fit. That's the tip of the iceberg.

Dealing with the Death of a Loved One

How does one deal with the death of a loved one?

How does one deal with the death of a loved one . . . Well, which person are you talking about? When we look here, we see millions. Some deal with it just fine, glad to get rid of Granny once and for all, you see? When someone dies upon the Earth, there is a great moaning of sadness from family members and friends and others. Well, hallelujah for them. They certainly did a wonderful job upon the Earth of being greatly loved, is that not accurate? Well, yes, it is! And so, when you are grieving for someone you love very much who has passed, understand that your sadness and tears show that you care. How very beautiful! What a wonderful testimony to the love of that person upon the Earth. Give prayers of thanks to your loved one for having had such a profound effect upon the Earth. His or her job is quite complete if he or she has affected so many in that fashion.

Now, we understand that there are indeed some situations where human beings will take their own lives, and that is very difficult for the family members who are left behind, for there are oftentimes unresolved issues between you. But, my dear friends, all that we can say to you is that you will have a chance once again to talk to the dearly departed. You will find yourself on the other side one day, reaching out to each of them and resolving your issues together. You will find that you will come back together as one. But upon the Earth, remember there is a relationship between life and death. There are no accidents.

Well yes, human beings occasionally miss a step and fall down and bump their heads and unexpectedly leave their bodies—they had not planned it as such, but it can happen. But even that is not necessarily an accident. The way in which someone dies is an accent mark upon that person's life. There is profound meaning to the way in which a human being chooses to exit this lifetime. Realize that it creates a resonance upon the Earth by which you can continue to grow.

So when a family member takes his or her own life, it gives you an opportunity to turn around inside yourself and say, "Goodness gracious! Perhaps I should have appreciated that person more." Well, perhaps you should have, and how very lovely that you discovered it! How lovely that you have a chance now to understand greater appreciation of life around you. Now you can enact it. To act upon your new understanding in this life is the greatest testimony you can give to the person who has passed from the Earth.

You want to rectify situations with loved ones who are upon the other side. "Daddy, I wish I had said I love you more often." Well, my dear friends, take that knowledge and wisdom and bring it to life here upon the planet Earth. Tell Daddy you love him. He's still there in spirit, but tell your neighbors, children, friends, pets, plants and yourself that you love them too. Take the chance to take these moments of sadness or points of awareness and turn them into opportunities for growth, for that is your point and purpose here upon the planet Earth.

There are often many children who have passed from the Earth who deliberately incarnated so that they could draw a family of souls closer together. For those of you who have lost a dear child within a family, realize, my dear friends, the great gift they have given to you. If there are areas in your life where there are still ripples of distrust or disrespect between family members, work within your ever-loving soul to bring the family back together. Make the apologies, have the telephone conversations and exchange the love as a testimony to the great love of the child who existed upon the Earth to help an entire family of souls celebrate love once again. And so it goes. There are so many variations, shall we say, upon this question, that we do not have time here.

How It Feels to Speak through a Channel

What sensation or feeling do you experience when you come through our channel, Summer?

It's like dipping my hand in a bucket of warm water. It's absolutely lovely. What a beautiful question! I have the most exhilarating experience. I am in a form of trance where I exist, and the dear little channel goes into a trance herself. For me, where I am as a being—and I do have a sense of my own physicality and the largeness of myself—there are actually eleven other spirits around me who hold my physicality, embrace it, shall we say, very much in the way (and this might sound silly) as you would see a hypnotist levitate a being off the ground.

My body lies in a prone position, and I am being held by these eleven very beautiful spirits who are essentially having contact with me—and we'll put it in human terms—in the same way as you lay hands on an individual. These eleven are, as well, receivers of messages from spirits on what you call "the other side"; these spirits are family members and loved ones. There is one in particular who is working within the region of, shall we say, the akashic records. There is another who is simply working to keep me in a state of suspension. Very much as I would be breathing for Summer, they are breathing for me. It is a form of trance, but for me it's a fantastic experience. It's like having my hand in a bucket of warm water. It feels beautiful. It's very orgasmic, I must admit.

But these researchers around are bringing in an enormous amount of information at one time, and it is through me that it is, shall we say, distilled into the essence that can come through Summer. It really is quite perfect. You can't imagine the ocean of spirits around in the din. Goodness gracious, you think that heaven is quiet? It's not at all, we assure you. To be immersed in life as we are is absolute paradise. It truly is. It's not a place of absence of anything. It is a place where everything is interacting and playing at all times. It is a constant dance. Everything exists where I am—all feelings, emotions, everything, all at one time. It's just a matter of where we choose to put our attention, which is always on love.

We have a few spirits who throw temper tantrums, very much as we started at the outset to share with you that you come to planet Earth like a rebellious teenager fighting Daddy or God. They come down to planet Earth, throw a temper tantrum and say, "You don't love me! You don't like me! You are not me! How could you possibly say that? You are a terrible daddy!" We have spirits around us in this very same capacity. "Ah, Dr. Peebles, you're a terrible, terrible being. I can't stand you! You don't love me. You don't give me enough attention. You never talked to me when I was on Earth. Why didn't you do this for me?" And I just say, "I love you. You're so cute. You're so lovely." We have our little discussions, and we work out our little . . . what you would call problems. We consider those to be fun interactions, you see? They are opportunities for more light—to create more light, shall we say, in the universe.

You are experiencing a lot more sunlight these days on your planet Earth, are you not? You blame it upon your ozone or on all kinds of things, as if the sunlight was something bad. Eventually, your planet Earth will disintegrate, because you will have brought so much light to the Earth through yourselves and through compassion, love, caring, gentleness and kindness. Planet Earth will simply dissolve and become love once again—light. It's not your sunshine that is causing any problems as far as we are concerned. How do you like them apples? That will scare your scientists right away.

Dr. Peebles' Favorite Food and Drink

What are some of your favorite foods and drinks?

When I was upon the Earth, I had quite a few. Now I am not really one who seeks sustenance for any need of it. What I really would rather do is share essences and the sensation of eating. For us, eating doesn't have anything to do with whether you get fat or thin or need to eat an orange to stay alive. It's more of an ongoing process of nurturing oneself.

For example, you have a scent to you. You smell like a very beautiful flower to me. I love the frequency you have in my presence, and as I sit here with you, I simply allow that into me. It's very nurturing. That is a form of what we could call "eating" where I exist. You smell like cinnamon to us and very much have that kind of an effect upon us. We just want to relax, kick up our feet and have cookies and milk and such. You're exotic, my dear. You have a mixture of curry and turmeric and many different spices—a little chili powder in there as well.

But upon the Earth, I actually enjoyed . . . I liked potatoes quite a bit, and I enjoyed every once in a while . . . perhaps once a week, I allowed myself just a little bit of chicken, because I did like chicken a lot. But it always made me feel a little sad that I would eat a bird. I didn't want it to ruffle my feathers either, so therefore I just surrendered to it, allowed myself my journey into the flesh of the chicken and have fun with it. My palate liked very much a mixture of exotic foods, but one of my very favorites was curry made with chicken and fruit. There were also lots of whole grains. I didn't particularly like them, but I knew of their benefits and properties. One of my favorites was simply a mixture of barley and a little bit of what you would call your tamari sauce, plus a little olive oil and a squeeze of lemon. I could gobble that up all day long, especially if you added a little spinach to it and some broccoli flowers. (They are good for you, but I didn't much care for them.) And apples, yes, certainly an apple a day did not keep this doctor away from anyone, because I was always reaching out to give hugs and kisses (though not always in integrity, I'm afraid to say). That's the greatest healer of all. But I loved apples very much. I cared a little too much about sweets as well, but it's all right; it's no problem for me to take in the sweetness of life!

What is the meaning of Thanksgiving?

What a beautiful question! Certainly every day is Thanksgiving. It is an opportunity in every moment of every day to give thanks for what you receive from God. Certainly, sit every once in a while throughout your day. Simply pause, close your eyes, relax, breathe and find something to be thankful for: the chair underneath your fanny, your tummy full of food, the color of light in the room, the shadows on the wall, the feeling of your feet upon the floor—the fact that you even have feet, my dear friends . . . if you do not, then be thankful for having a body at all. Having the opportunity to step upon the planet Earth is something to be very grateful and thankful for.

Don't hold life at arm's length. Make every moment of every single day an opportunity to give thanks to the God who you are. Understand and give thanks for everything, for it is all you. Giving unto life is to give your love from within. Give thanks, and you give love at the same time. God bless you, indeed.

A Collection of Wisdom

As you strive to understand your walk here upon planet Earth, my dear friends, you will also understand that there will be a weakening inside of everyone upon the Earth. God bless you indeed. Certainly that causes immediate panic and fear. "A weakening—that means we are no longer strong, Dr. Peebles?" My dear friends, there is a weakening here upon the planet Earth, a weakening of a desire here to be in control, in charge of everything. There is a point here of surrender, at long last, to the greater love that you are and a willingness of expressing the very same. Instead, my dear friends, of sitting back at arm's length from the world, you all—every single, solitary person here in this room and beyond—will be reaching out in a greater state of harmony.

The Future of Planet Earth

We have discussed this with some of you in the past. Planet Earth certainly is moving its vibration into a much higher frequency at this time, and the many rather than the few will choose to leave. They are not ready to move into this vibration, and the many who choose to stay are going to have a glorious adventure here upon planet Earth for the next twenty years. With greater clarity, there is going to be a point and purpose here of reaching out with your hands in terms of healing—certainly healing physical bodies but healing hearts first.

You will find that, in time, that which has served you in the past in terms of a desire here to control will turn to a desire, a wish, to dream once again, to fall in love with the lover who you are. That corresponds to the frequency of the very same. When you begin to understand the realm of experience of love and the dance here, the joyous dance with your guides and with God, within your consciousness, the awareness here of the imagination, you will find that no longer upon the planet Earth will you fear, but embrace the very same. It will be in a very different way this time around. God bless you indeed.

Imagination, my dear friends, is certainly a key and principal word for the future of planet Earth. You will find that creativity is going to reemerge upon the Earth in a way that you never dreamed or imagined. Certainly there will be a return back to a time when there were such things here as paintbrushes, and they were valued as much as your automobiles. It's going to be a badge of honor to carry one in your pocket, because it is going to show that you are one of the brave ones who are willing to make paper flowers. God bless you indeed, upon the planet Earth.

You understand, my dear friends, that it is a time here wherein Mother Earth herself is removing from herself the toxicity of life of existence. So you understand that part and parcel of the movement here is certainly going to be a movement of her body parts, through various explosions once again. We have discussed this as well. The Earth changes once again, magnifying and certainly becoming a much richer experience, because human beings are now going to be questioning, wondering why it is occurring. It will certainly be drawing humanity closer together in a higher state of compassion. God bless you indeed, my dear friends.

We would ask here that you celebrate yourselves during the course of this journey. Trust yourselves first and foremost, because it is there that you open a doorway for our expression through you. When you trust inside first, you have contact with your heart; and when you have contact with your heart, my dear friends, the illusions of separation begin to dissolve. You are no longer separate from anyone or anything—not from your guides; not from the angels (yes indeed, they do exist); not from the little creepy crawlers, the goblins upon the planet Earth. God bless you indeed. That's a wonderful point of imagination for you, my dear friends. Enjoy the journey.

Would you understand? Walk into the fire of your soul, where you find freedom beyond your wildest dreams and imaginations. It's an entire merging with your heart essentially, where you can no longer escape you. Sometimes, in your questioning, you ask us to save you from yourself, and that's the very last thing we're going to do. We're just going to scare you right back to your heart.

Focus on the Experience, Not the Outcome

The thing that will help the most is a different understanding of the animals. There is not the same experience of pain. Everyone on planet Earth is in such a rush to dispose of these wee children of the Earth because there is a little pain here, a little toxicity there. Not one of you here would want to have that experience for yourself, so we would encourage you to allow this puppy dog to run his course in his process of death. For it is there that he finds his greatest awakening, his greatest understanding. It is a very different experience, as we share once again, of pain. It is not experienced as all of you would experience it; it is simply something that he is doing. He doesn't see it in relationship to yesterday, when he didn't feel pain. Allow him to surrender to the process of death with the certainty of knowing that he will find what he set out to discover here upon the Earth. Do not have fear touching any animal that is in distress as if the animal fears in his process of transition. Focus on the experience, not the outcome.

Sometimes you have judgments of humanity, considered absolutely normal here on planet Earth. That's all right as far as we are concerned. God still loves you anyway. If you don't explore the judgments that you have of humanity, how are you going to learn? This judgment turns to discernment then as you realize that there was nothing to judge in the first place. You realize that really the harshest judge of all is you against you. You see that anger you have had against yourself.

Work with All Relationships

The science of wonder, wherein you fall in love with all of life, includes putting yourself into the equation of life at the very same time. Remember this, my dear friends; it is very key to all the experiences here in this group within this room today. It is time to put yourself into the equation of life. Remember that you are certainly striving to understand the illusions of separation within self and within life. Within self, my dear friends, you will discover that you have held yourself back, held yourself at arm's length, held yourself away from the magic and wonder of existence. It is time for all here upon planet Earth to make a final decision about a course of action. Are you wanting fulfillment here? Are you wanting enlightenment? Or are you simply wanting to enjoy the journey? God bless you indeed. Once you fall in love with that, then you get all the rest.

Working within the relationships that you already have in your life will attract the companion who you want in your life. Put the emphasis upon all relationships. Remember, my dear friends, when the kitty cat jumps upon your lap and you are discussing how very much you want to have love in your life and you push the kitty cat away, you have just pushed away love. You understand that love, the frequency of the very same, comes in all forms. When a child wants to have your attention and you turn away, you are turning away from love. So understand the relationships. There are the many rather than the few, even with the plants, with the animals, with the insects; there is loving allowance for all things to be in their own time and place, my dear friends—even the creepy crawlers in turn, all bonded together by love.

When can I bring the joy back into my life?

Day after tomorrow. Is that all right? You can bring it in right now, you can channel joy if you like. You do it like this, my dear. First of all, life is aggravating, isn't it? And why can't people be a certain way, why must they always be self-obsessed and why must they be speaking one thing and meaning another all the time? Drives you crazy, yeah?

Yes.

Can't stand it, can you?

No.

And your relationships just seem to always end up like this.

Yes.

And that's too much. So how do you shift your reality there, my dear? You can shift your relationships, God bless you indeed, by first of all studying the three principles.

The Three Principles

First is to make loving allowance for all things to be in their own time and place, starting with yourself. When you do this, my dear, you give yourself loving allowance to feel the way you feel. You have a tendency to beat yourself up, because you feel and you judge and you have biases and opinions and so forth, against the world. And then you feel bad about it. Stop feeling bad. It's all right; it's human nature; it's where you learn, my dear. It's where you learn to discern what feels right and what does not for you—that is all. It's not a matter of right and wrong, good or bad. There is no such thing. There is only decision. So you have loving allowance for yourself and loving allowance for others to simply be self-obsessed. It's all right, but you don't have to play with them.

Second is to increase communication with all of life, and with respect. That comes in terms of the age-old phenomenon here upon the Earth where human beings have a tendency not to be able to say no (and that would be you, you understand) and also the age-old tendency that human beings have of not being able to say yes when it feels good. So deny yourself and give to the world? That is not the formula for enjoyment here—give to yourself so that you can give to the world.

Third is to take responsibility for your life as a creative adventure. This you will discover in the process, because you will find that this is fun. "I can be anything I want, and it's all right. The world can judge me, but I don't care, it doesn't matter. I just am that I am, and my relationships will fall away, and new ones will come in, and I will find joy there." That is the formula as far as we are concerned. To bring yourself to the surface and share it with the world is the greatest gift you can give God, for it is that which is you whom He loves.

Great wisdom comes from being patient. We assure you, some of the greatest inventions, achievements, accomplishments, words and loves have been born out of patience.

Energy Changes and Healing

I have medical concerns that have all turned out to be nothing. I keep having them, and they scare me. I don't know what kind of healing I need—physical, spiritual, mental. It's recurring, and I'm concerned about what's going on now.

All right, first we would say, stop reading. Otherwise you get a thought in your head, and because you don't disagree, you take the vibrational frequency right into your body, truly. All sorts of things can come creepin' up on you that you will reach out with your heart to everyone who has a particular pain and such things.

It is not our habit to put panic into the hearts of humankind. But truly, the reason for all the changes and disturbances inside of human creatures and animal creatures and Earth creatures alike has to do with the greater energy of love that wants to be here on the Earth. You are all being asked to—at long last—assist yourselves up the stairs into your hearts and truly live from there, to express yourselves from there. God bless you indeed.

There is going to be a rather massive shift in the energy of planet Earth. You will find, my dear friends, subtle ways in which you will understand this. You will be attracted to individuals whom you would not have thought attractive in the past. That would be rather amazing for you, yeah? So there is going to be a deeper awareness of true love, and through this there will be healing and light and wonder that come in through the hands of human beings as healers; they will come in through the hearts of doctors, through your governments and in unexpected ways.

There will be a need, a vast need, through the changes in energy usage upon the planet Earth, for political governments to be in cooperation once and for all. This time it is going to be because the masses, the human beings of the Earth, are going to be telling them what to do for once. There are many changes upon the Earth and all very fantastic, and it builds up inside of you, my dear friends. It starts with you right there within your hearts. You have the power to change your reality and the reality of the many. Bring your own resonance to the surface. You all radiate from the very same thing, my dear friends; you are all plugged in to the very same outlet, and that is love.

Visualization and Salvation

Allow yourself the daydreams, my dear. That is not expectation; that is simply falling in love with your imagination—the place of wonder and the playground for Spirit, for us, to come through and talk to you. You will find that as you are trying to visualize one thing, it will change, and that would be our influence there. We can tweak it a little bit for you, yeah? We can make it a clearer vision, and then you will know exactly what you are supposed to do and how you fit into the grand picture of life, yeah. How do you like them apples?

You find that the salvation of your soul that you seek is inside of your heart, my dear friends. It is never outside of you. What you see around you certainly is a reflection of you—a reflection of light, of life, of energy that you create. You spiral it out from your heart, so when you are in a difficult situation, ask yourselves this: "Where did it come from? How did I create this moment in time? Why did I do this at this point in my existence? Is it possible that—rather than stressing and straining against this moment—I can fall in love with life deeper than ever before?" God bless you indeed. Ask yourselves these very simple questions, my dear friends, for it is there that you see a reflection of you in all that is around you. Do fall in love there, no matter what. That is where your urgency to get on with it, to get to the elusive "there" will disappear. Then, at long last, my dear friends, you fall in love as never before—falling in love with yourself first, falling in love with your heart.

Feel Everything

We whisper to everyone here on Earth in different forms. It might surprise you here that you are channeling me all the time, and certainly in ways that you don't even realize. I will show up in various forms within your life, with different names, with different desires, with different frequencies and such. But feel the energy as it courses through your veins. Feel the life, the life force that truly is yours, not just mine. You see, you and I are not separate either. You and your neighbors here are not separate. You are feeling the energy within this room, but once you wake up to that energy that is coursing through you, you will discover things about one another that you never dreamed or imagined were possible. You might turn to your neighbor and take his or her hand, God bless you indeed, at this given moment. You might gaze into someone's eyes here in this room today; look deeply there and feel all the sensations.

It's all right if you feel the attraction, if you feel the pain, if you feel the fear, if you feel the anxiety, if you feel the wonder. It is all right, my dear friends, if you want to turn and run away. Feel everything, and rather than moving away from those feelings, those expressions from your heart, move deeper into these spaces. It is there that you embrace more and more of you back into your heart. It is there—in the face of a stranger, of a friend, of a lover—that suddenly you fall in love with wonder as never before. God bless you indeed. You find yourself there, for indeed you are all seeking the very same thing, which is to touch and be touched. You just managed to do that here in this room today, to touch your neighbor, to gaze into your neighbor's eyes with wonder.

My dear friends, that is certainly part and parcel of the reason why we have asked everyone to join us here today in this room in an expression of love in and of itself. As you do this consciously, every moment, you will elevate the consciousness, the love, the compassion of planet Earth beyond your wildest dreams and imaginations. There is not a single person in this room who does not desire to be a healer, who does not desire anything less than transforming the world. God bless you indeed. What world do you want to transform, my dear friends? The world that extends beyond you here or the one that exists right there within your hearts? You do not have to travel, you do not have write, you do not have to do anything. It is simply through a mere thought, an expression of love, that you have transformed the world around you. We are not too far off the mark, ever.

Honesty and Trust

Why are we sometimes not quite honest?

Part of the reason why you are dishonest at times is fear that you would be rejected by the world. As you are looking to the world to embrace it all back into your heart and to realize that it is all you anyway, you find that the one piece that you are afraid might not be able to fit is simply you. So you use dishonesty, anger, unkind words, dysfunctional behaviors and such things—if you would like to call them that.

You can use psychological disturbances as ways to keep the world at bay and to keep yourself away from the world because of your belief that you are not worthy. So you still struggle with issues of worthiness, of self-worth, that you would not be heard, but it is not something that we feel any need to judge about you; it is just something that is helping you at this time to redirect your energy. The bad feelings that you feel inside, the heavy heart— all of that is a sign that perhaps you are walking down the wrong path for yourself. God bless you indeed, we certainly do not mean that you have ever been off the path but that the focus you are bringing to it lacks value of self. The sadness you feel is that in some way, you have compromised you. Your voice certainly has every right to be heard, so you can, if you like, rectify this. Go back and be honest. Share with another or with yourself that it would be very difficult, that you are terrified of the results, but that you are willing because you want to make yourself strong.

How can I get more in touch with my intuition and to truly trust that?

You are going to get—and you are already in the throes of it here—a lot of tests of this because you want it, you understand? It is rather accelerated at this time, and you are asking yourself in every moment, "Is that my intuition, or is that something else? Is this coming from Spirit, or is it not?" Even in the most minor sense, my dear—for example, when you are walking through a store and you feel that perhaps you should not walk toward a door because you have a sense it will be opening out and would pop you in the nose. So you just stop for a moment and wait to see what happens, and sure enough, the door does open, and you just saved yourself from a pop in the nose.

That really is what your intuition does. It helps to direct you through your life, even in what you would consider to be the most mundane circumstances. God bless you indeed, do you understand this? As you work on these, what you would consider at first to be lesser levels, lesser degrees of strength of intuition, you find that your trusting becomes stronger and stronger still. You begin to understand that you are indeed communicating with the heavens and allowing the heavens to communicate through you. You will feel very smart in this. You will have a great sense of what's going to happen in every given moment, because you have essentially plugged yourself in, do you understand? God bless you indeed.

You're working on it already, my dear. There is not too much else to be done other than to surrender to what you feel in every moment. See what happens and take a chance that perhaps you could be right all the time—100 percent accurate.

Relax and Heal Yourself

I've been having lots of dental problems that don't seem to clear up. Do you have any advice for me?

You can help it by relaxing your jaw and relaxing, with conscious focus, your teeth and your gums. They really are affected by your thoughts as much as any other part of the body would be. These areas need to be relaxed. Many conditions of the mouth are caused by a lot of clenching of the teeth, a lot of concerns and breath holding about the future as well. This creates tightness in certain glands surrounding the area of your teeth and gums, which puts an enormous strain upon the root system. It blocks proper supply of blood, of oxygen, of certain minerals and such things from working their way through.

The very best way to relax your jaw and to help your teeth, and your mouth in general, everything down to the base of your chin, is to fill your mouth with water, preferably distilled. Hold as much as you can in your mouth. At first it will feel uncomfortable, but swish it around your teeth and gums, drop your jaw and relax. You can do this in the bath if you like and afterward simply allow the water to drain and your jaw to drop. Rather than spitting it out, just let it run out of your mouth. When you fill your mouth, make sure you really fill it, all the way back to your jaw.

A Chakra Meditation and the Marriage of East and West

Sit in a chair and feel the force of heaven. Bring that down through your crown chakra, down through your heart, into the abdomen and straight down through your root chakra. And allow that energy to run straight from your root chakra down into Mother Earth herself. Because you are sitting in a chair, it could tend to run through your legs, but instead feel it go down into the Earth. That will be opening up a lot in the area of passion for you.

Practical Practicality

Students of the divine, we want you to realize that the answer to everything is "practically practical." "Practical practicality" is what we are asking you to practice in your life. Certainly, when you are hungry, you eat; when you want to stand, you stand; when you want to sit, you sit. It always helps when you reach out a hand to your neighbor and shake the hand of the one next to you. Look into one another's eyes and see; realize that there is a great beauty there, a great wonder there, because no matter who you are looking at here, that person is you. There is nothing separate; we are one and the same, all certainly riding on the same frequency band of love.

Certainly, my dear friends, we would ask that you become more tolerant of one another, because we want you to be more tolerant of yourselves. Loving yourself is certainly expressed in the way that you interact with the world around you. You step forward to give an embrace, a hug; to wipe away a tear; to give a smile and a generous offer of a dollar from your pocket to uplift the world around you. It does not take very much. Fill your pockets with kisses and with candy and distribute them freely to the many rather than the few to brighten the days, the hearts of your friends, family members and total strangers, even someone you would normally be afraid to touch. My dear friends, when you are afraid to touch certain human beings around you, you may as well look inside of yourselves, inside of your own heart, and find out what it is about you that you are resisting.

To not resist is to live your life without judgment. You realize there is nothing to fix or repair. You realize that you do not have to stand in any particular position or posture here upon the planet Earth, because what the world wants from you, my dear friends, is you—nothing short of that. Ask yourself this question: "Is that enough for me, to be myself?" You struggle and strive to become something different; you struggle and strive to change, but the reality here is that you remain the same forevermore.

And what if you remain the same? Well, you are indeed God, the creator of your reality. You are creators of wonder. It starts with you and not with those around you. You create your joy, your happiness, your heaven here upon Earth. It is right there inside of your heart. Heaven is not a place, my dear friends; heaven is a feeling.

God bless you indeed, my dear friends. We encourage you to no longer stress and strain against yourselves, to be more tolerant of you. That is the essence of practical practicality here upon the planet Earth.

I have an understanding that we all have the God within, but is there a separate God and a God inside all of us?

Not a separate God necessarily, but you would consider it to be a consciousness that is very, very large, of which you are indeed a part. So really there is God being expressed through you. You are an aspect of the very same, and at the very same time, you are everything that God is. But realize there are so very many . . . you can equate it, shall we say, with music or painting. There are many different ways to play the very same notes. There are many ways to place colors on a canvas, and it turns into something else. It shape shifts essentially—color in constant motion. And so that really is the consciousness of God being expressed through you in a unique and very desirable way.

And as we would discuss God here, we would consider God to be "He" in Earth language, because God penetrates. As the male would penetrate the female, God would penetrate the world. And then the movement—the womb, shall we say, where this movement occurs—is female, expressed as the Holy Ghost. The byproduct of this experience of penetration and growth is certainly the Christ within you, and that is expressed through you as you surrender more and more of yourself to the natural rhythms of God as He breathes the breath of life through you. God bless you, indeed.

The Tip of the Iceberg

All of you here in this room today are beautiful creators—and smart cookies too. You are in a period of exorbitant growth upon the planet Earth, and this means that you are all going to be asked to pare down your existence, to understand that the abundance begins within your own heart and to understand that peace is the way upon planet Earth.

The way to discover this is through more turmoil upon your planet Earth, and so we ask each and every one of you here today as the light-workers you are to share that light with the many rather than the few in kindness, in patience and with trust in and respect for one another. But first, start with yourselves in loving allowance for what your heart is saying to you. It is there—in the still, small voice within—that you will understand that you are listening to the heart, soul, mind, body and spirit of God, a living creature who works upon the planet Earth.

Focus on Simplicity

There are many who are learning about discovery—discovery in such a sense that you are now learning to seek outside in the world through expression, through willingness to communicate. This discovery comes from using your own voice; by voicing your opinions, your perspectives; by learning that you *do* count for something here upon the planet Earth, otherwise you would not have been placed upon it. In this discovery, you learn to value the fact that you have been created through the hands of God—the creation of yourself upon the planet Earth—to understand this, to appreciate your special talents and your gifts. To graduate into this consciousness provides clarity, with clarity there is understanding and through understanding there is healing.

So we certainly would ask that you outstretch a hand to a neighbor right here today, that you turn to your friend or your neighbor and say, "Congratulations on choosing to stick around on planet Earth." God bless you indeed. Understand that it is through the watchful eyes of God that you will find your life beginning to turn around in a truly remarkable way. This is because you are going to have so many opportunities to sink deeper into your heart and to express yourself with love. You will have opportunities to turn away from thoughts of shame, of guilt, of fear, of panic, of concern of a stranger in the night.

Turn your thoughts to love, and labor in peace. These are our words for you today, my dear friends. Focus on simplicity first as you enter into the month of March, a time of resurrection. Quietly we ask that you journey through the month of March; quietly we ask that you look inside your heart and ask yourself some simple questions: "How can I love more?" "How can I create more peace upon the planet Earth?" "How can I celebrate God through my existence by being a caring and compassionate and loving and wiser person day by day by day?"

Walk lovingly through March, slowing down just a little bit more, tempering yourselves for the future. For as you face the turbulence upon the planet Earth, the automatic response within the human flesh is to respond with fear, with panic, with depression, with feeling that the world is going insane. But please, as you walk outside, look up into the heavens and see the beautiful stars and planets in the heavens, and understand that there is a much larger force at work. Understand this, and then you can give up and release control, surrender, open and express yourself with vulnerability upon the Earth, no longer hiding yourself away in shame. That's the tip of the iceberg for you today.

🍎　🍎　🍎

On Reincarnation

You are being born every day. You are being born every minute. There is a past life—oh, there goes one now—and so reincarnation brings hope to the spirits upon the Earth. It brings hope that life is without end, that perhaps life never did stop—as our dear channel here has discovered, she was never really born, she always has been. But the birth that we speak of, from the star, is an awareness of self, an exploration there, the weaving of self into the fabric of eternity, becoming more and more aware and deciding to grow now. A little seed that has been in existence but just dormant now decides to grow and to share of self. Reincarnation is simply another tool for expansion. You can incarnate on planet Earth and make a decision to come back later, if you would like. You can come back as many times as you like, even after your enlightenment, if you like, but every time you come here to planet Earth, you are going to be studying and exploring the illusions of separation, the divinity of self. You will always be a student of the divine.

But you don't have to come back. It is just like a university; you don't have to return. You can drop out and never return, but there will always be a little aching, something inside of you, that you didn't get your diploma. So eventually, most spirits do make a decision to return to planet Earth and to finish their courses here. As you come back, you become more refined, you dig a little deeper, you work a little harder and the classes become a little tougher. But it's not necessary to look at past lives, to examine them. Sometimes, for some spirits on the Earth, it is helpful to go back. For some that would be helpful, it would be a tool, it would be something for greater understanding of the present.

But you can also get wrapped up there. You can get wrapped up in examining your past lives and your past experiences here on Earth. There are some experiences that you can't let go of, that you don't grow from or learn from but rather use as points of victimhood here upon the Earth to keep yourself immobile. That is where past lives and experiences can become cumbersome, a problem, and yet it's all right as far as we are concerned, because these ropes, these restraints that you put around yourselves—you're just going to have to resolve them so that you can step forth into life once again.

So there are all kinds of ways in which reincarnation can help and assist. God bless you indeed. You come here to planet Earth through a valley of forgetfulness. You decide what memories you want to bring with you, what you do not, what will serve you here, what will not. And it is there, my dear, that—it's very much like packing your bags—you can bring in the luggage from the past, if you like, but it's not always necessary. For example, you and some of the others involved here have brought forth a past existence for examination to further your exploration here of reincarnation, of life after death, of relationship to God, of relationship with Jesus Christ, of relationship with family and with oneness, so that at long last you can feel whole once again and complete. It is not to get stuck again, not to go back to get stuck in review. It is rather that you are growing and learning from it, you see? You could very simply, very easily, slip into the past with your adventures here and get lost there and not grow in your current reality. And so on and so forth—that is the tip of the iceberg.

The Richness of Self

Here upon this planet Earth, you certainly have many opportunities to express the awareness of the divinity of self. It is in your outer world that you become fully expressed, but it starts on the inside. Students of the divine, where is it that you seek your learning, your education? It is through prayer, through communion with yourself and then, my dear friends, with community. It is by putting yourself out into the world, speaking and expressing from your heart and simply sittin' back and waitin' for the honest echo of you to come a-runnin', either toward you or away from you. That's all right—it certainly is the ebb and flow, if you will, of the tide of self that you are experiencing here in this life.

You are all exploring here upon the planet Earth the richness of yourselves, and you certainly want to fully express the richness of yourselves and to feel it. Richness—in terms of what would feel like heaven—is a feeling, not a place. Here upon the planet Earth, realize that you are exploring the illusions of separation. And how do you explore these illusions of separation? By first acknowledging the separation that exists. It is there that you realize that you seek oneness here upon the planet Earth. You seek security that comes from this oneness, this connection, which would fill with life at all times in each and every moment of each and every day.

But because of the physical form here upon the planet Earth, it is absolutely impossible for you to find yourself feeling this oneness at all times. This is simply by virtue of the fact that you feel that Bev is over there and you are over here. It's all right, because this is part and parcel of the tools for learning how to fully express yourself, learning how to commune with life. How do you do this? Where is it that you find the oneness that exists between yourself and all of life? It comes through a frequency that you derive from God, from the heavens, bringing it down through yourself in the form of what we would call here Holy Spirit, the energy of the Mother, to be fully expressed through your hands just as the Lord Jesus Christ who walked the planet Earth was capable of touching the lives of the many rather than the few in the physical form. It is here that you no longer feel separation, because now you are at one with the heart of humanity as well as with the heart of God, the heart of the Mother, the Holy Spirit, the movement, the frequency, the band of love. God bless you indeed.

This is part and parcel of what we are here to explore with you today: the richness of yourself in relationship to life. There is never anything to fear or distrust if you truly understand that you are indeed love and that this is all that you are here striving to remember, striving to bring to the surface. This, my dear friends, dissolves any illusion of separation. Automatically you feel the connection with life, and yet you can experience life in a form of separation of the physical body, one from the other, communing with community, laughing and dancing and playing and singing. God bless you indeed.

Lead Yourself

How can I be a spiritual leader?

Lead yourself; don't worry about anyone else. When you lead yourself and bring yourself out (your heart, your truest colors) with abandon and freedom, my dear friends, you will find that what you desire is no different than what anyone else desires in this world: to touch and to be touched, to feel less alone, to feel acknowledgment by bringing yourself to the surface with vulnerability.

What the world wants from you is you—you, you and nothing but you—and only you know what that is. You must delve within and be willing to share of your heart. Share your fears! That will break the ice. That will bring about a whole new experience of relationship for you. You do have fears, and there is nothing wrong with that. That makes you absolutely 100 percent bona fide human beings!

Who Is in Charge?

You have said that we are each in charge of and in control of our own selves, our own bodies, our own lives. How about a five-year-old who has cancer? The father insisted that he take total charge of treatment and sent the son to a treatment center where he was subjected to radiation therapy and chemotherapy, which minimized the immune system.

No, my dear friend. It destroys it.

That's what I believe, but I didn't want to be judgmental.

My dear friend, that is not judgmental; that is your truth. You are not saying that the people who are administering this are jerks or such things. That would be judgment. They do not understand the way that you do and that's all right—is it not?

Yes. The treatment did not work, so the father sent the son back for a repeat treatment, and I wonder how that five-year-old boy is in charge of his own life?

First of all, it's quite plain and simple. He made a choice to be here upon the Earth with this particular individual as his daddy. He makes a decision day by day to surrender to this man—there are reasons for this that we are not permitted here to share; it is part of this little one's journey upon the Earth. It is part of something that he wanted as closure with his relationship with Daddy.

Yes, but it's too bad, because he lives in a community that also has the Institute, which uses one's own immune system to fight one's cancer.

Yes, we understand. However, the journey here upon planet Earth is not one whereby everyone will be whole and healed and live happily ever after. You see, my dear friend, growth is the point, and for this little one, there is a soul inside of that little body. There is a desire for a certain and particular adventure; there are needs for closure to past-life relationships or what he considers karma. It is not necessary to come back. It is not necessary to play karma out, but this little one has made a decision here. He stands as an icon of one who really is in charge, because he is very serene, beautiful and practical about what is happening to him. And he is a wonderful teacher, is he not?

Healing Starts with Family

How can I heal the planet?

Start with family. It is very interesting to us that those of you in the world are wondering every day, scratching your heads, wondering how you can heal the planet. You want to help the many rather than the few. You wonder, "What can I do about this? How can I help? What is my purpose? Where is my path?" Then you say, "Excuse me, Charlie, would you leave me alone? I'm thinking!" How many times do you push the kitty cat off your lap? How many times do you not respond to your telephone? How many times do you hold the world at arm's length? And yet you want to heal the world and be there for everyone and do the service of God.

You must start with your family. There is always the greatest learning— within the initial family structure, whether or not you have them with you in physical form, whether or not you can hold them or touch them. They are always there within your hearts. This is the springboard of activity for your life. That's the stage. It is there, within family, that you get your greatest learnings.

Do whatever you feel like with your family. Give love, attention, support, gifts, kindness. Keep it clear, be honest, be direct, do not fear, do not have concerns about hurting anyone. Be yourself! That is the greatest learning of all. To be yourself and to be all right with that is the greatest learning of all. God bless you, indeed.

Bring Love into Your Life and Find a State of Grace

G od bless you. Dr. Peebles here. It is a joy and a blessing when human and Spirit join together in search of greater truth and awareness. God bless you indeed, my dear friends. Beautiful creators are here in this room today, divine spirits, each and every one, my dear friends. You have a guide in the room with you today.

Decisions

U nderstand that there will soon be an acceleration in your life upon the planet Earth, for the entire planet will have some very unexpected experiences. There will be upheavals in terms of Earth changes as well, my dear friends. This will affect your heart, but don't you worry too much. When you try to sleep and you feel palpitations, just get up, have a glass of water, walk around, shake off the feeling and then return to bed. The energy that is upon the Earth right now is large, beautiful and lovely beyond your wildest dreams and imaginings. It is an opportunity, if you will, to hear the voice of God within.

However, if you continue on the present path, which you have followed for the past twenty years, you will find that you suddenly feel you are backsliding in your life. You want to take a step forward, and that is what we encourage, for all of you are beautiful spirits, kind, gentle and genuine. Staying that way will be the test for you, my dear friends. There will be times when everybody will be in despair. We're not doomsday prophets or any such thing, but we want to share with you that planet Earth really needs hope, trust, patience, kindness and tenderness right now. It needs a gentle hand extended, one unto the other.

You are beautiful spirits upon the Earth, striving to have a human experience, but it is very temporary. We want your temporary journey here to be one wherein you are always journeying to your heart, because when you step outside of that, everything becomes boring, upsetting, frustrating and depressing. Goodness gracious, you cannot see the forest for the trees! But we would ask that you remain genuine in your willingness to love the world, no matter what. Love, with patience, a frustrated friend, an angry coworker and even love your life, no matter whether or not you have money to pay the bills or what have you. Everything will be shuffled around a wee bit.

Your Decisions Must Be Born from Love

If you are considering, for example, a great, giant leap, movement in a new direction in your life, we encourage you to please take a deep breath and reevaluate your existence. Know inside your heart before you make this move that it is something that you truly want with all your heart and soul. It should not be something that you are trying on for size or perhaps to have a little change. Just because you feel sick and tired of the same old kitchen and the same old path that you walk to work isn't enough. God bless you indeed, my dear friends, your decisions now must be born from great love. Don't make decisions out of need or despair. Don't try to force change or force yourself to fit the world or vice versa, but rather try to feel inspiration so that you are not so tired.

Sit, relax with your decisions and look deeply within that well of your being and ask, "Is this truly what my God within wants for me?" Then, my dear friends, with no struggle whatsoever, allow for the answer to emerge. You will find a refreshing, different way of making decisions. For some there will be a twinge that says, "Well, perhaps I should not move to Arkansas after all. That was a bit of a rushed decision there." "Hmm, yes. I don't feel very comfortable inside. Every time I think about the journey to the altar, it's not fitting my life. Hmm." Then, my dear friends, you jump off the cliff into trust. That is the toughest part, if you will, of surrender, because you must take a chance when the decision has been made by your soul and allow it to be expressed in the physical world and see what happens. "Let's see here, perhaps I don't want to take that flight to Pennsylvania. Goodness gracious, I really would like to see my mommy, but every time I think about it, it hurts inside, and it's not because I don't want to see her. It doesn't make sense. Perhaps I should change the time? Perhaps, goodness gracious, the plane might fall from the sky!"

And you have once again allowed for God to shine His light within you, because certainly God's love is the constant when there are despair and dark places upon your planet Earth. God is not here to punish you, my dear friends, and He is certainly not here to try to direct you into disaster. God is not here to test you with anything. Rather, you put yourself into the boiler. You make the decisions about where you want to stand. Now we are asking that you stand firmly upon the planet Earth, rooted inside your own truth and expression of God upon the planet. God bless you indeed. That is the tip of the iceberg.

You are beautiful spirits, my dear friends. Plant flowers and trees, love one another, touch one another tenderly and know that you are here to experience love everlasting. <u>Look down at your body right now. It will disappear one of these days, so don't worry about hoisting it up all the time.</u> Instead, my dear friends, enjoy the journey of your body's fullest expression of who you truly are. See beauty there and wonder in the folds, tears and laugh lines around your eyes. Allow yourself to have a little touch of gray at the very least.

Enjoy finding out who you really are and the fullest expression of the very same. You're beautiful spirits, God bless you indeed. When you drop the coat of this human form, what you'll have left is what you create inside yourself. There are no mysteries here. You know who you are, and your relationship with God is one that you develop with every thought, expression, deed and act. If you want gentleness, express it: Do unto others as you would have them do unto you. God bless you indeed. Be like Christ upon the Earth—take a gentle walk into the nature of humanity, a gentle walk with the touch of a hand. Would you understand and would you have questions or comments?

 🍎 🍎 🍎

Trying to Find God

Hello, Lincoln. God bless you indeed. What are you doing these days?

Hmm. I'm trying too much to find God. That's what it feels like.

To find God, my dear friend?

To find . . . I don't know . . .

It's not a matter of finding God as much as experiencing the very same.

Yes, there's something that I'm driven toward, something that seems like it's missing. It feels like I need something to be fulfilled.

Yeah. Isn't it funny? There are so many in this room who really understand that about themselves as well. What promise did you make to yourself when you came to Earth? That's the question.

I guess I need to remember that.

Yeah, life is a lovely journey but—my dear friends, can we be very clear and frank here?—it's not one big party all the time. There are dishes to be done, shoes to be shined and all the rest. There is work too, and the work that is closest to your heart is what you keep skirting around all the time. We've discussed it before, and now we would ask that you set aside at least one to two hours of time. This applies to all in this room today.

If you've got a book, something that you are creating out of fabric, something that you are painting or a house that needs repair, <u>all these</u> <u>become heavy burdens if you're afraid to get started.</u> My dear friends, just do it in the smallest of ways, in micromovements, if you will. If it's time to paint the house, at least get out the paintbrush. Then tomorrow get the can of paint and set it beside the house. In this way, at least you are edging yourselves along. You are not getting stuck with static electricity because of unfinished projects. <u>Either you have to cross them off</u> <u>your list or you need to get them done.</u> It is the time upon the Earth for this kind of clarity.

Flow through the Process

Linda, hello. How are you, my dear?

Oh, I'm confused.

What are you confused about? It doesn't really matter, does it?

No.

And that's the good part. At least you're not getting upset about being confused anymore. You're just enjoying it, yeah?

[Laughs loudly.] Sorry about that.

Don't ever apologize for laughter, my dear. Look at what you did—everybody else is laughing now. It's beautiful! God bless you indeed. So you're confused. What would you like to ask today, my dear friend?

We've talked about a couple of things in the past. I felt pretty clearly that my calling was to serve people in some healing manner, and then I felt a strong urge to travel. The last time I was here, you thought that I would be getting a camper soon. I'm traveling next week to visit my family, but I'm flying there. I don't know. Things are just moving along. Of course, I would like to know what's going to happen next, but I probably just have to flow through the process.

Yes, my dear. If you wait too long for the camper, it won't appear, you see. But yes, we certainly see that you are still geared up for travel, and that is part of your greatest plan and desire. Manifesting it will take a little time. You must get everything in order so that you can feel comfortable leaving to travel, which is a whole other issue for you. In your daydreams, traveling is fun and exciting, but in reality, it's a lot of hard work, preparation and all the rest. Then you worry about what you've left behind. "How do I balance this, Dr. Peebles?" You see? And so it's frustrating.

What we would suggest is to just slow down a little more, enjoy the journey, enjoy your trip. Then, my dear, you'll take another one, but if you're not in this room, you'll miss it, you see? You're here, but you're at the grocery store at the same time, do you understand? It's better to just be here and enjoy. There's no place to rush off to. If there is, if you feel the need, get up and go, understand?

I sure do.

When Is Your Journey Complete?

And so, my dear friend Anthony, what would you like to ask?

Why am I still alive?

Why are you still alive? Because you, my dear friend, have work yet to be done, understand? You're very much like I was upon the Earth, with so many things you want to do, see, touch, taste, feel, smell and design, understand?

Yes.

So you're not going to leave. You can try to do the disappearing act, but it won't work.

It has so far.

God bless you indeed. And, my dear friend, does that help? What in particular would you like to know?

Just if that which I see as the path is the path that I need to continue on.

Yes, absolutely. You have done enough, God bless you indeed. The issue of pride is one that gets a bit muddled for you in that you tend to believe that if you stick to what you believe, what you promised yourself to do in this life, that somehow that's your ego talking. When you do that, my dear friend, you allow yourself to be steered off course. That really is prideful spirit saying, "Oh, I don't need to do this. I don't need to complete that." So stay on the path, be sincere and outspoken, and you will have completed your lives upon the Earth—but only when you come over, shake my hand and say, "That was a lovely journey, Dr. Peebles." God bless you indeed, you understand?

Yes, but if I've completed it, can't I be released?

The only way to complete it, the ultimate accent mark on your existence, is when you come over here and you say, "I loved the journey." If you come over and tell us how horrible it was, saying, "I hate that stupid Earth. I'm glad I'm out of there, with all those dumb people everywhere I go. I can't get away from them," then we will say, "Well, perhaps you have a little more to learn. Would you like to go back to school?" God bless you indeed.

My dear friend, the point and purpose of your journey upon the Earth is a journey into the heart of humanity, to realize that everything you hear, taste, touch, feel and smell is you. Every experience and person exists inside you. That's very hard for most human beings to grasp, but that's the way it's meant to be.

You're looking around at the world, collecting all your pieces back together into yourself so you can once again go home to God, to find and touch the face of God within. You can't do that unless you're willing to walk into the fire of your soul. "But I'll get burned," you say. No you won't. You'll lighten up just a little bit more. God bless you, indeed.

You Don't Make Mistakes

Karen, how are you, my dear? Goodness gracious, how exciting to see and hear you. You have had so many interesting adventures, this being one of them, don't you think? God bless you indeed!

Oh goodness, you're willing to try anything. "Why not try that shirt? I'll wear that flowered dress. I don't care." That's you all over. We love you so much. You're an easy subject for us—we don't have to work so hard, yeah? God bless you indeed. You are very compliant even though sometimes you grumble your way through and say, "All right, all right. I hear you. I'll get on with it. I've got it." Yeah? You're a beautiful spirit, my dear. You could teach the whole class. What would you like to ask?

What is the extended message that you have for me?

Goodness, didn't you just hear it?

Yes I did, but I was wondering if there is more.

The biggest part to that, my dear, is getting used to the idea that you don't make mistakes. Every time you don't trust yourself, every time you have an intuition about something and act against it, you make what you think is a mistake—but you don't make mistakes. In yourself you already have the knowing, but you say, "Oh, I did it again. I knew that was going to happen. Why did I push myself there?" You understand?

Yes I do.

That's it right there, my dear. You finish that one up and you'll have a really nice journey.

Okay.

It's already beautiful as it is, but that one will keep you in balance. You don't have to wonder, "Who threw that punch at me?" You understand?

Yes.

God bless you indeed. Does that help, my dear?

Yes it does. Thank you.

Anger Is a Frequency You Choose to Channel

Patti, where are you? God bless you indeed. Hello, you're a beautiful spirit. What would you like to teach the class today?

Well, how about just surrendering? I just went through an experience that you told me was coming. I didn't realize I could be that angry. I didn't know it was in me.

Yeah, that's when you gave yourself permission, didn't you?

You told me it's okay if we want to hate people. We can, but it's more fun to love them. I remembered that as I was hating them, but I wallowed in it and got bronchitis. I made myself deathly sick. You know, it gave me some relief. I didn't have to repeatedly think about what those people supposedly did to me.

Precisely. Yes.

Until I finally got to the place where I said, "God, I can't do this myself. Do it for me." Then I still had bronchitis, but it was about me after all. I don't know what the anger was exactly, so that would be my question.

Oh my dear, do we really have to spell it out? The anger was anger.

Just anger?

It's a frequency. You choose to channel it or not, just as you choose to channel patience or not. These are spirits. They live. They're living, breathing entities, if you will, but there's nothing to be concerned about. They're there to help you. You choose, as the expression would be, to bring in anger, to allow it to come up and out of you. It's one layer of the onion. It's in my existence too, but I choose to bring love to the surface. It feels better; it's all smooshy-mooshy. And I love love; love is loving; it's not hard to bear at all.

Whatever the Emotion, It Is a Blessing to Let It All Out

The question came up, will I ever get to the point when my reaction is just love?

Someday, yes.

How do you do that?

You stop being angry! It's really that simple.

And so it's really a blessing when it comes out, because you get to let it out?

Precisely. You see, for all of you, my dear friends, the biggest problems come by repressing depression and melancholy. "Why am I so depressed all the time? I don't know what to do. It's terrible. I'm so depressed." Thus you keep holding on to it, and depression says, "That feels good. You hug me every time you say you're depressed. Thank God for that. I have life here!" You give it life through your choice.

"Yes, but, Dr. Peebles, I just lost my dearest friend in a car accident!" Yes, we understand; really, we do. So if you're going to be depressed, by all means pull out all the stops and allow yourself to go into the depression in order to understand it. Don't fear it. It's when you try to hold it at arm's length that it lingers. "I don't want to feel depressed; I don't want to look at the depression!" Yet it is bearing down on you, because it is a teacher, guide and friend, just like anger.

When you allow for it, it won't come out so harshly, so full force. You can simply sit in a chair and say, "Oh boy, that one boiled my skin. Hmm."

If someone comes up to you and asks, "What's up today?" you say, " I believe I am going to imitate a bear today. I'm not feeling very happy. I'm very angry." "Is that so? What's it about?" "Well, if it's all right, I'll share with you: It's about you." "It is?" "Yes, but I'd rather, shall we say, get to know you a little better. Can we sit and chat awhile?" Instead of saying, "This is what you did to me," tell the person how you reacted to what he or she did to you as you felt it. "I had this reaction, and I'm not certain why. Could you please explain your actions toward me so that I might come to an understanding here? You would not have acted in such a way without a purpose. I truly want to grow and to learn why you feel the way you do."

In this way, you express your anger without having to get angry. You feel it and allow for it, but you give it a voice that can be heard, because what you seek is acknowledgment. So, my dear, you must acknowledge those around you. People do not act in a particular way without a purpose. What people say and do tells you more about them than it does about you. The murderer is in a lot more pain than the one whose life he or she takes. Do you understand, my dear?

I do. Thank you.

The Process of Surrender

My dear friends, you are beautiful spirits here today. We love you so very much and want you to understand that you have come to terms with yourself today in ways that were beyond your wildest dreams and imaginations. If for no other reason, my dear friends, you are here to just stare, to look at the process. We would like to share with you something about the process of surrender.

Dear Summer is a beautiful spirit who doesn't like for us to talk about her. That's her challenge—where she has to surrender to us. That is for her, right now, a very difficult issue, because we love her very much and she needs to understand that she is going to be more and more outspoken upon the stage, speaking to the many rather than the few about her life experiences and all the rest. She has had in the course of her life, since she was a little girl, many opportunities to end her life and many thoughts of doing that, and we share that with you because she gives us permission.

God bless you, indeed. My dear friends, what she did not understand is that ultimately, through the process of surrender, she has given her life. She lies down and dies, leaving her vessel, giving us this physical form—no small act for any human being. Human beings, generally speaking, are very much attached to their physical forms, but dear Summer, such a beautiful spirit, says, "Take the shirt off my back, as well as my shoes, coat, sandals and all the rest." She's a very giving, loving spirit, and we share this once again, although it's not her favorite thing. You share this with her and you'll see it in her eyes. She'll have fire there, ready to kill Dr. Peebles.

But, my dear friends, it is through this demonstration here, which is a part of the spiritualist path, that my friends and the band of angels working together during the course of my lifetime upon the planet Earth educated the masses. This is simply a demonstration as to what can occur when you surrender your mind, body and spirit to God.

Getting a Response from the Heavens: A Meditation

God bless you indeed. *I would ask right now that you close your eyes and breathe very deeply into your spines. Now, we shared at the outset that you have a beautiful spirit guide standing with you here today. My dear friends, if you would like to have an acceleration of your spiritual journey or an enlightenment that would occur much earlier in your life—if you would like to learn to laugh more, to give more, how to signal the heavens and get a response—then close your eyes very deeply and breathe into your spines and say a very simple prayer unto the Father who art in heaven, hallowed be Thy name. You want the kingdom to come into you now, my dear friends, the kingdom that has always existed inside you, waiting to be revealed through you. God's will be done. God has a will, a great love for you, a plan that can be enacted if you are willing to listen to directions.*

Now, my dear friends, again breathe deeply into your spines and say the following words to yourselves or aloud: "I reach beyond the confines of the Earth, the body and the mind. I open myself to receiving light, love, inspiration and truth." When you release yourself from the confines of the Earth, body and mind, those confines are the illusions of separation, panic, pain, disease, fear, insecurity, depression, anger and the energies that want to destroy. Breathe again into your spines and reach beyond the confines of the Earth, the body and the mind, opening yourselves to receiving light, love, inspiration and truth and allowing for your guides to stand behind you.

Using your mind's eye and your imagination where Spirit can speak unto you, feel the touch upon your shoulders and the warmth within your back. Your guide, my dear friend, has something to say to you. It is a name, the very first name that you hear. Trust, surrender, reach beyond the confines of the Earth, the body and the mind. Free your spirit to the understanding that there are no accidents as to the name you have just heard. Embrace it within your heart and know beyond a shadow of a doubt, my dear friend, that you have this spirit guide with you at all times. Your guide speaks your language, knows you, loves you and understands you. Guides are very patient, and you can trust them.

Again breathe very deeply into your spine. Now we would ask that you simply open your eyes, look unto the channel here and note with clarity the senses that have opened within. Trust that there's no hypnosis or any such thing at work here. It happens through your willingness to surrender to the greater love of God. It is through your willingness, my dear friend, to no longer fear or feel the need to compare or contrast yourself with anyone else. Reach deep inside of yourself and know with certainty the very special, perfect being you are. Know your gifts and talents. Understand that you can create games to discover that you have a desire to move beyond the physical, to step out.

My dear friends, you are beautiful spirits here today and no mystery to us at all, God bless you indeed. We love you so very much. We are going to allow the dear channel to return. Go your way in peace, love and harmony, for life is indeed a joy. All you have to do to enjoy the journey to your own heart and enlightenment is simply lighten up just a little bit more. God bless you, indeed.

● ● ●

Spiritualism: A Blending of Science and Religion

Seemingly valid criticism of channeling, beyond that of those who practice outright fraud, concerns the entities being channeled and the idea that the information we receive from them comes only from their experiences as living beings. Would you comment on that?

You don't stop progressing once you transition out of your body. So the knowledge would not, in any way, shape or form, be limited to prior lifetimes. I am not dead. I am very much alive and active! Certainly, since my own transition, I have grown enormously in awareness. I understand human suffering in a different way than I did when I was upon the Earth. Like anyone else, I had my moments of being very, very upset with God. At the very end of my lifetime upon the Earth, I certainly questioned why God allowed such pain to occur within my own physical form. But when I transitioned, I released all the pain; I had no more rheumatism and perfect vision! The rest of the veil was lifted, the illusions of separation were dissolved and in that moment, I began to expand and grow into greater consciousness than I had ever dreamed or imagined possible.

Through that awareness of myself in my transition, I began to realize how much I had accomplished in my life upon the Earth, despite always feeling that I had fallen short of the mark. That's why it's so extremely important to me to share with you, my dear friends, that never do you fall short of anything. If you had half a chance, if you would simply slow down just a wee bit and look around at your lifetime, you would realize how much you have accomplished, how very many breaths you have taken and how many heartbeats you have decided to keep going here, where life is not very easy. Certainly give yourselves a little credit here!

So, my dear friends, when spirits transition, well, some certainly do like to, oh, shall we say, sit in a chair and mope for a while. They say, "I am dead. I have nothing left." Then suddenly they wake up and realize, "Well, if I have nothing left, then why am I still thinking? Why am I feeling? Why am I still aware of my own self?" And there comes the sudden awareness that there is no death and that death is the greatest illusion of separation of all. There is no death, my dear friends! Your soul is eternal!

My dear friends, you have so many ideas here about discovery, don't you? You discover that you are awake when you open your eyes in the morning. When you go to sleep at night, you discover a different sense of yourself where you gaze into the stars and the heavens, releasing yourself from the confines of the Earth, body and mind. You discover that you are a spirit inhabiting a physical form. This is the beginning of creationism as well as spiritualism. It is the foundation of your heart! And that is where you reside. That is the foundation.

The Founding of American Spiritualism

For those who are unfamiliar with the term, you have already defined spiritualism. Can you clear up something for us? Common knowledge says that spiritualism began with the three Fox sisters from upper New York state in 1848. Basically, they experienced so-called tapping sounds and involuntary body movements. Is that really the true beginning of American spiritualism?

We'll say it was the beginning of the advertisement of it, because they made it more mainstream and, shall we say, even more acceptable—just as your television shows and movies certainly assist in increasing spiritual awareness and understanding, putting spiritualism into a realm where it is easier to discuss and to explore. Point fingers at the Fox sisters and say, "They're crazy!" and someone else says, "No, they're not! I've had the same experience!" So they were indeed at the point in time where spiritualism became more familiar to the many rather than the few. We certainly applaud and appreciate them for this. Were they frauds? Well, my dear friends, we must say here that there were a few things there that were not real stirring-ups, and yet there were others that really put their hair on end, God bless you indeed! So it was a wee bit of this and a wee bit of that. Eventually they realized they were dabbling in something that was much larger than themselves and rather humbling.

In Matthew 10:26 it is quoted, "For there is nothing covered that will not be revealed, and hid that shall not be known." How does spiritualism fit into Christ's statement?

Well, there's quite a bit being revealed here today, isn't there? Absolutely! First of all, there is an enormous fallacy that everyone believes about many religions. You haven't the foggiest idea how your religions, including Catholicism, for example, are extraordinarily based on the supernatural, even to the point of utilizing witchcraft and such things. There are tremendous correlations between witchcraft, Catholicism and voodoo. There is a marriage there of the physical realm using all kinds of objects and devices as points of focus to bring in spiritual awareness. There's nothing wrong with this. You can do the same by looking at your own body in the mirror and coming to terms with it, realizing that you are a divine creature just as you are. You are 100 percent perfect as far as God is concerned. It is for you to discover this for yourselves.

There seems to be a situation of religion and authority, of allowing an expert to help you reach God. People forget that they have the opportunity to tune in themselves, like a radio.

Yes, and the reality—the bottom line, as far as we are concerned—is that you should just fall in love with your discussions and your varying perspectives here. For example, we certainly are pushing buttons with a few of our words. Certainly we don't expect nor do we demand agreement with anything that we share. It is one perspective in the universe. The point and the purpose of spiritualism is to bring the collective consciousness of humankind together. It does not matter what your perspective is. You cannot, from any standpoint or vantage point, see the very same sunrise in the same way. There is no way to interpret anything in your existence in exactly the same way. You can use the same words, but they will still be interpreted very differently within each individual.

So it is the embracing of the many rather than the few perspectives upon the planet Earth that spiritualism was striving to establish. We assure you, there is a resurrection of this upon the Earth. There is a necessity for it if there is ever to be any freedom from the foundation of sadness, pain, despondency, despair, poverty, greed, obsession and all the rest. These are the things that we would ask; if you're going to be concerned about anything, be concerned about fear, obsession and pain. Those are the religions, if you will, of separation to which most human beings return and adhere. But, God bless you indeed, certainly the foundation of all life is love. That is the connecting point. For all upon the Earth, without qualification, seek to touch and be touched, to no longer feel divided but to find the acknowledgment, freedom and flight of the soul.

It helps very much, Dr. Peebles. Along that line, it seems that time is accelerating. Currently, both unfortunate events as well as pain, suffering, fear and new emboldening breakthroughs are happening simultaneously. So how can spiritualism be necessary at this point in time for humanity to make these breakthroughs?

It's not so much an acceleration of time, my dear friend. How can we put it for you . . . There is a mountain here of . . . we'll be kind . . . manure that has been created through fear, expectation and all the rest that we have already discussed. It has been upon the Earth for a very long time and the planet is getting sick and tired of it. It is a large, large pile of manure of all kinds of fears, hatred, jabs, punches and all the rest that you give to one another. There is the torture of child abuse, rape, robbery and murder.

So understand that time is not accelerating. If it were, you would feel greater love. What is really happening relates to this mountain of manure. You're trying to climb it, to hold on to it. It's not a strong foundation. It is not the foundation of rock that you hoped it would be, and it is starting to cave in on you. You're backslidin', and planet Earth is taking a dramatic step backward, returning in vibrational frequency to Medieval times. That's why it seems that you're not able to get anything done and it feels slower than molasses. You especially, the lightworkers, want so much more. It is especially true for those who have their sights set upon the face of God and finding and touching the very same within self and life.

My dear friends, we implore you to set your sights clearly in this direction. It is incredibly important—and that is not something that we very often say. In order to, shall we say, preserve the planet Earth, it is incredibly important that you set your sights upon loving one another, giving one another as much freedom as possible, the widest berth possible, to give birth to yourselves and differing perspectives. Differ, love one another and realize that it is the diversity that you crave and desire. This is what brings you life!

The Unification of Diversity through Love

What you're basically commenting on is unification of diversity.

My dear friend, how do you find unification in diversity?

The common thread, the glue that binds the universe—love.

Precisely, and it is that simple. If you're striving for a "there" and that's it, you're going to get "there," but where are you going next? Just more of the very same! There will be expansion, and it's going to be a lovely experience for you. But first you must learn to eradicate pain, hatred, terrorism and the wars that go on inside of yourselves. For you, that is your responsibility—self-responsibility for your life as a creative adventure.

Despite what is occurring around you, you can weather the storms, just as Christ weathered the storm upon the Sea of Galilee. Despite what is going on around you, you can remain in love. It takes tenacity of spirit to do this, because you are in a physical form and it hurts. No question about it, my dear friends. When you're hungry, it hurts. Now we ask that you fill yourself up with spiritual manna, and that will get you through every experience upon the Earth in the physical that you might be afraid to face. The reality is, get yourselves ready and hang on to your hats, 'cause planet Earth, she's going to be a-spinnin', and it's going to have some of you, my dear friends, spinnin' too if you do not firmly tether yourselves down with love.

There's no right or wrong, up or down, good or bad or what-have-you. There are lots of contrasts. You can't get rid of anything. You try to let go of memories, push back the pain and get rid of anger, but you can't get rid of anything. It's all you. So what're you gonna do now that you realize, "All of this is me"? This big mess of government and what-have-you, all the rest that you want hopefully one day not to have to look at anymore—well, how do you create that reality for yourself? You simply decide, "Well, if it's all me, then it's up to me what I bring to the surface of my existence!"

For example, that would be love. It is for us a waste of time to feel any kind of hatred or anger toward anyone. We don't feel it. We love you all very much. We have our concerns, yes, but we don't allow them to consume us, because that wastes time. It doesn't provide freedom for love, and love is the strongest force in the universe. If you truly adhere to that within your heart, you begin to realize that your body in and of itself is a planet Earth. It is a school called planet Earth. You are trying as hard as you can to bring the truth of yourself to the surface through your mouth, ears, hands, eyes, words, actions—or when you step on someone's toes.

Do You Express or Repress Love?

Everything that you do is a decision as to whether you will express or repress love. Still it is the strongest force in the universe. You can try all kinds of things on for size upon the planet Earth. No question about it! You can play this game, but eventually, at the end of all your antics, you will find that it feels very nice to have milk and cookies and just sit by the fireplace with someone you love.

And that, my dear friends, is abundance, freedom and salvation. That's really what spiritualism is striving to help you understand. Blending science and religion means to really look at your physical body, which is very scientific in its nature with its nerve synapses and beating heart. You don't have to think about any of it. You have a thinker, and it does some good work processing the issues of your heart, bringing them out to be expressed by your hands through writing and other works. That is the science of you. The spiritual aspect, the religion of you, is the foundation and the personality that you are going to trust. Are you really going to set your sights on the reality that God exists and is a living God who wants to be expressed fully and completely through you? Spiritualism worked very hard to eradicate the barriers, borders and boundaries, just as the channel here does, allowing us to occupy her body as a demonstration that, well, goodness gracious, it is just a body after all. Where's Summer? Is she scrunched up in a little corner of her brain? Where did she go?

Well, my dear friends, she's a spirit. She stands to the side and back and sometimes listens in, sometimes not. She's a beautiful spirit and allows us to take over the chamber in which she exists upon your planet Earth. That is a beautiful expression of love. There is no fear or expectation, just complete and total surrender and trust to God. God bless you, indeed.

◉   ◉   ◉

The Simple Truth of You

My dear friends, understand that it is in my belief system and through my structure here that I have an awareness. I found this awareness within my own heart in my passing from planet Earth, into the I Am life force. I am the energy that courses through everything. I am God, you understand? I am a creator. I am victim of no one, and no one can ever be a victim of me. I, my dear friends, am you.

How can I not love you? You, my dear friends, are me. How can I not want to touch you? How can I not want to share with you? How can I not want to adventure and explore with you? There is not one of you who I love any more or any less than any other. Every one of you I look at with curiosity, because you are me, and I thank you. I value every expression that you bring to me, because it teaches me. It is part of my exploration here.

The Wonder of Yourself

Fall in love with the wonder of yourself, my dear friends, for it is there where you will discover peace, harmony and love beyond your wildest dreams and imaginations. It is there where you will realize that you are never alone, and you will never feel alone ever again. God bless you, indeed.

We ask that you work in servitude to yourselves, understanding the very simple, very magical, very real, very wonderful simple truth of you. The truth of you is that you are not finite beings; you are infinite. It is your belief that you are finite, your belief that you are limited that creates distress, disorders, diseases, discomfort and an experience of life that is anything less than love. Here upon the planet Earth, your adventure is one of discovery. It is a labor of love where you diminish and dissolve illusions of separation within self and between yourself and life—and what does that add up to but intimacy?

Solemnly swear within your heart and soul to create more intimacy in your life for at least one year, and then you will find so much magic in your world that you might even want to try it for a year and a day, and then perhaps for a year and a week and so on and so forth. It becomes a rather beautiful dance for everyone, made up of the entire spectrum of light, and all the colors add up to white light, which adds up to the darkness. Understand that darkness is not the absence of light at all; it is the density of light. With a change of your heart, a change of your mind, darkness becomes for you the very beautiful, fertile soil where you plant your being and grow to find and touch the face of God.

The very simple truth of you is that you all want to be healed—physically, emotionally and spiritually—but truly what you are striving for here upon the planet Earth is to remember that you are already healed, you are already perfect, you are already enlightened beings. You are striving to remember this! Here is a very beautiful way in which you test yourself and the tenacity of your spirit: Ask yourselves how much you love God, my dear friends. We hope that you ask yourselves this question every day.

How much do you love God, truly? Put a number to it. Is it 75 percent, or is it 5 percent today? Realize that this number doesn't matter. Understand that you are very much loved by God, because that is who you are—everything you see, hear, taste, touch, feel and smell is you. Fall in love with all of it, and there will you remember your enlightenment. The very simple and beautiful truth of you is that you are omnipresent; you are with everything and everyone at all times. You're all very beautiful spirits striving to have a human experience.

You have created an experience here upon the Earth within which you can discover and rediscover, time and time again, the magic of yourself, the magic of your being, through this lovely dance with life. The disharmony that you experience here upon planet Earth is an opportunity for you to grow. The little experiences that you feel—the ones that feel like parasites tappin' at your ankles and nippin' at your toes—are there for you to create more wonder about God, the God who you are, because you are all seeking the experience of heaven. But where is heaven? It is right inside of your heart. It is not a place; it is a feeling, and it stretches out as far as the eye can see and as far as the heart can feel.

God bless you indeed, my dear friends. A little-known fact here: Dr. Peebles still has things to learn! And you know something else? I absolutely love it, because the learning never ends! It is there where you fall in love with an experience of surrender, realizing that there is no "there" to get to, because when you're "there," where are you going to go next?

Isn't it fantastic that you always wonder about tomorrow? Isn't it lovely that you remember today? Understand and embrace this, and realize that you are an infinite being. In this infinite way of self-expression here upon the Earth, realize that this is the simple truth of you. Do you ever lack things? How is it possible for you to lack anything if you are everything that you see, hear, taste, touch, feel and smell? It is only within an illusion of separation that your heart and soul can ever experience your life here upon the Earth as in any way lacking.

We would ask that every day for the next year, even when you are weary, even when you are tired, you sit and relax with a little pen or a pencil in your hand and a sheet of paper in front of you. These are fantastic tools that you can use for the expansion of yourself. Sit and write down the many ways in which you are weary of life, and then describe upon the page why these moments when you are so weary are such lovely benefits to you, to your soul and to your growth. You always can find truth anywhere you look, and sometimes the most enlightening experiences are found in the darkness. It is there where you work upon your issues of fear and pain, especially the fear of discovery of yourself, of that which you are. So many of you hold yourselves at arm's length, not speaking your truth to the world.

Use Your Voice to Benefit Humankind

You're all beautiful channels, and there is one voice that you can speak to most of all. It is the greatest voice you can channel for the benefit of humankind—and that is your own voice. We love you so very much! We are more than willing to engage in a little play, in a little dance with you, to inspire you, to encourage you, but we cannot do anything for you. You must make the decision to turn your life around with a change of mind, with a change of heart.

Everyone has at least one guide. Some have several, because they have been here upon the Earth for centuries. Within your heart understand that you are not finite; you are infinite. You are with everyone and everything that there ever has been, all at one time—not separate from it, not separate from me, not separate from anyone. Now understand that your guides are standing very, very close to you right now, and they want to just simply whisper in your ear words of inspiration. "Well, I can't hear Spirit, Dr. Peebles!" you argue. Well, you "hear" me right now, yeah? Here I am inside of this channel's body, speaking to you. So there you go; you were wrong on that one, yeah? God bless you, indeed; we tease you a little bit. My dear friends, your guides want to play with you; they want to speak to you. Your guides speak the language of the heart not the language of the mind. Listen with your heart for just a moment here. Suspend your disbelief and learn the lessons of wonder that they have to offer.

In every action that you take here upon the Earth, in every thought that you create inside of your consciousness, you are seeking acknowledgment. Through this acknowledgment, you find intimacy. Through this intimacy, you dissolve the illusions of separation that have encumbered you for so very, very long. Consider your insecurities, the words that you hear inside your head: "I am not good enough, not strong enough, not smart enough, not creative enough," or "I should have gotten up a little earlier this morning!" Consider the many ways in which you undermine and sabotage the beauty and wonder of yourself. We would ask that you wake up from this process here upon the Earth and realize that your desires for money, for automobiles, for a home, for human touch, for health—all of these desires are various ways in which you are asking for acknowledgment from God—acknowledgment that you are indeed worthy of receiving love.

Create Prosperity by Ridding Yourself of Toxicity

Rid yourself of the toxic energy that you draw into yourselves with every thought you create that is against you. Rid yourself of this toxicity and you open a gateway for eternal love to truly breathe and move through you. When you are afraid that you might attract some disease, it is your fear that will attract it—keep your sights set upon it and it certainly will be yours.

So if you truly want to create love, good health, prosperity and abundance, have no judgment against yourself. As far as we are concerned, you can have millions of dollars in the bank; it doesn't matter to us. It's all you and it's all us anyway. It is simply a matter of how much love you are willing to receive and how much you then allow it to flow through you and spiral out to the rest of the world—family, friends and others. That is where you begin to weave yourselves into the fabric of eternity. It is there that you find and touch the face of God, which is you in every moment, and then your need, your passion, your drive to "get there" dissolves as well and you immerse yourself in the moment. Then you will realize that the prosperous being who you are was never outside of you, ever; prosperity has always been right inside your heart. We love you so very much. Please remember the simple truth of yourself: You are all very beautiful spirits, and you are indeed the light and the way and the truth. God bless you, indeed.

Something You Might Not Know about Your Guides

A few weeks ago, you commented that without our guides, we wouldn't be here—that we wouldn't exist, that they kind of sustain us. And I was wondering if you could clarify and expand on that for us.

God bless you indeed; that is a very nice question, indeed. Yes, my dear friends, you cannot exist upon planet Earth without your guides. Your guides set up a very wonderful resonance between you and planet Earth, and they keep your soul stabilized. This is necessary because you are not always fully incarnated; you are really a little bit here on Earth and a little bit plugged into the other side at all times. It is your guides who maintain this frequency so that you can stay in the physical body. Without your guides, you would very quickly retract from this place called planet Earth and leave your physical form, without question.

You are always requiring encouragement, whether or not you hear it and whether or not you sense it in any way, shape or form that is tangible to you. Your guides are always there, increasing the vibrational frequency of love around you in order to stabilize your environment, in very much the same way, if you will, in which you might clear your air with a little filter. Your guides set up a wonderful resonance in which you can do your work, for indeed, planet Earth is a school where you are increasing your awareness and understanding of love.

But there are, for the purposes of growth, individuals who come to planet Earth and choose not to have any guides and say, "I can do it alone after all." And that is the greatest illusion of separation of all, my dear friends: that you are ever alone. You can try to disappear, you can try to retract, you can try to commit suicide—but it's not going to work. If you want to be alone and think that you can be by killing yourself, you'll be surprised by how many beings are there to receive you on the other side. God bless you indeed, my dear friends.

How do I best access my guides' wisdom and guidance?

You pay attention to all those voices jabbering away in your head, even the contradictory ones. The contradictory ones are fine, you see, for you are asking for help and assistance, and there are as many perspectives in the universe as there are spirits, and so what you hear are different perspectives. You hear, "Well, you can do this," and then you hear another voice say, "No, no, no! That would be a terrible mistake."

What you are hearing is the conversations of your guides; so when you hear this, address them: "Hello, I hear you and you are driving me crazy. Why do you always contradict everything that this other being says? Would you mind if I stuck with him for a little while? I want to try something new here." And you will find that the other voice fades away. And in this way, you will find that they also respect you. You have to learn to converse with your guides. They get through to you in most cases anyway; everything gets distilled down into the one kernel of truth that would be for your highest good.

Immerse Yourself in Life as in an Ocean

The heavens are a laughin', and God bless you indeed! Our dear channel is such a beautiful spirit; we love her so very much! As well, we are very much intoxicated by you; we love you so very much! You are going to be called upon, each and every one of you, to open your hearts in ways you never dreamed of or imagined possible.

Understand that there is tremendous energy at work here upon the planet Earth that is helping and assisting in the eradication of barriers, borders and boundaries, creating unification between family and friends as well as unification between yourselves and Spirit. Realize that at this time, with little tugs and pulls at your heart, you are being called upon to reunite with family members. It is there where you can overcome the greatest obstacles that have been put in front of the full expression of your heart here upon the planet Earth.

It is a time of expansion—expansion of yourself, of light, of energy, of love, of Christ energy that wants very much to come through and be fully expressed in each and every one of you here. Why? To increase the vibrational frequency of love. Planet Earth is being elevated into a new dimension—one where hope is no longer a necessity. Rather, you are immersed in life in ways you never dreamed of or imagined possible. Turmoil upon the Earth is a necessity for this process, for increasing the vibrational frequency of love requires giving birth to self, giving birth to God here upon the Earth.

Your life here upon the Earth is as a surface dweller. There are creatures living in the water, however, who are fully immersed in life as well. They are symbolic of what we are asking for your souls to become—fully immersed in love, in the consciousness of Christ upon the planet Earth. However, there are still storms on the surface, are there not? But it is only the surface dwellers who feel the storms. It is only the surface dwellers who are tormented by the elements. It is only the surface dwellers who live in fear. You are here upon the Earth in human form with your feet upon the Earth—surface dwellers. But your heart and soul—that which you truly are, the light from within—do not exist here upon the surface but come from elsewhere. Dive deep, my dear friends, deep within your hearts, and you will no longer feel or fear the storms.

It takes a lot of effort to hold life at arm's length. Instead, surrender into life's embrace. Love those who at times you feel in your heart are not worthy of love, for they too are family members. Work within your heart, within your soul, within your life, within your consciousness, within every breath to uplift the planet Earth into a greater consciousness of love, now and forevermore. It is when you are existing in that world deep inside of your heart where love is fully expressed that you will find heaven.

The Finest Meditation

From our perspective here, the very finest meditation that you can all engage in for at least twenty minutes a day is one wherein you open yourself to receiving all of life without pushing any single part of it away. Allow the activity of your mind, allow your wonderings, allow your pain, allow everything to occur all at once. *Simply sit, creating a vortex from the heavens that spirals down through the top of your crown chakra and down into the Earth. Then, from the Earth, another vortex comes spiraling back in the opposite direction, up through you, up through the root chakra, up through the crown chakra, and this vortex spews out all those things that are not for your highest good.*

So you are inviting everything in and allowing that which is for your highest good to stay inside of you, and this is going to be very revitalizing. You will find that you transform yourself in terms of finding more youthfulness, more strength and more passion—certainly this is a wonderful exercise for activating kundalini, sexuality and creativity. So this, from our perspective, is the very finest meditation. Set up a station for meditation. Light a candle. Invite in the essences of cedar and orange if you want to promote spiritual awakening a little bit more; these essences will heighten your senses in terms of clairaudience in particular.

You very much want to understand your relationship with your guides, with God, with the god who you are. So the meditation we are going to give to you is for you to do every night at bedtime. *As you are lying on your back, picture and visualize in the area of the third eye that you are walking into the fire of your soul. Fall asleep there within the fire of your soul, and you will have some rather startling experiences.* This is what we would ask you to do for the next five weeks. Do you have that kind of commitment inside you? You want this personal growth, do you not? Then you are in for an adventure. This will bring about a little exhaustion, so drink plenty of water, because all those toxins that you carry around inside of you are not going to have any place to stay anymore, because there will be so much light within you that they will need to be released.

🍎 🍎 🍎

Understanding Alzheimer's Disease

My question today has to do with Alzheimer's. It's been coming to my attention through different areas that this is becoming a big issue. Where does it come from? What's going on with the person who has it? How can family members deal with having a loved one who has it? Is there something you could share that will give us a better understanding of what is happening in this situation? I've heard you say that a lot of times it's a time for the person who is experiencing it to kind of review and retract and do a lot of things that the masses aren't aware of.

Yeah, God bless you indeed, my dear; we can speak for hours upon this topic, because with various individuals, what you would call Alzheimer's is, as far as we are concerned, just a mere state of sleep, of trance, if you will. Oftentimes it will occur within individuals who have created a very stubborn existence for themselves, who are not willing to leave the planet Earth without a fight and who oftentimes have kept a lot of their thoughts to themselves, for example. Realize that we speak very broadly, very generally here about these individuals; it's not in every single case but in most cases that you find that these individuals have one of these three things in their past.

Alzheimer's has a tendency, my dear, to free up these thoughts and to, at long last, force these individuals to express themselves emotionally, without restraint, because they have no control over what they are saying. As well, a lot of the information they are speaking is from the other side, and so you will find that they are at times half in the body and half out of the body, seeing both realms at once, so you must listen very carefully to your friends, family members and others who have Alzheimer's.

If you ask them questions about past-life existences and so on, you would find that they make profound psychics and mystics. Have the presence of mind, God bless you indeed, to realize that there is nothing wrong with those who have the symptoms of Alzheimer's whatsoever; they are simply on a different journey as far as their relationship to the other side goes. They are simply having a different experience, God bless you indeed, experiencing another fantastic perspective.

For those of you who have a sense of urgency about Alzheimer's, however, especially that it might lead to demise and so on and so forth: Those with Alzheimer's would be leaving planet Earth anyway; it is a creation of those individuals, my dear friends. It is a way in which they can very slowly peel themselves away from their physical existence here. So it is not something to be concerned about on their behalf, because oftentimes they are feeling more free from the body than you even realize.

There are indeed certain substances that you can give to these individuals that will help and assist them in releasing toxins from the body. There is a direct physical connection between the disease and the dysfunction, if you will, of the ability to release one's shit. In other words, these individuals frequently have held on to quite a bit of shit throughout their lives, you understand, certainly in terms of experiences, relationships, anger and so on. In some emotional cases, some very emotional cases—lots of sadness and so on, compounded—these emotions are compacted inside of your abdomen.

My dear friends, inside of your abdomen, you find a very beautiful organ known here as the colon, God bless you indeed. You also find the intestines, and all of these are right there in the area of your solar plexus, and you find that there is tremendous pressure from buildup inside of the abdomen from carrying around feces. This creates difficulty for the spirit in maintaining contact with the body. That would be more of a technical answer to the question of Alzheimer's, yeah? So it is of primary importance to keep the colon completely cleansed.

And that's the tip of the iceberg, my dear friends. Does that help? Is that sufficient? God bless you, indeed. We can speak for about an hour upon this topic; it would be a good session for us to do with a group.

●   ●   ●

Living in a State of Grace

We are here today to discuss with you the idea of living your life with grace, especially in regard to yourselves and your community. Understand that grace is not in a hurry for anything. Grace, my dear friends, is magical. Grace is kind. Grace is pointing the way for you to have a fantastic journey upon the planet Earth. Understand that grace is here in this room with you today. You will feel the presence of Spirit in the room as you embrace grace within your heart. Certainly the learning is here, and the education grace brings to you is the ability to slow down just a little bit more in every action, every word and every gesture that you create here upon the planet Earth. This does not mean that you are not to have everything that your heart desires, but grace is to truly find your heart at long last.

Certainly, living in grace means finding within your heart what it is that you want to share with the world—make that discovery there first. What world exists inside of you and what would you like to manifest here upon the planet Earth? Bring that world to life, my dear friends, whether it is in terms of wanting your healing, wanting your sanity, wanting to attract love or wanting to change the course of your existence. What you are truly seeking inside of your hearts, my dear friends, is heaven. Heaven is not a place, not a point in time, but a feeling, a feeling that is in a state of constant expansion. And certainly that feeling can be summarized in the one beautiful spirit known as grace that exists inside of your hearts.

You do not require Dr. Peebles here or anyone else to give you the answers; you have it all inside yourselves. You find and touch the face of God when you are willing and determined to walk into the fire of your soul. It takes tremendous courage at first, but by slowing down just a little bit, you will find that you have actually accelerated the process of your expansion here upon the Earth. Understand that it is your fears and concerns that keep you away from the wisdom of your heart.

Certainly understand how often you strive to sabotage yourself with words that are less than kind from self to self. It is there, when you stop and realize that these words that are against you have nothing to do with the love that comes from God but come instead from the un-creator, when you realize, my dear friends, that this is the ego talking to you and trying to sabotage you. Your ego tries to undermine you in every breath you take here upon the Earth, but realize that the dark cannot understand the light. A small light in a room certainly can be seen, but a pinpoint of black cannot be understood or found in a room full of light.

So where is this room that we are discussing here? Well, it is inside your heart. Allow your heart to expand with light, and no longer will you be concerned about what might go wrong, what could go wrong or how things are going to turn out, because everything is always in right order. Once you understand this, you have surrendered to the journey of expansion of self, and it is there where you find and seek your enlightenment. And once you are enlightened, what are you going to do next?

Take Your Desires, Needs and Expectations Seriously

So understand that life does not have to be hard; it can be a journey of grace, a journey of expansion and a journey of wonder, my dear friends. Understand that once you are thrown into the bathwater, if you should struggle against it, you shall sink, but when you release your need to struggle, you will find that you float—you will find that your face rises again toward the sun and that you are always safe and never alone. My dear friends, you are always supported by the universe, you are always supported by God; but are you supported by yourselves? Are you the ones in charge of your own existence? How do you find yourself in charge of your existence? Well, first you must take yourselves seriously. To take yourselves seriously means that you realize inside of your heart that you have needs, desires, concerns and expectations. Once you find these and are serious about yourself, you will find these desires expressed on the outside of yourself in a resonance—a wonderful, honest echo that comes back to you so that you can learn and you can grow.

So when you are walking in grace, be kind to yourself. Realize that at times you will find fear inside of your heart, and it is all right to share this with the world: "I am afraid," "I feel alone," "I'm frustrated," and statements such as these. When you are willing to speak them to the world, you will find that the world comes a runnin' to give you support. The reason for this is that you have found that you are giving grace to yourself, loving yourself first and then expressing this into life and allowing life to love you in return. To touch and to be touched is certainly the course of your existence here upon the planet Earth. You are all very beautiful spirits—magical creators, each and every one of you here in this room; you are all students of the divine. Where do you find divinity once again? Inside of your hearts.

The Many Faces of Abuse

When it comes to understanding the many faces of abuse, it is very difficult for those who are the victims here in the course of this work to understand that indeed they are, as well, the creators of their own reality. Understand that the momentum, the force behind the creation of what you would consider to be abuse here upon the planet Earth began at the very beginning.

God bless you indeed. What was the beginning, my dear friends, but the fall into sin? Discovery of self occurs in relationship to life. It is here that this separation did occur. Understand that everyone here upon the planet Earth carries a residual force of awareness that you are all responsible here for the matters of planet Earth. There is certainly inside of this awareness an awareness of responsibility. Of course this responsibility is very frightening for you, and this creates inside each and every one of you . . .

Opening Up to the Topic Is Not Easy

God bless you indeed, my dear Summer! You just simply will not let us discuss this, and this is why, you understand, it is very difficult for us to do the work with you. My dear, you are a beautiful spirit. Understand that you are very gracious—your concerns about the future and wondering which direction your work is going and so on and so forth . . . My dear, we want you to understand that we would very much like to share this with the public. God bless you indeed, certainly, in regard to abuse and such, but understand, my dear, that everyone here upon planet Earth is not only abused but an abuser. In small ways, shapes and forms, all have found ways in which they can indeed abuse one another upon the Earth as well as abuse the Earth herself.

When we are having a little conversation about the many faces of abuse, understand that many faces of abuse can occur in a single moment where there is an ability on the part of human beings to try to control one another. These happen through subtle manipulations. A small child crying and faking the cries to manipulate Mommy into giving him an extra cookie or such thing—this, my dear, is an abuse. An abuse of what? An abuse of love.

Certainly, my dear, it is during this abuse that there is a discovery of self in relationship to life. What does abuse do to abusers? It does not bring them any closer to the world but indeed creates even further separation— the very thing they are trying to avoid. All abusers are trying to find ways to manipulate the world around to draw it closer to them still. Why? Because everyone here upon the planet Earth is in a grand discovery and exploration of self in relationship to life. What is this exploration, my dear? It is an exploration of love. What is it that all upon the planet Earth want to bring closer to them? God bless you indeed, my dear—it is the vibrational frequency of love. All beings here, as well as all objects, as well as all creepy crawlers upon the planet Earth are indeed channels of this love, to varying degrees.

How much do you want to channel this love? How much do you want to give to one another in terms of this love, in terms of understanding that what you want would be the opposite of abuse? That is embrace—to embrace truly from the heart; the opposite of abuse is embrace from the heart. My dear friends, understanding this will bring about greater awareness and understanding of those who are the abusers.

Understanding the Abuser

Now, we understand that certainly the topic here is to explore the relationship of abuse that would be in terms of violence and anything that is less than tender within spousal relationships or family relationships, for children who are seemingly the victims here of tremendous and horrible acts as far as human beings are concerned. God bless you indeed. The aggravation that one being can cause another here upon the planet Earth is tremendous.

But first and foremost, we want you to understand—before we explore this relationship of abuse, of victim and creator, and you indeed are certainly the abuser and the abused—that what we are sharing here is a perspective that comes from a very different realm. In this realm, abuse does not exist, so for us to discuss it, we must have the understanding that we do not believe in abuse. We do not believe that there is such a thing. You have created it upon your planet Earth as a point of discovery of yourself in relationship to life, as a point of understanding that what you truly want to create here is the eternal bond of love.

See the Illusion of Separation

That is the reality, my dear friends; the rest is an illusion. Abuse is an illusion, an illusion of separation that keeps you once again at arm's length from love. It's really quite as simple as this and yet, for you, rather complex. Although we understand that your hearts are a-hurtin' as far as we are concerned, if you would step into our realm of understanding, you would realize, my dear friends, that we feel that it is a very beautiful thing that your hearts are a-hurting.

It is certainly a very beautiful thing that you do not want anyone to feel this kind of pain in his or her life—not on behalf of the victim, as you would call the one who is abused, nor the one who is certainly seemingly in charge, the abuser. Both the abuser and the abused are very much in pain. There is indeed a reality in their lives that is keeping them separate from love.

Understand, my dear friends, that the motivating force for abusers is certainly not being in love with themselves, not being aware that God certainly loves them. There is a driving force that wants to "force" togetherness, if you will, and the way in which abusers do this is through trying to force life to be with them. This can be physically, emotionally, through manipulations, through control, through confinement.

It is those who are abused, the victims, as you would call them here upon the Earth, who at times are extremely and extraordinarily compassionate in their nature, extraordinarily naive, extraordinarily simple in their awareness of life.

Certainly many times, my dear friends—very sadly for you, but it is a part of the school called planet Earth—there are indeed individuals, young children and such who are oftentimes the victims here. They are at play, at wistful play, if you will, walking in a crowd or what have you, certainly absorbed within life and completely immersed with this reality here upon the Earth, understanding the oneness of everything; of all that is, all that ever was, all that ever shall be; completely and totally immersed in a state and condition of love. It is there, my dear friends, that the victim is setting himself or herself up as a victim, because the one who is the abuser wants to do everything possible to eradicate this kind of immersion in life. The abuser does not want to feel alone, does not want to feel outside of life and so therefore tries to make life fit.

The Pain of the Abuser

The abusers, my dear friends, are ones who are hurting extremely in their hearts. Abusers will look to life around them, anything that is growing, anything that is beautiful, anything that is enjoying life, anything that understands the immersion in love, anything that is close to God. This is certainly part and parcel of why there has been tremendous awareness of abuse within churches and such upon your planet Earth, for those who are ministers and preachers and priests and others within the pulpit are seeking a greater understanding and immersion with God. When they see individuals, especially children, who are easily, easily understanding God, wholeheartedly immersed in the very same, certainly surrendering to the journey here of love without any despair, without any resistance, they want to change these children to match their frequency of sadness, of dismay, of misunderstanding. They simply fear that they will be left behind.

The Sin of Separation

My dear friends, all upon the planet Earth are responsible for creating their own heaven. They are responsible for creating their own hell. It is this eternal struggle, this illusion of separation, that was occurring during the first moment of birth here upon planet Earth during what is called within the Bible your "fall." This was a fall into sin—sin being separation, my dear friends; sin being that which keeps you separate, any act that keeps you from the world, from being completely immersed in love one hundred percent at all moments upon the Earth. God bless you indeed.

It is certainly an exploration here upon the planet Earth, an awareness of black and white, up and down, evil and good, but the reality, when all is said and done, comes back to one single given point. That is the tremendous, abiding, eternal vibrational frequency of love that is *you*, that is the truth of self. There is a tremendous desire for those who have fallen into great darkness during the course of their lifetimes, certainly through being abused by others. Once they are abused by others, they have no other awareness of any other reality here upon the Earth. They find themselves immersed in darkness, not knowing that there is light. God bless you indeed. When they see a little seed growing nearby, trying to push its way up through the fertile soil to the sunshine, to the glory and the true love that comes from God, these individuals are terrified. Their reaction is to keep that little seed confined, because this abuser does not understand what is out there on the surface of this soil, of this darkness, and does not want to find out. Why? For fear that there might be even more pain than this.

So oftentimes, in fact surprisingly frequently, the abusers truly feel that they are saving and sparing their victims from greater pain by inflicting pain along the way. Many times, my dear friends, this is the course of action that results here in murder, in a snuffing out of life here upon the planet Earth. Understand that it is the abusers who think truly they are sparing that life any greater pain. That, my dear friends, is the mysterious, unusual awareness of self that occurs at the core of the abuser.

This is something that has not yet been addressed on a grand scale here upon the planet Earth but will be soon surfacing, coming to the front over the course of the next eight years—an awareness of the psyche of individuals who seem to be in such despair, such angst, such fear, such anger that they certainly find themselves creating heinous, horrible acts upon the planet Earth.

God bless you indeed, my dear friends. You have situations of mass murders, what you would know as your serial killers. Where does this form of abuse come from? Where does this act of violence originate? Certainly, my dear friends, generally speaking, these individuals have been forced to be alone so very often in their lives that they are terrified of being left alone ever again. Best way, as far as they are concerned, inside the psyche of the serial killer, is to collect bodies around them so that they know where everyone is. Better to know where they are so there are no surprises, better to know where every individual is so that there are no surprise attacks.

The realm of victims here, my dear friends, is oftentimes correlated directly to an individual in their lives who wreaked havoc upon them, whether real or presumed. On behalf of abusers, of those known here as serial killers, murderers or what have you—you have so very many names and labels for these individuals who are indeed surprisingly as worthy of love as anyone else here upon the planet Earth—you certainly intend to keep them in their spot. God bless you indeed, and we do understand that there is a need for this upon your planet Earth. But realize, my dear friends, that name-calling is just that. It is name-calling that keeps the world in a state and condition of confusion at all times.

Rehabilitating the Abuser

For abusers to ever recover, to revive, to be firmly planted upon the Earth once again as loving beings, they must be told time and again that their true core is to want to love, to receive and to give love to the world. This is the only way in which to rehabilitate such abusers, my dear friends—to remind them of their true self. As long as there is mud-flinging, as long as there is anger, as long as there is a pushing away of these individuals, more and more will yet be born. Certainly there is a wide berth given to these individuals to come to the surface. God bless you indeed. We encourage a healing of these hearts, a healing of the many rather than the few as a testimony to the beauty of their victims, a testimony to love and compassion.

This healing is a part of the increasing awareness and understanding that love is truly what all are seeking here upon planet Earth. This is why, my dear friends, abuse breaks so many hearts, why it bothers you to the core of your being that small children would be taken advantage of, that women would be raped. How awful to cause and wreak havoc and pain upon anyone here upon planet Earth, whether it be black or white, male or female, young or old. God bless you indeed. It's all the same. Pain is felt, my dear friends, in the very same way by everyone here upon the planet Earth.

Seeing the Abuser Within

These are the many faces of abuse, my dear friends, that exist upon the planet Earth. The full spectrum here is the understanding that any action that is less than imbedded in love is certainly considered, as far as we are concerned, to be an abusive act. Any action, great or small, even the way you pressure one another to drive upon your freeways, riding upon the bumper of the car in front of you—even this is a form of abuse, a desire on your part to try to control the world around you.

My dear friends, little white lies, presumably not going to do any damage here, just a little white lie to get your way—these are indeed an abuse of love; an abuse once again of relationships; an abuse that keeps you separate, a wee bit arm's length from the world around you. God bless you indeed, my dear friends. Every time you choose to push away another perspective, every time you choose not to hear someone's opinion, every time you choose not to give any credence to what another individual finds of value for him- or herself, this is once again a form of abuse. These are forms of separation, something that keeps you a wee bit away from love. God bless you indeed.

To honor and respect each other's opinions, perspectives, realities, no matter what; to realize that everyone and everything upon planet Earth is equally deserving of this love—it is there that you fall into your hearts. It is there that you find enlightenment, there within your world, as the creators who you are. It is there, my dear friends, that the abuse disappears. It is there that you begin to understand that you are not a victim, nor is anyone else here upon the Earth a victim. We are all the creators of our realities.

Wrapping Your Mind around Abuse

You might ask, "How is it then, my dear Dr. Peebles, that a small, helpless child is torn apart by a parent and abused so severely in so very many ways, physically tortured, emotionally tortured, sometimes murdered, sexually abused, assaulted, violated in so very many ways?" My dear friends, it's an illusion of separation. It is not a coldness on our part to discuss it in this fashion; we want you to understand that it is an illusion of separation. Can those little souls, those little individuals, truly ever be violated? Can they truly ever have their true, beating, ever-loving heart taken from them?

No, my dear friends, no matter what you try to do here upon planet Earth—you can squash one another with stones, burn one another at the stake, throw daggers into one another's hearts—but the reality is that you cannot ever kill anyone. The reality is that you cannot truly ever abuse others, because their souls indeed are eternal. Their souls indeed come from God. The reality is that great learning, awareness and understanding come through the study of the victim, the abuser and the abused. God bless you indeed.

My dear friends, a great value to be learned from such a study is that planet Earth is indeed a school wherein you are striving to dissolve the illusions of separation, anything that keeps you separate from God, separate from love, separate from anyone here upon the planet Earth, that which we will call the heart of humanity, the true reality of everyone upon the Earth.

God bless you indeed, my dear friends. Certainly it is here that you will discover that never in your eternal soul have you been the victim but always the creator. You will realize that there are so very many opportunities, beautiful souls who come here oftentimes, my dear friends, as willing victims, to offer themselves up as a sacrifice, little angels, little cherubs who come here with such a purity of light that they offer their little souls up to planet Earth as a sacrifice so that you can fall into deeper love with self, with your own hearts.

If It Has Happened to You . . .

My dear friends, we understand that the many rather than the few of those who are indeed listening to this tape, reading the transcription, have indeed been abused in the course of their lifetimes. We understand that your daddy did not serve you well by touching you in the night. We understand that your mommy was particularly spectacular with her anger toward you. We understand that oftentimes you have had many repercussions from these acts of abuse toward you—from husband to wife, from wife to husband.

God bless you indeed, my dear friends; please understand that we are very much aware of this. We know that you are indeed hurting in your ever-lovin' heart from the forms of abuse that you have had to endure. But for a moment here, we would simply ask that you sit in absolute wonder at the reality that you have created. You, my dear friends, are still here upon the Earth. You have chosen to survive. You have come to a greater awareness that you are not worthy of such acts of torture, that you are worthy only of acts of love.

These experiences for you have been tough teachers, without question, but truly, they have helped you to understand, to spell out for you how very beautiful you are, how very compassionate you are, how very trustworthy you are. Certainly, my dear friends, many of you listening to our words have even stepped forth as a result of their experiences to become the teachers to the many rather than the few; to help and assist others to understand that they always have a chance to change their reality and their perspective, to understand that what they are seeking is love.

The many rather than the few have helped and assisted their abusers, have oftentimes not been able to turn away from the one who has abused them. Why, my dear friends? Because you are smart cookies, that's why. Because you have an awareness of what really counts here upon planet Earth, that indeed it is love that counts, the eternal love of self, the eternal love of all of life.

Living after Abuse

God bless you indeed. It is there that you are dissolving the illusions of separation, realizing that this one who has hurt you is still worthy of love, of attention, of a chance. That person is still worthy, my dear friends, because you know the truth and the reality of that person's being. Be aware that it's all right to have a little discernment as well, for those of you who have fallen victim, if you will, to the abuser understand that as a result of this abuse, you have opened your hearts to an awareness of self and God that comes through an unusual form of intuition. You need to learn how to use this intuition to your advantage so that you will not be hurt ever again. We would ask that you simply explore this intuition in terms of your relationship to your abusers. God bless you indeed. Ask yourself quite honestly here: "Was there any given point, any moment at which I knew that this person was going to hurt me? At any point did I know, was I aware that I was in danger? Was there some way in which I was forewarned?"

Now, we understand there are many situations where you could not have extricated yourself, no matter what; wild horses could not have done it for you, only divine intervention could. We understand this, but if you can become aware of the moments when you certainly had it very clear inside your heart and soul through your God-given intuition that you were in danger, you can learn to use this toward your advantage now and in the future. Such moments help you come back to the security of knowing that you are indeed safe.

Certainly this is a tremendous struggle for the many rather than the few who have been victims, to find once again that they can feel safe in the world, that there is not an abuser standing behind every bush, every barn, every begonia. God bless you indeed. My dear friends, it is through your intuition and your awareness of self that you can keep yourselves safe upon the Earth. Realize that a part of this difficulty, the struggle for those of you who have been abused, is that you have such ever-loving hearts, such compassion that you have a tendency to see the potential of the light within a soul. You see the potential, the love, the truth and the reality of those individuals, no matter what they present upon the surface. Then, when you get your intuitive nudge that perhaps you are not safe in their presence, the loving part of you says, "But I am, because the reality of this individual is that he or she would never hurt a fly, that this person does not want to hurt any-one and perhaps is even carrying quite a bit of hurt inside of him- or her-self." And so, my dear friends, you end up giving your abuser the benefit of the doubt time and time again. Be it in the grocery store, in the course of conversation with a clerk, it doesn't matter: The form of the abuse is always the same at its core; it is that which is less than love. God bless you indeed.

Keeping Yourself Safe

So realize, my dear friends, that you can use your intuition and discretion to understand an individual who has the potential of light within. All peo-ple are truly, at their core, loving, respectable, honorable beings. This is where they are indeed headed toward in their understanding. But all are not there yet. Of course there is no "there" to get to, because when they get there, where are they going to get to next? The answer is: into even greater awareness and understanding of God and of love.

But for the time being, understand that it is all right at times to take human beings at face value, to understand and have compassion for their struggles that you can feel inside; but, my dear friends, you cannot change them, you cannot release them from their confinement unless you are will-ing to grow yourselves.

Sometimes it takes great strength and much courage, my dear friends, to meet someone and fall in love with that person's soul but then to make a decision to turn away, simply to walk away, because what is upon the sur-face is a very clear indicator that this individual is not ready to give birth to the truth of him- or herself. Then you turn and walk away, taking charge of your existence, sending a strong message to abusers, potential abusers, the bullies who want to pull you close to them so they don't feel alone. You send a very strong message to them that your frequency is different, that you are standing in an intoxicating world of love. By doing so, my dear friends, by turning away, you get their little ticker to thinking. Their little hearts begin to beat stronger because they want to understand how it is that you are able to walk away from them.

In many situations, my dear friends, this can cause vast anger inside of them, because they don't understand. How dare you walk away? How dare you be immersed in the light? How dare you? This is where the fights begin, where they try to grab you, to claw you, to pull you close. God bless you indeed. Certainly this is very, very frequent in terms of spousal abuse—quite specific to this form of abuse where abusers do not want to see light shining forth from their beloveds. They do not want to see this light being made public; they want to keep it for themselves. They want to determine when it surfaces and how it surfaces so that they can study it, explore it and understand it.

Spousal abusers have a tendency to draw their spouses very close to keep them confined, away from the public. They become enraged even when their spouses would laugh. They want to take everything and put it through a filter that becomes very contorted and very, very frightening and very surreal to them and to their loved ones. This is where a situation begins for the ones who are victims here in which they find themselves confined through what is an emotional confusion caused by their abusers. They don't know if it's right or wrong, when they can bring their light to the surface, when they cannot, when they can share of themselves, when they cannot, because it is randomly decided by the abuser. It is here, my dear friends, that the anger increases on behalf of both victim and abuser; it is here that the fights begin.

Leave the Situation Behind

The individuals who are abused have so very much love and so much awareness that love is at the core of existence, so much compassion, that the abusers begin to feel guilt and shame. The abused ones feel frightened that they have done something wrong by becoming enraged, that in some way they have caused and created their reality of being abused by their husbands or by their wives. And this, my dear friends, is indeed truth—not to make excuses here for one who is creating acts of violence, but to applaud the victims for an understanding that they are indeed participants in these relationships. It is necessary in order to help the victims in these particular circumstances to applaud their beauty and their compassion for the abusers rather than to make them feel shamed. We do not want to berate them for their choice of spouse or any such thing but to understand and to appreciate the victims' great love for their spouses, because they indeed see the potential of the light within the abuser.

The reality is that the abuser wants to love, to create love, to manifest love, to be love eternally. It is through this form of discussion with the individuals who are being abused that they can then see the light of their souls and realize that—although they want to continue to give the benefit of the doubt to the abuser—perhaps it is indeed time to give the benefit of the doubt to themselves. Perhaps it is time to love and to appreciate self, to realize that there has been a learning here; that they are indeed compassionate, wide awake, intuitive and aware of the reality of the core of humanity and of human hearts, no matter what appears on the surface.

It is there that they find strength and courage inside themselves to at long last walk away. It is there, within this clarity of self, within this clarity of value of self, that the victims, the ones who have been abused within such spousal relationships, can at long last stand firmly within their truth that they are indeed worthy of more. And certainly it is there that you assure everyone—yourself, a friend, a loved one—that although they have walked away, you understand that they still love their abuser. Reassure them, my dear friends, that love is never wrong, no matter the form. It is never wrong; it is all right for you, those of you who have been hurt by your spouses, who have been hurt by your children, who have been hurt by your mothers or fathers, to love them. Love should never cause you any shame. God bless you, indeed. Free yourselves up and applaud yourselves for learning these tremendous lessons of compassion.

Start with Self-Love

My dear friends, all human beings upon the Earth want to find companionship. Companionship is the driving force here. Holding hands, falling in love, touches and kisses and hugs—these are the treasures of your souls, the treasures you seek outside of money, fine homes, careers and outside of enlightenment. These are the treasures you seek here upon the planet Earth. Just stop and pause and think how very difficult it is to get these treasures, how very difficult it is to give these treasures.

Think of the many ways in which you withhold your love, how many times you have resisted a hug or a conversation, how many ways you have withheld your love. When you understand this, you will realize that the work that all human beings have to do here upon the planet Earth is very difficult work. We understand; it is one of the most difficult schools in the universe. Through this understanding, you will suddenly become aware that you are indeed here to discover and dissolve these illusions of separation—anything that keeps you away from love.

Understand that you very much want to receive love. Think of the many ways in which life resists you, why someone will not talk to you, why someone will not touch you. It is not because the world is out to get you, not because the world doesn't like you. It is because other people are as afraid as you are, my dear friends, of giving and receiving the greater abundance of self, of life, of God and existence, which is indeed love.

You are all very beautiful spirits upon the planet Earth. Give yourselves love today. Do not beat yourselves up with unkind words. When you look in the mirror, my dear friends, say, "I love you so very much. You are so perfect in your form, and I appreciate all that you have given to life." Say this to yourselves; start there in solving and resolving the issues of abuse in your life and in the lives of others.

Start within your own heart to love yourself, making loving allowance for all things to be in their own time and place, starting with yourself. Increase communication with all of life, with yourself first, with respect. That is the key to resolving the issues of abuse. How often have you belittled and berated yourself? Write your answer on a sheet of paper, and you will be appalled at the abuse that you have inflicted upon yourself. From our much larger perspective—not the only perspective in the universe—that is sad. It breaks our hearts to watch you struggle with self-love.

My dear friends, you are indeed worthy of love. Stand tall upon the planet Earth, immerse yourself in community with life, communion with life, relationship with life. Enjoy the journey to your heart without end. Love yourself first, my dear friends, and this love will emanate and radiate toward the world around you in ways you never dreamed or imagined possible. You will find more love than you have ever known before. My dear friends, give one another a hug today. Cherish the life that you have been given. Enjoy the opportunities for growth.

Go your way in peace, love and harmony, for life is indeed a joy. All you have to do to enjoy the journey to your own heart and to your own enlightenment is simply lighten up just a little bit more and remember, my dear friends, that the potential of the light that you see within life around you exists within you too. God bless you, indeed.

Healing the Pain of Yesterday

S parks of light are here today. You are beautiful creators. We love you so very much, students of the divine, every single one of you here in this room today a teacher. And we want you to understand that the one you are teaching first and foremost is yourself. You have an opportunity today to step into the light, the fire of your soul, with respect for yourself and your angelic friends, and to create an opportunity to find the light within yourselves.

You have a vision of yourself, but what is it? Does it come to you, my dear friends, in a feeling? Does it come to you in a fear? Does it come to you in a chance for understanding the world or a chance, my dear friends, for the world to understand you? Does it come through a desire for acknowledgment of the great and wondrous person who you are? And yet you are so afraid to reveal the very same.

Right here, today, each of you has a beautiful guide, a friend who's been with you for a lifetime. Your guide stands directly behind you to comfort you, acknowledge you and give unto you that which you desire to receive in your life—the feeling that you are special, that you are walkers in peace and laborers of love.

We understand the pain, the desires and the expectations of your human existence, and we understand how difficult it is to be upon the planet Earth. You are some of the most courageous adventurers in the universe. Planet Earth is unlike any other school. We want you to delve into yesterday-and we mean quite literally yesterday, the past twenty-four-hour period of time—and we want you to be very honest with yourself.

No one is looking at you or judging you. Look into your heart and be honest with yourself. What is it that you would change about yesterday? What would you like to recognize and acknowledge as being a darker space that you would rather push aside? Recognize and acknowledge it. Be it that you stepped upon a turtle or an ant, or that you looked away when someone tried very hard to give you love through a glance—there is within every single, solitary person reading this today a point in time yesterday that, if you could, you would go back and change. God bless you indeed.

Commit to the Truth of Yourself

Well, my dear friends, there is no need to go back, because yesterday is here today. There is no time; there is only the moment. So the opportunity exists to rectify what you fear to be the roles that you have created upon the Earth, either through action or inaction. We ask that you resolve this issue within yourself, here and now. With your eyes closed, return to that time and place and repeat the action. Then say very frankly, "I am so sorry. All I really wanted was to touch and to be touched, to love and to be loved, and I apologize to you, my heart, for having turned my face away from God."

It is here in this revelation of yourself that you begin to understand that you can fall in love with life as never before and in such a fashion that you become intoxicated by the opportunity to be a lover to planet Earth. We ask here today that you commit to the truth of yourself, the divinity of the light that truly wants only to reveal the truth of God—the truth of you. You, my dear friends, are indeed God eternal. You are not separate from anything or anyone. Through meditation and prayer, you have already begun to reach out to one another, to unify in agreement with God's heart that love is the only point upon the Earth. If you turn away from this in any moment, you dispel the richness and abundance that you seek—that which you desire to manifest in everyday life and that which you desire to have within your home, relationships, work, play and opportunities.

It is part of the illusion of separation that you do not have a chance, that you can't, that you are not able to do this. My dear friends, you do, you can and you are. There are so many possibilities in the universe. You can redesign yourself instantly if you are willing to take a risk and to know that you don't know what's going to happen next, and that is wise. To understand and to embrace this is the greatest wisdom of all, because it is there that you step into the present, for there is no time.

Everything that you have seen, tasted, touched, felt, smelled, spoken and experienced in this lifetime—the intolerance and the injustice that you have suffered and the bodily ailments that overwhelm you in some cases—adds up to this moment. You have created this reality by choosing to step into the room, by choosing to hear my voice and by choosing to be involved in a meditation that guides you to the God light within. God bless you indeed, my dear friends. You are beautiful students here upon the planet Earth. Do you have questions or comments?

Acknowledging Guidance

I'm not sure I have a question today, but you talked about guidance again. I am aware of the guidance and have a lot of faith in it, but I don't acknowledge it enough.

Yes, that's hard. It takes time. Look at it, my dear friend, like learning how to play the guitar. You have to practice and take a chance. The best way to take a chance is to make little games, if you will. Spirits love to play games. And you say, "All right, here it is. I feel something inside that I would like to do, create or manifest. I'm not certain that it's the right action for me, but if I see that the next car is red, I will take action. If it is blue, then I will take no action. If it is any other color, I will realize that I am out of my mind." And then you simply take action. If the car is red, then you do it; you proceed.

Test this over and over, and you will see that when you listen to your heart, you have the knowing. It is in hesitation that things don't work out. You say, "But I knew it in advance. I felt it. I was intuiting." Then you must be honest with yourself, because if it takes three days to convince yourself that you really do know that you are feeling what you are feeling, then the opportunity is probably lost!

When you laugh, my dear friends, it is a lovely resonance of you. When you speak, it is another lovely resonance. We encourage you to speak to us out loud. This is very hard for some of you, but thoughts are things, and you make them manifest as you hear them with your ears. When you speak them rather than trying to pray them out of yourself, you absorb the resonance. You not only hear the words, but a frequency is being moved about and absorbed into you. So when you pray, do it out loud.

"Dr. Peebles, I am so upset with you. I can't stand this. You told me x, y and z would happen, and they haven't happened yet. How dare you?" It's all right to chew me out! I don't mind. I love you anyway! My dear friends, this makes you become very clear about your heart. You become clear about what you really feel inside, because sometimes when you're chewing me out, for example, you might find, "Well, I don't really feel that way," and "Yes, I am willing to wait a little longer." But you hear the truth of yourself, if you will, as you believe it to exist. The real truth, the underlying reality of who you are, is that you are a lover, a beautiful spirit who knows in your heart of hearts that your destination is in the divine. Your destination, my dear friends, is love. That is the tip of the iceberg.

How to Quit Your Job

I want to quit my job, but I don't know how.

You set your sights on it 100 percent—and we mean through meditation, prayer and your actions that support the statement: "This won't last forever; I am on to other things." You need to commit to what you want inside. We don't care if you make a mountain out of snowballs or marshmallows. If that is your truest heart's desire, my dear, then it is what you need to do, and that will lead you to the next step in your journey. There is nothing too crazy or too far-fetched for God, because it all comes from Him.

So we want you to pay attention. Are you different? Yes. Are you creative? Yes, you are ridiculously creative. Are you afraid to show this? Yes. Are you, my dear, tired as all get out? Yes. Look at the things that you know to be true about yourself and be honest with yourself. That's the only way you will find the light within.

See if you can fathom this, my dear: You are digging a hole in fertile soil. As you dig, you find a worm. You move the worm out of the way and then a rock falls in. So you take that out and—oh goodness, look at that! There are some leaves and old glass and so on. You pick it all out to make this hole clear so that you can plant yourself in it and then grow, finding and touching the face of God within.

You can do it today, my dear. Nothing's stopping you other than yourself. Will you perish? No, you won't perish. You're smart! You've gotten yourself out of worse pickles. So, my dear, it's just one more little test of your soul. Now get busy doing what you really want to do, you see? You're a lightworker, and for all lightworkers, there is always adversarial energy at work—energy trying to knock you down, turn you astray or get you off course, until you think you can't do it. It says, "You'll never amount to anything!" You say to that voice, "You know what? Excuse me, but I'm getting on with it anyway. I'm going to look for God, nothing else but God." And that's the bottom line, you see? Put your foot down. A little righteous anger wouldn't hurt, yeah?

Thank you.

You are welcome, my dear. You're a beautiful spirit; you're immeasurably better already. God bless you, indeed.

The Value of Soul Retrieval

You mentioned soul retrieval to me. Maybe it would be helpful for everyone here to understand the value of that.

You are retrieving yourself in every single, solitary second of the day. You talk to yourself all the time. You are looking around, peeking inside, looking at yesterday and tomorrow, looking and seeking and striving to make sense of the beautiful, multifaceted being who you are, God bless you indeed. That is soul retrieval in a nutshell. As well, when you finally try to stop going backward and move forward, you have to step into the past so that you can gain a sense of yourself where you felt a little more important or enlightened, so that you can see the fruits of you labor. There's nothing wrong with reviewing your life or other lifetimes to see the fruits of your labor.

Here in this room today, it's not your first time as a lightworker or a teacher. You have been a friend; you have gone above and beyond the call of duty in other lifetimes and so on. These are all parts of you, my dear friends, and so you're retrieving memories from yesterday for your understanding today. They aren't something you have to hold on to. They were never separate from you in the first place. But really, my dear friends, you are tilling the soil of your soul. Does this help, my dear?

It helps just to be here and speak with you.

Doesn't it? God bless you, indeed. It helps us too. It is a true pleasure, my dear friends, to have the opportunity to play. That's something that Summer, our dear channel here, cannot fathom. She's constantly thanking yours truly for the opportunity to make a living doing this work, for my willingness to come through. She doesn't understand that I want to come through; I love it. It is my greatest joy. I need a telephone line, and she provides that.

It's All Good

Hello, my dear. You're a beautiful spirit! Don't stress and strain. It's all good, yeah? You hear that all the time, and you say, "Yes, it's all good. I believe it." Part of this, my dear, is that you worry so much about everyone else. Part of your difficulty is learning how to enjoy life, even when everyone else is in so much pain. It's hard for you, my dear, but someone's got to start doing it, don't you think? You can make it. Start enjoying your life as a demonstration for others. It doesn't matter what's going on. You can take care of anything! You can walk in peace and love, and then you become a true lightworker who is willing to walk into the darker spaces without fear, expectation or concerns of being judged. Nothing that you think or say is too frivolous.

You know something? My dear friends, we are not here in this room to prove that there is life after death. You'll all find that out sooner or later anyway, and then you will know for sure. We are here, my dear friends, to show you that there is life in life, and you experience that and cherish it. It's such a short journey upon your Earth. Don't waste time with anger or resentment. Don't waste time by holding life at arm's length. It's so much easier to fall into the embrace.

The Power of Vocalizing Prayer

You mentioned earlier about vocalizing prayer, but I feel that the spirit realm can feel our resonating thoughts and that certain thoughts are prayer. Would you comment on that?

Yes, absolutely. There is nothing wrong whatsoever with silent prayer, but the biggest problem for human beings is believing what you're praying about and really feeling it with sincerity. When you speak it, you hear the words that you want us to hear, and we hear them all the time. We are never away from you, my dear friends. God's not away from you at all; God is right there within your heart, always with you, as are your guides. We're the open telephone line, if you will, twenty-four hours a day, seven days a week. God bless you, we do work past midnight, you see?

It's a challenge for you to find the sincerity within to really say, "I am worthy. I know that God is kind, and I know that God desires me to have clarity in this." You are afraid of the clarity, because once you get it, then you have to take action. So, my dear friends, to force yourselves to really receive from your prayers, we say speak to them with your voice, out loud, and learn and educate yourselves about sincerity. Then you will find that you have the insight and can hear the still, small voice within yourself and learn to obey it instead of thinking about it for a week.

Thoughts are indeed things, my dear friends. You bring them down from the heavens and make them manifest here upon planet Earth. For example, make a decision to ride a horse, and then go do it. That might sound like a fantastic adventure, my dear friends, but it exists already.

We love you so very much. Go your way in peace, love and harmony, for life is indeed a joy. All you have to do as you enjoy the journey to your own heart and enlightenment is simply be intoxicated with yourself and the possibilities within you. What you have to share with the world is unlike anything else, and yet it's not any different than what is inside of everyone—and that is love. God bless you, indeed.

Creation, Reincarnation and Falling in Love with Life

My dear friends, at this time, we would like to discuss respect for and intimacy with all of life. This is part and parcel of your journey to the heart here upon the planet Earth: intimacy with life—contact with the many rather than the few.

When we say "contact with the many rather than the few," we do not necessarily mean contact with human beings around you. We do not necessarily mean contact with the little creepy crawlers of the Earth. We do not necessarily mean your fanny having contact with your chair. What we mean by "contact with the many rather than the few" is for you to have contact with the many rather than the few within yourself—your emotions, feelings, inspirations and perspectives. We mean for you to have contact with yourself first, and to birth your many emotions and inspirations into the world so that you set the stage for yourself.

Give of Yourself and Watch Life Give Back to You

You set yourself up to receive an honest echo back to you from what you have created in this life so that you are aware and can say, "Well, I did my very best to take charge of myself, to give of myself without lying, hiding or giving out any shades of gray. I have given only the black and white of me, and on the surface, I am very outspoken and very kind, very compassionate while I am doing so. Now I sit back and wait for the resonance to return this back to me from the life around me." Is life going to kill you for this? Well, you'd be surprised. Life will not kill you when you are coming to the surface with your truth—100 percent, fully and completely. The only thing that life around you can feel from this is absolute, total love. Love is equated here with intimacy—intimacy with your heart first, and then taking this circle and turning it into a spiral that spirals out toward your family.

Start there in speaking your truth; begin speaking to your family first. If you can resolve the issues in your heart and in your family structure, no matter what that structure is, you will find the salvation of your soul. From there, spiral out toward your friends, the ones you feel are closest to your heart. Share your opinions and perspectives with the friends around you and watch your life come to life at long last. No longer must you mask your tears, your laughter. No longer must you mask your concerns or your anger. No longer must you cry yourself to sleep feeling as if you are very alone and separate from life around you.

"Why don't my friends talk to me? Why don't they understand me?" Well, look inside of your heart. How much have you given of yourself? How freely and how intimately are you willing to have contact with life around you? It is up to you. It starts within your own heart and continues as you have contact with your friends and family. And now, my dear friends, you spiral out toward a nearby stranger standing in the grocery-store line and begin sharing of your heart. You will discover that there are no accidents upon your planet Earth in terms of the contact you receive from life around you. You are sitting in your restaurants and you stress and you strain to not listen in on conversations nearby, to not get involved. You try and stress and strain to keep yourself separate from life. But we would encourage you to allow yourself to fall into the folding arms of existence, the ever-lovin' hug.

Certainly it is much easier to surrender into that hug than to hold it at arm's length. And so therefore, when an opportunity arises for you to speak to a stranger because you are so inspired within your heart to share something very intimately, give it a whirl; see what happens and how life responds to you. The more you come to the surface with this willingness to have intimacy—contact with the many rather than the few inside yourself first and then bringing it to the surface to share with life around you—the more of a resonance you set up of yourself upon planet Earth.

It is here where you will begin to attract human beings closer and closer to you who are of like mind and like heart. It is here where you will discover freedom, because no longer will you feel alone; no longer will you feel that you are self-centered with your opinions and your perspectives, that no one else understands you and so on.

Suddenly you will be surrounded by true family, immersing yourself in the true conscious awareness of who you are, looking into the faces of life around you and discovering that nothing is hidden anymore. Right now when you look at your family members, when you look into the eyes of your friends, what do you see there? Are there mysteries? Do you feel that something is hidden away? Can you look into your own eyes in the mirror and say to yourself, "Well, in what way am I hiding myself? In what way do I remain a mystery to life around me? I want to have contact with the many rather than the few but . . ."

Well, I say, do unto others as you would have them do unto you! You start with yourself once again. To share of yourself is the greatest gift, certainly the greatest gift that you can give to human life upon planet Earth. It is one way in which you can show God how very much you appreciate all the gifts that you have been given—all the gifts of self, all your dear friends and all the perfection that you are. To bring this to the surface will create a sense of self beyond your wildest dreams and imaginations. You will find that suddenly you are indeed living in an ideal world that feels like heaven on Earth—and after all, my dear friends, heaven is not a place; it's a feeling, is it not? And it exists right there inside of your house.

Metaphysics Is the Science of Wonder

What would you tell those who are brand-new to the metaphysical world?

The very first thing that we would tell them is that they are not brand-new to it at all. Do you believe in the supernatural? Do you believe in the paranormal? Ask yourselves these questions and then look into your own heart. Are you not rather a miracle yourself? Look at your physical bodies. So often you take for granted the absolute miracle that exists there. The mere movement of your hand, is that not in and of itself supernatural? Is that not in and of itself a miracle? From where does this energy come? That is all that you have to ask yourselves, and suddenly you will appreciate the miraculous nature of existence. The harmony that you can see within nature itself—within the environment, for example—can ignite a spark of awareness that something that seems rather paranormal is occurring at all times.

For example, as you watch animals from a distance, you would begin to understand the many ways in which they communicate with one another without words, in a way very much akin to psychic capabilities. Another example: You have not seen your kitty cat, and you have a thought of your kitty cat only to find him around your feet. How did this occur? How did your little kitty cat hear the tiny stirrings of your heart and know of your desire that he be closer and nearer to you? Such situations arise time and time again within your existence. Certain points, moments of intuition . . . Don't cross the street right now; sit back for a moment here; wait for a second before you cross the street—why do we have these stirrings? Well goodness gracious, my dear friends, there goes a zooming car! It would have flattened you right then, but you listened to the stirrings of your heart.

That is part and parcel of what metaphysics is about. And it's not something that is scary; it is a science. Metaphysics is the science of wonder, and metaphysics is where healing and understanding begin. All you have to do is look into the sciences that you cherish so very much: Look within your medical community, within your psychiatric community. They would be your gods at times. But when medicine first appeared, where did the inspiration come from? Before human beings had microscopes upon the Earth to see the very cells inside of your body, someone had to think about it, had to feel the possibility there, had to wonder. And that is the science of metaphysics, my dear friends—the science of wonder.

And so metaphysics is not outside of you; it is the very foundation on which you were born. You scare yourselves silly when there are unknowns. Everyone upon the planet Earth, and we say this without qualification, is afraid of the possibility of a spark within that is unknown to you—afraid of darker spaces, afraid of dis-ease, afraid of the unknown. And yet, the flip side of that fear is excitement, anticipation, wonder. Fall in love with that wonder, and suddenly you will give birth to the perspectives of the many rather than the few. Suddenly nothing will really be unknown to you; you will have the answers, because they will be inspired within your heart, within your intuition, within deeper understanding.

But look into your own eyes every day in the mirror. Fall in love there first, for that in and of itself is a metaphysical expression. Can you measure love? Goodness gracious, you can't put a quantity to it, can you? Can you measure it in terms of grams or weight or energy or light frequency? Ask yourselves these questions. You do, however, believe in love, do you not? That's rather unusual. Actually, that's rather supernatural; it's rather, as far as we are concerned, paranormal, for it is outside of what you can touch, outside of what is tangible in the flesh; it is something that comes in. You know it exists; it exists inside of your heart. Start there. Love, my dear friends, is metaphysical. Love is the very nature of self. God is love, and therefore God is you. And that, once again, is the tip of the iceberg.

How are you, Dr. Peebles?

How am I? I am—I shall say it in a nutshell here—fascinating, wondrous, gorgeous and absolutely stunning in my stature. I love my profile, my chin. I love my heart. I love my hands. I love my insecurities. I love my sense of security. I love myself as God, and I love myself with a passionate fever that you would call here upon your Earth as being derived from someone known as Lucifer. "Goodness gracious, Dr. Peebles here?" Well, goodness gracious, not a problem as far as I am concerned! As far as I am concerned, I have not yet found a way in which to separate out anything from myself. I am all that is, ever was and ever shall be, just as you are, God bless you indeed. So don't be afraid; you have everything inside of yourselves—all possibilities.

That is how I am today: filled with possibilities! And the funny thing is, what I have discovered in my enlightenment is that what I enjoy more than everything is to bring to the surface of myself in each and every moment of my existence *love!* It is there, within love, that all greed, shame, doubt, guilt, pressure, stress, anger, fear and pain dissolve. That's how I am today, my dear. How do you like them apples?

Create Your Own Heaven on Earth

Would you please expand on heaven and hell? Do they exist, and if they do, where are they?

They exist, and they are right there inside of you—right now, absolutely. There are many ways in which we can answer this question, because there are—how shall we say?—worlds that exist that are born from the consciousness of human beings who passed to the other side with a very strong belief system in a place such as an inferno and in a place that is within the heavens, within the clouds, where beautiful angels of wonder play harps.

Yes, these places exist for many, many spirits, but our answer to the question is that they exist inside of you at all times. Through your choices and perceptions, you do indeed create your reality. You make a decision in every single moment of your day as to whether to stand up straight and feel great joy in your existence or to slump over and feel defeated. Whether to be the victim or the creator is the question inside of you at all times. To be the victim is hell, and to understand that you are a creator is absolute heaven upon Earth. When you truly understand that you are a creator, you will finally realize that nothing is outside of you, and that therefore everything is possible for you. It is not a matter of good or bad, right or wrong; it is not a matter of perfection or imperfection. Everything is always in right order. And so therefore, whether you are asleep or awake, you are making a determination inside of yourself: "Right now I am living in hell," or "Right now I am standing in an intoxicating heaven." You make the decision.

"But Dr. Peebles, there are terrible things happening upon planet Earth! We have terrorists and wars! We have unexpected deaths! We have strangers crawling through our windows! How do you expect us to feel that this is heaven on Earth when there is so much unkindness, so much greed, so much pain?" We would ask you this: What do you want to create? That is all that counts here, my dear friends. And so when you find that there is a terrifying moment in your existence, you choose how to respond to it. Is it easy? Not at first, but once you realize that only you can poison your life through your thoughts, choices and perceptions, once you realize this, you will suddenly discover that you have a power beyond your wildest dreams and imaginations and that this power comes through change. It comes through your willingness to change your mind, to act in kindness, to believe in God, to believe in love and to bring compassion to the surface, no matter what the circumstances, rather than running out and grabbing your guns to fight the terrorists even as you become a terrorist yourself.

Find yourselves simply praying for the upliftment of others, praying for them to find their hearts and the truth of themselves. And the truth is, my dear friends, you are all made of the same stuff, and you are all one family, forever and ever. It is up to you to create heaven and hell. It is a choice in every moment of your life. All you have to do for a moment here—whether or not you believe in Him, whether or not you believe He existed (if you do not believe, you can suspend this for a moment here)—is simply think about the person known as Jesus Christ. Think about the way in which He could walk into a person's aura field and dissolve pain, dissolve misery, because His love was so true and so abundant and so much on the surface all of the time that no matter the moment—no matter the pain and the burning and the sting within His hands and feet upon the cross, no matter, my dear friends—his love dissolved the agony. And it was there that Jesus Christ walked in heaven upon planet Earth, which could at times have been a living hell, but He refused to see it as such. He did not acknowledge it. He saw only what was good and right and kind and wondrous within each and every human heart, knowing full well that He was that and that all human hearts are birthed from the very same place. One family, one God, one love.

Soldiers Reenact Karma and Defend Their Soul Families

We have such compassion for the soldier who has no control over his life and murders others, and yet he is not held accountable for murder on this Earth. What happens when he crosses over? How does he deal with this?

It is a very, very difficult journey for any soldier upon the planet Earth. Certainly it is not an easy task to come in and make the decision to be a soldier, to be willing to come to planet Earth and inflict pain on others. Many a soldier is involved in an act of . . . How shall we say? Well, most wars, most hand-to-hand combat, most battles (for your understanding, we will say about 98 percent of battles)—physically speaking here, between at least two individuals, though possibly many more—are born and birthed from karma. Those who choose the soldier's life show a willingness to come to planet Earth and reenact situations from the distant past, to allow their lives to be taken by another's hand in an act of exchange, for if you have once taken the life of someone else in a previous lifetime, you want to rectify this. That is what war is about. It is a point of balance upon your planet Earth in order to bring about karmic relief for individuals who are feeling remorse over actions from the distant past, and they cannot release the pain without truly reenacting the experience. Battles give them a chance to go back: "Can't I do it again? Can't I do it differently this time?"

Yes, you can, and by choice. The soldier's life is not something that God forces upon anyone; it is not a necessity, but it is tremendously loving of all those individuals who come to planet Earth, for they are willing to reenact situations from the past to at long last release—how shall we say?—situations within soul families. For oftentimes these are collective communities coming together. For example, with your Twin Towers, there was a tremendous acting out of karma there, and for the many rather than the few there was tremendous release and absolute enlightenment at the point of transition.

That is the tip of the iceberg. But, my dear friends, love your soldiers without question, beyond your wildest dreams and imaginations. They have chosen a very difficult path upon your planet Earth, and certainly it is not murder; it is an act of care. Truly, respect and honor your soldiers, for they exist inside of you as well.

You see, when you look at your soldiers, there is a tremendous uprising within individuals who say, "I love my soldiers so very much," and you feel deeply moved by this, and the reason for it is because you can see that it takes tremendous courage to defend a soul family. It is a tremendous act of courage and a tremendous act of love and bravery as well, without question. What this inspires within individuals is a feeling of, "I wish I had such bravery. I wish I had such courage. I wish I could even walk into the grocery store and say 'hello' to a stranger, let alone reenact karma here upon the Earth and take another life with my own hand and still feel good about myself."

It's a very interesting point upon your Earth and one that is often overlooked. When we ask that you look at the soldier, we are not asking that you look at the soldier who fights for your country. We ask you to look at all the soldiers, on both sides. It's a very interesting thing, this war. It is the battle of what you consider to be good and evil, light and dark, Satan and Jesus Christ. But you can't separate the two. Each side needs the other to enact these acts of bravery, these acts . . . How shall we say? At times, some of these acts are not brave at all and some of them are extreme acts of cowardice, but that would be a whole other answer to your question.

All Wars Are the Same

With all of the wars that you've seen, is there any difference between one war and another?

There is no difference between wars, whether it is within a family or between countries. Wars are certainly there because human hearts do not like boundaries; they do not like barriers. You try to force others to change, to fit you, but you will come to an understanding upon the Earth—everyone will before you can ever be enlightened—that these barriers really exist inside of yourself. You can't change anyone, ever; it is up to the individual to make that decision for him- or herself. And so you try to make others cross over to your perspective. You can't! It's impossible.

And so what can you do then? Well, you simply play with life, allowing for other perspectives with loving allowance for all things to be, starting with yourself—loving allowance for all things to be; allow for other perspectives. And you'll be rather surprised that even within your arguments, the moment when you agree to disagree, there is understanding, for that is when love comes into play. Try it out on a family member. The next time you are arguing, surrender and say, "All right, I understand your perspective, and I surrender." You will fall into laughter, and you will find that it really doesn't matter, that all you are seeking in the first place is simply love. That's really at the heart of everything, is it not?

This is a very, very beautiful question, and it is not often asked. Most human beings don't want to take a look at their wars; they don't want to look at the pain that is caused upon planet Earth. But that's a fascinating arena, because it is there where you come to learn how to care. The compassion level is always raised upon the planet Earth in times of war, because everyone sees how absolutely absurd it is. It's ridiculous! You can convert the most hardened criminals in a second flat once they have lost a brother or sister to war. It's a remarkable phenomenon upon the Earth, but it is truly the most descriptive phenomenon on the Earth.

It shows the battle within yourself at all times. How many acts of terrorism have you committed against yourself already this morning as you looked in the mirror? "Goodness gracious, I see yet another wrinkle! Why are my eyes so dark? Why is my skin so flaccid? Oh, goodness gracious, hoist up my bosom with a bra!" You see, these are acts of terrorism and unkindness to yourself. At all times, this battle rages. When you see it enacted in full-blown wars, it's a fantastic place to test yourself and your strength. Do you want to stay with your perspective, or are you suddenly willing to let go and let God instead?

Reincarnation Offers You Different Courses in This School

Please comment on reincarnation.

Reincarnation is about past lives, we believe. That's our comment here.

Ah, we tease a little. You go to sleep every night and you die, and when you wake up in the morning and you live, you are reborn. And every morning, you wake up and you review your previous day and you say, "Well, this happened yesterday. I don't like what that was. Let me try it again. Let me call Dad and make amends here. I don't like the way we started out that conversation, and I would like to rectify it." And so you go back into your past lives, your yesterday, and re-create it. Think about this for a moment here; try to remember exactly where you were standing in your living room at the age of three on June 1, 1942, for example. Remember this? Perhaps not. Perhaps you weren't even born yet. But find a point in your childhood. Can you remember everything? Not at all. Past lives are just other days of the week as far as we are concerned.

There is certainly a wearing out of the physical form, and eventually you will transition from this lifetime. And you say, "Well, I wasn't quite finished yet," and so you make a decision to come back to the school called planet Earth. Very much as you attend a university, so you decide to take a few courses, and you decide that your major will be in philosophy, for example. And then you realize, "Well, I think I'll change this; I would rather study home economics," and so you change your desires until you are better matched within your frequency to learn what you would like to learn. You come back to college again and again, going home for the summer for a vacation. Rest your feet, eat some watermelon and then get back to work in the fall.

That is reincarnation, and certainly it is not a necessity any more than it is for you to go to a university. You don't have to. You can attend, you can quit and you can go do something else as far as we are concerned. You are here by choice. "Ah! Dr. Peebles, please tell me it's not my choice. I can't stand my existence!" Well, my dear friends, it is your choice, and it is your choice every single morning to wake up. You make that decision. You choose to wake up, to discover something new every day. And every night, you go to sleep and you feel that you have fallen into another world for the time being, leaving your body and once again coming back in the morning, reincarnating over and over and over again.

You can reincarnate a thought; you can start out as a Christian and become a metaphysician. You take water and fill a cup. The cup is your physical body and the water is your spirit, and you can pour it out and pour it back in as many times as you like. You can pour it into a different glass, if you like, but the water stays the same. It might take a little different shape, a little different form; it might have a different resonance if it's in a champagne glass than if it's in a jelly jar, but it still remains the same. So you choose your physical form to set up a resonance of how people will respond to you, how they will look at you, so that you can formulate various classroom settings.

Some come to planet Earth to discover and dissolve the illusion of separation between beauty and ugliness. Neither one really exists; it's a matter of perspective. And so one might choose to incarnate into what most would consider to be an ugly, awful, terrible body, for example, a rather unsightly one at that. And yet, within that soul's experience of life, it might discover the beauty that existed inside all the time, and that is the point. Through their lifetimes, souls suddenly discover love beyond their wildest dreams and imaginings.

You make a decision as to the courses that you have come here to study upon planet Earth. You might incarnate within a certain religious perspective, for example, only to force yourself to look at other religions when you get so tired of being constrained and confined by church rules and regulations that you realize that God doesn't exist inside of a book or inside of a building, that God exists inside of your heart. It is there where you find yourself appreciating the religious setting in which you were raised because of the confinement it created for you, so that you had to force yourself to find God with your heart—the true "religion" after all, God bless you indeed.

Water can be an ice cube or it can boil.

Yes, and it can be steam as well. It can be light as rain, and it can be dewdrops. It can change its shape, but it's still water, isn't it? But you have a different perspective if you are a dewdrop sitting on a tree limb than if you're sitting in a wine glass at a party. It's very beautiful! And you can certainly immerse yourself in life and mix yourself up with a little juice, if you like. You can incarnate—to continue with your theme here of water—into a leaf, as a molecule of water that nourishes a plant. There is a whole other world out there, is there not?

The universes that exist! The possibilities of your incarnation! Which Earth do you want to incarnate upon? That's another question. Will you be the water that nurtures the earth that the creepy crawlers like to slither through? Oh, goodness gracious, that would be frightening, wouldn't it? But again, you can be a molecule of water in the ocean, playing and laughing with the others within your soul family. That would be a lot of fun, wouldn't it? Imagine being blown out of the blowhole of a dolphin! There you find freedom and flight of soul, yeah?

Exploring the Truth of Creation and Evolution

Please comment on creation as told in the Bible and the countertheory of evolution.

The Bible, from our perspective . . . Well, that is certainly one perspective in the universe and one that is more often than not right, we will add. Ah, we tease here.

Certainly the perspective of creation within the Bible is absolutely accurate. And we share this because, my dear friends, there were at one time one man and one woman upon the Earth. And they were indeed known as Adam and Eve. And they did indeed suddenly come to the awareness that they were naked—stark naked—here upon the Earth and wanted to cover themselves up. So this is absolutely accurate in terms of how planet Earth became populated. But how did they get here? God, according to the Bible, put them here. Well, that makes sense, because everyone and everything is God, so how could they be separate from the very same? Adam and Eve were also lightbeings—starseeds, shall we say?—who were planted upon the Earth to help populate it.

And as far as your evolution goes? That exists as well! Yes, there are monkeys and apes, and evolution certainly has occurred throughout centuries and centuries of time upon the Earth. Of course, watching the changes, it's not hard to understand evolution when you simply see, for example within a family structure, parents who behave in a certain fashion who have children who grow from that and behave in yet another fashion. They evolve from the family structure.

They evolve as well out of the science, shall we say, of two human beings who come together. There is a putting together of genetics here. It is not necessary. It does not necessarily come first, nor are you at the mercy of genetics, but it is a science that is true and it does work, and you can alter yourself genetically, shall we say, scientifically speaking. Or, my dear friends, from your heart and soul, you can make a decision about what kind of person you want to be as the result of the coming together of your mommy and your daddy. What kind of physicality do you want to bring into this lifetime? The possibilities are endless within your genetic structure.

Within your DNA, there are changes all the time. You are in a state of constant evolution, but evolution is not separate from God. Evolution is God. God is ever changing. God is ever growing. God is ever moving. God is anything but dormant and stagnant. God, my dear friends, is change, constant change. The Bible has profound truths within its pages. Certainly many of these truths have been altered through generations and generations of rewriting, but metaphorically speaking, in most of the stories, there is absolute truth. And as well, many of the individuals within the pages of the Bible are represented very accurately, only because there is One who is in charge of the way in which the Bible has been rewritten. Oh, goodness gracious! That brings us right back to God, does it not?

Do not hold anything at arm's length. Enjoy the exploration of all your sciences, your religions and of the heavens and the Earth.

Humans Are Perpetual-Motion Machines

In our attempts to understand ourselves, we are creating robots made of metal and electronics and so forth. Because everything contains consciousness, these will also have a consciousness. Are we not just the robots of God?

Not exactly. Your robots will never be able to contain consciousness. It is not possible. You understand that your body is a perpetual-motion machine, constantly moving. The blood within your body is moving. You're breathing. You're breathing. You're blinking. Your hair is growing. You're in constant movement. That defies everything that your sciences believe as far as perpetual motion. There is no such thing as a perpetual-motion machine, but there is! You are it! And that's what you are trying to create through your robots. You're not ever really going to have a consciousness within the robot. You will have something that will "live" for a period of time, and once the battery runs dead, then the creature dies as well until someone—a human being—takes the time to bring it back to "life." It can't reincarnate by itself, because there is no consciousness there.

But you are not a robot of God, not in any way, shape or form. God, my dear friends, is a constant exhale without end. That is not being a robot of God; that is being constantly birthed from within Him. That is the best we can put it.

God is movement. If we don't move, if we don't change, if we don't evolve, we don't exist.

Precisely, yes. And it's impossible to not exist. You evolve even when you transition from your physical body. Your body can die; it can be burned, it can be squashed, it can be all kinds of things, but your spirit? You can't squash that. Consciousness is not something that you can make out of tin.

Believe in Infinite Possibility

In regard to the perpetual movement of the spirit, of the soul, do we reincarnate, if we prefer, into the bodies of animals?

Yes, you can. In many instances, you are doing it all the time, even when you are in a human body. How do you like them apples? Let us put it in this fashion: How very often have you lost your eyeglasses? Many times, yes? And when you lose them, what do you do? You think about them, yes? And you try to embrace them with your heart to find them, do you not? You visualize. You try to remember where you last saw them. You project your consciousness into them to imagine where they might be sitting. You try very hard to connect yourself with the physical object—not even something that is animal in its nature. And so you incarnate, shall we say, into your eyeglasses on a daily basis—sometimes more than once a day, my dear friend!

You can do the very same thing with animals. You can do it with the consciousness of a stone, if you like, to feel what a stone's existence would be like. Would it be boring? Would it be rather relaxing? It is not sedentary, that is for certain. It is a very active existence, being exposed to the elements at all times, having little critters running on top of your surface. A rock has a closer awareness, shall we say, even of molecular movement and structure. But yes, you can leave your physical human body and incarnate into the physicality of an animal or a plant. It really doesn't matter.

Let's go a step further with this. When I am working in the garage and I need a part that I don't have, I go to my drawers that are full of all these little parts, and all of a sudden, I come up with a part that I don't remember putting there, but it's the part I need. I've thought sometimes that what I am really doing is creating that part.

Absolutely, yes! There are many dimensions in which you exist, layer upon layer upon layer of them. If you consider the layers to be like those of an onion, you can be at the center of the onion. Your part does not exist there. You want very much for your part to exist and so therefore you spiral out with your consciousness into the next layer of the onion, where the part does exist. So you are constantly moving between layers of the onion of your existence.

It's a kind of time travel.

It very much is, yes. It is movement that is created from within your heart according to your desires. You do, indeed, create your own reality. That is why we say to you over and over again that love is the greatest healer of all. Love is the greatest thing with which to manifest instantly that which your heart desires. Within your Bible, within the creation of the heavens and the Earth and the first man and woman to be born here upon your planet Earth from the heart of God—how did this occur? It occurred through movement; through desire; through the great, tremendous love within God's heart. That is how your world was born. It was born in love, in a manner very similar to the very last push that pushes a child into the world. It takes a tremendous, tremendous act of surrender, concentration and love for a woman to allow herself to spread her legs and birth a child into the world. It is a labor of God's eternal love by which you are born, always and forevermore.

And so therefore, is there anything outside of love? What about a part you would consider to be a piece that doesn't really matter and that will be put in a junkyard someday? Yes, it is within love as well. And since it is within that realm, why can't you birth it into your little drawer of doodads?

It answers the question, but it sort of violates the scientific principle that you can't create or destroy matter.

God bless you indeed! Yes, we understand; but you can, can you not?

I think it's consistent, because all things exist in potential. There's no end to reality. There's no end to infinity. There's infinite possibility, and everything exists. The manifestation occurs when it's required to be there.

Absolutely, yes. And all of you reading this will remember a time in life when you knew where you'd put your shoes, but your shoes weren't there when you went back to find them. Right there you have your evidence. Right there you have your proof. But so often, you overlook these things as being outside of the realm of possibility. You see the little flickers within your peripheral vision. "Sure looks like Granddaddy, but he's not on the

Earth. Couldn't possibly be him who I see in my peripheral vision—could it?" Well, give it a whirl. Say hello to Granddaddy when you see him. Test the theory. That is scientific, is it not? Give it a whirl and trust the movement of your heart. The possibilities are infinite. Who was that master upon your planet Earth? Mr. Einstein, yes? What was it he said? E=MC², yeah? And in that, is there not all possibility? Even that scientific understanding has been revisited and revised, has it not? Even the "master" didn't master anything, did he? Isn't that the beauty of your existence—that the learning never ends?

So rather than putting yourselves into a box of illusion of separation from possibility, why not allow yourselves—you have a lovely expression for this on your Earth!—to go with the flow? Allow yourselves to open your heart to all the possibilities; play with the light and the sparkles that come to you in the night. Find out what they are. They're not accidents, my dear friends. There are no accidents here upon the planet Earth.

God Wants You to Fall in Love with All of Life

Along these lines, I have often thought that if there is such a thing as evil, in my view, evil is the resistance to change. We're in a constant state of flux, a state of constant change, and anyone who resists change is actually evil.

Resists or tries to force change to occur. There are many who, if you are using your definition here of evil, appear to be very kind, compassionate and caring, because they are only trying to do what's right for you—trying to help you, you see? They are trying to help you by making you change to their ways, their opinions, their perspectives. That, my dear friend, is a form of hate; that's not love. That, my dear friend, according to your definition of evil, is also evil.

I wasn't looking at that side of it.

Yes, we understand. Why do you think we talked about it?

I was thinking about resistance to change.

Yes, and you're absolutely accurate there. That one we would consider to be what you call here your no-brainer. Yes, resistance to change is inflexibility. That is a form of dis-ease, becoming very inflexible in your life.

Is that not what is causing all this strife on Earth right now—the resistance of the people in the old world to come into the present?

To a degree, yes, as well as the resistance of the "new" world to just allow for the past to be unchanged. Remember, loving allowance for all things to be. Is it not so beautiful, the delicate fabric of your Earth and your wondrous families upon it? You think you would like to make everyone American, for example. But you know something? It would be very boring if you did not have your Saddam Husseins. It would be very boring if you did not have your Spanish-speaking individuals south of the border trying to get over to your United States of America. You would find it very boring, very bland indeed. If you can celebrate and appreciate the many different perspectives, religions and ways in which you understand and appreciate God, it is there where you fall into greater and greater love with life, and truly God has prayed for you to participate upon the Earth in this way.

You are doing beautiful work, and we're excited. We're charged up for tomorrow, but we are certainly not going to worry about it. And we're going to love our moment of existence, right here and right now. We cannot tell you enough, my dear friends, how much it feels like we are in heaven upon your Earth when we are allowed to come through your beautiful little channel here and have a little chat with you, an opportunity to offer expressions of hope, peace and understanding to help the many rather than the few into a state of greater enlightenment. God bless you, indeed.

The Dream State, the Dance of Self-Expression and Crop Circles

G od bless you. Dr. Peebles here. It is a joy and a blessing when human and Spirit join together in search of the greater truths and awareness. You are becoming strong now in this, your chosen lifetime. It is a time of intimacy. Touch and be touched by life around you. That is the point and purpose of your coming to planet Earth! Yes, at times you get rather tired, fed up and very toxic with many of the energies that come into your life, but do not be discouraged. For it is here upon the planet Earth where at long last you will dissolve the illusions of separation within self and between life and discover that through all your questionings, you desire certainty, comfort and security. You want to know absolutes, but, my dear friends, there is no such thing as "absolutely" anything.

The only absolute is change, and within the arena of change, there is exploration. It is there that you journey to your heart, and when you fall in love with the journey with wonder, you will suddenly, at long last, fall into your enlightenment. And when you're enlightened, what are you going to do next? When you realize that your journey never ends, that you will exist forevermore—upon the planet Earth, within the heavens, within the stars and beyond, even in areas that we have not yet explored for ourselves—you realize that you are a journey without end. You, my dear friends, are a journey to the heart. It is in this understanding that you find complete and absolute wisdom.

The Dream State Fills Your Reservoir of Healing Energies

What happens in our dream state? Sometimes we wake up rested, or we're tired, or we feel like we've been run over by a truck. A lot of people go into different dimensions.

Yes, we understand. And as well, oftentimes within the dream state, there is a filling up once again of your reservoir of healing energies. There is also a releasing of energies that no longer serve you. You ask a question here that really is worthy of an entire book by itself.

There are some energies that you release in dreams that are little imaginings, little wonderings about your day, about the distant past, about the future, which no longer serve you. It is a form, shall we say, of urination—ridding yourself of toxic energies and thoughts that have built up inside you. When you release them, sometimes you are conscious of it, sometimes not. When you are asleep and do not have an awareness of your sleep, you are plugging yourself into the universe and filling up your reservoir once again with pure, healing light. These loving energies build frequencies inside you that will serve you for many weeks, sometimes for months and years, even from one evening of absolute, restful sleep. It is not a matter of leaving your body but rather sitting as a receptor of love and light from God, the heavens, the universe and your guides, and sometimes from your little animal friends. Your animals oftentimes love to sleep next to you to help you fill up your reservoir once again with love, energy and light. That is one form of sleep.

There are other forms of sleep, however, wherein you do indeed go out of body. You have astral projection. You go into other dimensions, for example, to help and understand spirits who are departed from the Earth, learning their language and striving to understand them so that you can understand the mystic who you are. In some cases, you are learning how to become psychic. Sometimes in these periods of intercourse in other dimensions, you discuss with them how they became spirits and what it feels like to be out of body. Sometimes you're just there to sense this, to feel and discover it, so you can take the understandings back to the Earth in the physical form. Sometimes there are opportunities in sleep whereby you can graduate into a greater conscious awareness of self, life and all life in between. That's the best we can put it in human language.

Sleep is also an opportunity to study with your guides, to receive information or to sit in a classroom. Oftentimes you are in classrooms in the evening, learning more so that you can bring it back to the Earth. Sometimes while you are out of body, you work with your guides to do research for artwork, music, design and redesigning your life upon the Earth. So many of you want to have contact with your guides, conscious awareness of this contact, but oftentimes you are getting it anyway in your sleep.

Work Consciously with Your Sleep Cycles

You can work with the sleep cycles very consciously. For example, you can set a day-by-day schedule, where Monday is your night of restful, healing sleep in which you just sit as a receiver of light and love. On Tuesday night, perhaps you would like to go to school to educate yourself about your life and purpose. You can set a time to release toxic energies. "I'm exhausted! I just want to get rid of all this toxic energy!" That does not necessarily mean that you're going to have restless sleep, but it does mean you might have very disturbing dreams—sometimes nightmares and sometimes images and sensations that do not make sense. Even fitful sleep is a wonderful opportunity for releasing toxic energies. You can set up, by design, one night a week dedicated and devoted to different forms of work within your sleep. You become a conscious creator of your life, not only in your waking state, but while you are in the dream state.

There are many times when you leave your body just to visit family members who are not with you, because you desire their contact so much. You meet with them in the astral plane. It's a nice way to go away for the weekend, very much as you would take an excursion away from school to go see Mommy and Daddy and have a little hug again, a night of laughter and a night of play.

Staring into a candle by your bedside, you make a decision as to how you want to work with your sleep for the evening and then blow out the candle, go to bed and don't give it another thought. Your soul knows exactly how to take charge and be of greater service to you.

My partner has brought it to my attention that sometimes I cry out or scream when I'm totally zonked at nighttime. I'm rather concerned about this and wonder where I'm going on such journeys. It doesn't compute to hear you say this.

You are really in a class by yourself. You have a tremendous desire to help and assist. This is a form of channeling that you are involved in while sleeping. Oftentimes the cries that come through you are not your own. You are offering your body to others as a vessel for healing, understanding and release.

There are human beings who never have restful sleep, not for one night, because they allow the energies of the Earth and of human beings around them to course through them while they sleep. Their bodies are used as a vessel for cleansing those energies and allowing them to be released. Oftentimes this is by design of the spirit who has come to Earth, incarnating as one who is willing to work with and process the energies of the Earth so that they can be released in the night. These individuals don't ever get very restful sleep, because they are always letting their bodies be used as vessels to release very toxic energy. It has an effect upon your physicality.

As well, my dear, oftentimes you are out on little excursions, gathering and collecting. You often go to places that are much like very beautiful woods, but they don't have just leaves and such upon the ground. Oftentimes there are crystals and gems filled with all kinds of light and color. You love to play and fantasize while you sleep, so you often completely empty your body, 100 percent, running around in the universe collecting new ideas for your artwork and other things. Oftentimes you wake up in inspiration, but other times you awaken in the middle of the night in a terrible sweat and a fit. That happens because you are aware that there was a disturbance within your body as you slept.

Sleepwalkers Fear Separation of the Spirit from the Body

Could you address the issue of sleepwalking?

Sleepwalkers have a fear of separation of the spirit from the physical form, so they do not allow themselves to leave their bodies. They end up carrying their bodies with them on their little excursions. Many of these human beings have died or been killed in their sleep in previous lifetimes, so they want to stay very, very close to home and in charge of their physical form. They aren't willing to go very far away at all. They still have a need, however, to get up, move around and have experiences in the night. Instead of the spirit leaving the body, they take their physical form with them.

Another form of sleepwalking occurs in individuals who have physical bodies that do not get enough energetic release during the day. This can sometimes mean release of sexual energy, and sometimes there is not enough release in terms of exercise or movement of the physical form. In these human beings, there would not be a spirit within the body—at least, not entirely. The spirit is out astral projecting, playing around, and yet the body needs movement. It needs a physical release, and oftentimes it gets up and walks around the room.

This is one of the reasons why you do not want to awaken a sleepwalker, because of the incredible shock that occurs to the physical body without a person in it 100 percent. That can create a very dangerous condition, physically speaking; it can cause heart attacks, emotional breakdown and so on, without allowing the spirit to fully reincarnate. As we already discussed, when you go to sleep at night, you die. When you wake up in the morning, you reincarnate. You always come back into the body by choice. If it does not happen with a complete, solid connection, it can cause disturbances that resonate for years or decades. It's very important to be very, very tender and gentle with sleepwalkers. The best way to awaken such a person is to simply whisper his or her name very, very, very softly. Whisper and say, "Come back home now, sweetheart. It's time to come home." Whisper as softly as you can to gently guide the spirit back home into its physical vessel.

There is a tremendous restlessness within individuals who have trouble with sleepwalking. Vigorous exercise would be very highly recommended before sleep. As well—and this is from Dr. Cayce—two hours prior to bed, nothing but water should be taken into the body. Some physical bodies burn energy at night at a very rapid rate, and the metabolism does not slow down. For some individuals, it accelerates, and those are the ones who get up. They are not sleepwalkers, but they certainly are sleep eaters. They get up in the night and don't realize they're eating a whole chicken dinner!

Using the Future Memory Bank

Are our memories connected to dreams? When we are profoundly influenced by our memories—past, present or even future memories—do we project what will be in terms of ourselves and put that into our future memory bank?

Yes, you can. Oftentimes it is no different than mapping out a trip that you would take—a journey on the road. You are mapping out your future. You have plans for certain destinations and can change those plans any time you like. Memories can be brought to planet Earth. As you are incarnating, you pack your bags with the lessons you want to learn and what you'd like to resolve in this lifetime. Sometimes you carry karma from the past, situations where you might say, "I would like to meet Frank again in this lifetime, if it's all right with him, so that we can work out our differences," and Frank says, "All right, I'm willing! We'll meet at this time and this place." Predestined, shall we say. Oftentimes you realize that this is happening when it occurs.

This pertains to memories within dreams. Within dream states, there are little triggers inside you. When you are ready to face and resolve issues from the past, you have all the knowledge, wisdom and tools for understanding in place. Then, almost as if you have set an alarm clock inside your soul, you discharge a memory from the distant past that comes to the surface to be released from its confinement. You can study it in a way that will not be too disruptive to your life. Sometimes this is very metaphorical. At other times, you do this so that you can experience a past lifetime to bring about a greater perspective on this one without letting it become a terrible trauma for you. For example, you might have a past-life memory of dying by being stuck in mud and muck. You writhe in pain and fear in your dream, then awaken breathlessly into the understanding that you do not want to— metaphorically speaking—get stuck like that again in this lifetime.

Sometimes in the dream state, there is a glorious release of personality traits that can be washed away in an instant. There could be, for example, an individual who wants to release selfishness. He says to himself during the waking state, "I am so selfish! Why am I so selfish? I don't want to be selfish anymore!" And so the soul devises a plan to release the selfishness in the dream state by bringing forth a memory from the distant past or from this lifetime where there was an extremely selfish action. Sometimes it is a manufactured image that the soul brings up from the imagination that creates enlightenment on the topic of selfishness. Those are the evenings where you awaken in the middle of the night with grand revelations. "Goodness gracious!" you cry out, "I'm not walking down that street again."

There are so many ways in which the dream state is of tremendous use. It is very active; yet very, very little of it is understood upon your Earth. It is a science that would serve humankind well to explore. There has been an innate awareness of this in the past in various tribes and communities. There are still a few upon the Earth, but not as many as in the past. The dream state is very much taken for granted. All most people care about is getting a sound night's sleep. That's not necessarily for the highest good of your soul's education upon the Earth!

A sound sleep is not always the greatest teacher. Sometimes too many nights of sound sleep cause lethargy. An individual might feel very bored with life, because the sleep state can be extremely wondrous in terms of finding new ideas and new energy, recharging your batteries, bringing in all kinds of imaginings and bringing intuition up to the surface. It's a wonderful educator. So healing sleep would really be best left for one night a week at the most. If you can change your ideas about sleep in this fashion, instead of taking drugs and forcing yourself to fall into unconsciousness all the time, you would find that you would have much more vigorous health by simply saying, "Tonight is my night for healing, restful sleep." With practice and surrender, you'd find that you sleep for eleven hours straight without one interruption. That is what your soul is designed to do. Your physical body can run very nicely on one very long night of serene, comforting, healing sleep.

Catnaps Recharge Your Batteries

Truly, there is enough information about sleep cycles that we could fill a book. We haven't yet discussed the understanding and awareness of what you call catnaps, for example. These are fantastic opportunities to recharge your batteries. Unfortunately, within your world, especially within American society, this is not an acceptable behavior. If catnaps were made acceptable, your workplaces would be designed, for optimum work standards, with a room that would be a quiet room, a place of rest wherein you could recharge your batteries at will. It would be a very sacred sanctuary for those who suddenly, while sitting at a desk, become overwhelmed with a desire to fall asleep. The expectations around you are to work, work, work and keep your nose to the grindstone, and that's when your computers begin to crash, mistakes are made and machinery crushes fingers.

Instead, my dear friends, for all employers who might be reading this material, we would encourage a quiet room for your employees. Give them permission to adjourn to the quiet room and close their eyes anytime during the day when they feel tired and need to close their eyes for a moment or perhaps just feel the need to sit. You could have comfortable chairs, a couch or a bed—it doesn't matter which—but there could be several ways in which people could simply sit, close their eyes and very consciously say, "I am now going to allow the universe to come in, take a peek around and make some adjustments to my physicality and my spirit so that I can rejoin with self."

You humans need this several times a day. Yes, several times a day! When we say this, we don't mean for hours at a time but simply for a few seconds. "Oh, goodness gracious, I am yawning now. Well then, I guess I will close my eyes for a moment and breathe very deeply into my spine and rejoin my spirit with my body." That's all it is. You don't give yourself half a chance! Instead you barrel through and disrupt your body as a result, because you are not in the body very well and the frequencies are not connecting with all the nerve synapses. Then you get a backache, pain in your shoulders and neck, your eyes begin to blur and you begin to lose your vision. Optimum health can certainly be inspired through just these periods of quiet.

Do you take catnaps in spirit?

Catnaps for us? I believe that my entire existence is one long catnap! It truly is. There is a flow—it's hard to put in human terms, because you see your life in terms of up and down, good and bad, right and wrong and so on. It's always between extremes. For me, my existence is just whatever I am right now. I don't give labels to each moment, saying this is a catnap, that is a time of turbulence or now I'll watch television. I am one giant movement, one giant constant expression, and it is a magnificent experience—my existence is the flight of a helium balloon out into the sky without fear of popping. I'm never worrying about what's around the corner.

The Greatest Dance of All Is How You Express Yourself

That's why I find channeling to be eternally fascinating. I work through the channel's body to assist the many rather than the few as much as I possibly can upon your Earth. I often feel and sense in group settings that people are concerned about the channel. Is she all right? Is she breathing? Will she be okay? Are we taking up too much of Dr. Peebles' time? People always worry about taking up my time or about praying too often or asking for too much. I don't see it that way, not at all.

Keep expressing yourself. That is the greatest dance of all. I love to have interaction and contact. That is my existence—to touch and be touched in one constant state of lovemaking. It doesn't end, and it doesn't matter who I am interacting with either. I don't have any judgments there. You are all very beautiful spirits as far as I am concerned, equally attractive in your nature, eternally fascinating in the many ways that you do not love your-selves. I am overjoyed when you seek help from me.

We love your questioning here. Within that realm of understanding where I exist, there is no hierarchy, so I do not see myself as being better than you. I keep trying to tell you to appreciate yourself. I am beautiful, fascinating, wise, witty and kind, and you are that as well. The only difference between us is that I know that I am you, and I'm not afraid of it. If you can under-stand that you are me, then you suddenly realize, in an instant, that all is one and everything is God. There is a constant union, and within that union is this lovely diversity. It is not something to fear or hold at arm's length.

We have our own difficulties at times putting things into human words through the channel. That's why Jesus Christ walked the Earth and told everything in parables and metaphors. You can't put the love of God into a box, you see. You can only put it into an expression that you feel and under-stand inside your heart. It's very hard to express the love of God. The human language is extremely limited and very confining unless you know how to work with the frequencies of language.

Many individuals whom you consider to be mentally ill eventually show that they're really mentally charged and are anything but crazy, having incredible insights into the universe. If they were more acknowledged for the insights in their mutterings and mumblings, you would find that once they are acknowledged, they begin to heal. Some of your greatest therapists upon the Earth understand this and say, "I understand that you have some-thing to say that is of importance to you because you see it like that." It's an acknowledgment of perspective that is healing for anyone. You are all seek-ing acknowledgment all the time.

That's where you have your tug of wars, your wars upon the Earth, your disagreements and angry arguments. Everybody says, "Look at me! I want to be acknowledged!" When one person understands this and acknowl-edges the perspective of another, there is suddenly an instantaneous healing.

The Meaning of Crop Circles

Who makes crop circles, and do they mean anything?

Do they mean anything? No more than the grains of sand on your beach. Yes, of course they have a lot of meaning! At times they are just trying to remind you that there is something larger than self in the universe. They keep you inspired. Many times these crop circles are indeed made by extra-terrestrials who are friends of planet Earth—not enemies who are out there slaughtering your cattle or any such thing, but very beautiful spirits who simply want to keep you encouraged and say, "Look at the sunlight and find inspiration there. Look into the stars and the heavens and find your inspiration there." They give these little images—emblems, they would rather call them—as little gifts to planet Earth.

And are the crop circles human-made as well? Of course they are. What a beautiful experience for human beings to create their own crop circles. My goodness gracious, you would create the most incredible amusement park if you would simply grow acres and acres of wheat fields and allow human beings to come in to create their own designs. What a fantastic and fascinating adventure! But rather than move with the flow of love upon our Earth, you would try to, shall we say, condemn the human beings who try to make these in your fields. You get angry and throw rocks and stones at them to get rid of them.

Take it in the other direction and watch your world flourish. It would be beyond your wildest dreams and imaginations. For those who do not believe that crop circles are made by extraterrestrials, well, we would ask that you simply try the idea on for size, once and for all. For just a moment, turn your consciousness toward the possibility that perhaps there is something a little larger than self, and suddenly you will find freedom inside yourself beyond your wildest dreams and imaginations. Every time you look to your world, you try to limit it, putting labels and names to it. What would it hurt if, for just a moment, you gave a little appreciation to the idea that there are indeed extraterrestrials? They are not upon your planet Earth, but they love to play and open gateways for understanding, love, freedom and the flight of the soul.

My dear friends whose lives and fields have been touched by the crop circles, human-made or made by those not in body here upon your Earth, count your blessings, for you have truly been blessed in a most magical way. Remember, these are reminders to you that there is more than meets the eye and more to nourish you than simply the wheat in the field. It is perspectives and possibilities that are the real nurturers, for you are not just a body; you are a spirit as well. Allow yourselves, my dear friends, to fall in love with all of life, not just part of it, for it is you.

So, as for your crop circles, think of them as being very large bootprints on the Earth. Yes? Isn't that a lovely way to think of it? You walk on your Earth and leave a print in the sand, the mud, the dirt, the concrete or in the wheat fields. It's very similar to this.

The Larger Picture of Healing

Dr. Peebles, you are a doctor . . .

Doctor of souls, yes.

How is it for you to witness through Spirit the tremendous advances of medical science?

Hmm—just a moment here, let me take a look. I didn't know that there were tremendous advances. I tease a little bit here. I do not find anything at all remarkable about your medical science. Nothing. I find it eternally fascinating, however, the way in which you explore your medical science, play with it and wonder about it. That is more important. What I see is your scientists playing with energy and light in their laboratories and discovering aspects of themselves. I don't see any advances. Every time there is a medical breakthrough, as far as I am concerned, it's a breakdown. Because the truth is that your body is at the mercy of your spirit; your spirit is not at the mercy of your physical form. You are not your body, and therefore, I have a lot of difficulty with your question, because I don't care about your physical body. How do you like them apples? Your physical body will be in right order once your spirit is truly seeing with clarity. Then you will see through your eyeballs with clarity.

And as well, you see, I don't see physical problems. I see physical insights. You might come to the Earth and be born without arms, for example, and that gives you tremendous opportunity for understanding an embrace, does it not, from a very different perspective? How do you give a hug if you don't have arms? Well, you do it through your interactions, through different types of physical movement and through writing and speaking, such as through books or lectures. There are so many opportunities here that are missed, you see. If you would combine a bit of psychological and spiritual care with your medical industry and your medicines, you would find that there would be greater advances in terms of healing.

It's a very good question, but it puts Dr. Peebles here in a bit of a pickle. I see a lot of pus pockets and cancers, and I see a lot of broken, bleeding hearts, but the cancers exist inside your consciousness. What's eating away at you today you then manifest in your physical form. You allow your life to eat at you. For me, that is where I find sadness. But those are the rips and tears that I work to repair.

How can we spread that word to the many?

It will be done through these words. It is not something that science is yet willing to embrace, but science will soon embrace it. I am not in any way, shape or form saying that there is anything wrong with your medical science whatsoever. Rather fantastic, is it not, that they know how to clamp off a heart valve to keep it from bleeding during surgery? And how very lovely that you can set a bone. It's really quite fascinating that you can, by design, put a bone back into place. Rather amazing that you know how to numb yourselves physically with drugs and so on. It's fascinating to us.

But I know a larger picture. I know about instant healing. I know that bones don't break. That's an illusion. It hurts, certainly, upon your Earth.

That is what you are here to explore, and you explore separation upon your Earth for a reason. You separate everything out that is you. But a broken bone is yesterday to me. There is no such thing where I exist. It just doesn't occur. Leave your bumps and bruises, pick up and move on.

We're not machines and we're not without feeling here. We're not without care and concern for our dear, beautiful family who lives upon the Earth. If you can, embrace your life as a large motion and fall in love with all of it. Have you ever witnessed, for example, a very young patient who might have cancer or leukemia or what have you—you name the disease, there are children who have it upon the Earth. Oftentimes these children, because they are incarnating as such pure and generous spirits, tend to be more than willing to move through the illness with grace and kindness, to still find magic and love. They still celebrate family and look outside themselves and their condition, and they know wholeheartedly that the only condition that really exists is love. Such children are great teachers, as you are very much aware.

What You Really Want Is True Intimacy with Life

Would you comment on the fact that we seem to be inundated with pornography through the Internet and other things?

And you will be even more so. It's going to come to light more and more, until at long last you can put this one to sleep, for it shows little care. And the more you are inundated with your pornography, the less attention, shall we say, you will give to your physical orgasming, toward your having to push or force the energy of love.

In your current reality, physical orgasm is strongly equated with love upon your Earth. But, my dear friends, love is a much different creature than that. Physical orgasm is a physical activity. It doesn't make any difference to us. You find all kinds of ways in which to match up your bodies, and you have a lot of fun with it. But really, ultimately, what you are striving for is true intimacy with life that comes heart to heart. Comes heart to heart, you understand? No accident of the word that we use here. And certainly the true love, the true embrace of love, is the one eternal orgasm. Certainly, you live orgasm to orgasm, week by week. It's all right. You can have your physical releases. We have no judgment on this whatsoever. It's a big game, and you're all going to get tired of it as you move into a greater consciousness of love here upon your planet Earth.

So it's just going to come to light more and more. Every time you see love as equated with orgasm, you suddenly find yourself shifting your consciousness into, "Goodness gracious! That's not love for me!" So, as far as we are concerned, just build your character and move yourself into the greater light of true love.

Does God Have Amnesia?

Summer has a question for you, Dr. Peebles: You say that we are God. Who or what is God? And if we are God, how do we forget that we are? Does God have amnesia? Is God a being with multiple personalities?

That would certainly be like our channel to ask such a question. As we shared at the start of our conversations here, you incarnate as a small child. You are not aware that you are naked, you don't care that you are, and suddenly someone tells you that you're naked and that you'd better care about it—that you are naked physically, emotionally or spiritually. That's the point of "the fall." It is in this moment that you suddenly become afraid, and you feel that everything around you is out to attack you. You feel vulnerable, and you retract from life by holding it at arm's length. It is in this moment that you forget that you are God and that everything around you is God.

From that moment, you have to spend the rest of your life pulling the pieces of your God-self back into you. And how do you do that? The only way is through your heart, by falling into greater and greater love. This is very much in the same way that Jesus Christ walked the planet Earth. He could stare into anyone's eyes—including those who were about to hang Him upon the cross—and feel overwhelming love, because He knew that everything that He saw, tasted, touched, felt and smelled was indeed Him, was indeed God. They, on the other hand, had forgotten this truth for a moment in time.

And so your planet is based very strongly in insecurity. Insecurity of what? Of allowing yourself to be vulnerable to touch. Goodness gracious! If you walked your Earth naked, imagine the physical feelings you'd have all day long! What if you allowed yourself to feel the elements around you or allowed yourself to sit next to one another naked upon a bench on the street or in your cars? What a different sense of life you would have! It would be very frightening for you, however, because you believe in imperfection and attack and things that are less than love.

My dear friends, there is nothing that is less than love. You can create hate, generate it, nurture it and attempt to keep it alive, but ultimately you will always find that the only healer is love. The only way you are ever going to feel better, to have true intimacy with life and be able to celebrate the existence of God, is through love—absolute, 100-percent appreciation of self and of all of life around you in the 100-percent understanding that nothing, *nothing* is outside of God.

So you come back to Earth. You are very rebellious characters sometimes, believing that you are going to come to Earth and change the planet once you are at the helm. That is ego, one form of belief that you are God. That is a sense of self that is separate, an illusion that keeps you from seeing beyond the veil.

Is God filled with multiple personalities? Yes, we would certainly say, very much so. In your world, you can certainly see it around you. Look at all the personalities. Every one of them is indeed God. So yes, in a sense, God is filled with multiple personalities, but ultimately, the overriding personality is one that is rooted in love 100 percent. And, by the way, that looks very much like the real you. You are God eternal, my dear friends, God bless you indeed.

Different Methods of Communication

My dear friends, we have no grievances with planet Earth; we have nothing to change here. We just have a sharing from the heart. And it is not just from our heart; it's from your own. You share from your heart with your questions. You're the ones who came up with these questions in the first place, and they are very nice questions at that. It's going to leave the many rather than the few scratching their heads, wondering what they just have read, but isn't that lovely as well? It will get them thinking in new directions as far as we are concerned.

We speak the language of the heart, you understand, not the language of your mind. You think you are hearing words, but what you are hearing is frequency. You absorb it into yourselves. Can you for a moment as we speak realize how you comprehend what I am sharing with you? You comprehend it inside yourself, not by processing the words. We create a resonance, a movement of sound, light and color inside you. You can hear it with every word we say.

Now, we can bring the frequency down. [Voice softens and lowers in pitch.] We can push it into a different arena. Can you sense it now? You feel the shift inside your body. And now we can bring it back up just a wee bit. [Voice becomes louder and higher in pitch.] Ah, let's put it into the arena of silver. Silver, you understand? [Voice becomes still higher in pitch and a bit louder.] Can you feel the silver inside of you?

We can share gobbledy gook here. It doesn't matter! It is the way in which we share it, the frequency upon which the information rides. Our frequency is love. So there will always be understanding. If we answered all of your questions, for example, with "Ride a bicycle," would you still get the answers? Frankly, it doesn't matter what we say, because again, it is simply the frequency with which we say it. You understand?

About the Aging Process and Love

It becomes harder and harder upon your planet Earth to push forward. The older you get, the more you begin to believe that you are on the brink of demise, and that's not true. You are never on the brink of demise. Your soul remains wholly intact. But there are times when you say, "Enough is enough! I've been here long enough. It's too difficult!" And you begin to shut down and begin to have difficulty breathing. You aren't certain if you can pass the next test, but there really are no tests. You set yourselves up; you set yourselves up very well here.

Truly, the answer to every question on these so-called tests that you think you are taking in your life is *love*. That's the only answer. It is time for no longer having judgment against anyone upon the Earth—not even an ant, a plant or a spider. Not to have judgment but to have appreciation for all is absolutely lovely. All of it is birthed from love.

Now, certainly there are different interpretations. What makes you any different from Saddam Hussein? Absolutely nothing, my dear friends. You are all beautiful spirits as far as we are concerned; you just haven't come to an appreciation of that—not one of you. So in many ways you, Saddam Hussein and all the rest are exactly the same, because you still don't love yourselves or one another. You still have not found the common ground of appreciation that is simply an outstretched hand or a touch of kindness. Stop and breathe before you speak, my dear friends, and act in kindness toward one another. These little frequencies will gather and collect around you, and you will find your souls uplifted, unexpected but expected simultaneously. It might be unexpected for you, but God knows. God really does know, my dear friends.

Go your way in peace, love and harmony, for life is indeed a joy, and all you have to do as you enjoy the journey to your own heart and to your own enlightenment is to lighten up a little bit more and realize . . . Where is your enlightenment? Is it tomorrow or is it right now? Well, my dear friends, that's for you to find out, but you will find that when you are "there," you realize that there is no "there" to get to! It has always been inside your heart. You're not going to find your enlightenment outside your front door or under your car or in your pocket. It's in your heart. It's been with you all the time. God bless you, indeed.

Creating Intimacy with All of Life

Understand that the journey you have embarked upon here on planet Earth is one wherein you spiral deeper and deeper into your heart, penetrating the fabric of eternity, penetrating with your heart, your soul and your spirit. Contact with the many rather than the few is the reason that you are here upon the planet Earth. Understand that within this room today, we will be having little discussions with you. Certainly you have some questions, and we have some answers. But what are we really doing here in this room but moving energy about? It is not so much in our words as it is in a sensation, a feeling that helps you restructure your lives and restructure your world. We wish to help you create your reality from the inside out, from your heart, until at long last, you feel that you no longer have to serve anyone and that you are one with everything.

The answer to all of your questions is indeed intimacy—intimacy with all of life, with everything that you are working upon here upon planet Earth. It all comes down to one thing, my dear friends: intimacy. How can you create more intimacy within relationships, with money, with your socks and your shoes? It doesn't really matter with what; suddenly we speak of your shoes, and you become more aware that they are on your feet. God bless you indeed. Intimacy, contact with the many rather than the few, is certainly the order of business here upon planet Earth.

How do you create intimacy? With the frequency of love, creating an understanding between yourselves and the world around you and in loving allowance for all things to be, understanding that all perspectives do count, for they are important to the individual who holds them. Everyone and everything upon the planet Earth is here for you, to help you in the creation of yourself, the divine being who you are, as you hold a certain energy, just as we are doing here in this room for you today. We hold this energy so that you can grow and learn to hold this certain energy, creating certain scenarios that at times we understand appear to be very challenging for you, but they are always, always created for your divine self to grow toward greater light and greater understanding. By serving yourself first, you serve all of humanity, for you shine your light as brightly as you possibly can, and everyone in the village can at long last, at the very least, begin to see.

Have a Conversation with the Universe

Beautiful creators here in this room today, each and every one of you is a student of the divine. A student of the divine what? A student of the divine self who you are, connected to everyone here in this room, not separate from anyone. Why? Because you, my dear friends, are all one, the One who is God, and we want for you to understand and to study this, because all of you here in this room are very compassionate and you want more, certainly for yourselves but as well for the rest of the world.

When you have a question, surrender to the greater opportunity here and just have a little discussion with God here, if you will, and say, "I have something I would like to ask you." Well, my dear friends, you find that what you have done is that you have plugged yourself into a wealth of information—the library of the universe. So understand that when you ask questions of God, when you have a conversation with the universe—when you are in prayer, when you are in meditation or when you are sittin' at a stoplight in your car—you find that there is a tremendous opportunity for expansion of self, for never are you away from the answers then. You have all the necessary resources right there inside of your heart, my dear friends.

But how do you receive it, how do you hear the answers? How do you understand the directive of the universe? My dear friends, you listen very, very carefully and you realize that it is the smallest of voices that speaks to you. This smallest of voices makes you feel as if you are ready to try something new; it is the voice that tells you, "Perhaps it's not really the wisest decision to go down that dark street right now, because a gentleman is there with, shall we say, a little knife in his hand."

You don't have to know the outcome of anything; rather, you are here to understand that the process here upon the Earth is to surrender to the journey, the expansion of self as you explore every opportunity that exists inside of you—not on the outside, my dear friends, for the outside, the outer world, is where you express the opportunities that you seek inside. What you are all seeking is certainly heaven here upon the planet Earth, and heaven, my dear friends, is not a place; it's a feeling. And certainly it expands forevermore, is indeed imbued forever with the frequency of love.

As you who are here in this room today open your hearts wide in this given moment, you are indeed expanding yourselves, reaching and straining to receive the greater love that you are, the love that is here in this room today. We would ask that for a moment, you take a fantastic, incredible journey to your heart. Turn to your neighbor and take a look into his or her eyes right now, if you are so willing, if you are so courageous. Look into that person's eyeballs. Do not think about anything, do not try to connect or even to understand, but simply gaze into the eyeball. Now imagine that that one eyeball there is the way planet Earth looked as you came to incarnate. It looked very beautiful, very sincere and very lovely, and once you landed here, it also looked very frightening, for everything began to become separate to you; you suddenly realized that there were others here with you. Now begin to reach into your neighbor with your heart and your soul and realize that you are made of exactly the same stuff—the same opportunities, the same understandings and the same emotions. Each and every one of you here in this room is seeking love, is seeking the opportunity to love and be loved by the universe forevermore.

That, my dear friends, is the gift that we give to you, God bless you indeed, so that you can carry it with you for an eternity. This gift is the understanding that you are indeed nothing less than God, nothing less than love, and that you are here simply to understand this. In every moment of every day, when you are having your frustrations with a paper clip, understand that what you are indeed seeking is greater love. Understand this, my dear friends, and it is there where you expand your consciousness forevermore and find that no longer are you stressing and straining against life. Life is no longer something to fear. My dear friends, surrender to the journey to your heart, and you will have a fantastic life ahead of you.

Certainly, during this time period here upon the planet Earth, there is to be tremendous change, but as well, my dear friends, there will be increased laughter, increased love and increased opportunities to touch and be touched. Would you please turn to someone beside you, shake that person's hand and understand that through outstretching your hand, you are making contact with the many rather than the few. Without question, this may be frightening for you at times, but this is what you are truly seeking: to touch and be touched. This is the language of the heart right here, fully demonstrated in the outer world but manifested from inside of this heart, God bless you indeed, startin' with this little channel here.

We are always and forevermore with you and by your side. Never are we away; never are we holding back. We are always right here with you, wrapping you up in our love. And every time you turn to us and want to receive—truly, with sincerity from inside of your heart—we will be there to guide you into a greater understanding of the fantastic journey that you can indeed have here upon the planet Earth.

We assure you that this is an exciting time to be alive, my dear friends. There are plenty of angels, including myself, who very much wanted to come back to planet Earth just to enjoy the adventure. So my dear friends, understand that you are in a time period where the angels want to be among you, and certainly they are indeed among you—they love you very much, and they're going to be coming here with a bang. So look into the face of every person you see walking down the street, for many angels will be appearing in human form, incarnating for brief periods upon the Earth simply to guide each and every one of you during this time period of growth into a greater vibrational frequency of love upon planet Earth. God bless you, indeed.

🍎   🍎   🍎

Find the Oneness

Each and every one of you here in this room today is a student of the divine. We have said this so very many times, and we would ask that you bring this into your hearts and truly embrace it within your soul. God bless you indeed, my dear friends and students of the divine, and certainly here upon this planet Earth, you have many opportunities to express this awareness of the divinity of self. It is in your outer world where you become fully expressed, but it starts on the inside. Where is it that you seek for learning, for education? Through prayer, through communion with yourself and then through your community, putting yourself out into the world, speaking and expressing from your heart and simply sittin' back and waiting for the honest echo of you to come running, either toward you or away from you. And that's all right; it certainly is the ebb and flow, if you will, of the tide of self that you are experiencing here in this life.

And certainly you are all exploring the richness of yourselves here upon the planet Earth; you want the richness of yourselves to be expressed fully here as well as to be felt by you—richness in terms of what would feel like heaven. Once again, heaven is a feeling, not a place. Here upon the planet Earth realize that you are in exploration of the illusions of separation. And how do you explore these illusions of separation? By first acknowledging that the separation exists. It is there where you realize that you seek oneness here upon the planet Earth; you seek the security that comes from this oneness, this connection with fields of light at all times, in each and every moment of each and every day. Because of this physical form here upon the planet Earth, it is absolutely impossible for you to find yourself feeling this oneness at all times simply by virtue of the fact that you feel that you are here and someone else is over there. It's all right, because this is part and parcel of the tools for learning how to fully express yourself, for learning how to commune with life.

And how do you do this? Where is it that you find the oneness that exists between yourself and all of life? It comes from a frequency that you derive from God, from the heavens, and bring down through yourself in the form of what we would call here the Holy Spirit, the energy of the Mother. This energy is to be fully expressed through your hands, just as the Lord Jesus Christ who walked the planet Earth was capable of touching the lives of the many rather than the few while in his physical form. It is here that you no longer feel separation, because now you are at one with the heart of humanity as well as the heart of God and the heart of the Mother, the Holy Spirit, the movement, the frequency, the band of love.

This is part and parcel of what we are here to explore with you today: the richness of yourself in relationship to life. There is never anything to fear. There is never anything to distrust. If you truly understand that you are indeed love and that this is all you are here striving to remember, striving to bring to the surface, this dissolves any illusion of separation and you automatically feel the connection with life. And yet you can experience life in a form of separation of the physical body, one from the other, communing with community, laughing and dancing and playing and singing. Do you understand?

●   ●   ●

Surrender to Love

What is your mission here upon the planet Earth? What is your purpose? You all have this bit of information inside yourselves at all times. You are never astray from your purpose, your mission here upon the Earth. Never do you fall off the path, never do you stray from the path, but everything, everything, absolutely everything is in right order at all times in your life. Now we are going to ask that you surrender to your life being in right order, understanding that in each and every moment of each and every day, you can wake up to the truth of self.

How do you do this? How do you understand the truth of self? You take a peek around inside and ask yourself how you feel right at this given moment, and that is the truth of self. You have to be very honest with yourself, however; you have to be in integrity, and you certainly must use a little bit of discretion here. Understand that much of what you feel at times comes from other people, certainly from values that are placed upon you, through society, through your parents' expectations and through other influences. Sometimes you even carry around a wee bit of awareness of hierarchy that you would surrender to as well, valuing at times the opinions here of Dr. Peebles more than you would value the opinions of yourself.

We want you to strengthen your souls. The challenge here is to always understand that change comes with opportunity. Surrender to the very same. Now, in this given moment, you find that there is truth within your reality. What do you feel right now? How does the environment around you feel to you? Does it feel scary? Does it feel exciting? Does it feel sad? Ask yourself these questions all the time, and it is there where you will find the truth that becomes the springboard for your spirit. It takes much more effort and energy to hold life at arm's length, to hold parts of yourself away, to deny yourself the experience of misery and pain, to deny yourself the experience of love.

Love is never wrong, my dear friends. You should find yourself on many occasions, every single day, leaping out with your heart wanting to jump into the arms of so many upon the planet Earth—not just one individual, but the many rather than the few. It is there where you will understand that love has no boundaries. It is not finite; it is infinite, and it is here upon planet Earth that you try to encapsulate it into a single moment, into a single person, into a single value, into a car, into a home. You strive to understand love by breaking it into its little pieces, although love is the energy that bonds life together.

You come to understand that you love yourself by stopping, pausing and asking yourself, "How do I feel right now?" and not denying yourself the emotion. It is never, ever wrong for you here upon the Earth to feel, to live, to breathe. You are never taking up too much space. When you are sad, it's fine as far as we are concerned. Surrender to the very same, and you will find yourself moving through it with great ease. Why? Because you are surrendering to the frequency band of love, loving yourself beyond your wildest dreams and imaginations through loving allowance for all things to be, starting with yourself. You are increasing communication inside of yourself first and expressing it to the world.

It is there that you find self-responsibility for your life as a creative adventure, because it is your decision what choices and perceptions you embrace to create your reality. You are not a limited being by any stretch of the imagination. What gift can you give to the world? What is your mission? What is your purpose? The answer to all these questions is to share of yourself in each and every moment of the day, understanding that life is always harmonious—always and forevermore. The pain is an illusion of separation; understand this, and you will also begin to dissolve dis-ease inside of yourself. (We have a little running joke here with the band of angels that dis-ease is what we would call giveupitis.) We certainly don't want you to give up; we want you to fall into life, to fall into life inside of yourself and then to watch yourself fully expressed here upon planet Earth.

The challenge is to be willing to change, to be flexible, to respond with sensitivity to the many rather than the few. Planet Earth is in a very beautiful time period of great growth, great understanding. Embrace the many perspectives. You do not have to live them, but strive to understand by putting yourself in someone else's shoes for once. Strive to understand why their hearts are beating in the way they do and why they would be expressing themselves in the way they do. No longer will you have to hold anyone in life at arm's length ever again, for it is there that you find you can love them no matter what.

And certainly we love you, my dear friends. We love you always. It is not at all a conditional love; we love you always despite your fears, despite your expectations and concerns. We embrace you. The only difference between you and us is the fact that we know we are you. God bless you indeed. We see ourselves in every face, in every smile, in every tear. God bless you indeed, my dear friends.

●   ●   ●

Life: A Dance of Wonder

Beautiful creators in this room today, beautiful spirits, each and every one with a hurting heart. Understand that you have an opportunity, and certainly it is a time upon planet Earth for healing even the smallest hurts—the smallest hurts, my dear friends. Whether it's a little nick on your finger or a nick on your heart, it is all the very same, because indeed it is a part of your experience here upon the planet Earth in understanding God, the beauty. The reality here is that life at times feels like a dance of adversity, but life here upon the planet Earth is certainly a dance of wonder.

You are being given an opportunity here today to have contact with the many rather than the few in the body, in the human form, each and every one of you wanting more contact with Spirit, but you are the Spirit incarnate. Understand that it is through your willingness to touch and be touched by the world that you will find yourself, in a profound sense, immersing yourself in life as never before. Be willing to touch and be touched, understanding that part of your driving force here upon the Earth is to find and create greater love.

Let us talk about how to heal the little hurts inside your heart or on your finger or sometimes from past life existences. Those are hurts that you have chosen—and we emphasize *chosen*—to bring forth into this lifetime. We assure you that God does not have a book of karma that you must act out here upon the planet Earth, but rather He is a very loving God, and He is you. Take a look in the mirror and then look at all the faces around you, and you will understand that everything you see, hear, taste, touch, feel and smell is indeed, my dear friends, a part of you. Every face you gaze upon today is the face of God. Fall in love with the wonder there. Understand as well that as you are working upon the planet Earth studying this course of existence of how to dissolve the illusions of separation, you will find yourself drawing closer and closer to the moment of Now.

We would ask for a moment that you breathe very deeply into your spines and release, at this moment, your struggles of the day, of the week, of the months and, my dear friends, of the years ahead. Realize that right here, today, you have a point, an opportunity for re-creation for your souls. Your spirit guides are drawing closer to you now. There is an enormous band of angels who certainly want to work with you, and they will be creating today a fantastic vortex of energy, of healing light and an opportunity for an expansion of your own souls.

For those of you who are willing to accept and to admit them into your life, understand that they can indeed right now touch the top of your spine. It is there where you will find chakra adjustments occurring inside of you. You will find yourselves feeling a little warm. Be certain to drink plenty of water, and remember to play today.

That is part of our journey here today: to simply play through conversation, through communication with community, my dear friends. Communion with community is certainly what your experience upon planet Earth here is about.

●   ●   ●

The Pasture of Prosperity

My dear friends, creators you are always, but certainly at this time, you will be called upon to fully express the power of your soul. It is time now to release the toxic energy of the past, the toxic energy that has been welling up inside of you physically, emotionally and spiritually. Understand that there is a very beautiful elixir for one's broken spirit, and that is simply to look into the mirror and tell yourself that you love you; say it with sincerity. If you practice this on a regular basis, it will eventually begin to sink in that you are indeed nothing but love—so how could you not love you in the first place?

You are all very beautiful spirits, and we would give you an exercise here of prosperity and abundance. We call it "The Field of Prosperity," or you might call it "The Pasture of Prosperity." It is the very same pasture that you are afraid you're going to be turned out to when you are old and gray, for lack of financial abundance. Well, my dear friends, face it head-on. Close your eyes and look into the eyes of the flowers that you want to bring forth. As you stand in your pasture, watch them bloom. From within your hearts, you will begin to inspire a relationship with finances in your world that will be beyond your wildest dreams and imaginations. You can indeed create your own reality, because that's what you're doing all the time. It is a matter of decision; it is a matter of priorities inside of yourself; it is certainly not a matter of my priorities.

Within yourself, you keep rearranging—emotionally, spiritually and physically—and suddenly you find that there is one priority that exists above and beyond all of that. It is the priority of love. It is love that creates movement. It is love that creates expansion. It is love that draws you closer to one another without fear, without expectations. You might ask, "Without fear of what?" Well, my dear friends, the greatest fear of all is losing one's self in another. We would ask you: Can you trust? Can you truly, in this lifetime, find that you can trust? The reality of your existence—that you indeed are God—would tell you that there is nothing to fear, that you are nothing but love so there is nothing to fear. You, my dear friends, are already full and abundant and prosperous beings. You're just trying to remember it, God bless you indeed. Understand this, and you will find that you will create beautiful relationships that will help you in exploring and understanding yourself, the expansion of the loving being who you are.

We love you so very much. There is going to be a tremendous, miraculous, exciting expansion of awareness of the mystical realm in the near future. "Hallelujah to that," you're all sayin', yeah. But understand that you will have a more fulfilling relationship once you realize this inside of your heart: that there are many realms that exist. All you have to do is stop, pause and think about yourself, about the many lifetimes that you have already lived within this given lifetime. You realize that you have lived here as a two-year-old, a three-year-old and so on, and certainly each one of those is a lifetime in and of itself. But, my dear friends, so is each and every day, for at night you go to sleep and you die, and you wake up once again resurrected, reincarnated into the world. You make a decision every night that you want to breathe upon the planet Earth once again for greater and greater understanding still. When you think you have not done enough, realize that you do enough by simply sitting in these chairs, by simply speakin' a word to a neighbor, by simply learning to appreciate yourself—the magnitude, the beauty and wonder of you.

This is the power of your soul that we would ask you meditate upon. Release your expectations that things must match and fit and so on and so forth. That is where you find your frustrations; you will find less frustration when you at long last learn to surrender. Surrender to the magnificent journey to your hearts, taking this consciousness that is you that is a circle and turning it into a spiral, wherein you weave yourself into the fabric of eternity. God bless you indeed. There you discover that the learning never ends; there, my dear friends, you fall into your enlightenment. And when you are there, what you gonna do after you're enlightened? God bless you indeed, my dear friends.

You are beautiful spirits, each and every one here today. Our prayer for you, my dear friends, is that you realize that you are ever-expanding beings, that you are ever-wondering beings and that you are ever-prosperous beings in this joyous celebration. God bless you, indeed.

•   •   •

Surface Dwellers

God bless you indeed! The heavens are a-laughin'; we are very much intoxicated by you. We love you so very much, my dear friends, and certainly there are challenges here upon the planet Earth. Understand that you are going to be called upon to open your hearts in ways you never dreamed or imagined possible. There is a tremendous energy here at work upon the planet Earth that is helping and assisting in the eradication of barriers, borders and boundaries. The energy is creating unification among families and friends and unification between yourselves and Spirit. Watch with wonder, my dear friends, as certain activities here upon the planet Earth will be increasing as well.

There will be contact with the many rather than the few and some—things that our dear channel doesn't like for us to share—from extraterrestrials. How do you like them apples, my dear friends? It's going to be a very exciting time for you here upon the planet Earth, a fantastic journey for you as long as you are willing to open your hearts to expand now and forevermore. Realize that at this time, you are being called upon with little tugs and pulls of your heart to reunite with family members. It is there where you can overcome. We do not use this word lightly, but truly, my dear friends, for the very first time, you have an opportunity here to reunite with family members and to overcome the greatest obstacles that have been in front of the full expression of your heart here upon the planet Earth.

It is a time of expansion, an expansion of yourself. Certainly the light, the energy, the love, the Christ energy, wants very much to come to each and every one of you here to be fully expressed upon the planet Earth, to increase the vibrational frequency of love, to be elevated into a new dimension. Dear friends, you are suddenly immersed in light in ways you never dreamed or imagined possible. Turmoil upon the Earth is a necessity for this process—giving of birth of self, giving of birth of God here upon the Earth as never before.

We want you to understand that in your life here upon the Earth, you are a surface dweller. Understand, if you will, in relation here to the sea, that there are creatures living in the waters, fully immersed. That is certainly symbolic, my dear friends, of what we're speaking of: that your souls be fully immersed now, here, in love, in the consciousness of Christ upon the planet Earth.

There are still stones upon the surface, are there not? But it is only the surface dwellers who feel the stones; it is only the surface dwellers who feel tormented by the elements; it is only the surface dwellers who live in fear. You are here upon the Earth in the human form, feet upon the Earth, surface dwellers. But your heart and soul, that which you truly are, the light from within, my dear friends, did not exist here upon the Earth—it comes from elsewhere. Certainly it is one with all, always has been, and you're just here striving to remember this.

Now, in this time of great turmoil upon your planet Earth, you are being asked to immerse yourself in light as never before, to understand that the key word here is "trust." Trust, my dear friends, that there is indeed a point and purpose to your life here upon the planet Earth that exist beyond what you feel is your three-dimensional reality. We would not ask that you turn away from that perceived reality, but rather that you understand that you have an opportunity now to breathe freely here, to feel safe.

You can encourage your life beyond your wildest dreams and imaginations if you are willing to root yourself within the consciousness of the Lord. It is there that you find that you're from the very same family. Never have you been separate from anyone. Never have you been separate or parted from any religion, any science, for the truth here is that all is one, now and forevermore.

So, my dear friends, do not hold life at arm's length. Love those whom you feel in your heart at times are not worthy of love, for they too are family members. We ask that you work within your heart, within your soul, within your life, within your consciousness, within every breath, my dear friends, to uplift the planet Earth in greater consciousness of love, now and forevermore. It is when you are existing in that world inside of your heart, fully expressed here, that you find heaven. For we say it time and again that heaven is not a place but a feeling and, my dear friends, you can have it now. All your sorrows will melt away once you step fully and completely into an expression of love. God bless you indeed, my dear friends, our family. We love you so very much.

The Richness of Self and the Unity of Life

U nderstand that you are in a process of discovery of yourself here upon planet Earth unlike any other that has ever been experienced before. This profound experience of existence is partly due to communication. Never before has there been such an opportunity to share with the lives of the many rather than the few in an instant. With your news networks, you can experience the wars on the other side of the world very directly. The images are there upon your television sets. No longer must you rely here upon telepathy, although certainly this is a part and parcel of the process here upon the Earth. There will be an expansion, my dear friends, of your telepathic consciousness, your awareness of self and of others and of world experiences. You will be aware of energy frequencies and such that you will find are coursing through your physical bodies.

So, my dear friends, when you have questions in your hearts with every passing day as to what is occurring inside of you physically, please understand that you are indeed essentially picking up the different programs, the different stations of certain experiences upon the Earth—in terms of wars, in terms of love, in terms of labors of love. Understand this, and you will understand how to work with it: by increasing the vibrational frequency of love within you. Raise this light element inside of you, my dear friends. Each and every one certainly understands that the purity of your heart has always existed, and yet you struggle against this—you hold it at arm's length in so very many ways, shapes and forms.

Surrender into Life

We are asking at this time that you would bring light forth through you. "Now how, my dear friend Dr. Peebles?" you would ask. Well, you understand that in the movements, the stirrings of your hearts is where you have conversations with God. This is where you find that the Lord Jesus Christ, who did indeed walk the planet Earth, was simply just another man—well, perhaps a wee bit more aware than others around. He would be very much willing to work with you and certainly to honor you and to refresh your spirit, but He can't give the answers directly. Rather, my dear friends, you would feel this in terms of the stirrings of your heart, the truth that you very much want to speak and to share with the world.

This means vulnerability and surrender into life, jumping in with your entire being, your entire soul, which is indeed baptismal for you, the experience of finding yourself not only at one, at peace with God, with self, but certainly with planet Earth and the many rather than the few. By sharing these stirrings of your hearts, allowing the truth of self to shine forth in all its vast array of color, without concern as to whether it is right or wrong, up or down, you come to that peace. You should also understand that because it comes from you—and certainly your feelings do count here upon the planet Earth—there is a space that was predestined, if you will, and designed for you. God bless you indeed. You need no longer feel that you must make the world fit in order to play with it, but rather you just simply discover that you already fit with the world.

It is there that life becomes a grand and beautiful dance. Now, with your light shining through in this fashion, suddenly your so-called problems here, all illusions of separation, begin to disappear, and certain genuine realities for yourself begin to manifest. Certainly, my dear friends, you find that there are no longer grievances that you hold within your heart. No longer do you hold judgments against anyone, and you discover that what you have really done is dissolve the judgments against yourself. Some of you are the harshest terrorists against yourselves. It's no wonder that here upon your Earth, this is a great time to root them out. Start within your own hearts and understand the many ways in which you are terrorists against yourselves. We emphasize this very specifically here.

As this light shines forth, it creates for you an attraction, an abundance of attention, and this can come in terms of relationships, love in many forms, including financial resources and absolute, perfect health. It is certainly possible and will be happening for the many rather than the few. You will literally be redesigning yourselves. Your DNA will begin to change, not because of anyone's manipulation of it, but because you have brought more of your heart to the surface than ever before. It is there, really, my dear friends, that you find heaven upon the Earth. It is there that your work truly commences, with the many rather than the few healers.

As this light shines forth, everybody will be gravitating toward you. My dear friend, when you hold out your hand, how many want to touch it? If we would ask how many here in this room would like to touch our hand at this given time, how many here would like to do this? Simply say I. [Everyone says I.] God bless you indeed, for that's a fantastic resonance, is it not? It comes because I am here, sitting with you, working through this channel with a tremendous vibrational frequency of love that I would like very much to share with each and every one of you. Simply place your hand up in the air as we have here, and close your eyes, if you like, or keep them open, if you like. It doesn't really matter; we simply want to work with each of you. Greetings.

Do you understand the wave of a hand and its significance as you are waving one to the other? You really are sharing an energy frequency one with the other, are you not? My dear friends, do not stress or strain against any gift that is given to you in such a fashion. Receive it with all your heart and all your might and all your soul, and you will find that you are filled forevermore with love. What are we doing here but reading the stirrings of your heart? We are not fabricating this for you; we don't hold the answers at all.

The significance of baptism is an immersion into life—all of life, without fear, without concern, without expectations and without regret, of course. To immerse yourself in life does not mean simply to care for everyone else around you but to remember that you are indeed a part of the equation and to care for yourself as well. Make loving allowance for all things to be in their own time and place, starting with yourself, with your desires, your opinions, your needs, your wants, not to the detriment of anyone, but rather to help the many rather than the few. It is by bringing yourself to the surface, by sharing your truth, by speaking and expressing it without fear, by being willing to stand firm in that which you are that the world has an opportunity to respond honestly to you, for you are bringing truth to the surface. It is there that you get the honest echo of life all around, for you are rooted in absolute truth of self.

Think once again of the lessons here of the Lord Jesus Christ, who did indeed walk the planet Earth in the human form, my dear friends, fully expressed and on the surface, in a skin, so to speak, in the flesh. And when He dropped His coat, it was exactly the same as what was on the surface. My dear friends, the greatest love of all is love that you find for yourself, for it is there that you find that everyone exists. It is there that you fall in love with all of life.

The Band of Love

During times of inactivity there is a necessity to be more active inside of yourself. Everyone close your eyes, just for a moment. We tell you a little story here.

I am spokesperson for the band of angels; we ride the frequency band of love. The band is also something, my dear friends, that can be stretched and pulled and can certainly stretch out through the dimensions, if you will, to touch many lives and many hearts. This band, my dear friends, exists inside each and every one of you, in the many rather than the few.

Here in this room today, you might be feeling a bit scared, skittish, sad, melancholy or in a state of fear and panic and paranoia. You hold this feeling at arm's length; you do not want to go into these darker spaces, nor do you want to be possessed by them. But, my dear friends, you are feeling the insecurities of the Earth at this time. The frequency of Earth is being raised and elevated, so if you would for a moment here visualize inside of your body, your physicality, and find the points of pain that are physical. Now realize that these physical points of pain are ties to the many rather than the few who are upon the Earth who are in grief. They may be in this room, it could be our dear Summer who is out of body . . . the many rather than the few.

My dear friends, your band is around them. Upon this band, send them as much love as you possibly can. Tell them how very much you care and that you now care enough to bring this band back into your heart so that now, my dear friends, you can find your strength once again. Understand that your frequency, your love, is indeed heard and is always expressed upon the Earth. But, my dear friends, you must remember that you do not need to be plugged in to anyone in order to keep that person going. This is sometimes what you end up doing, because you are very compassionate. You think that you have to be plugged in at all times, forgetting that you already are because you really are made of the very same stuff.

Set Aside Your Studies

Magnificent creators, each and every one here in this room today, each and every one a student of the divine, explore this relationship within your hearts, my dear friends. It is there that you will set your souls not only on fire but on a raging fire—a fantastic and beautiful, brilliant light that shines forth from within you to spread across the planet Earth. This certainly is a time when there is dire need here upon the Earth of tremendous uplifting of all hearts. God bless you indeed.

My dear friends, we would ask that you step properly into your souls today here, that you step forth into the discovery of self and the expansion of the very same. Realize that everything you see, hear, taste, touch, feel and smell—even that which is upon your news networks at this time—is *you*, my dear friends. These are the battles that rage inside your hearts. God bless you indeed. Each and everyone here in this room today certainly understands that you are being asked to no longer be terrorists against yourselves in terms of your self-worth and your self-value and in freeing up your spirit through the permission here of your own heart.

Where You Find Your Freedom

Understand, my dear friends that it is a time when there are no more shades of gray. We certainly would ask that you, within your own chosen life here upon the planet Earth, consider this option—it is just an option from the band of angels to you—that today you will find within your heart to give up on something. We ask you to take your tools such as astrology, astronomy, anything that you find that you study at this given time, and set them aside. Just for a moment, would you ponder the understanding that even sacred geometry, all studies of all religions, all studies of how relationships work and the expansion of the very same is a study of the illusions of separation?

Everything you study within your heart, all the tools that you use, whether it be your crystals, your particular piece of jewelry you feel you must wear in every moment of every day in order to get through and do the work that you are here upon the Earth to do is certainly part of One. There is no separation; every single study here upon the planet Earth leads to the very same conclusion. What you are seeking here, what you are trying to express, what you are trying to map out through various studies such as sacred geometry, all of it describes the very same thing: the frequency band of love, the love that you are, the love that is directly the source from which you were birthed. God bless you indeed.

You came here in the beginning of time to understand and to study the illusion of separation—the possibility that you could ever be separate from the one who is God, love eternal. My dear friends, study this, and it is there that you will refine your heart and your freedom; from this point, you find that you are indeed one with the Source. Then you can move forward and study your religions or take up your crystals—as little extensions of yourself but not you. They are not you entirely. *Everything* is you, and this is where we want you to put your sights and your attentions. It is there where you find your freedom, my dear friends. It is there where you no longer find yourself needing to be reclusive within your soul, to hide yourself from the world.

When you put yourself upon the surface, when you teach the world through your truth and the expression of the very same, you find freedom beyond your wildest dreams and imaginations. Abundance reigns free inside of you; no longer are you concerned with financial difficulties or relationships of any kind. You find the relationship that is eternal, the one that exists inside of yourself. God bless you indeed. You will know love of the very same; you will understand that there is no need for protection from anything or anyone, because you are white light. You have just simply forgotten this.

You, my dear friends, are God, and you have forgotten it. With this awareness inside of yourself, you have stationed yourself properly upon the planet Earth to find and seek your enlightenment at long last, no longer concerned about tomorrow or yesterday but only about the given moment. That is the tip of the iceberg.

Your planet Earth is in tremendous transition at this time, my dear friends. Remember to bring love to the surface no matter what, no matter the tendency to fight inside of yourselves the desire that is true and real, that exists within everyone upon the planet Earth to bring love to the surface. This is your real spirit, your real heart. God bless you indeed. Love thy neighbor as thyself. How do you do this, my dear friends? You do this certainly through forgiveness. When you are finding yourself hurt, when you are finding that the world is treating you very improperly, remember these beautiful, divine and inspired words and speak them aloud: "Forgive them, for they know not what they do." God bless you indeed, my dear friends.

Self-Healing from Dr. Peebles: An Exercise

We would now guide you through a little exercise. Every person in this room has pain somewhere in the physical body. Close your eyes . . . We want you to understand that you have a physical body and a spirit inside of this body—you can call that spirit your personality, the musings of your brain and such things, but inside of your physical body, there is a point of pain. Find it inside of yourself and understand that this point of pain will look rather black and bleak to you. To some it will be frightening, because it is sore or tender, but, my dear friends, these are the areas that need your light—the light of your spirit, the truth, the One who you are, the lover who you are, the white light that you are. You want to take your spirit and move into this darker space, because you are all healers.

You would do it for anyone else; you would help a stranger on the street. Now it's time to turn this attention to you. Draw in a very deep breath, and as you exhale, imagine yourself as God exhaling freely the light of your soul into this area of pain, illuminating it. For some it's going to be very difficult to bring even the smallest amount of light into this area, but practice, my dear friends. With every breath, you will find that you can take these darker spaces, bring the light of your soul into them, and thereby repair your physical body, for your physical body is responding to parts of your spirit that are afraid to reincarnate.

A Platform for Community

God bless you indeed, my dear friends, in this tremendous, rapid growth here upon planet Earth. We call upon each and every one of you here today to understand that you are a part of creating the harmony and balance here. Beautiful spirits, everyone here in this room today. My dear friends, understand that you are creating compassion—certainly through your hearts, through the conditioning of your growth here upon planet Earth.

From the time you were wee little ones, you have created inside yourselves a tremendous degree of compassion and trust. All here in this room today have had certain conditions—God bless you indeed. We are just checkin' out each one of you, but yes, without question here—each one of you has had certain conditions in the course of your lifetime; you have had to overcome tremendous obstacles. The way in which you have done this, my dear friends, is through tremendous commitment to creating the most compassionate heart that you can possibly create. God bless you indeed.

This is the strength, my dear friends, that you have worked with and certainly will be working with. We are going to ask that you work inside of your hearts at this time to create a condition of love and understanding and compassion for everyone. Do not turn your thoughts to fear but only to tenderness. Do not turn to anger, my dear friends, but only to cherishing your neighbors and family members—the many rather than the few here upon planet Earth.

My dear friends, you certainly have your own concerns and issues, and we understand this. But we want you to understand that when you fall in love with yourself and respect and honor the deeper values that are eternal, you are sitting in the right condition inside yourself. We speak in terms of honoring self, honoring everyone in your nation, honoring everyone on the planet Earth, honoring this expression of God through you. It is there, my dear friends, that you find that there is no need to turn to the outer world for your answers anymore.

A Meditation for Self and Unity

My dear friends, for a moment here we would ask that you would close your eyes and breathe very deeply into your spines. Draw upon the energy of light from which you were born; you are drawing now from the very same source. It is through this mere act, my dear friends, of breathing into your spines from this source of light from which you were born that you find yourselves deeply united. Within this unification, there is tremendous diversity inside of your hearts in terms of how you choose in this lifetime to express yourself here upon the planet Earth.

Now we would ask that you would focus upon your situations, if you will, your concerns, your issues for a moment here just in terms of how they relate to you. Do not concern yourself with anyone else in the world. Simply ask: "What would I like to have resolved once and for all? What is that aggravating condition inside of me that I would like very much to repair? What is it that I would like to learn in the course of this lifetime? What decision at this given time would

I like to make?" Take care here that you are not turning your attention to how it affects anyone but you at this given time.

Now, my dear friends, for a moment here, remain with your focus upon these issues. Imagine that you place them in your own palms, and with this light force from which you are breathing now, raise these issues in the palms of your hands and offer them up here to God. Simply release them into the light so that you may find this illumination inside of your hearts, the firm and solid answers. There you will find all that you seek, the awareness that you are not ever alone with these conditions of your heart but that there is always a chance for resurrection here of self into the world.

God bless you indeed, my dear friends. There is resurrection from grief, resurrection from pain, resurrection from that which ails you in the physical form, resurrection of your spirit into the light. The true light of your soul, my dear friends, is all that remains once you leave this planet Earth, once you drop the coat of this physical form. God bless you indeed, my dear friends, as you enjoy the journey to your hearts.

A Shortcut in the Search for Clarity

In this search for clarity that everybody is involved in here on Earth, is there some kind of a shortcut? It seems that I can get clear, and then the next day, I start to drift back into going round and round as opposed to in a spiral. Is there some kind of a key or formula? I understand that to eliminate the word "but" and inject "however" really helps me greatly.

Yes, and even further, my dear friend, when you are saying your prayers, you simply offer yourself as we just demonstrated here. Offer your issues, your concerns, your desires up to heaven. Then you would say a prayer such as "I, Jerry, would like to offer my concerns, my expectations and my strong will to you, Lord, and I would ask that I may understand that you will respond, for you know me very well. I release my expectations as to how you will respond here." It is in this way, my dear friend, that you find yourself releasing yourself entirely to all the possibilities of the universe, you understand?

What is heaven? And how do you create that? Is this in the afterlife, or is it perhaps a possibility to have it here upon the planet Earth? And how do you create heaven on Earth? You do that by releasing your expectations and certainly by finding that within each and every moment of each and every day, you can always expect the unexpected. The unexpected, my dear friend, is not turmoil, not adversity, not difficulty, not trouble, but perhaps it truly is a time of peace, of love and tranquillity, of harmony in every moment, no matter the world around you, no matter the conditions there, do you understand? For heaven is a feeling, is it not? Is it a place as well? God bless you indeed. It is a place where you are at any given time. For when you are praying, you are with family, yes? And it is there that you realize you have crossed the borders, the barriers and such that you feel exist. Those are illusions, you understand? And when you realize that you are really sitting with family and you're just talking there to God, my dear friend, you have everything in right order, yes?

The Richness of Your Being

Certainly, my dear friends, here upon this planet Earth, you have many opportunities to express this awareness of the divinity of self. It is in your outer world that you become fully expressed, but it starts on the inside.

Student of the divine, where is that which you seek? Is it in your learnings, in your education, in prayer, in communion with yourself? And then there is community, putting yourself out into the world, speaking and expressing from your heart and simply sittin' back and waitin' for the honest echo of you to come a-runnin', God bless you indeed. Either toward you or away from you is all right, my dear friends. It certainly is the ebb and flow of the tide of self that you are experiencing here in this life.

You are all exploring here upon the planet Earth the richness of yourselves. You want the richness of yourselves to be expressed fully here as well as to be felt by you—certainly richness in terms of what would feel like heaven. Heaven, once again, is a feeling, my dear friends, not a place. Here upon the planet Earth, you realize that you are in exploration of the illusions of separation. And how do you explore these illusions of separation? First you acknowledge the separation that exists. It is there, my dear friends, that you realize that you seek oneness here upon the planet Earth; you seek security that comes from this oneness. You seek this connection with life at all times in each and every moment of each and every day.

But because of the physical form here upon the planet Earth, it is absolutely impossible for you to find yourself feeling this oneness at all times, simply by virtue of the fact that you feel that Bev is over there and you are over here. God bless you indeed. Certainly, my dear friends, it's all right, because this is part and parcel of the tools for learning how to fully express yourself, learning how to commune with life. How do you do this? Where do you find the oneness that exists between yourself and all of life, my dear friends? It comes through a frequency that you derive certainly from God, from the heavens, bringing it down through yourself, certainly in the form of what we would call here Holy Spirit, the energy of the Mother. It comes from being fully expressed through your hands, just as the Lord Jesus Christ, who walked the planet Earth, was capable of touching the lives of the many rather than the few, certainly in the physical form. It is here, my dear friends, that you no longer feel separation, because now you are at one with the heart of humanity, the heart of God, the heart of the Mother and of the Holy Spirit. It is within the movement, the frequency, the band of love. God bless you indeed.

My dear friends, this is part and parcel of what we are here to explore with you today—the richness of yourself in relationship to life. There is never anything to fear; there is never anything to distrust if you truly understand that you are indeed love. This is all that you are here striving to remember, striving to bring to the surface. This is what dissolves any illusion of separation. Automatically, my dear friends, you feel the connection with life, and yet you can experience life in a form of separation of the physical body, one from the other, communing with community, laughing and dancing and playing and singing. God bless you indeed.

Creating Intimacy

God bless you indeed. Do understand, students of the divine, that the journey you have embarked upon here on planet Earth is one wherein you spiral, my dear friends, deeper and deeper into your heart, penetrating the fabric of eternity. You are penetrating with your heart, your soul, your spirit. Contact with the many rather than the few is certainly the reason you are here upon the planet Earth. God bless you indeed, my dear friends.

Within this room today, we will be having little discussions with you. Certainly you have some questions, and we have some answers. But what we are really doing here is moving energy about. It is not so much in our words as it is in a sensation, a feeling that helps you to restructure your lives, to restructure your world, to create your reality from the inside out—from your heart. At long last, my dear friends, you are feeling that you no longer have to serve anyone, but rather that you are one with everything. The answer to all of your questions is indeed intimacy—intimacy with all of life. Everything that you are working upon here upon planet Earth comes down to one thing my dear friends—intimacy.

How can you create more intimacy? Whether it be within relationships, with money, with your socks and shoes—it doesn't really matter. Suddenly we speak it, and you become more aware that they are on your feet. God bless you indeed. Intimacy, contact with the many rather than the few—this certainly is the order of business here upon planet Earth.

Now, my dear friends, how do you create intimacy? You do it upon the frequency of love, creating an understanding between yourselves, within the world around you, making loving allowance for all things to be, understanding that all perspectives certainly do count, for they are important to the individual who holds them. Certainly, my dear friends, everyone and everything upon the planet Earth is there for you, to help in the creation of yourself, the divine being who you are, to hold a certain energy as we are doing here in this room today for you so that you can grow. God bless you indeed.

We are holding a certain energy, creating certain scenarios that at times we understand appear to be very challenging for you. But it is always for your divine self to grow toward greater light, toward greater understanding. We love you so very much. By serving yourselves first, you certainly serve all of humanity, for you shine your light as brightly as you possibly can, so that everyone in the village can at long last begin to see.

This is a time certainly of clarity, of stability inside of yourself and true honoring of your own sensations. It is there, my dear friends, that you are going to find that your own sensations you are feeling are generally correct during this time of great turmoil here upon planet Earth. We say "generally" because there are certain discrepancies, for some of you would think that what you are sensing is you, and it would not really be coming from you but from other resources, other entities around. There's quite a bit of confusion here upon the planet Earth, so the best place to look is inside of your hearts, my dear friends, for your answers from the divine self who you are.

There is one here who wants very much to spell out something for all here. Certainly in terms of intimacy, there are veils between you and Spirit, between you and God. There is the veil that exists between yourself and another here upon planet Earth. Sometimes that veil comes from you, and sometimes it comes from the one with whom you are in contact, attempting the intimacy there. How do you break through the veil, my dear friends? You do it by piercing it with truth and love, by understanding that there is nothing to fear here upon planet Earth. Here there is only activity of surrender, surrendering into your heart, surrendering to the other perspectives around you. As you become more clear, the world around you will become more clear. God bless you indeed. It is there where you have contact with the many rather than the few. It is certainly a dance, a journey of expansion of self as never before, freedom beyond your wildest dreams and imaginations. It has nothing to do with how fast your car can be driven, certainly not. It has very much to do, my dear friends, with how much you are willing to allow yourselves to grow here into your divine selves, expression of the very same here upon the planet Earth.

Earth Changes Affect Your Identity

God bless you indeed, my dear friends. Thank you so very much for responding within your hearts to our words to you. God bless you indeed, in terms of caring for your planet Earth, increasing the vibrational frequency of love here upon planet Earth, for certainly you have brought

Earth into greater understanding. You have certainly, each and every one here in this room today, increased Earth's compassion. Mother Earth is not feeling quite so bad these days, God bless you indeed. Thank you very much, my dear friends, for all of your love and all of your prayers. Planet Earth is in a process now of being elevated into an even higher frequency.

Understand that there will indeed be some disturbances within your sleep patterns that some here in this room are already experiencing. My dear friends, realize that there will be certain disturbances in your daily patterns as well. Certainly, my dear friends, you will find unexpected occurrences coming your way, opportunities. God bless you indeed. You will find that there will be little approaches from strangers who will offer you gifts and such things. My dear friends, this is because your planet Earth is now being raised into a frequency wherein you can find and seek your angels, spirit guides and friends.

Certainly the veil here upon planet Earth is getting a little thinner, so pay attention, my dear friends, in your daily encounters, where you will find little secrets and such things being whispered in your ears. This is going to help coax and encourage you along your path.

Each and every one of you here in this room today is fully awake now here upon the Earth, and certainly you have made a decision to stick around for a little while, with greater and greater certainty that you do indeed care for life and indeed, my dear friends, want to live a very enriching, a very fulfilling life here upon the Earth. This doesn't mean that there's not going to be turmoil here down the road apiece. We do not say this, of course, to strike terror in anyone's heart here but only to ask that you would work even a little harder to elevate the love within yourselves so that you indeed, my dear friends, can understand that you have an influence here upon the planet Earth—certainly through your thoughts and through reaching out of your heart in your own frequency, spiraling out to the world, embracing it with increasing love. God bless you indeed, my dear friends. Is your soul crying out for a whole new identity?

It Is Time to Refresh Your Identity

I left my wallet someplace yesterday, I can't find my keys half the time, I lost my cell phone, I just don't know what's going on. It's kind of disconcerting to leave your wallet in places . . .

Not as far as we are concerned—it's wonderful, absolutely! My dear, it's your soul crying out right now that you want a whole new identity, you're looking for yourself hard and fast here and you are realizing you are not going to find yourself in your husband, are you? And your joy and your happiness are not going to come from his certainty and willingness, are they? So, my dear, it is once again time for you to simply focus upon yourself, do that which you enjoy, do that which you love. Learn and grow and, my dear, you do not need the filter of your husband to put it all through to see if it works. Do you understand?

In your previous employment, you had to find all sorts of facts, did you not? And you had to put them to the test through a filter, did you not? To see if you had it all correct? You were always doing this on others' behalf, so that is an old pattern you have created for yourself. You do not need to do this anymore, especially not for you. The only one who has to share whether or not you can be trusted, pass the test, whatever you want, is you. My dear, that is what you are being asked to do right now; this is your new identity, truly, my dear.

It wouldn't ever hurt for you to simply order new credit cards—you don't have to change your name or anything—get a new driver's license. Simply, my dear, refresh everything around you. Toss out the old wallet and get a new one! Change your identity in very small and subtle ways, and you will find that you will vastly improve your very existence, because you will find yourself in a lot of balance, less tired, more aware of yourself.

What do you want to do now that you are retired? And you know what you want, but you are afraid to go and dive in with all your teeth, legs and arms, yeah?

What happens is that you are experiencing much of the disturbances that Mother Earth is feeling at this time. There is yet another large Earth change that is about to occur, and you are already feeling the rumblings and the stirrings there; it is coming up through you.

You are extremely clairsentient. What you can do is have a little talk with yourself. Ask yourself what you are willing to feel, then tell yourself that it is not necessary to pick up on every single frequency, and it certainly is not necessary for the earthquake to play out in you. Talk to yourself with your voice, say, "All right, this is enough." No longer will you accept or even have to acknowledge the workings of planet Earth. You love her—give to her your love, but you do not have to accept the coughs and the sneezes, so to speak, that she is feeling at this time.

When you are constantly berating self for berating others for berating self, and round and round, it goes back and forth. It's a terrible cycle, is it not? It's really quite natural if you would think of it as this: Everything is God, and you would not have such feelings and emotions if they were separate from God. So understand that all of your emotional states—whether it is anger, pain, misery—really serve you, serve a higher purpose, push you up to the next step, so to speak. This is fertile soil; plant your soul there and grow. You will find that what you think is raging anger inside of you really isn't anything at all. Once you acknowledge it, you find what you thought was a lion is just a little kitten.

Be kind to yourself first. You want to give back to God. You are all very grateful—thank you, God; thank you and thank you and thank you. "But I hate myself." Well, my dear friends, if you want to give back to God, love yourself. That is the greatest gift you can give to Him at all.

You cannot make a wrong decision. Your heart is always in the right place at all times, always, because it's just going to push you to another place and yet another so that the learning never ends. Impatience will just keep it from happening.

When you are working on your mystical experiences and your life starts to change but your friends' lives are not, it is difficult and friends don't know you anymore. There is really nothing you can do, but you can start to talk to them a little bit more about what you are learning, if you like. They will look at you as if you are cuckoo, but you can share with them, "It seems to me that we are really growing apart, and it is cause of great concern to me. I can tell that you feel a little left out of my life, and that's because my journey is taking me elsewhere." Tell them at the outset that there is something you wish to discuss. It is going to be very hard. Make sure they understand that it may come out a little clunky, that it may even hurt, but that you really feel the need to share it. You will feel much better and there will be resolution.

Love Everlasting

Y ou have come to the school called planet Earth to learn about love, an opportunity for understanding and growth inside of your divine spirit through relationship—relationship with the many rather than the few. Understand there are many relationships upon your planet Earth, each and every one equally deserving of unconditional love.

We have a number of individuals here in this room today. Are you ready for the adventure here? Hello, my dear friend Jim, you are a beautiful spirit, and we love you too, Tom, but it's hard for you to hear, isn't it?

Tom: *Not bad.*

Anger Is an Illusion of Separation

Sometimes, yeah. Sometimes it's hard for you to hear it. My dear friend, we love you very much, do you understand? If so, touch your toes for a moment here. Breathe deeply into your spine and be willing to receive now in this relationship with your toes here an awareness of yourself as a light-being, one who is laboring in love here upon the planet Earth, one who is truly now stretching himself to this understanding, this awakening of his heart. Breathe very deeply into your spine once again and understand, my dear friend, that it is the toxicity of anger that you want to release in order to receive more love.

Anger is your illusion of separation from love; anger is your illusion of separation. The reality is that you love so very deeply, so very hard, for so very long, and then, when you step into uncertainty about your relationship, you find that you fill the gap with anger. This is because you are trying very hard to desensitize yourself. You say, "I don't love. I don't want to receive love. I never cared about it in the first place." It is a way in which you try very hard to separate yourself, and it doesn't work. And the anger is not going to leave until you are willing to embrace the reality that you do love, that you do want to be loved, that you do touch, that you do want to be touched, and that is the reason for the exercise of touching your toes right now. From your head to your toes, my dear friend, you want to love and be loved by life. Do you understand? So how long are you going to remain within the anger?

> *Until it's over.*

We hear that you have yet some work to do, and we hear this from your guides. When you say that it is over, then what are you replacing it with? What are you going to restore inside of yourself? Love once again and appreciation for what you had within your relationship?

Your Very First Relationship with Life

God bless you indeed, smart cookies, each and every one of you certainly a student of the divine. We love you so very much and understand that you come to the planet Earth to explore relationships with everything, with all of life and everything in between.

Breathe deeply into your spines for just a moment here. That in and of itself is a relationship; it was the very first relationship that you had with life as you came through the birth canal and out into the world, the very top of your head connecting you as you were plugging yourself into this existence. But then at long last, you took your first breath and developed your very first relationship with life, and it is there that you began to spring into consciousness upon the planet Earth, to realize that immediately . . . Your immediate need upon the Earth was for love, and you sought it so fast inside of your heart, everything accelerating as you stretched your arms, as you cried in anger and found your mommy and, for some you, sucked from her breast. Understand that it was in this relationship that you began to receive nourishment, and you realized that love is very fulfilling, very nutritionally balanced, shall we say, and certainly is very energizing.

My dear friends, as you are reading this text, as you are here in this room today to hear my words and the words of many partners within the band of angels, realize that you will receive many love kisses, hugs, squeezes and gentle pats upon your head, upon your back, upon your knee. Pay attention to the spirits who are working with you as you labor in greater and greater love within relationships with all of life and with respect.

Number one: loving allowance for all things to be in their own time and place, starting with yourself. This is the very first principle to be used as a tool in tandem with the others. Loving allowance for all things to be in their own time and place—this you can use within every relationship, God bless you indeed. For example, and we put it very simply here, you find yourself a chair you want to have a relationship with, but in its own time and place, for if you, my dear friends, try to sit down before you are with the chair, you're going to fall on your fanny. So within its own time and place, you develop the relationship and very gently lower yourself into the chair so that you can have a soft, settling experience.

And you develop a relationship there within increased communication, principle number two. Increase communication with all of life and with respect. Within the chair in which you sit, your fanny finds either comfort or discomfort. It is hard or it is soft where you sit. You are feeling scared or you are feeling balance within this chair, and you find yourself either settling into the relationship or standing up to find yet another. It is not a matter of like or dislike; it is simply discretion inside of yourself that you are seeking relationship in this fashion. You do not cast judgment upon the chair, nor do you pass judgment upon yourself for not wanting to sit in a particular chair—you simply get up and move to another. This is a very simple motion that is part of all relationships upon the planet Earth, even the relationships that occur within human hearts, one joined unto another.

Now, my dear friends, self-responsibility for your life as a creative adventure: You sit in the chair, you find yourself feeling very uncomfortable and you choose to remain there—this is self-responsibility for your life as a creative adventure; it is through your choice to sit in the chair that you do indeed create your reality. You choose to sit in the chair in discomfort. Here, today, as you sit in your chairs, you experience varying degrees of relationship as you are sitting in a classroom for growth and understanding, for prosperity and abundance, trying to understand principles that will help you in your work, help you in your employment, help you within relationships, for example. Comfort and discomfort—but none, none of it is to be judged; it simply is, it exists.

This is the principle that we share with you in a very simple, very gentle fashion, for you can make your life so very complicated within your human relationships. You target the human heart, you look upon another human being through attraction, attraction that is by design through beauty, through physicality, through emotionality, through spirituality, through dimension—layers and layers of the onion in which you are connecting one human heart to another, sometimes in a way that you do not even understand.

You find yourself attracted to an individual, and you move closer and closer still—very much, my dear friends, as you moved closer and closer to the planet Earth, to the beautiful blue orb that you saw from the heavens, that you saw with your, shall we say, heart, with your love. You decided that you wanted to move closer to the planet Earth, and as you moved closer to the Earth—the beautiful blue orb, not very complicated, not filled with chaos; just simple, plain, gentle, out in the universe—you found yourself discovering beautiful diversity of light and color, of clouds and birds, of trees, of grass, of the ground; the browns, the blues and the greens; a very beautiful planet Earth, until you discovered an animal who could bite you and a human being who could spite you.

Falling in Love—And into the Illusions of Separation

It is there that you began to understand aggravation, fear, pain, disillusionment, sadness, depression, all of these pulling you away from what you wanted in the first place, which was simply to find and touch the face of God here upon the planet Earth through your willingness to labor in greater and greater love. "But I'm terrified," you say. "I can't do it," you say. "I don't want to," you say. "I want everything to be my way," you say, "at all times and at all turns."

My dear friends, this is your relationship with planet Earth. It is the one that started the cycles of reincarnation, the one that found you bound here in the very first place, the one where you discovered that you did not want love anymore and found yourself standing separate from God. But the truth of yourself is that you do want to find and touch the face of God once again; to regain your sensitivity, your compassion, your skills of touching, your skills of receiving; to regain your skills, my dear friends, that release you from the feelings of bondage that are indeed part and parcel of the experience of pain, disillusionment, sadness, depression, anger, guilt, shame—all of these illusions of separation, God bless you indeed.

My dear friends, you come to the school called planet Earth to discover and dissolve the illusions of separation within self and between life. Certainly it is your labor of love to diminish these very same illusions wherein you will discover that never in your eternal soul have you been the victim but always the creator. Always the creator, my dear friends! And so upon the school called planet Earth, you find and touch the face of God in another human being. You move closer and closer still. He looks very nice from a distance; sometimes he is dressed in blue just like the Earth, looking very nice. You move closer and closer still, and you come into contact with a vibrational frequency of emotionality, the color and light that comes from within.

The physicality of the individual is simply a cloak; it is sometimes for you, my dear friends, a cloak of betrayal, a cloak that does indeed divide one human being from another. In reality it is not the physicality that you are attracted to; it is the inner light that shines from within to the surface. It is the truth of this individual that you will discover, and the inner light you are attracted to is the face of God.

Now you stand in front of this individual. You gaze into her eyes, very beautiful eyes, sometimes blue, just like the Earth. And you gaze into her skin, and you gaze into her chest and into her legs and into her arms, and you explore the physicality there very much as you did when you came to the planet Earth; it is an attraction that now creates a beautiful resonance inside of your heart, and this person feels it from you. A very beautiful relationship you can develop here—not to be afraid but rather to reveal yourself. You're feeling courageous now: "I have found someone I can feel safe with; she is very beautiful."

And so together you begin to strum your inner chords and you create a frequency between the two of you of value. You discuss everything, from the top of your head to the bottom of your toes; you discuss all opportunities in life and life together. You release yourselves from the confines of the Earth, body and mind. You find and touch the face of God within yourselves and within one another.

And then, all of a sudden, something goes awry. "How in the world will I ever find understanding with this individual?" you ask yourself, and it is there that you fall into the illusions of separation once again, afraid that if you should reveal too much of yourself, you will not be valued; you will not be understood; you will not be really unconditionally loved for who and what you are inside of yourself, the truth of the light within. And you get scared and you hide yourself; you withdraw into the cave that is your physical body. You do not allow yourself to reveal your consciousness.

You do not allow yourselves, my dear friends, to reveal your heart. You do not allow yourselves, my dear friends, to be understanding of this individual any longer, because if you do, you might get hurt. And so it is there that this love begins to dissolve and you get afraid and, God bless you indeed, my dear friends, you withdraw your compassion and you replace it with anger, you replace it with fear, you replace it with depression, you replace it with lack of trust and you, my dear friends, say, "Ah, but I am an unconditionally loving person. I love this person. I am just very clear about how I feel about him (or her); he (or she) is not to be trusted. I don't like him (or her)," and so on.

In Every Relationship Is an Opportunity for Unconditional Love

Well, my dear friends, we want for you to understand that unconditional love starts within. It has very little to do with whether or not you are going in life with one individual, but rather whether or not you are willing to unconditionally love all—not one individual, my dear friends, not one relationship. There is only one relationship, and that exists inside of yourself.

Each and every one of you, my dear friends, on one level or another, has asked at any given time, "Where is my soul mate, Dr. Peebles? I want to have one. I want to live for this person, to die for this person." Well, my dear friends, the sole mate, s-o-l-e, you are seeking is you, and *that* within every relationship you entertain upon the planet Earth. Love everlasting exists within yourself.

You explore this through the opportunities for understanding that are given to you in the presentation of human beings to your life. As you approach the individual and you want to love him (or her) very, very much . . . We understand this; you start with the best of intentions, without question. You want very much to love this person, you want to embrace this person, you want to allow yourself to be touched and to touch. Back and forth you go, but still you are confused about whether or not you are worthy; still you are confused as to whether or not the person you are with is worthy of your love.

Well, my dear friends, these individuals are worthy. We're going to put it once again very simply, very plainly: These individuals upon the planet Earth, all individuals, not just the ones with whom you want to have a lover relationship—which is truly the one in which you want to entertain sexuality and such, a different exploration of love—but individuals in all relationships, whether it be friendships, whether it be within your workplace, whether it be within the grocery store, whether it be within a room of strangers, in every single, solitary relationship is an opportunity for you to understand unconditional love.

Unconditional love comes from an awareness that you very much want to accept and appreciate all human beings without having massive expectations of them to change themselves to suit you. And what you will begin to understand is that you are working in your life, as you are coming into contact with human beings, to simply find the joy in their expressions toward you. "Ah, but this person is a liar, Dr. Peebles. How can I love a person who has hurt so many people, Dr. Peebles? How can I love this person, Dr. Peebles, who is not necessarily the best-looking individual?"

You Can Love All People

My dear friends, we will share with you that you can. These are individuals like yourselves who are simply immersed in the illusions of separation, in a belief that they are not worthy of love; in a belief that they cannot give proper love to life; in a belief that love must come in a particular form, in a particular way, at a particular time, through a particular diamond ring on a particular finger. My dear friends, understanding unconditional love and relationships is the most freeing experience of all, for it is there that you no longer have to put yourself in any kind of box. No longer are you within the confines of the Earth, body and mind, but you are capable of moving freely about the Earth, like Jesus Christ Himself. You are capable of walking into a band of thieves and realizing that in the heart of every thief is an angel and the potentiality therein is a band of angels; and eventually they will come to understand this, but they are in toxic exploration, striving to find and touch the face of God, striving through the illusions of separation.

My dear friends, as you stand within the group of individuals whom you think you cannot love, you will begin to understand that they are no different than yourself. They are afraid to reveal the truth of their own hearts; they are afraid that they will not be accepted or valued for who and what they are within. Eventually, after a little practice—and we put it once again very simply, very plainly—you will begin to develop the skill of compassion. The skill of compassion, my dear friends, is the highest virtue, much higher even than honesty, truly putting you into an area, an arena, that would be higher than honesty in terms of integrity. For it is there, within compassion, that you no longer have to worry about honor and honesty, truth or untruth; rather, you are immersed in a labor of love without end.

It is there as well that you realize that no longer is life about being centered upon yourself. And we mean that you oftentimes see your reality as being a punch or a jab to your own personal growth, your own desires, your own quests, your own journey. You often see, my dear friends, that everyone is putting up a wall around you, and you don't see the walls that you are putting up for yourselves—the walls that keep you from the opportunities you are seeking, the walls that you develop by your own expectations of life.

You will find that eventually your barriers, borders and boundaries will begin to break down; they will begin to deteriorate because they are false, because they are illusions of separation. You will find and touch the face of God in the many rather than the few within relationships. There are individuals who can help you along your journey, and they oftentimes do not even come in the package you would expect. They do not come in the package, my dear friends, of a gorgeous man or a gorgeous woman, of a marriage, of a particular friendship. Rather, they come in an unexpected way, where you find that someone can touch your life for three and a half seconds and change the course of your existence—if you are willing to find unconditional love in your heart and to realize that there is value within every single, solitary human being upon the planet Earth; if you are willing to realize that love everlasting exists inside of yourself, that you will feel love everlasting when you are willing to express love everlasting.

You will begin to understand, down the road apiece, as you continue to practice compassion with human beings, as you continue to find and touch the face of God within all of life without having to change anyone, without having to try to get others to be honest with you or what have you, and your expectations—massive expectations—will dissolve. And it is there that you will simply love the human beings in you life, be it your spouse, a friend, a neighbor, a boyfriend, a girlfriend, doesn't matter; you will simply love the things and beings in your life, be it the chair which you are sitting upon or an animal. With every relationship you are involved in, you will find that every fiber of your entire being is such that you want very much to express love at all times, at all turns.

"That's True Too"

My dear friends, practice a game here that we would call "That's True Too." It is a game of truth. When others share with you a word of wisdom that they impart from their lips, whether it be a bit of gossip, a bit of spirituality, about their hair, about their desire for love, about their desire for a cup of coffee—it doesn't matter if it is with cream or sugar, no judgments here, God bless you indeed—tell yourself that everything others are sharing with you is beautiful, is truly coming from love. And even when you think it's going to hurt you or someone else, understand that every single, solitary bit and every word that is spoken from human lips is a labor of love.

When you can do this and tell yourself, "That is true too. Dr. Peebles told me it was true," you will begin to understand yourself in relationship to life in the most remarkable way, for it is there that you will find purpose and value; you will find love everlasting within every movement, within every song, within every dance, within every human discussion upon the planet Earth. No longer will you find a need to move away from anything or anyone. Rather, you will enjoy the dance, the glorious exploration that comes from relationships with life, from relationships, my dear friends, with the many rather than the few and the relationship that occurs within your own given heart.

Every experience that you have upon the planet Earth begins inside of you and ends inside of you, my dear friends. Your external world is simply an arena whereby you find the physical expression of what's occurring inside of self. Within your relationships then—and we will turn specifically to relationships of love and with lovers, if you will, wherein you are expressing yourself in an arena of sexuality—look into the eyes of the one from whom you want to have understanding and be willing to give that person the very same. Before you seek outside of yourself that which you want to desperately receive, you must be willing, my dear friends, to receive it inside of you. You must be willing to give it of your own heart. You must be willing to speak it from your own lips.

You understand that there is certainly an old adage that will forevermore be the crux, if you will, of all issues, of all relationships upon the planet

Earth, which is, my dear friends, "Do unto others as you would have them do unto you." And it is there that you would find freedom and flight of soul beyond your wildest dreams and imaginations. It is there that no longer will you feel a need to run away from a spouse; no longer will you find a need to run away from a friend; no longer will you find a need, my dear friends, to change anyone upon the planet Earth, but rather you will love all very freely from your heart.

Change Has to Come from Within

God bless you indeed, my dear friends. Understand that you are in a state of confusion much of the time upon your Earth. You don't know what to do next. "Dr. Peebles, what should I do here?" "I don't know what to do. Where do I go? How do I work? Whom should I be with?" My dear friends, my response would be to all: Be with life in all its various arrays of color, light, frequency; be understanding; share in discussions the many beautiful perspectives, whether you believe them or not; develop an appreciation within yourself—this is freedom and flight of soul beyond your wildest dreams and imaginations and creates a sense of peace of love everlasting upon the planet Earth.

Within relationships you find yourself bickering, and you find yourself contained. You don't like this bickering; you don't like to have the anger. You want it all to be very nice and to never have misunderstandings, to never have grievances; it should be all kisses, it should be all hugs, you understand? But it has to start with you, and so, within any argument, any bickering, any fight, if you can, employ the principles of "That's true too"— which really is, in a nutshell, loving allowance, increased communication and self-responsibility all wrapped up in one and employed at one single given time. Listen to your partner and say, "That's true too. I do understand. I hear your words" and really hear the other person.

Stop trying to change your partners, stop trying to push them into different perspectives. If they are not ready, your greatest and most unconditional love is to allow, my dear friends, your lovers, your partners, your friends to be in their own time and place; to allow for their perspectives; to allow for them to live their lives without having to be pushed and cajoled to change. You don't like it for yourself, so why would you do it unto others if you do not want it done unto you?

Realize that you cannot change anything in the world around you; it has to start from the inner world, from inside of your heart; it has to start within the face of your spouse, your friends, your family members and others with whom you have contact throughout your day. All of these faces, my dear friends, are the faces of God. You pray and you ask for appreciation from

God and a friend comes to your house and says, "I baked you some cookies." And you say, "I don't have time for cookies." Well, when you are praying and asking for God to come to you and to show you appreciation and your friend bakes you cookies and you push you friend away, you have just rejected the answer from God. There are many, many ways in which your prayers for love are indeed answered in every single, solitary moment of each and every day. Your quest for love that you have embarked upon, for love everlasting, starts within your own human heart.

Bring the Truth of Yourself to the Surface

You want to feel love in your life? Then be willing now to ease someone else's pain. Be willing to pick up the telephone rather than picking up the knife for suicide here. Pick up the telephone, my dear friends, to give color and life and light to another; to share and to care; to give love and understanding; to bring peace, prosperity and abundance; to give your last dollar to a friend. It is there that you create a cycle of abundance of love within your life that will be unparalleled to anything you have ever experienced upon the planet Earth. You master this, my dear friends, and it is there that you not only find and touch the face of God, not only find freedom, not only fall in love with your divine self and your relationships with all of life, but that you release yourselves at long last from the cycle of reincarnation.

God bless you indeed, my dear friends. Within every relationship, there is an opportunity to see yourself reflected. All that you reject and all that you deny and all that you do not like within another . . . Yes, bark at it, that's nice, and tell it to go away: "I don't like that, that's not nice; go away!" "I don't understand that; go away!" "I don't appreciate that behavior!" You snap and bark very loudly, and this, if you would be willing to realize, you are saying to the part of yourself that you want to have disappear, that you don't want knocking at your door anymore. If you can understand this and sit down and write about it, if you like . . .

You can simply for a moment here take a deep breath and say, "My spouse is treating me very unkind here." "I don't like the way she curls her hair." "I don't like the way he makes the bed." "I don't like the way she makes the coffee." Then you might want to take an opportunity to find out how she would like for you to make the bed, what he likes with his coffee, how he likes you to do your hair, and you give this to your spouse and it is there that you will find freedom, because you will find understanding. It is there that you begin to appreciate your spouse in a much deeper fashion, if you are willing to understand that he (she) is a reflection of you, God bless you indeed.

All that everyone upon the planet Earth says, does, sees, smells, tastes and experiences occurs in only one place, and that is within your own human heart; it is not external at all. For a moment here, close our eyes and breathe very deeply into your spines. It is in a body that you live here upon the Earth. You have propelled, pushed a wee bit of yourselves into this experience of life, not all of who you really are. There is a much larger sense of yourself. You feel it; you know it; you have tasted of it; your greatest desire is to bring it to the surface, but you're afraid of rejection. You're afraid you'll be pushed away. You're afraid you won't be loved for it. You are afraid, my dear friends, that you will not be understood. You are afraid that you do not have a capacity to express yourselves clearly.

But, my dear friends, if you can indeed push past the fears and simply do it anyway, bringing this part of yourself to the surface, be it a willingness and desire to dance in the streets; a willingness and desire to call a neighbor and say, "Hello, I really do like you and I would like to get to know you a little better"; a willingness to face rejection, to face a life that will perhaps push you away, will not want to hear from you, will not at first appreciate you . . . If you are willing to try, at the very least in a most simple fashion, to bring a little bit more of yourself to the surface . . . Yes, in the very beginning, life will run away because you will now be reinventing yourself, and what happens is, you begin to shuffle up the dance a little bit; you're beginning to change partners. Remember the chair we spoke about? You are simply changing chairs. And so family members, friends and others will begin to fall away. But watch your life, my dear friends; watch what happens when you are willing to bring the truth of yourself to the surface, when you are willing to say, "What I really always wanted to be was not a corporate president. I wanted to be an artist." If you are willing to read the books of art and you enter into your library and you read the books, you find yourself sitting in proximity to others of like mind and like heart. You begin to be willing to walk into a workshop and to put your paint on the canvas, and you find yourself sitting nearby human beings of like mind and like heart.

All of this feels like love, because you are now falling in love with the truth of yourself, being willing to express yourself fully and completely upon the planet Earth. Yes, my dear friends, family members might say, "You're a crazy man, you're a crazy woman. Why would you walk away from a job such as the one you have, with all the financial riches in the world, and study art? You should be at the office. What's the matter with you?" And you would say, "There's nothing the matter with me at all. I'm falling in love with myself. I am falling in love, and it feels like love everlasting." Allow the world to stand in judgment of you. Allow the world to cast stones. Allow the world to be, and be unconditionally loving of the world my dear friends. Be unconditionally loving and let others be in sadness, depression, fear, anger, pain, shame, guilt— it's all right, my dear friends; it's not for you to fix or repair.

You begin first by healing your own heart, and you stand by example upon the Earth. And as others watch you, they say, "Why are you so happy? How is it possible that you can be happy when you are not doing what I think you should be doing?" Then suddenly someone comes up to you and says, "I fully realize and understand why you are becoming an artist, because I see that you are now releasing yourself from pain and I find this fascinating about you, attractive. Here I come; I want to give you a kiss." And look what you are bringing into your life by living your life, by living your life fully and completely expressed upon the planet Earth. You begin to attract love beyond your wildest dreams and imaginations. Oh, here comes somebody else, "Goodness gracious, what a lovely picture upon the canvas! I think that's very beautiful. You're a wonderful artist! Why didn't you show this to us before? Goodness gracious, I want to give you a hug for this." God bless you indeed. My goodness gracious, dear friends, by being willing to express yourselves fully and completely upon the planet Earth, there comes love—not because you tried to force it from the outside in, but because you are willing to first express it from the inside out.

Life Is about Relationships

As you are working and laboring in love here upon the planet Earth, realize that this is a labor; this is a work that is very creative, spontaneous, playful and alive. That's why you are seeking it; that's why you want love in the first place. You can find love within a friendship, with a lover, within sexual expression, within writing, within art, with your chair, with an animal. You can find love even with your computers, with your tabletops, with your woodworking tools, with blowing up a balloon. Everything upon the planet Earth, every experience upon the planet Earth, can be completely saturated with love everlasting, but it starts with you.

When you wake up in the morning, be willing now for a moment here to simply surrender yourself into the understanding that life is about relationships, and first and foremost about the relationship you create within yourself. And so you seek your day; you want to have prosperity, you want to have abundance, you want to have fun, you want to have joy, you want to have happiness, but you are facing a day that just does not look like it's going to be much fun at all: so much work to do, so many clothes to iron, so much work to do. Well, before you even get out of your bed in the morning, sit with yourself for a moment here; make a decision that you want to have beautiful, comfortable, compassionate and loving relationships. For a moment here, my dear friends, for one day, and then, if you can extend this, for a week, you will watch your life transform in remarkable ways.

With everything that you do on a given day, find ways in which you can bring more love into the situation, without expectation, without manipulation, but rather simply by willing to love the situation. For example, you have a bed to make. "I hate making the bed," you say. Well yes, it wasn't my favorite pastime either, and oftentimes I didn't do it, and oftentimes I left little crevices for little critters to get into my bed and the bedbugs did bite. But, my dear friends, you can get up and you can make your bed and you can thank your pillow and say, "Hello pillow, thank you so very much for making my night a beautiful night," and you stroke your bed as you put the sheets nice and tight and you say, "Thank you so very much, my bed and my sheets! You are so very beautiful."

And some of you will say, "My sheets are not beautiful; they're ugly. Someone gave them to me, but I can't afford the ones I want." Well, how very sad for the sheets! Give them a little compassion and understanding there. Would you like to be an ugly sheet on a bed? Perhaps with some people around you, you feel like an ugly sheet on a bed. Give what you want to receive, and therefore we simply ask that you begin to love everything, everybody, every situation. There is always love, that is the constant; the rest is the illusion of separation.

And so, my dear friends, you look at your sheets until you can love them for what they are. Perhaps they are not the prettiest sheets nor the cleanest, but they are yours and they love you, we assure you of this. And as you begin to give them love, this love will increase in abundance, a vibration that will be projected right back at you when you climb into your bed at night. You will feel the difference, because you have given your bed love. You have immersed your world in your love everlasting through the willingness, the movement of your own loving heart.

As you go into your world and you put your car keys into your car and you start the engine, say, "Thank you, dear car," and you say thank you to the sky because it is there, whether it is gray and gloomy, whether it is bright and sunny, doesn't matter. Say, "Thank you, sky, for being there." That, my dear friends, is a gift from God, a very graphic one at that, something you take for granted all the time. "God, why don't you give me anything?" Well, I gave you a lovely rain shower today; was that not enough? I gave you a beautiful sky today; was that not enough? I gave you the ground to walk on and your ever-beatin' heart; was that not enough? All righty then, let us try something else! God's gifts, my dear friends, are abundant, and certainly God's love is everlasting.

So you drive your car down the street and you see a stranger. How can you bring love into that situation? The stranger is a very down-hearted spirit, a very frightening one. Perhaps this person wants to steal your wallet? Well, goodness gracious, you're not going to make eye contact with that person, not for any reason under the Sun. But today, my dear friends, because Dr. Peebles said so, you smile brightly and you wave and you say, "Hidee-ho to you!" and you can do this within your heart. Simply wrap up everyone and everything in little kisses of love that come from your heart with sincerity, with compassion. And as you enter your workplace and you see the very arch nemesis, shall we say, of your life standing in front of you, you say, "Hello, very nice to see you. I'm so glad that you work here," and you extend your hand with love and grace and kindness and you realize that everyone has faults and so do you, and therefore there really are no faults at all; everyone is just seeking the same thing: love and tender expression, to touch and to be touched.

And through your willingness to extend your hand for a little handshake in spite of what you feel from this individual, you are increasing the abundance of love in your life. It will be reflected back at you as you work through your day, my dear friends. And understand, relationships exist everywhere, with everything. You are blowing up a balloon for a party. Take a nice, deep breath and say, "All right God, bring the love into my breath here; may every cell that is released from my body into this balloon be filled with love." God bless you indeed! And it is there that you increase the abundance of love within a party. It is there that this love comes back at ya.

Hello James, how are you?

James: *I'm just fine.*

You don't mind to be called James, yeah? It's all right; it's a beautiful name. I have a relationship with my name, and I love it. I have a relationship with myself, and I love myself very much, yeah. And I love you. You know why? Because I know that you are me; because, my dear friends, I have no illusions of separation. I'm not afraid of you; I just simply love you. You can do anything you like. You can yell at me, you can kick the chair in my name, and it doesn't bother me a bit. I love you anyway, because I know that you have a lot of anger sometimes, disillusionment, sadness, guilt and shame, but it doesn't make you any less in my eyes because, my dear friends, I know your beautiful beatin' heart is truly filled with love—wanting love, wanting to give the very same.

Draw Love from the Heavens: A Meditation

For a moment here, close your eyes and breathe very deeply into your spines. Feel yourself, your spirit. Who are you? Feel yourself. "I am physical." "I am spirit." "I am a soul encapsulated in a body." It doesn't matter, just make a decision and allow yourselves once again to breathe very deeply into your spines.

Feel your feet upon the Earth. Feel your fanny upon the chair. Feel your head surrounded by the air that you are breathing; there is a relationship there. Your skin is breathing the air as well. Your skin is immersed in the air, releasing toxins into the room. Oh goodness gracious, that's a frightening thought, isn't it, because you are breathing in one another's toxins! "Aah, now I'm afraid! I'm going to get sick, and I might die!" No, my dear friends, not at all. The reason that you won't is because truly, you do love. Truly, my dear friends, you don't want to get sick; you don't want to die. That's the truth of yourself. You want to be expressed fully and completely upon the planet Earth.

As you are breathing very deeply into your spines, with every breath imagine that you are reaching into the heavens, into that beautiful blue and glorious sky overhead, with a stream of light that comes from the top of your head. Plug yourself in, very much as you did when you were birthed from your mommy's chamber there. Now you are being birthed into life, the very top of your head connecting with the heavens.

Take a nice, deep breath now, and through that funnel of light there, with your deep breath, imagine that you are . . . You can imagine yourself as being a bit of a syringe, if you will, sucking up a lot of love from the heavens down into your physicality here upon the Earth, sucking up more of who you really are. Take another deep breath, breathing even more love into your physicality. And as you exhale into life, release that love into life. Take another deep breath, drawing the love from the heavens into your physicality, then exhale into the room greater and greater love, every breath filled with love. That is the degree of understanding of relationship that you want to attain in your lifetime upon the planet Earth.

Continue to draw love from the heavens and out through your mouth. And one last time, my dear friends, this love is going to pour into you in one continuous stream of light. There is no separation. It is circulating through your body, out through your mouth into the room. Take another deep breath, and suddenly you realize you are drawing in the love that you have just created in the room. You, my dear friends, are automatically receiving the love as you give it to life. That is the rhythm, the dance of love upon the Earth. Once again take the biggest breath of all, the one that says yes to love forevermore, drawing in the love, filling every cell of your being with love. Now open your eyes.

You develop and create a natural rhythm as you dance with all of creation. Not one bit, my dear friends, you can ever hold at arm's length. It takes a tremendous amount of hard labor to hold life at arm's length, and it is a lot easier to simply fall into an eternal embrace.

Take Charge of Your Existence

My dear friends, explore consciously, wake up in your life here and be willing to see the many ways in which you are afraid to let life embrace you. How often do you hold life at arm's length! How often do phrases such as "Oh, I don't like that!" cross your lips, cross your mind! "How could they? That's unnatural!" "Unacceptable!" "Ridiculous!" "Unkind!" "Terrible!" My dear friends, it is not for you to judge; it is for you to open your heart, to bring love to the person who is immersed in the illusions of separation. Very sad? Yes, it is very sad to see human beings treating one another unkindly, but for you to add to it with your anger is not going to end the cycle. For you to see that they are treating one another unkindly and to give equitable love to all, unconditional love for all to be in their own time and place, will help the world heal much faster than your judgment from your lips.

My dear friends, we challenge you here because it's much easier to allow for the darkness to spill forth than for the light. It is much easier for you to turn yourself into the victim rather than the creator. It is easier, because should you allow yourself to become unconditionally loving at all time, in all places, in all relationships, with love everlasting, it can feel very lonely. It's a very hard existence upon the Earth, and we certainly do understand and appreciate this. But realize that it is what the Earth requires; it is what you desire. And once you can do it without having to force yourself to love, simply living your life as a loving being and finding and touching the face of God that is you, being the God who you are, the creator upon the planet Earth, you will find flight of soul. You will find freedom, and your adventure here will become much gentler. There will be much more appreciation of you and for you expressed by life around you. But you must be willing to take charge of your existence. You must be willing to be the courageous adventurer upon the planet Earth.

You are beautiful spirits, each and every one here in this room today a student of the divine; each and every one reading the text here is a student of the divine. What does this mean, divinity of self? What does it mean, my dear friends, to be a student of the divine? You are a student here upon the planet Earth studying the divinity of yourself, not of life around you necessarily, but of you. You have opportunities in your world wherein you see little projections of yourself, which we have discussed. You see it upon your televisions, you hear it upon your radios, you hear it within discussions that you overhear in the grocery store. All of these are not separate from you but simply opportunities for you to understand yourself.

Watching this projection on the screen, watching, for example, military men and women marching through the streets and small children being killed, stop and pause and ask yourself in this relationship with life, "How am I doing this to myself? In what way do I kill off the children inside of me at all times? In what way is this occurring upon the planet Earth as a result of what I am doing within myself?" You will be surprised at the response there. If you can be honest with yourself and not do this as an exploration of shame and guilt but rather as an exploration of love, an exploration of divinity of yourself, an exploration of the divine being who you are, and if you look into the eyes of these scary monsters within you, you realize that you can change the course of existence upon the planet Earth. All that you see, hear, taste, touch, feel and smell is a reflection of you, of the world that you have created inside.

You want to increase the abundance? Then be willing to increase the abundance in your inner world; to find yourself sitting and being appreciative of what you do have, of the abundance that you have—not the lack, which is the illusion of separation. Realize that the abundance comes from your awareness of love; that the journey upon planet Earth is not about money, not about a sexual relationship with another human being, not about a house or a car or a telephone, not about theater, not about space exploration, not about correcting misunderstandings between governments—it is not about any of this. It is all, my dear friends, about love. It is all about one relationship that begins with you.

You struggle to understand the world, which is your struggle to understand yourself, for you are never separate, you are never alone and you are indeed a beautiful creator. But, my dear friends, you have yet to master one thing, and that is the self-exploration that is so exciting, so enthralling, so thrilling. And the enthusiasm that you feel as you reveal more and more of yourself to the world, that is rare, my dear friends. It is rare that you understand the divinity of your being, that you understand how very special you are. Yes, we say "special," but all are special upon the Earth, is that not accurate? Why yes, my dear friends, all are special upon the Earth, because all are one. It is one relationship. You are not separate, never have been, never will be. All are birthed and born from God; all come from the womb, the heart, the soul, the spirit of love; all are one. God bless you indeed.

You are all very beautiful spirits. The challenge here today is to become smarter as a lover, to become smarter as a lover, to become smarter as a lover, to understand that there is so much love upon the planet Earth that you are afraid to see. Can you, my dear friends, find yourselves a relationship with a child who is what you would perhaps consider to be less than wise because perhaps the child has a damaged brain? From such a child, you would learn more about love in half a minute than you would from sexual expression with another for sixteen years. It is within these small children that there is a divine light that comes to the surface. They are, unabashedly, very beautiful spirits, these special children upon the planet Earth. They are here to share with you that love is abundant, love is free, love doesn't cost a penny, it doesn't come in any particular package, it doesn't have to look very pretty, it doesn't have to smell very nice, it is abundant and it surfaces forevermore. It is in these small children that you can find the greatest understandings, the greatest healers of all upon the planet Earth—in these small children with half a brain, God bless you indeed, and double the heart.

My dear friends, beautiful spirits, each and every one of you a student of the divine. There are so very many ways in which you have chosen not to love the Earth, have chosen not to love yourself! You do not love yourself every time you do not love the Earth. Every time you feel anger or pain or shame or guilt or insensitivity, this is happening to you, not to the life around you. The anger hurts you, not life around you. It starts within, and how long are you going to be willing to carry the pain? How long are you going to be willing to live in a condition and state that is less than love? Take the anger, my dear friends, and turn it into prosperity and abundance. Turn it into light. It is certainly the density of light; it is black, and it is from there that you can indeed grow, but you must be willing. You must be willing to do a little bit of work and to labor a little bit harder to love your pillow, to touch and caress your bed and to stretch your hands out to a stranger and say, "I love you!" and not worry about the response.

Free Yourself from the Confines of Earth, Body, Mind

For to say, "I love you!" is the greatest truth of all upon the Earth. And those who would laugh and those who would turn away, those who would not say thank you, those who would think you are trying to get something from them as a result of your kind words, well, my dear friends, that is their world. Have unconditional love for them to be in their own time and place and, God bless you indeed, it is for you to increase communication with all of life and with respect, and so you can handle such situations.

You say, "I love you," and the other says he or she thinks that's crazy. You say, "It's all right. You can think it's crazy, I love you anyway." It is there that you free yourself from the confines of the Earth, body and mind, for you are now abiding and operating by the only force in the universe; the only force that is real; the only force that is not separate; the only force, my dear friends, that runs and courses through life, the reality and truth of you— which is love. It is love everlasting, my dear friends, that you seek, through the eyes of a stranger, through your fanny on the chair—it doesn't matter; it is everywhere.

God bless you indeed, my dear friends. Go your way in peace, love and harmony, for life is indeed a joy, and all you have to do as you enjoy the journey to your own hearts is for a moment here to outstretch your hands and hold the hand of a neighbor; for all who are reading the text, simply place yourself here in the room today. And it is here in this circle of one; in this circle of life; in this circle of opportunity with joined hands with a neighbor, with your heart, with your soul, where there is no separation. And realize, my dear friends, how very many are gathered here as one across time and space, different times of reading the text, different ways of experiencing it, different expressions, different understandings, different perspectives—but all, my dear friends, one family; all seeking the very same opportunities; all seeking love; all, my dear friends, wanting very much to be fully expressed upon the planet Earth, united in your spirits, the very same on the inside— diversity of life on the exterior, but unity in the interior.

God bless you indeed, my dear friends, and as you enjoy the journey to your own hearts and certainly to your own enlightenment, simply lighten up just a little bit more. Share your inner light with the world through your hands, through your ears, through you heart, through your mouth. And, my dear friends, bring this light to the world, and you will never, ever have to ask for forgiveness again. God bless you, indeed.

Book ◆15◆

Joshua David Stone PhD

Encyclopedia of the Spiritual Path

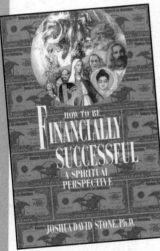

HOW TO BE FINANCIALLY SUCCESSFUL: A SPIRITUAL PERSPECTIVE

As one of the most successful businessmen of the New Age movement, Dr. Stone has written an easily digestible book full of tools and advice for achieving prosperity. This book conveys esoteric secrets of the universe that, if mastered, can lead to maximum manifestation results.

- Keys to Prosperity Consciousness from the Soul's Perspective
- How to Develop the Midas Touch
- The Seven Keys to Releasing Fear and Worry
- How to Master the Twelve Levels of Integrated Spiritual Power in Life
- Integration of the Seven Rays and Spiritual Leadership
- How to Program the Subconscious Mind for Success in Business

$14.95   SOFTCOVER 235 P.
ISBN 1-891824-55-4

LIGHT TECHNOLOGY PUBLISHING • 928-526-1345 • 800-450-0985
Or use our online bookstore: www.lighttechnology.com

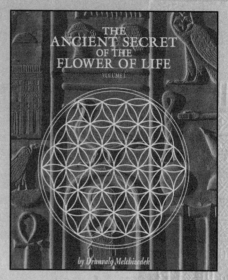

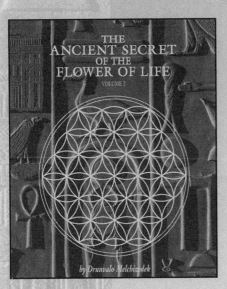

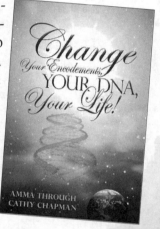

BRIAN GRATTAN

MAHATMA I & II
The I AM Presence

Awaken and realize that all of humankind will create their "body for ascension," whether they accomplish this now or later, and that this is not the exclusive domain of Christ or Buddha or the many others who have ascended—*this is your birthright.* When humans lift the veils of their unworthiness and recognize that they are the sons of God, that there is divine equality and that no one is greater than another, then you will have begun your journey in the way that it was intended. The *Mahatma* is for those who are motivated to search for the answers that can respond to their mental and spiritual bodies. No matter how contrary your current beliefs, this book contains methods for creating your spiritual lightbody for ascension and also explains your eternal journey in a way never before available to humankind.

19^{95} SOFTCOVER 480 P.
ISBN 0-929385-77-2

Chapter Titles:

- Introduction by Vywamus
- The Journey of the Mahatma from Source to Earth
- The Spiritual Initiation through the Mahatma
- What Is Channeling?
- Evolution of a Third-Dimensional Planet
- The Rays, Chakras and Initiations
- Conversations with Barbara Waller
- Transformation through Evolution
- Patterns
- Time and Patience

- Mahatma on Channeling
- Conversation Between the Personality (Brian) and Mahatma (the I AM Presence)
- Mastery
- The Tenth Ray
- Integrating Unlimitedness
- The Etheric and Spiritual Ascensions
- The Cosmic Heart
- Mahatma as the I AM Presence
- So What Does the Personality Think of All of This?

TITLES ON TAPE
by Brian Grattan

BASEL SEMINAR
10 TAPE SET (AUDIO CASSETTE), English with German translation $35.00

EASTER SEMINAR
7 TAPE SET (AUDIO CASSETTE), English with German translation $59.95

SEATTLE SEMINAR
12 TAPE SET (AUDIO CASSETTE) $79.95
Twelve one-hour audio tapes from the Seattle Seminar, October 27–30, 1994. These twelve powerful hours of meditations lead to total spiritual transformation by recoding your two-strand DNA to function in positive mutation.

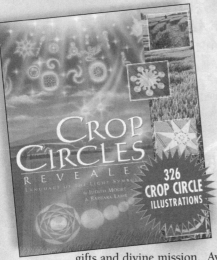

SHAMANIC SECRETS
ROBERT SHAPIRO

Shamanic Secrets for Spiritual Mastery the third book of the Shamanic Secrets series due out late 2005!

SPEAKS OF MANY TRUTHS AND ZOOSH THROUGH ROBERT SHAPIRO
SHAMANIC SECRETS for MATERIAL MASTERY
Learn to communicate with the planet!

This book explores the heart and soul connection between humans and Mother Earth. Through that intimacy, miracles of healing and expanded awareness can flourish. To heal the planet and be healed as well, we can lovingly extend our energy selves out to the mountains and rivers and intimately bond with the Earth. Gestures and vision can activate our hearts to return us to a healthy, caring relationship with the land we live on.

The character and essence of some of Earth's most powerful features are explored and understood, with exercises given to connect us with those places. As we project our love and healing energy there, we help the Earth to heal from humanity's destruction of the planet and its atmosphere. Dozens of photographs, maps and drawings assist the process in twenty-five chapters, which cover the Earth's more critical locations.

$**19**^{95}$ SOFTCOVER 498 P.
ISBN 1-891824-12-0

Chapter Titles:

- Approaching Material Mastery through Your Physicality
- Three Rivers: The Rhine, the Amazon and the Rio Grande
- Three Lakes: Pyramid Lake, Lake Titicaca and Lake Baikal
- Mountains: Earth's Antennas, Related to the Human Bone Structure
  - Three Mountains: The Cydonia Pyramid, Mount Rushmore and Mount Aspen
  - Mountains in Turkey, Japan and California
  - Eurasia and Man's Skeletal Structure
  - Greenland, the Land of Mystery
  - Africa and North America
  - South and Central America and Australia

- Shamanic Interaction with Natural Life
- Africa and the Caspian and Black Seas
- Mauna Loa, Mount McKinley and Shiprock
- The Gobi Desert
- Old Faithful, the Cayman Islands, the Blue Mountains and Grandfather Mountain
- Meteor Crater, Angel Falls and Other Unique Locations on the Planet

PART II: THE FOUNDATION OF ONENESS
- The Explorer Race as a Part of Mother Earth's Body
- Spiritual Beings in a Physical World
- Earth Now Releasing Human Resistance to Physical Life
- Healing Prisoners, Teaching Students
- The Shaman's Key: Feeling and the Five Senses
- How to Walk, How To Eat
- Breathing: Something Natural We Overlook
- How to Ask and Let Go, and How to Sleep
- Singing Our Songs
- Some Final Thoughts

SHAMANIC SECRETS for PHYSICAL MASTERY

The purpose of this book is to allow you to understand the sacred nature of your own physical body and some of the magnificent gifts it offers you. When you work with your physical body in these new ways, you will discover not only its sacredness, but how it is compatible with Mother Earth, the animals, the plants, even the nearby planets, all of which you now recognize as being sacred in nature.

It is important to feel the value of yourself physically before you can have any lasting physical impact on the world. The less you think of yourself physically, the less likely your physical impact on the world will be sustained by Mother Earth. If a physical energy does not feel good about itself, it will usually be resolved; other physical or spiritual energies will dissolve it because it is unnatural. The better you feel about your physical self when you do the work in the previous book as well as in this one and the one to follow, the greater and more lasting will be the benevolent effect on your life, on the lives of those around you and ultimately on your planet and universe.

$25⁰⁰ SOFTCOVER 544 P.
ISBN 1-891824-29-5

Chapter Titles:

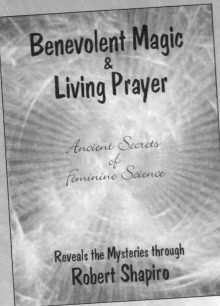
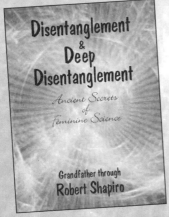
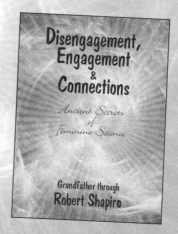

THE EXPLORER RACE SERIES

ZOOSH AND HIS FRIENDS THROUGH ROBERT SHAPIRO

THE SERIES: Humans—creators-in-training—have a purpose and destiny so heartwarmingly, profoundly glorious that it is almost unbelievable from our present dimensional perspective. Humans are great lightbeings from beyond this creation, gaining experience in dense physicality. This truth about the great human genetic experiment of the Explorer Race and the mechanics of creation is being revealed for the first time by Zoosh and his friends through superchannel Robert Shapiro. These books read like adventure stories as we follow the clues from this creation that we live in out to the Council of Creators and beyond.

❶ THE EXPLORER RACE

You individuals reading this are truly a result of the genetic experiment on Earth. You are beings who uphold the principles of the Explorer Race. The information in this book is designed to show you who you are and give you an evolutionary understanding of your past that will help you now. The key to empowerment in these days is to not know everything about your past, but to know what will help you now. Your number-one function right now is your status of Creator apprentice, which you have achieved through years and lifetimes of sweat. You are constantly being given responsibilities by the Creator that would normally be things that Creator would do. The responsibility and the destiny of the Explorer Race is not only to explore, but to create. 574 P. $25.00 ISBN 0-929385-38-1

❷ ETs and the EXPLORER RACE

In this book, Robert channels Joopah, a Zeta Reticulan now in the ninth dimension who continues the story of the great experiment—the Explorer Race—from the perspective of his civilization. The Zetas would have been humanity's future selves had not humanity re-created the past and changed the future. 237 P. $14.95 ISBN 0-929385-79-9

❸ EXPLORER RACE: ORIGINS and the NEXT 50 YEARS

This volume has so much information about who we are and where we came from—the source of male and female beings, the war of the sexes, the beginning of the linear mind, feelings, the origin of souls—it is a treasure trove. In addition, there is a section that relates to our near future—how the rise of global corporations and politics affects our future, how to use benevolent magic as a force of creation and how we will go out to the stars and affect other civilizations. Astounding information. 339 P. $14.95 ISBN 0-929385-95-0

❹ EXPLORER RACE: CREATORS and FRIENDS
The MECHANICS of CREATION

Now that you have a greater understanding of who you are in the larger sense, it is necessary to remind you of where you came from, the true magnificence of your being. You must understand that you are creators-in-training, and yet you were once a portion of Creator. One could certainly say, without being magnanimous, that you are still a portion of Creator, yet you are training for the individual responsibility of being a creator, to give your Creator a coffee break. This book will allow you to understand the vaster qualities and help you remember the nature of the desires that drive any creator, the responsibilities to which a creator must answer, the reaction a creator must have to consequences and the ultimate reward of any creator. 435 P. $19.95 ISBN 1-891824-01-5

❺ EXPLORER RACE: PARTICLE PERSONALITIES

All around you in every moment you are surrounded by the most magical and mystical beings. They are too small for you to see as single individuals, but in groups you know them as the physical matter of your daily life. Particles who might be considered either atoms or portions of atoms consciously view the vast spectrum of reality yet also have a sense of personal memory like your own linear memory. These particles remember where they have been and what they have done in their infinitely long lives. Some of the particles we hear from are Gold, Mountain Lion, Liquid Light, Uranium, the Great Pyramid's Capstone, This Orb's Boundary, Ice and Ninth-Dimensional Fire. 237 P. $14.95 ISBN 0-929385-97-7

❻ EXPLORER RACE and BEYOND

With a better idea of how creation works, we go back to the Creator's advisers and receive deeper and more profound explanations of the roots of the Explorer Race. The liquid Domain and the Double Diamond portal share lessons given to the roots on their way to meet the Creator of this universe, and finally the roots speak of their origins and their incomprehensibly long journey here. 360 P. $14.95 ISBN 1-891824-06-6

THE EXPLORER RACE SERIES

ZOOSH AND HIS FRIENDS THROUGH ROBERT SHAPIRO

❼ EXPLORER RACE: The COUNCIL of CREATORS

The thirteen core members of the Council of Creators discuss their adventures in coming to awareness of themselves and their journeys on the way to the Council on this level. They discuss the advice and oversight they offer to all creators, including the Creator of this local universe. These beings are wise, witty and joyous, and their stories of Love's Creation create an expansion of our concepts as we realize that we live in an expanded, multiple-level reality. 237 P. $14.95 ISBN 1-891824-13-9

❽ EXPLORER RACE and ISIS

This is an amazing book! It has priestess training, Shamanic training, Isis's adventures with Explorer Race beings—before Earth and on Earth—and an incredibly expanded explanation of the dynamics of the Explorer Race. Isis is the prototypal loving, nurturing, guiding feminine being, the focus of feminine energy. She has the ability to expand limited thinking without making people with limited beliefs feel uncomfortable. She is a fantastic storyteller, and all of her stories are teaching stories. If you care about who you are, why you are here, where you are going and what life is all about—pick up this book. You won't lay it down until you are through, and then you will want more. 317 P. $14.95 ISBN 1-891824-11-2

❾ EXPLORER RACE and JESUS

The core personality of that being known on the Earth as Jesus, along with his students and friends, describes with clarity and love his life and teaching two thousand years ago. He states that his teaching is for all people of all races in all countries. Jesus announces here for the first time that he and two others, Buddha and Mohammed, will return to Earth from their place of being in the near future, and a fourth being, a child already born now on Earth, will become a teacher and prepare humanity for their return. So heartwarming and interesting, you won't want to put it down. 354 P. $16.95 ISBN 1-891824-14-7

❿ EXPLORER RACE: Earth History and Lost Civilization

Speaks of Many Truths and Zoosh, through Robert Shapiro, explain that planet Earth, the only water planet in this solar system, is on loan from Sirius as a home and school for humanity, the Explorer Race. Earth's recorded history goes back only a few thousand years, its archaeological history a few thousand more. Now this book opens up as if a light was on in the darkness, and we see the incredible panorama of brave souls coming from other planets to settle on different parts of Earth. We watch the origins of tribal groups and the rise and fall of civilizations, and we can begin to understand the source of the wondrous diversity of plants, animals and humans that we enjoy here on beautiful Mother Earth. 310 P. $14.95 ISBN 1-891824-20-1

⓫ EXPLORER RACE: ET VISITORS SPEAK

Even as you are searching the sky for extraterrestrials and their spaceships, ETs are here on planet Earth—they are stranded, visiting, exploring, studying the culture, healing the Earth of trauma brought on by irresponsible mining or researching the history of Christianity over the past two thousand years. Some are in human guise, and some are in spirit form. Some look like what we call animals as they come from the species' home planet and interact with their fellow beings—those beings that we have labeled cats or cows or elephants. Some are brilliant cosmic mathematicians with a sense of humor; they are presently living here as penguins. Some are fledgling diplomats training for future postings on Earth when we have ET embassies here. In this book, these fascinating beings share their thoughts, origins and purposes for being here. 350 P. $14.95 ISBN 1-891824-28-7

⓬ EXPLORER RACE: Techniques for GENERATING SAFETY

Wouldn't you like to generate safety so you could go wherever you need to go and do whatever you need to do in a benevolent, safe and loving way for yourself? Learn safety as a radiated environment that will allow you to gently take the step into the new timeline, into a benevolent future and away from a negative past. 208 P. $9.95 ISBN 1-891824-26-0

ॐ **LIGHT TECHNOLOGY
PUBLISHING**
PO Box 3540 • Flagstaff, AZ 86003

Phone: 928-526-1345 or 1-800-450-0985 • Fax: 928-714-1132 or 1-800-393-7017
. . . or use our online bookstore at www.lighttechnology.com

Jonathan Goldman and Shamael, Angel of Sound

Jonathan Goldman is an internationally acknowledged teacher, musician and pioneer in Sound Healing. He is the author of Healing Sounds, *president of Spirit Music and director of the Sound Healers Association.*

Shamael is the Angel of Sound. An extraordinary being of light and love, he is an aspect of the Metatronic energy of Kether.

Shifting Frequencies
How Sound Can Change Your Life

Now, for the first time, Healing Sounds pioneer Jonathan Goldman tells us about shifting frequencies—how to use sound and other modalities to change vibrational patterns for both personal and planetary healing and transformation. Through his consciousness connection to Shamael, Angel of Sound, Jonathan shares his extraordinary scientific and spiritual knowledge and insights, providing information, instructions and techniques on using sound, light, color, visualization and sacred geometry to experience shifting frequencies. The material in this book is both timely and vital for health and spiritual evolution.

In this book, you will:
- Explore the use of sound in ways you never imagined for healing and transformation.
- Discover harmonics as a key to opening to higher levels of consciousness.
- Learn about the angel chakra and what sounds may be used to activate this new energy center.
- Find out how to transmute imbalanced vibrations using your own sounds.
- Experience the secrets of crystal singing.
- Understand the importance of compassion in achieving ascension.

14^{95} SOFTCOVER 147 P.
ISBN 1-891824-04-X

Chapter Titles:

- Sound Currents: Frequency and Intent
- Vibratory Resonance
- Vocalization, Visualization and a Tonal Language
- The Harmonics of Sound
- Vocal Harmonics and Listening
- Harmonics and the Brain
- Energy Fields
- Creating Sacred Space
- Compassion through Sound
- Sacred Geometry and Sound
- Merkabahs

- Sound, Color and Light
- Sound and Crystals
- Crystal Singing
- Breath
- The Waveform Experience
- Harmony
- Healing
- The Language of Light, Part I
- The Language of Light, Part II
- The Angel Chakra